D1004083

**Public and
Urban
Economics**

Public and Urban Economics

Essays in Honor of William S. Vickrey

Edited by
Ronald E. Grieson
Columbia University

Lexington Books
D.C. Heath and Company
Lexington, Massachusetts
Toronto   London

Library of Congress Cataloging in Publication Data
Main entry under title:

Public and urban economics.
   1. Finance, Public–Addresses, essays, lectures. 2. Urban economics–
Addresses, essays, lectures. 3. Vickrey, William Spencer, 1914–   I.
Vickrey, William Spencer, 1914–   . II. Grieson, Ronald E.
HJ141.P76   336   74–31877
ISBN 0–669–98400–0

Published simultaneously in Canada

Printed in the United States of America

International Standard Book Number: 0–669–98400–0

Library of Congress Catalog Card Number: 74–31877

dedicated to William S. Vickrey,
"Mc Vickar Professor
of Political Economy,"
Columbia University

Contents

Part I
Public Economics

1

Quantity Adjustments in Resource Allocation: A Statistical Interpretation

Kenneth J. Arrow

1. Introduction and Summary

Resource allocation is part of the general theory of constrained optima. Any method of successive approximation seeks to approximate a solution of the Lagrangian conditions (if we ignore non-negativities and the possibility of slack in the constraints).

The following notation is used:

x is a column vector of n *decision variables*; $\hspace{2cm}$ (N-1)

$f(x)$ is the *objective function*, to be maximized;

$g(x)$ is a column vector function defining constraints, specifically, $g(x) = 0$.

f_x is the gradient of x, the row vector with components $\delta f/\delta j$;

g_x is the matrix of gradients of the constraint functions, with components $(\delta g_i/\delta x_j)$;

primes denote transpose.

Then the optimization problem is,

maximize $f(x)$ subject to $g(x) = 0$. $\hspace{2cm}$ (1-1)

If the matrix g_x has full row rank, then the solution to (1-1) satisfies the Lagrangian conditions, namely, there exists a row vector p such that,

$$f_x + pg_x = 0, \hspace{4cm} \text{(1-2)}$$

$$g(x) = 0. \hspace{4cm} \text{(1-3)}$$

In the standard discussion of decentralized resource allocation, attention is concentrated upon adjustments in the Lagrange parameters, p. At each stage, an

---

The author wishes to acknowledge the support of Contract N00014–67–A–0298–0019 between the Office of Naval Research and Harvard University.

approximation to p is given. Then x is chosen to satisfy (1-2); this can be interpreted as choosing x to maximize.

$$L = f(x) + pg(x), \tag{1-4}$$

if $f(x)$ and $g(x)$ are assumed concave. However, unless p is already that associated with the constrained optimum, (1-3) will not be satisfied. The deviation of $g(x)$ from 0 is used to guide changes in p. A specific adjustment process in differential equation form is suggested by interpreting $g_i(x)$ as the excess supply of primary factor i when the productive activities are determined by the decision variables x. Then we wish to lower p_i if $g_i(x) > 0$ and raise it otherwise; specifically, the adjustment process might take the form,

$$\dot{p} = -g(x), \tag{1-5}$$

where the dot denotes differentiation·with respect to time.

This process will in fact converge to the constrained optimum under suitable hypotheses, which we will not investigate here [2, pp. 70-71, 84-85]. The idea is standard in the theory of market socialism. It is usually defended on the grounds that not only does it converge, but it is also informationally economical. At each stage, the decision on x requires knowledge only of the gradients of $f(x)$ and $g(x)$ (which can be interpreted as marginal productivities and marginal input requirements). The decision to adjust p, in turn, requires only the simple reflection of the x-decision on resource limitations through $g(x)$.

Marglin [6] challenged the view that price adjustments have any unique virtues. He considered a very simple case, with one resource: decision variables were taken to be the allocations of the resource to different uses, so that,

$$g(x) = r - \sum_j x_j, \tag{1-6}$$

where r is the total resource availability, and $\delta f/\delta x_j$ can be interpreted as the marginal productivity of the resource in its jth use. In the price adjustment process, satisfaction of (1-2) implies that all the marginal productivities are equal throughout the adjustment process. Marglin suggested instead that at each stage the allocation x be chosen so as to be feasible (to satisfy (1-3)). Then, if the allocation is not optimal, (1-2) will not be satisfied. He suggested that each x_j be adjusted so as to increase L, i.e.,

$$\dot{x} = L'_x, \tag{1-7}$$

where L is defined by (1-4); in computing L as a function of x, p is to be so chosen that feasibility is maintained when x is adjusted in accordance with (1-7).

In his special case, Marglin argued that the proposed quantity adjustment system is guaranteed to converge and that the amount of information transmitted at each stage is comparable to that in the price adjustment system.

One interesting implication of the Marglin process is the adjustment equations can be stated in statistical terminology. Specifically, (1–7) turns out to say that x_j should be adjusted in proportion to the difference between the marginal productivity of the resource in its jth use and the average marginal productivity of the resource in all uses. Further, the rate of increase of the objective function is proportional to the variance of the marginal productivities, which, naturally, falls to zero when (1–2) is satisfied.

Do these conclusions generalize to the case of many resources? In particular, what is the generalization of the "statistical" interpretation of the Marglin process?

Actually, the notion of quantity adjustments had appeared earlier in studies of methods of approximating constrained optima; see Forsythe [4] and Arrow and Solow [3, Section 3]. Their interest lay rather in the fact that convergence was valid under less stringent conditions than in questions of informational economy. However, the results developed earlier can be reinterpreted to give rise to a generalized statistical interpretation.

Specifically, the tentative prices and the quantity adjustments in a quantity-adjustment process can be thought of as determined by a regression. Each "observation" is taken to correspond to one component of the decision vector. For the jth observation, the value of the dependent variable is taken to be $\delta f/\delta x_j$, while the value of the ith independent variable is $\delta g_i/\delta x_j$. I.e., given any tentative values for the decision variables, the marginal gains to the different decision variables are regressed against the marginal inputs. The regression coefficients can then be interpreted as the (tentative) prices, while the residuals in the regression are the rate of adjustment of the decision variables. Finally, the rate of growth of the objective function is precisely the square of the standard error of estimate multiplied by the number of decision variables.

In section 2, the Marglin model is reviewed in the present language. In section 3, the generalization to any number of resources is given, and the results in the preceding paragraph proved. In section 4, some comments are made relating the quantity adjustment process to decentralization and informational economy.

2. The Marglin Quantity Adjustment Process

We reexamine Marglin's model in somewhat more general form. He assumed that $f(x)$ was additively separable, an issue important for decentralization (see section 4 below) but not necessary to his main results.

If $g(x)$ has the special form (1-6) and if we insist that the resource allocation be feasible at every moment of the adjustment process, i.e., that (1-3) hold
throughout, then we are requiring that,

$$\sum_j x_j(t) \equiv r. \tag{1-8}$$

This condition will hold if and only if the following two statements are valid:

$$\sum_j x_j(0) = r; \tag{1-9}$$

$$\sum_j \dot{x}_j(t) \equiv 0. \tag{1-10}$$

From (1-6), the Lagrangian can be written,

$$L(x, p) = f(x) + p\left(r - \sum_j x_j\right), \tag{1-11}$$

where p is now a scalar, so that,

$$\delta L/\delta x_j = (\delta f/\delta x_j) - p,$$

and the adjustment process for any component x_j is defined by,

$$\dot{x}_j = (\delta f/\delta x_j) - p. \tag{1-12}$$

To make sure that (1-10) holds, p has to be selected appropriately at any
time t. Substitute (1-12) into (1-10), and solve for p.

$$p = \sum_j (\delta f/\delta x_j)/n, \tag{1-13}$$

i.e., p is the *average* marginal productivity of the resource in all uses.
    Then (1-12) asserts that the rate of change of the resource allocation to any
use is the difference between its marginal productivity in that use and the average
over all uses.
    We will also compute the rate of growth of the objective function itself.

$$\dot{f} = \sum_j (\delta f/\delta x_j)\left[(\delta f/\delta x_j) - p\right] = n\,s^2,$$

where s^2 is the sample *variance* of the marginal productivities about their mean.
    So long as the Lagrange condition (1-2) is not satisfied, the marginal pro-
ductivities will not all be equal. Hence s^2 will be positive, and therefore so will $\dot{f}$.
It is clear, then, that the process can only come into equilibrium at a point where

(1–2) is satisfied as well as (1–3). Since the path is a path of resource allocations, it must be bounded and therefore must have a limit point. It is easy to see that $\dot{f} = 0$ at any limit point, and from this it can be shown that an adjustment path starting from any initial point is feasible, i.e., satisfies (1–9), will converge to a point satisfying (1–2) and (1–3).[a]

3. The General Case Without Non-negativity or Slack

Let us revert to the general constrained maximization problem. We follow the discussion in [3, section 3] but reinterpret the results.

We now wish to require that (1–3), the feasibility condition, hold throughout the adjustment process and therefore as an identity in time.

$$g[x(t)] = 0 \qquad\qquad (1\text{–}14)$$

(1–14) will hold for all t if and only if (a) it holds for $t = 0$, and (b) its derivative with respect to time is identically zero.

$$g[x(0)] = 0; \qquad\qquad (1\text{–}15)$$

$$d\, g[x(t)]\, /dt \equiv 0. \qquad\qquad (1\text{–}16)$$

By the chain rule, (1–16) becomes,

$$g_x\, \dot{x} \equiv 0. \qquad\qquad (1\text{–}17)$$

From (1–4), the definition of L,

$$L_x = f_x + p\, g_x.$$

Hence, the adjustment process for the resource allocation (1–7) is,

$$\dot{x} = f'_x + g'_x\, p'. \qquad\qquad (1\text{–}18)$$

---

[a]The adjustment process (1–7) is arbitrary with regard to the choice of adjustment speeds. The rate of change of any particular x_j could be thought of as proportional to $\delta L / \delta x_j$, rather than equal to it. However, in that case, a suitable change of units in measuring x_j will restore the form given.

The vector p is to be chosen, at any time t, so that (1-17) holds. Write (1-18) as,

$$f'_x = -g'_x \, p' + \dot{x}. \qquad\qquad (1\text{-}19)$$

We are, then, seeking a linear combination of the columns of a matrix, $-g'_x$, such that the difference between a given vector, f'_x, and the linear combination is orthogonal to every column of the given matrix (note that the rows of g_x are the columns of g'_x). This is precisely the defining characteristic of the vector of regression coefficients estimated from a sample, where the columns of the matrix represent different independent variables and the given vector represents the dependent variable.

In more detail, let a regression of y be fitted to variables $z_1, \ldots, z_m$. Let u_j be the residual in the jth observation. Then the linear regression model asserts that, for each $j \; (= 1, \ldots, n)$,

$$y_j = \sum_i \beta_i \, z_{ji} + u_j,$$

where β_i is the regression coefficient of z_i, z_{ji} is the jth observation on the independent variable z_i, and u_j is an error term. Let b_i be the least squares estimate of β_i and v_j the jth estimated residual. Then, by definition of estimated residual,

$$y_j = \sum_i b_i \, z_{ji} + v_j,$$

or, in matrix-vector notation,

$$y = Z \, b + v. \qquad\qquad (1\text{-}20)$$

The estimates b satisfy the normal equations,

$$Z' \, Z \, b = Z' \, y,$$

which can be written,

$$Z' \, (y - Zb) = 0,$$

or, from (1-20),

$$Z' \, v = 0. \qquad\qquad (1\text{-}21)$$

The analogy is now obvious. In (1-20) and (1-21) replace y by f'_x, Z by

$-g'_x$, b by p', and v by $\dot{x}$; then (1-20) translates into (1-19) and (1-21) into (1-17) (after multiplying by -1).

Hence, at any stage t, there is an approximation, $x(t)$, to the optimal alloca-tion. At this value of the decision vector, compute the marginal benefit vector, f'_x, and the marginal input vectors for all inputs, forming the matrix $-g'_x$. Take the regression, across decision variables, of marginal benefits on marginal inputs. The estimated regression coefficients are the approximation at stage t to the resource prices; the calculated residuals are the rates of adjustment of the in-dividual decision variables.

Further, we can easily relate the rate of increase of the objective function to the standard error of the residuals. With the aid of (1-17) and (1-19), we have,

$$\dot{f} = f_x \dot{x} = (\dot{x}' - pg_x)\dot{x} = |\dot{x}|^2 - pg_x \dot{x} = |\dot{x}|^2 = ns_E^2,$$

where

$$s_E = [(\sum_j \dot{x}_j^2)/n]^{1/2},$$

is the standard error of estimate (since the regression has no constant term, the deviations are taken from zero rather than from the sample mean).

As in the simple Marglin case, the objective function continues to increase so long as the regression does not fit perfectly. The path cannot come to an equilibrium unless the Lagrange conditions (1-2) are satisfied. Suppose the ad-justment path is bounded. Then by standard use of Lyapunov's second method (see [5, pp. 7-9] or [1, Chapter 11, section 4]), with $f(x)$ as the Lyapunov function, $x(t)$ must converge to a limit at which condition (1-2) holds; (1-3) has been required to hold for all points on the path. Under suitably concavity con-ditions (or even quasi-concavity conditions), conditions (1-2 and 1-3) are suf-ficient as well as necessary for a constrained optimization.

When will the adjustment path be bounded? Let,

$$F = \left\{ x | f(x) \geqslant f[x(0)] \right\}.$$

Since $f[x(t)]$ is increasing $x(t)$ must belong to F for all t. Hence, the bounded-ness of F is sufficient for that of the path $x(t)$.

Alternatively, it has been insured by construction that $x(t)$ is feasible for all t. If the set of feasible resource allocations is bounded, then again the path must be bounded.

THEOREM. Let g_x have full row rank. Then the quantity adjustment process defined as a path $x(t), p(t)$ satisfying the conditions,

(a) $g[x(t)] \equiv 0,$

(b) $\mathring{x} = L'_x,$

where $L = f(x) + p\, g(x)$, is well defined if the initial point satisfies the condition $g[x(0)] = 0$. If, for each $x = x(t)$, the regression across decision variables of the components of the gradient of f on the corresponding components of the gradients of the constraint functions $g_i(x)$ $(i = 1, \ldots, m)$ is taken, then the estimated regression coefficients are the components of $p(t)$, and the estimated residuals are the components of $\mathring{x}$. If s_E is the standard error of estimate (about zero), then $\mathring{f} = n\, s_E^2$.

If either the set $\left\{ x \mid f(x) \geqslant f[x(0)] \right\}$ or the feasible set, $\left\{ x\, g(x) = 0 \right\}$, is bounded, then the path converges to a point that satisfies the Lagrangian condition, $L_x = 0$, as well as the feasibility condition, $g(x) = 0$.

4. Observations on Decentralization, Information, and Computation

Let us take the case most favorable to the possibility of decentralization, that in which both the objective function and the constraint functions are additively separable, i.e.,

$$f(x) = \sum_j f^j(x_j), \, g(x) = \sum_j g^j(x_j). \qquad (1\text{-}22)$$

Here, x_j might be interpreted as an activity level, and, for given j, the functions $f^j(x_j)$ and $g^j_i(x_j)$ $(1 = 1, \ldots, m)$ define the final output and intermediate outputs (or inputs, with sign reversed) of a nonlinear activity. In that case, the information in the jth "observation," i.e., $\delta f/\delta x_j$ and $\delta g_i/\delta x_j$ $(i = 1, \ldots, m)$ is solely a function of x_j and hence can be determined by the jth activity manager without other information. Therefore, the information can be transmitted to the central authority. Indeed, in some sense, the information transmitted is less expensive than the demands and supplies needed under a price adjustment mechanism, for the latter requires optimization and hence global knowledge by the activity manager, while the former requires only information on the production structure of the jth activity in the neighborhood of the present point.

Hence, from the information point of view, Marglin's thesis is valid in the more general case. The information to be transmitted by the activity managers is not greater and may even be less in the quantity adjustment process than in the price adjustment process.

But a different valuation must be made when we consider computing costs at the center. In the price adjustment model, all that is needed is aggregate excess demand; this is computed by simply adding up the excess demands of the individual activities. In the quantity adjustment model, *per contra*, the central authority has to fit a regression, a much more complicated operation. Indeed, it involves, among other steps, the inversion of a matrix whose order equals the number of resources. The Marglin model, which involves only one resource, thus gives an unrepresentatively favorable impression of the computational problem, since the regression estimation reduces to computing mean.

It should also be noted that any commodity which enters into the production of another commodity is a "resource" from this point of view; that is, the resources which are constrained include both primary resources and intermediate goods. Thus, the number of resources is apt to be almost the same as the number of commodities.

These cursory remarks to leave some issues unresolved. For example, if the production structure is marked by constant coefficients (as in a Leontief structure) then the inversion need only be done once, not repeated at each iteration. It is clear that we need a more sophisticated theory of computational and informational efficiency, in which a priori knowledge of production and utility structures is used to reduce the need for calculation. But if we stick to the conventional rules for evaluating alternative optimal resource allocation mechanisms, in which the central authorities know no more of the activity structures than what is transmitted to them, the quantity adjustment process appears to be inferior in terms of the computational load on the center, though not in terms of the costs of information transmission.

References

1. Arrow, K.J., and F.H. Hahn. *General Competitive Analysis.* San Francisco: Holden-Day, 1971.
2. Arrow, K.J. and L. Hurwicz. "Decentralization and Computation in Resource Allocation." In R.W. Pfouts (ed.), *Essays in Economics and Econometrics.* Chapel Hill, North Carolina: University of North Carolina Press, n.d. Pp. 34–104.
3. Arrow, K.J. and R.M. Solow. "Gradient Methods for Constrained Maxima, with Weakened Assumptions." Chapter 11 in K.J. Arrow, L. Hurwicz, and H. Uzawa, *Studies in Linear and Non-Linear Programming.* Stanford, Calif.: Stanford University Press, 1958. Pp. 166–176.
4. Forsythe, G.E. "Computing Constrained Maxima with Lagrangean Multipliers." *Journal of the Society for Industrial and Applied Mathematics* 3 (1955): 173–178.
5. Letov, A.M. *Stability in Nonlinear Control Systems.* English translation. Princeton, New Jersey: Princeton University Press, 1961.
6. Marglin, S. "Information in Price and Command Systems of Planning." Chapter 3 in J. Margolis and H. Guitton (eds.), *Public Economics.* New York: St. Martin's Press, 1969. Pp. 54–77.

2 The Income Tax Treatment of Charitable Contributions

A.B. Atkinson

Introduction

One of the many areas in which Bill Vickrey has been a pioneer is that of the economics of charitable contributions. His essay "One Economist's View of Philanthropy" presented, among other things, an analysis of the motives for charity, and a critique of the tax treatment of contributions. The conclusion he drew was that the "haphazard array of subsidies that result from present special tax privileges call for replacement with more uniform and explicit arrangements" (1962, p. 56). One particular recommendation for reform which he had made fifteen years earlier in *Agenda for Progressive Taxation* was that the deductibility of contributions under the United States personal income tax should be replaced by a flat-rate tax credit (1947, p. 131), a proposal which of late has received widespread attention (see, for example, Andrews (1972), McDaniel (1972), Pechman (1971), and Surrey 1972)). The aim of this chapter is to describe a simple theoretical model of contributions to charity. This embodies some of the insights contained in "One Economist's View" and pays particular attention to the redistributive consequences of philanthropy. The model provides in turn a framework for examining the income tax treatment of contributions, and whether tax deductibility should be replaced by a proportional tax credit as Vickrey proposed.

1. Redistribution and the Motives for Charitable Contributions

There are many motives for charitable contributions, and this is reflected in the wide variety of types of charities. People give to support religious institutions, to provide educational or medical facilities, to encourage cultural and scientific activities, or to help disadvantaged groups. These forms of charity may have quite different distributional consequences, and indeed Vickrey (1962) has argued that in many cases the redistributive impact of philanthropy may be relatively slight. In what follows we consider two rather different views of the

I am grateful to A.J. Culyer, M.S. Feldstein, R.E. Grieson, and M.K. Taussig for their helpful comments on an earlier version.

13

motives for contributions and their role in redistribution. The first is that individuals give to charity solely on account of the utility associated with the act
of giving. They are not concerned with the end use of the funds, although it may
be the case that some part performs a redistributive function. At the other extreme is the view that charitable activity is purely redistributive. Individuals give
because they are concerned about the welfare of disadvantaged groups.

In the model described here, this is formalized as follows. There are two
groups in society. The first is the working population, who consume X, spend a
fraction L of the day working, and make charitable contributions G. They are
assumed to have identical utility functions, but differ in the wage rate they can
earn (w), and this is continuously distributed with density $f(w)$ and $w \geqslant \underline{w}$,
where $\int_{\underline{w}}^{\infty} f \, dw = (1 - \mu)$. The second group has zero earning power, and is reliant
on state financial provision and on private contributions. A proportion μ of the
population is in this group, which is denoted as group A (for the Aged).

On the first view of the motives for charity, the level of contributions G
enters the individual utility functions of the working population, and they
maximize

$$V^I(w) \equiv U(X, L, G). \tag{2-1}$$

The resulting total of contributions by the working population is given by

$$\Gamma = \int_{\underline{w}}^{\infty} G(w) f(w) \, dw \tag{2-2}$$

and of this some fraction may go to group A, whose utility is denoted by U_A.

The second view—that charity is purely redistributive—means that G does
not enter the individual utility function; on the other hand, individuals are concerned about the level of consumption of those in the disadvantaged group A.
This concern may be represented by individuals in the working population
maximizing

$$V^{II}(w) \equiv U(X, L) + \delta U(X_A, Q) \tag{2-3}$$

where X_A denotes the consumption of Group A.[1] Their altruism is limited in
that only the welfare of group A enters their maximand (they are unconcerned,
for example, about fellow workers with a lower wage) and that the utility of
group A is "discounted" by δ (where $0 \leqslant \delta < 1$). It is them assumed that
individuals perceive X_A as being related to their charitable contribution G
according to:

$$X_A = \gamma G + G_0. \tag{2-4}$$

It should be emphasized that this is the *perceived* and not the *actual* relationship between X_A and G. This formulation of charitable behavior is based on Vickrey [1962], who emphasises the importance of interdependence between donors:[2]

> (it might be claimed) that in the case of a voluntary contribution the donor, on balance, gains in satisfaction at least as much as he would by spending the money in other ways . . . in practice however we are in a situation akin to that of monopolistic competition where one's own behaviour is expected to influence that of others . . . . A will expect that B and C may also be induced by his gift to contribute . . . . The combined effects of A's original gift plus that of the induced gifts . . . will provide for A a level of satisfaction equal to what he would have obtained had he kept the amount of his contribution for himself."
> (pp. 40–41).

Two comments should be made about this formulation of the two views of charitable motives. Firstly, it is clear that (2–3) and (2–4) together are a special case of (2–1), so that in a formal sense the analysis is equivalent. The difference lies in the interpretation of the results, as is discussed later in the chapter. Secondly, this representation of charitable behavior is obviously not the only one which could be adopted, and the reader is referred to the discussion by, among others, Boulding (1962), Hochman and Rodgers (1969), Ireland and Johnson (1970), and Becker (1974). But although the model is a rather special one, it seems worth exploring and, as shown below, it can lead to equations determining the level of contributions which are not dissimilar to those estimated in econometric studies by Feldstein (1973) and others.

2. The Framework for Policy Decisions

Much of the previous discussion of the policy implications has been concerned with the "efficiency" of alternative tax treatment of contributions, where this is measured by the amount of additional contribution received by charities per dollar of potential tax revenue foregone. In the case where there is a constant marginal tax rate t and full deductibility, this focuses on the level of $(1 - t)\Gamma$ and it is for this reason that particular attention has been paid to whether the elasticity of Γ with respect to $(1 - t)$ is greater or less than minus one. In the present context however we take the rather broader view of the government's objectives represented by the additive social welfare function

$$\mu U_A + D\int_{\underline{w}}^{\infty} V(w)f(w)dw \tag{2-5}$$

where $0 \leqslant D \leqslant 1$. The case $D = 1$ corresponds to a utilitarian objective, whereas $D < 1$ means that the government attaches greater weight to the utility of group A. In what follows it is assumed that the transfers to group A are never sufficient to raise their utility (U_A) to the level achieved by a worker with wage $\underline{w}$:

$$U_A < V(\underline{w}). \tag{2-6}$$

This means that $D = 0$ corresponds to the Rawlsian case where the government is concerned *only* with the welfare of the least advantaged group (Rawls, 1972).

The consumption of Group A is financed by the revenue raised from income taxation (R) and by charitable contributions (Γ). (It is assumed that the only government expenditure is on transfer payments to group A.) In both cases administrative costs and inefficiencies in allocation may mean that the total received is less than that collected. Denoting the relative effectiveness of charitable contributions by h, we have

$$\mu X_A = \eta(R + h\Gamma) \tag{2-7}$$

where $0 < \eta \leqslant 1$ and $h \geqslant 0$ are constants.[a] A number of considerations are likely to affect the value of h, and two of the most important here are the type of charity supported and the effectiveness of charitable organizations. In the former case, the value of h is likely to reflect the motives for charity. Where individuals are motivated by the utility derived from giving, and where the redistributive consequences of philanthropy are limited (as argued by Vickrey, 1962), the value of h may be very low. On the other hand, where the main motive for charity is redistribution, the value of h depends on the efficiency of the charitable organizations. Those who attach great importance to the disbursement of funds by private bodies rather than state agencies may feel that h is greater than 1. On the other hand, those who are concerned about the high proportion of collection costs in private charities, or about their patterns of allocation, may argue that h is substantially less than 1. To sum up, h is only likely to exceed 1 if most charitable activity is redistributive and if it is at least as effective as state income maintenance programmes.

The main aim of the subsequent analysis is to examine the desirability of tax preference for contributions in the light of the social welfare function (2-5) and differing views about the value of h. This may be contrasted with the "efficiency" objective usually considered, which in the present context is equivalent to assuming that $h = 1$ (i.e., private charity and tax revenue are perfect substitutes) and that $D = 0$ (a Rawlsian objective).[b]

---

[a]The assumption that h is constant is not necessarily realistic, since the effectiveness may depend on factors such as the size of gifts.

[b]It also assumes that pre-tax incomes are independent of the tax treatment of contributions. For further discussion, see Boskin (1975).

As explained in the Introduction, the principal question with which we are concerned is the choice between tax deductibility and a tax credit. This means that the assumption of a constant marginal tax rate, frequently made in the literature on income taxation, would rule out the interesting aspects of the question, since the two approaches would then be equivalent. At the same time, there are advantages in adopting a relatively simple form. For this reason, we assume that the tax system is given by

$$T(Y) = Y - Y^\beta E^{1-\beta} \quad \text{for} \quad Y \geqslant E$$

$$= 0 \text{ otherwise}$$

where Y denotes income (wL) and $0 \leqslant \beta \leqslant 1$. The adoption of this function is particularly appropriate in the present volume, in view of its use in Vickrey (1947). As he showed, it has the property that if M denotes the marginal tax rate, then $1 - M = \beta(1 - T/Y)$, so that the marginal rate starts at $(1 - \beta)$ where $Y = E$ and rises as Y increases. If we now introduce the possibility of deducting a proportion Θ of charitable contributions, and a tax credit rate ρ, then the tax schedule becomes (for $Y - \Theta G \geqslant E$)

$$T = Y - (\Theta + \rho)G - (Y - \Theta G)^\beta E^{1-\beta} \tag{2-8}$$

where $0 \leqslant \Theta \leqslant 1$ and $0 \leqslant \rho < 1$. The cost of a gift of \$1 in terms of a loss of net income is \$$(1 - \rho)$ with the tax credit, and \$$(1 - \Theta M)$ with the tax deduction, so that the cost declines with income in the latter case.

3. An Explicit Model

In order to simplify the analysis we shall consider the special case where the function $V(w)$ takes the following form (identical for all individuals):

$$V(w) = \log X + b \log (1 - L) + \delta \log G. \tag{2-9}$$

Although a special case, it is of some interest. Not only does it allow an explicit solution which throws light on the issues involved, but also it leads to a price elasticity close to that estimated in recent studies. The relationship to $V^I(w)$ and $V^{II}(w)$ may be seen as follows. On the first view of charity, V is a logarithmic individual utility function with δ the exponent associated with gifts and U_A equals $\log X_A$. On the second view, $U(X, L) = \log X + b \log (1 - L)$, and it is assumed that $G_0 = 0$, so that δ is the discount attached to the utility of group A as perceived by the donors.

The maximization problem for a person in the working population subject to tax may be written in terms of the Lagrangian

$$L = \log X + b \log (1 - L) + \delta \log G + \lambda \left\{ wL - \Theta G)^\beta E^{1-\beta} \right.$$

$$\left. + (\Theta + \rho)G - X - G \right\}$$

(the consumption good is taken as the numeraire). This gives first-order conditions:

$$X^{-1} = \lambda$$

$$b(1 - L)^{-1} = \lambda w(1 - M)$$

$$\delta G^{-1} = \lambda[(1 - \Theta - \rho) + \Theta(1 - M)] = \lambda(1 - \rho - \Theta M)$$

To avoid unnecessary taxonomy, we assume that all the working population are subject to tax: i.e., $\underline{w}$ is sufficiently high to ensure $T > 0$ for all w. It may be verified that the second-order conditions are satisfied.

It follows that the level of G may be written as

$$G = \frac{\delta X}{(1 - \rho - \Theta M)} . \qquad (2\text{-}10)$$

This equation for G in the case of tax deductibility ($\Theta = 1$, $\rho = 0$) may be compared with the empirical evidence in the United States. Analysis of the data presented by Vickrey (1973) shows, for example, that the ratio of the net cost of gifts ($(1 - M)G$ in the case of tax deductibility) to disposable income (here taken as X) was broadly constant over the range from $10,000 to $200,000 of adjusted gross income in 1970. As Vickrey pointed out, the evidence is consistent with both the price and the income elasticities being unity, and although he himself felt that the price elasticity was less than 1.0 (and the income elasticity greater than 1.0), more recent econometric studies which have attempted to isolate these elasticities give results close to those implied by equation (2-10).[3] The equation used, for example, in Feldstein and Clotfelter (1975) to examine alternative tax policies (equation 2-6) has a price elasticity of 1.15 with a standard error of 0.20. Some of the estimates obtained by Feldstein (1973) indicate a price elasticity significantly greater than unity; on the other hand, those found by Schwartz (1970) were typically rather less than unity.[4] It should also be noted that our formulation implies that all those in the working population are donors. In the sample used by Feldstein and Clotfelter, "almost every individual" made gifts. Their sample excluded a number of groups, and therefore was not representative of the population as a whole. However, the excluded groups corresponded at least in part to group A in our model (e.g., they omitted the lowest fifth of households by income), so that the assumption made here may be unreasonable as a first approximation.

Solving the first-order conditions gives the following results for the two cases of particular interest:

Full tax deductibility, no tax credit ($\Theta = 1, \rho = 0$)

$$X = \frac{w\,(1 - \tau)}{(1 + (\delta + b)/\beta} \equiv X_1 \tag{2-11a}$$

$$L = \frac{1 + \delta/\beta}{1 + (\delta + b)/\beta} \equiv L_1 \tag{2-11b}$$

$$G = \frac{w\delta/\beta}{1 + (\delta + b)/\beta} \equiv G_1 \tag{2-11c}$$

No tax deductibility, tax credit ($\Theta = 0, \rho \geqslant 0$)

$$X = \frac{w(1 - \tau)}{1 + \delta + b/\beta} \equiv X_2 \tag{2-12a}$$

$$L = \frac{1 + \delta}{1 + \delta + b/\beta} \equiv L_2 \tag{2-12b}$$

$$G = \frac{\delta\,w(1 - \tau)}{(1 - \rho)\,(1 + \delta + b/\beta)} \equiv G_2 \tag{2-12c}$$

where τ is defined as the average tax rate, expessed as a percentage of taxable income, before allowing for the credit ($\tau = (T(Y) + \rho G)/(Y - \Theta G)$).

4. The Optimal Level of Tax Credit

In comparing the tax deductibility of contributions with the alternative of a tax credit, we have to consider the rate at which the credit would be set. Most of the discussion has assumed either a zero rate (the complete abolition of tax preference for contributions) or an arbitrary positive rate, typically around 20–30 percent (Vickrey (1947) suggested 25 percent). In this section we consider the optimal choice of the rate of credit (ρ).

The government's objectives are assumed to be represented by the social welfare function (2–5), and in the present context this is equivalent (using (2–7)) to maximizing

$$Z \equiv \mu \log(R + h\Gamma) + D \int_{\underline{w}}^{\infty} V(w)f(w)dw \qquad (2\text{-}13)$$

where R and Γ denote total revenue and gifts respectively.

Differentiating with respect to ρ, we obtain (in the case $\Theta = 0$)

$$\frac{\partial Z}{\partial \rho} = \frac{\mu \Gamma}{R + h\Gamma} \left(\frac{h-1}{1-\rho} \right) + D \int_{\underline{w}}^{\infty} \lambda G f dw \qquad (2\text{-}14)$$

where use has been made of the relationships

$$\frac{\partial \Gamma}{\partial \rho} = \frac{\Gamma}{1-\rho} \quad \text{and} \quad \frac{\partial V}{\partial \rho} = \lambda G$$

and it may be noted that the labor supplied is independent of ρ.

It is clear from equation (2–14) that where $h \geqslant 1$ we want to have the largest tax credit possible. The subsidization of charitable contributions is Pareto-improving, since it raises both the income of group A (the aged or handicapped) and the utility derived from giving by the donors. It is assumed that there is an upper bound to the possible level of credit, and in particular that the net revenue received by the government is always positive. The credit is therefore set at the upper bound $\rho_{\max}$, and

$$\rho_{\max} < \frac{R_0}{R_0 + \Gamma_0} \qquad (2\text{-}15)$$

where R_0, Γ_0 denote the total revenue and gifts when $\rho = \Theta = 0$ (the no tax preference case).

To see what happens where $h < 1$, that is charitable contributions are less "efficient" than state provision or are not directed at redistribution, we may rewrite (2–14) using (2–12a) and (2–12c).

$$(1-\rho)\frac{\partial Z}{\partial \rho} = D\delta(1-\mu) - \mu(1-h)\frac{\Gamma_0}{(1-\rho)R_0 + (h-\rho)\Gamma_0}$$

so that $\partial Z/\partial \rho$ has the sign of

$$\gamma - (1-\gamma)(1-h)\left[\frac{\Gamma_0}{(1-\rho)R_0 + (h-\rho)\Gamma_0} \right] \qquad (2\text{-}16)$$

where $\gamma = D\delta(1 - \mu)/(\mu + D\delta(1 - \mu))$. This is a decreasing function of ρ (for $0 \leqslant \rho \leqslant \rho_{max}$). It follows that the optimal value of ρ is given by

$$\max \left[0, 1 - \frac{(1 - h)}{\gamma(1 + R_0/\Gamma_0)} \right] \text{ subject to } \rho \leqslant \rho_{max}. \tag{2-17}$$

The term γ has the following interpretation where charity arises for redistributive reasons. In that case, the welfare of the disadvantaged group may be seen as entering Z both directly with weight μ and indirectly via the utility functions of the working population with weight $D\delta(1 - \mu)$ (i.e., incorporating both the social discount factor D and the private discount δ). The value of γ is a measure of the indirect importance of group A relative to their total weight in the social welfare function. If the government's concern arises largely because of private charitable feelings (γ is high) then the credit will be higher than if the weight attached to group A arises largely from their direct effect on social welfare (γ is low). If the government is concerned solely with the disadvantaged ($\gamma = 0$), then there should be no tax credit.

The condition for a positive tax credit may be written as

$$h > 1 - \gamma \left(1 + \frac{R_0}{\Gamma_0} \right) \tag{2-18}$$

The possibility that a positive tax credit may be desirable even where $h = 0$ (i.e., that the right hand side of (2-18) may be negative) can be ruled out where the following conditions hold:[c]

$$X_A < X(\underline{w}) \text{ and } \eta = 1 \tag{2-19}$$

If therefore charities perform no redistributive function ($h = 0$), the case for any tax preference has to be based on the inefficiency of transfers through taxation ($\eta < 1$) or on the marginal utility of consumption group A being lower than that of the lowest paid worker.

From (2-17) it may be seen that the optimal rate of tax credit is higher, (i) the larger the value of h (the more effective charitable contributions), (ii) the greater the indirect importance of group A (γ), and (iii) the smaller are gifts as a proportion of tax revenue when there is no tax preference (Γ_0/R_0). To give some idea of the magnitudes involved, suppose that gifts in the absence of tax preference would be one-quarter of revenue (bearing in mind that this relates to revenue raised for redistributive purposes), and that the proportion of the popu-

---

[c]At $\rho = 0$, $\delta(1 - \mu) = \int(G/X)f\,dw \leqslant \Gamma_0/X(\underline{w}) < \Gamma_0/X_A$ where the first part of (2-19) holds. From (2-7) where $h = \rho = 0$, $\Gamma_0/X_A = \mu\Gamma_0/\eta R_0$. It follows that $\gamma/(1 - \gamma) < (\Gamma_0/R_0)$ where $\eta = 1$, so from (2-16) $\partial Z/\partial\rho < 0$ at $\rho = 0$.

lation in group A is one-fifth. A value of 0.05 for δ would imply that net gifts constituted 5 percent of consumption. With these values, $D = 1$ implies that γ equals one-sixth and that a positive tax credit is desirable where $h > 1/6$. Where $h = \frac{1}{2}$, the optimal level of credit would be 40 percent. On the other hand, $D = 1/3$ would mean that the optimal policy was one of no tax preference where $h \leqslant 11/16$.

5. The Choice Between Tax Deductibility and a Tax Credit

The choice clearly depends on the value of D, or the relative weight attached to the welfare of the two groups. The simplest case to consider is the Rawlsian case $D = 0$, where the government is only concerned with the disadvantaged group A. The difference, denoted by Δ, between the level of social welfare in the situation with tax deductibility and that in the case of a tax credit is then given by (using (2-13) and the fact that total gifts with the tax credit are $\Gamma_0/(1 - \rho)$)

$$\Delta = \mu \log \left[\frac{R_1 + h\Gamma_1}{R_0 + \dfrac{h - \rho}{1 - \rho} \Gamma_0} \right] \tag{2-20}$$

The effect of the different tax treatment on the income accruing to group A from the two sources may be seen from the equations (2-11) and (2-12). In particular, [d]

$$wL_1 - G_1 < wL_2 < wL_1 \tag{2-21a}$$

$$(1 - \rho)G_2 < G_1 \tag{2-21b}$$

In other words, gross income is higher with the tax deduction but *taxable* income (net of gifts) is lower. Revenue would therefore be lower than with a zero

---

[d]The second of these is obtained from (2-11c) and (2-12c), where for any given w

$$G_1 \gtrless (1 - \rho)G_2 \text{ as } \frac{\beta + \delta\beta + b}{\beta + \delta + b} \gtrless 1 - M$$

or

$$M \gtrless \frac{\delta(1 - \beta)}{\delta + \beta + b}.$$

Since $M \geqslant 1 - \beta$ it follows that $G_1 > (1 - \rho)G_2$.

tax credit $(R_1 < R_0)$. On the other hand, the level of gifts is higher with the tax deduction than with a zero credit $(\Gamma_1 > \Gamma_0)$.

The government has therefore to balance the effect on revenue against that on charitable contributions. As noted in section 2, this is typically done by considering the total of revenue and gifts: i.e., the case where $h = 1$. The present tax deduction is then preferable according to the "efficiency" criterion where[e]

$$R_1 + \Gamma_1 > R_0 + \Gamma_0 \tag{2-22}$$

(although in empirical applications it is typically assumed that Y is unchanged, so that no allowance is made for the effect on the tax base). As argued earlier, h is only likely to equal or exceed 1 if most charitable activity is redistributive and it is at least as efficient as state income maintenance. Where $h < 1$, the optimal rate of credit is zero (since $D = 0$), and Δ is reduced as h falls below 1. In the limiting case where $h = 0$, Δ is clearly negative, since $R_1 < R_0$. Condition (2-22) implies therefore that there is a critical value of h below which tax deductibility ceases to be desirable. The critical value

$$h^* \equiv \frac{R_0 - R_1}{\Gamma_1 - \Gamma_0} = \frac{\text{loss of revenue from deduction}}{\text{increase in gifts from deduction}}.$$

This, and condition (2-22), depend on the effect of the tax deduction on pre-tax incomes and on the degree of progressitivity (β). (It is assumed throughout the chapter that β is unchanged, although variation in the tax treatment of contributions might well affect the optimal degree of progression.)

In the case where $D \geqslant 0$, that is the government attaches some weight to the welfare of the working population, the difference between the level of social welfare with the deduction and that with the credit is proportional to

$$\Delta = (1 - \gamma) \log\left(\frac{R_1 + h\Gamma_1}{R_0 + \dfrac{h - \rho}{1 - \rho}\Gamma_0}\right) + \gamma I \tag{2-23}$$

where

$$I = \int_{\underline{w}}^{\infty} \frac{\hat{V}}{\partial(1 - \mu)} f\, dw \tag{2-24}$$

---

and $\hat{V}$ denotes the difference in utility between the tax deduction and tax credit situations (and is a function of ρ).

We are interested in the conditions under which $\Delta = 0$, or the government is indifferent between the two policies. It may be shown (see the Appendix to this chapter) that condition (2-22) implies that the possible contours for $\Delta = 0$, regarded as a function of h and γ, are as shown in figure 2-1. Where $\gamma = 0$, we have the case discussed in the previous paragraph with $\rho = 0$. Condition (2-22) means that the top left hand corner has a Δ positive, and $\Delta = 0$ at h^* as indicated. Where $\gamma > 0$, we have to allow for the possibility that the optimal level of credit determined by (2-17) is positive. In the figure it is assumed that the conditions (2-19) hold, so that the boundary $\rho = 0$ is given by the lower dashed line. The value of ρ is zero to the left of this line, and then rises as one moves in a counter-clockwise direction around ($\gamma = 0$, $h = 1$), until it reaches ρ_{max} at the upper dashed line. Where $\rho = 0$, $I > 0$ (see Appendix) and the $\Delta = 0$ contour slopes down from h^*. Two possible paths are then shown. If there is a feasible level of credit such that $I = 0$ (i.e., it compensates for the abolition of the deduction),

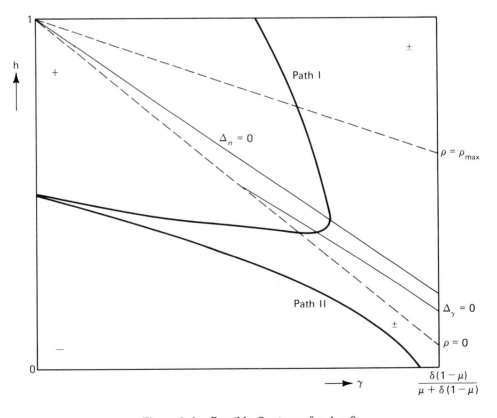

Figure 2-1. Possible Contours for $\Delta = 0$

then the contour cuts the line $\Delta_\gamma = 0$ horizontally and rises as indicated on Path I. In such a case, the tax credit would be preferred to the tax deduction in the upper right-hand corner. This would not imply that the credit made everyone in the donor population better off; indeed one of the features of the credit is that it redistributes *within the donor class.* Where this level of credit cannot be attained, then we have Path II and Δ is positive in the upper right-hand corner. These results may be summarized as follows:

	Low γ	*High* γ
High *h*	Tax deductibility desirable on basis of condition (2–22)	May be case for tax credit at maximum rate to secure equity among donors
Low *h*	No tax preference	?

The above analysis suggests that the case against the tax deductibility of charitable contributions can be made in two main ways. Firstly, if the government is largely concerned with the welfare of the disadvantaged group (γ is low) and if it believes that the redistributive effectiveness of charitable contributions (as measured by *h*) is low, then there should be no tax preference for contributions. Secondly, if the government attaches more weight to the welfare of the donors (γ large) and believes that charitable contributions are both directed at redistribution and reasonably effective (*h* is high) then there *may* be a case for a tax credit at a relatively high rate to bring about greater equity between donors. The replacement of the deduction by a tax credit benefits the middle and lower income donors at the expense of the wealthy, and if this can be achieved without a serious reduction in total giving, then such a redistribution may be considered desirable.

6. Concluding Comments

The aim of this chapter has been to provide a framework within which the arguments concerning the income tax treatment of contributions may be made more precise than is commonly the case. At the same time, it hardly needs emphasizing that the model considered here is a very special one. As recognized earlier, the model incorporates only some of the considerations influencing charitable behavior, and it focuses on charities as redistributive agencies. More specifically, it does not allow for different views about the stimulus to giving provided by tax preferences, since it is assumed that the price and income elasticities are both unity. While this is consistent with recent econometric evidence Vickrey himself has argued that the price elasticity is less than 1.0. The reason for taking the unitary elasticity case is that it is clearly a critical value, and that it allows us to focus on the other elements affecting the choice between tax deductibility and a tax credit. In particular we have tried to go beyond simple "efficiency" considerations (in the present notation these correspond to $h = 1$, $\gamma = 0$) and to set the analysis in an (albeit simple) general equilibrium model, incorporating the impact on decisions other than those about giving.

Notes

1. This formulation has certain similarity to equation (1) in Mirrlees (1973); see also Sen (1966). The treatment by Mirrlees emphasizes the role of charities in the provision of collective goods, an important aspect which is not discussed here.
2. It is of course only one aspect of interdependence and more generally we might expect G_0 to depend on the gifts by others. For interesting attempts to test this empirically, see Schwartz (1970) and Feldstein and Clotfelter (1975).
3. There have been a number of papers following the early econometric study by Taussig (1967), including Schwartz (1970), Feldstein (1973), Feldstein and Clotfelter (1975), and Feldstein and Taylor (1975).
4. The results of the different studies using income tax data are compared in Feldstein (1973), where he explains why the earlier finding of a low price elasticity (around 0.1) by Taussig (1967) is likely to be misleading.

References

Andrews, W.D. "Personal Deductions in an Ideal Income Tax." *Harvard Law Review* 86 (1972): 309–385.

Becker, G.S. "A Theory of Social Interactions." *Journal of Political Economy* 82 (1974): 1063–1094.

Boskin, M.J. "Estate Taxation and Charitable Bequests." *Journal of Public Economics* (1975, forthcoming).

Boulding, K.E. "Notes on a Theory of Philanthropy." In F.G. Dickinson (ed.), *Philanthropy and Public Policy*. New York: Columbia University Press, 1962.

Feldstein, M.S. "The Income Tax and Charitable Contributions." *National Tax Journal* (1973, forthcoming).

Feldstein, M.S. and C. Clotfelter. "Tax Incentives and Charitable Contributions in the United States." *Journal of Public Economics* (1975, forthcoming).

Feldstein, M.S. and A. Taylor. "Taxation and Charitable Contributions." Harvard discussion paper, 1975.

Hochman, H.M. and J.D. Rodgers. "Pareto Optimal Redistribution." *American Economic Review* 59 (1969): 542–557.

Ireland, T.R. and D.B. Johnson. *The Economics of Charity*. Blacksburg: Centre for the Study of Public Choice, 1970.

McDaniel, P.R. "Federal Matching Grants for Charitable Contributions." *Tax Law Review* 27 (1972): 377–413.

Mirrlees, J.A. "The Economics of Charitable Contributions." Paper presented at the European Meeting of the Econometric Society, August 1973.

Pechman, J.A. *Federal Tax Policy*. New York: W.W. Norton, 1971.

Rawls, J. *A Theory of Justice*. Cambridge, Mass.: Harvard University Press, 1972.

Schwartz, R.A. "Personal Philanthropic Contributions." *Journal of Political Economy* 78 (1970): 1264–1291.

Sen, A.K. "Labour Allocation in a Cooperative Enterprise." *Review of Economic Studies* 33 (1966): 361–371.

Surrey, S.S. *Federal Income Taxation*. Mineola, N.Y.: Foundation Press, 1972.

Taussig, M.K. "Economic Aspects of the Personal Income Tax Treatment of Charitable Contributions." *National Tax Journal* 20 (1967): 1–19.

Vickrey, W. *Agenda for Progressive Taxation*. New York: Ronald Press, 1947.

Vickrey, W. "One Economist's View of Philanthropy." In F.G. Dickinson (ed.), *Philanthropy and Public Policy*. New York: Columbia University Press, 1962.

Vickrey, W. "Private Philanthropy and Public Finance." Unpublished mimeo., 1973.

Appendix 2A

The contours for $\Delta = 0$ are given by $\Delta_h\, dh + \Delta_\gamma\, d\gamma = 0$ (where it may be noted that $\Delta_\rho\, d_\rho = 0$). Differentiating with respect to h, it may be seen that Δ_h is proportional to

$$(1 - \rho) \left(1 + \frac{R_0}{\Gamma_0} \right) - \left(1 + \frac{R_1}{\Gamma_1} \right)$$

which is positive where $\rho = 0$ (since $R_0 > R_1, \Gamma_0 < \Gamma_1$). Substituting for $(1 - \rho)$ from equation (2-17), where $\rho < \rho_{max}$, Δ_h is proportional to

$$1 - h - \gamma \left(1 + \frac{R_1}{\Gamma_1} \right)$$

The line $\Delta_h = 0$ passes through $(\gamma = 0, h = 1)$ and

$$\gamma = \left(\frac{\Gamma_1}{R_1 + \Gamma_1} \right), h = 0.$$

The contours $\Delta = 0$ cut this line vertically. Differentiating with respect to γ, and evaluating at $\Delta = 0$, the curve $\Delta_\gamma = 0$ is given by

$$(1 - \gamma)(R_0 + \Gamma_0) = R_1 + h\Gamma_1 \quad \text{for} \quad \rho > 0 \quad \text{and} \quad h = h^* \quad \text{for} \quad \rho = 0.$$

Where condition (2-22) holds, this has the form shown in figure 2-1. The $\Delta = 0$ contours cut $\Delta_\gamma = 0$ horizontally. (The intersection of $\Delta_h = \Delta_\gamma = 0$ is at $(\gamma = 1, h = -R_1\Gamma_1)$.

Since V is a strictly increasing function of θ, it follows that $\hat{V} > 0$ for $\rho = 0$ and hence that I is strictly positive for the region where $\rho = 0$.

3 Cumulative Averaging and Neutrality

Martin J. Bailey

In (1939) and (1947) Vickrey proposed a cumulative averaging formula for the personal income tax, and claimed that it would eliminate any incentive to accelerate depreciation or to convert ordinary income to capital gains. In (1964) Samuelson offered a theorem claiming to prove that present values, and by implication investment incentives, will be independent of the marginal income tax rate of the individual taxpayer if and only if the depreciation allowance for tax purposes always exactly equals economic depreciation—the loss of value of the depreciable asset with the passage of time. These two positions contradict each other: Vickrey was right and Samuelson wrong, if we accept the usage of calling Vickrey's proposed tax a form of income tax. However, Samuelson relied on an assumption, not expressly stated in the premise of his theorem, that would rule out Vickrey's formula. That assumption was that the taxpayer's marginal tax rate remains constant over time. Therefore, the sufficiency half of Samuelson's theorem is true, ("if"), but not the necessity half ("only if"). Vickrey's formula provides a counterexample to the latter. With a constant tax rate, neutrality requires accurate economic depreciation for tax purposes; with the Vickrey formula, which varies the tax rate over time in a way chosen to assure neutrality, the depreciation allowed is immaterial so long as it is limited to a cumulative total of 100 percent of original cost. This chapter proves these assertions and enlarges upon them.

By "neutrality" we refer to the absence of announcement effects that would directly alter resource allocation among different industries, or that would affect an investor's choice among financial instruments, depreciation procedures, and so on. Any non-neutral effects of the tax system on saving versus consumption or on labor versus leisure we largely ignore, inasmuch as, to a first approximation, they are unaffected by depreciation, capital gains taxes, and interindustry neutrality for a given effective marginal income tax rate.

Vickrey proposed that for some large number of years—age 21 until death, if possible—each taxpayer should carry forward his cumulated income and tax payments, the latter with interest. Each year his cumulated tax liability would come from a tax table calculated from the present annual type of table using the number of years the taxpayer had been in the system. (That is, the IRS would send a two-year table to all taxpayers aged 22, a three-year table to taxpayers aged 23, and so on. Students and other special cases would have special rules.) The rate brackets in the k-year table would be approximately k times as wide, the exemptions k times a large, etc., as they are in the one-year table, and the cumulated k years of income would determine the gross tax liability. From this liability the taxpayer would subtract his past taxes paid, with interest, to find his net tax due in the current year. The exact rate bracket lines would be set so that each year's net tax due would work out the same as it does on the basic annual table if the taxpayer's income stream over time fits a chosen standard pattern, such as a constant, unchanging income.

Vickrey and others have fully explained the merits of averaging, and he has pointed out the neutrality advantages of his cumulative method. Here we offer proof of this neutrality, and establish it as a counterexample to the Samuelson theorem.

Vickrey properly proposed to include in the taxpayer's cumulated income the interest credited to his past taxes. This step equates the taxpayer's after-tax interest on paid-up taxes to his after-tax yield on competing investments, for every taxpayer regardless of marginal rate. It is necessary for our claimed results. However, instead of adding to income the interest on past taxes, we obtain exactly equivalent results by cumulating and discounting with the after-tax rate of return appropriate to his rate bracket. In effect, we pay each taxpayer tax-exempt interest on his past taxes using an interest rate that declines with the taxpayer's marginal tax rate so as to be equivalent to the same taxable interest rate for all taxpayers. This equivalent procedure greatly simplifies the mathematics compared to that required to represent the Vickrey procedure more precisely.

Where the pertinent interest rate is r before taxes, we allow the taxpayer a cumulated credit $C(t)$ his past taxes at time t as follows, where for simplicity we use continuous flows and a force rate of interest:

$$C_1(t) = \int_0^t T_1(z)e^{r'(t-z)}\, dz \tag{3-1}$$

where $T_1(z)$ is the tax payment at time z and where $r' = r(1 - m)$ is the taxpayer's after-tax rate of interest, his marginal tax rate being m. Although our proof does not depend on any restriction on the formula for cumulated tax liability $L_1(t)$ except that it be independent of the timing of income, we shall for convenient illustration approximate the Vickrey proposal as follows:

$$L_1(t) = \bar{m}(t)Y_1(t) \tag{3-2}$$

$$= \frac{m}{t} \int_0^t e^{r'(t-z)}\, dz \quad \int_0^t y_1(z)\, dz$$

$$= \frac{m}{t} \frac{e^{r't} - 1}{r'} \int_0^t y_1(z)\, dz \tag{3-3}$$

where $y(t)$ is current net taxable income at time t, $Y_1(t)$ its total since time zero, cumulated without interest, and $\bar{m}(t)$ is the effective tax rate per formula (3-3). Once again for simplicity and without loss of generality we tax all the taxpayer's income at the one rate $\bar{m}$, and we use a single interest rate r' through time. (The expression (3-3) differs from Vickrey's because we leave interest on past tax payments out of taxable income.) Now

$$L_1'(t) = \frac{dL}{dt} = Y_1(t)\frac{d\bar{m}}{dt} + \bar{m}y_1(t)$$

$$= \frac{Y_1(t)\,[\bar{m}(t)e^{r't} - m]}{t} + \bar{m}(t)\,y_1(t) \qquad (3\text{-}4)$$

and taking the derivative of (3-1) we have

$$C_1'(t) = \frac{dC_1}{dt}$$

$$= T_1(t) + r'C_1(t). \qquad (3\text{-}5)$$

If we require the taxpayer to pay

$$T_1(t) \equiv L_1'(t) - r'C_1(t) \qquad (3\text{-}6)$$

at every time t, then

$$L_1'(t) \equiv T_1(t) + r'C_1(t)$$

$$\equiv C_1'(t) \qquad (3\text{-}7)$$

for all t. Inasmuch as

$$L_1(0) = C_1(0) = 0$$

(3-7) implies

$$C_1(t) \equiv L_1(t) \qquad (3\text{-}8)$$

for all t. That is, the flow of tax payments (3-6) exactly keeps the taxpayer paid up on his cumulated liability.

Consider now the same taxpayer's position if he changes his depreciation formula, or any other practice affecting the timing of income, as he looks forward to the end of useful life of the pertinent asset (or to the end of any time period zero to t in which his total undiscounted taxable income will be the same under the new practice as under the old.) Then his cumulated tax liability for the new taxable income stream will be

$$L_2(t) = \bar{m}(t)Y_2(t)$$

$$= \bar{m}(t)Y_1(t)$$

where the second right hand side equals the first by assumption. Then by (3-2) we have

$$L_2(t) = L_1(t)$$

and so the present values are also equal

$$L_2(t)e^{-r't} = L_1(t)e^{-r't}. \tag{3-9}$$

By (3-8) and (3-1), (3-9) shows that the present values of the two entire tax streams $T_1(z)$ and $T_2(z)$ from time zero to t are equal, proving Vickrey's claim. The taxpayer gains nothing, if he discounts the future using r', by accelerating depreciation, by charging some capital costs to current expense, or the like, under the Vickrey plan.

Now consider the particular result that follows if the taxpayer's "new" accounting leads to an income stream $\bar{y}$ that remains constant from time zero onward. Then (3-4) says that his tax liability works out to be

$$L_2(z) \equiv \frac{m\bar{y}}{r'}(e^{r'z} - 1) \tag{3-10}$$

and we have

$$L_2'(z) \equiv m\bar{y}e^{r'z}.$$

By (3-8) we have

$$C_2(z) \equiv L_2(z)$$

for all z, and by (3-6) we may write

$$T_2(z) \equiv L_2'(z) - r'L_2(z)$$

$$\equiv mye^{r'z} - r'\left[\frac{m\bar{y}}{r'}(e^{r'z} - 1)\right]$$

$$\equiv m\bar{y} \qquad\qquad\qquad (3\text{-}11)$$

The taxpayer pays the constant tax rate m on his current income, just as if the tax were a conventional non-averaged one, when his income stream is constant, conforming in this respect also to the Vickrey plan. Suppose that the taxpayer's new accounting uses economically true current expenses and depreciation $h_2(z)$, to be deducted from his cash flow $g(z)$, to arrive at taxable income.

$$g(z) - h_2(z) \equiv \bar{y} \qquad 0 \leqslant z \leqslant t. \qquad\qquad (3\text{-}12)$$

His net cash flow after tax is

$$g(z) - m[g(z) - h_2(z)] = g(z) - m\bar{y}$$

whose cumulated present value is

$$V_2 = \int_0^t [g(z) - m\bar{y}]e^{-r'z}dz$$

$$= \int_0^t [g(z) - m\bar{y}]e^{-r(1-m)z}dz. \qquad\qquad (3\text{-}13)$$

Because m is constant over time and because the taxpayer arrives at his taxable income using true economic depreciation, this example satisfies all the assumptions used in Samuelson's proof, whose "if" part we may therefore use to conclude that

$$\frac{\partial V_2}{\partial m} = 0 \qquad\qquad\qquad (3\text{-}14)$$

where r' varies with the tax rate m, while r remains constant. Now (3-13) gives us

$$V_2 = \int_0^t g(z)e^{-r'z}dz - L_2(t)e^{-r't}$$

and we have from (3-9) that a change in the taxpayer's accounting such that depreciation is no longer economically true has no effect on the present value of expected taxes under the Vickrey plan; hence

$$V_1 \equiv \int_0^t g(z)e^{-r'z}dz - L_1(t)e^{-r't}$$

$$\equiv V_2 \tag{3-15}$$

for every value of m. Together (3-14) and (3-15) imply

$$\frac{\partial V_1}{\partial m} = 0$$

completing the proof that we have a counter-example to Samuelson's (1964) theorem, which stated,

> *Fundamental theorem of tax-rate invariance.* — If, and only if, true loss of economic value is permitted as a tax-deductible depreciation expense will the present discounted value of a cash-receipt stream be independent of the rate of tax. (Italics in original.)

The "only if" of the theorem is false; when tax is assessed using Vickrey's cumulative averaging, the present discounted value of the cash receipts stream will always be independent of the rate of tax regardless of depreciation practice, provided that all income is eventually taxed and that the pre-tax rate of return r is independent of the rate of tax.

In defense of the correctness of the Samuelson theorem one might argue that the Vickrey tax is a wealth tax with annual installments, not an income tax. However, that is a question of usage, not substance, and I think that in face many tax scholars have been misled by the Samuelson theorem given their own concept of an income tax.

In private correspondence Samuelson has kindly reminded me of another case that appears to be a counter-example to his theorem: allow the taxpayer to write off each investment (take immediate 100 percent depreciation) against taxable income at the time of the investment. This procedure, also, is neutral between industries, and in addition is neutral between consumption and saving. A counterargument to it is that this procedure is equivalent to a consumption tax, which is not an income tax, and hence is not a valid counter-example to the Samuelson theorem. However, that may be, it is in fact neutral while departing from true economic depreciation, and is therefore pertinent and interesting.

It is pertinent to explore further the relationship of tax neutrality to the challenged theorem. We know that competitive investment markets neutralize net present value of all investments at zero for those who hold them, the price of a claim or security being the same for everyone. Inasmuch as any person in any tax bracket may own any investment, the after-tax rate of return (internal discount rate) r' must be the same for every person in any particular tax bracket. By a "neutral" tax system we will mean one under which in competitive equilibrium all pre-tax rates of return r_i equal the same value $\bar{r}$. Without loss of generality, we assume that there exist fully taxable reference investments for which $r'_i = r_i(1 - m)$; also, we assume that the marginal tax rate m can be zero for at least one investor. We assume also that any less-than-fully-taxable investment is similarly privileged for every investor in a non-zero tax bracket, and that no investment is taxed more heavily than a reference investment. (However, with a non-neutral tax system a given privilege will be worth more to taxpayer in one tax bracket than to those in another (see Bailey 1974).

Assume that the tax system is neutral, this is $r_i = \bar{r}$ for every investment i. Then also

$$r'_i = \bar{r}' = \bar{r}(1 - m) \tag{3-16}$$

for every i and for every m. For suppose the contrary. Then there is an investment j such that $r'_j > \bar{r}'$ for some value of m, if $r_j = \bar{r}$. Because all have equal access to tax privilege, as just noted, it follows that $r'_j > \bar{r}'$ for every value of $m > 0$. However, in this circumstance investors with non-zero m would bid up the price of a unit of this investment, driving down its r_j below $\bar{r}$, contrary to the assumed neutrality. It follows from (3-16) that if the tax system is neutral, the present value of every investment is invariant with respect to the tax rate m.

Now assume that the present value of every investment is invariant with respect to the tax rate m. It follows that $r'_j = \bar{r}'$ for every investment of every value of m. Because there can be an investor for whom m is zero and so for whom $\bar{r}' = \bar{r}$, it follows that $r_j = \bar{r}$ for every j. Thus we have proved the

> FUNDAMENTAL THEOREM OF NEUTRALITY. *If, and only if, the present discounted value of the dash-receipt stream from every investment is independent of the rate of tax will the tax system be neutral.*

In his discussion of his misleading *Fundamental theorem,* Samuelson implied but neglected to establish the present theorem. It would be a useful characterization of neutrality if we could readily verify his form of tax rate invariance; unfortunately direct verification can be difficult. However, the proof of the present theorem also proves its useful

> COROLLARY. *If, and only if, there is a non-zero tax rate* m *for which* $r'_i = r_i (1 - m)$ *for every investment* i *will the tax system be neutral.*

That is, we need consider only a single tax rate and establish the absence of tax privilege for every investment for that tax rate to establish neutrality, and so, incidentally, to establish "invariance." It is straightforward to apply this test to

Vickrey's cumulative averaging proposal, where for neutrality we must of course also have consolidation of the corporate and personal income taxes and must allow the deduction from taxable income of exactly 100 percent of true expenses and investment outlays for any investment.

To illustrate the point that cumulative averaging allows the taxpayer complete freedom to allocate his legitimate deductions over time without disturbing neutrality, consider the case of a steady stream of (true) income that the taxpayer elects to covert to "capital gain." As noted in equation (3-11), if the taxpayer pays tax currently on a steady true income of $\bar{y}$ his tax stream is a steady stream equal to $m\bar{y}$. If the present value of the investment is V_o, the taxpayer has the pre-tax and after-tax yields

$$r = \frac{\bar{y}}{V_o}$$

and

$$r' = \frac{\bar{y}(1 - m)}{V_o} = r(1 - m).$$

Now instead of reporting his true economic income suppose that the taxpayer elects to claim extra depreciation and report zero income until time t, at which time he must report in one sum for tax purposes all the income previously masked by accelerated depreciation. Suppose further that his investments and true income are unaffected by this change in his accounting. Then his taxable income at time t will be

$$y(t) = \bar{y}t.$$

Under cumulative averaging his tax, from equation (3-3), will be

$$T(t) = \bar{m}(t)\bar{y}t$$

$$= \frac{m}{t}\left(\frac{e^{r't} - 1}{r'}\right)\bar{y}t \tag{3-17}$$

$$= m\bar{y}\left(\frac{e^{r't} - 1}{r'}\right) \tag{3-17}$$

and this tax is precisely the amount required to keep the discounted present value of the net income stream unchanged:

$$V_o = \int_0^t g(z)e^{-r'z}dz - m\bar{y}\left(\frac{e^{r't} - 1}{r'}\right)e^{-r't}$$

$$= \int_0^t \bar{y}e^{-r'z}dz - \frac{m\bar{y}(e^{r't} - 1)e^{-r't}}{r'} + V_o e^{-r't}$$

$$= \frac{\bar{y}(1 - m)}{r'}$$

as before, so that the after-tax rate of return is the same as it was on the steady stream of (fully reported and taxed) true income.

This result depends on having a tax rate that rises with time for deferred income, as it does in (3-17). If the law merely required the full inclusion of capital gains in ordinary income under the present annual type of income tax, the taxpayer would still get a higher rate of return by deferring realization. (Bailey 1969).

The treatment of capital gains helps to highlight one obscure but possibly important feature of cumulative averaging: for any given tax rate m, the Vickrey plan aggrevated tax disincentive to saving/investment compared to a flat-rate annual income tax. Under an annual income tax at the rate m, the discrepancy between the social rate of return r and the private rate of return r' to investment is simply mr, regardless of the time path of income:

$$r' = r(1 - m) = r - mr.$$

If the taxpayer wishes to reinvest the after-tax earnings from an investment whose income he accurately reports for tax purposes, his accumulated capital at time z under the flat annual income tax will be

$$V(z) = V_o e^{r'z} = V_o e^{rz}e^{-rmz}. \tag{3-18}$$

His income for tax purposes will follow the time path

$$y(z) = rV(z)$$

$$= rV_o e^{r'z} \tag{3-19}$$

and his tax will follow the simple path

$$T(z) = my(z)$$

$$= mrV_o e^{r'z}. \tag{3-20}$$

In contrast, under cumulative averaging he pays the tax rate m only on a level income $\bar{y}$; with a growing income his tax rate $\bar{m}$ will grow as we have already shown, as in equation (3-17). Therefore, as time passes the taxpayer who re-invests his after-tax income will find his capital and income will fall below the paths (3-18) and (3-19), yielding him a net after-tax rate of return less than r'. To illustrate this point simply, suppose that for a certain period zero to t he accumulates and reinvests his earnings without reporting them for tax purposes, and then reports the entire amount and pays on it, as in the case of the "capital gain" example just given. Before tax his capital at time t will be

$$V(t) = V_o e^{rt}.$$

His tax will be

$$T(t) = \bar{m}\,[V(t) - V_o]$$

$$= \frac{m}{t}\left(\frac{e^{r't} - 1}{r'}\right) V_o (e^{rt} - 1). \tag{3-21}$$

To give the same outcome as under the flat-rate tax, the tax at time t would instead be

$$T^*(t) = V_o e^{rt} - V_o e^{r't}, \tag{3-22}$$

which incidentally would have to be the amount of tax to eliminate the incentive to defer realization of capital gains under a flat-rate annual income tax. It can be shown that the tax in equation (3-21) is greater than that in (3-22) for every positive t and m, as is intuitively clear when we note that $\bar{m} > m$. Therefore, the after-tax rate of return to saving is less than r' under cumulative averaging.

It might seem that the after-tax rate of return to saving could be made equal to r' for the typical saver if we normalized $\bar{m}$ so that it was equal to m for a growing income stream, such as that in (3-19); and indeed the formula for $\bar{m}$ can be adjusted to make the tax on that stream work out to be equal to that in (3-20). This adjustment would change (3-21) and make it equal to (3-22). However, in that case the tax rate on a level income stream $\bar{y}$ would *decline* with time, falling below m; it would give the taxpayer the option of a slowly growing after-tax income stream even though he was not saving. Therefore, the rate of return to saving, taking into account his true after-tax gain from saving, would still work out to be less than r'. Hence, for given total government revenue from the income tax, cumulative averaging imposes a greater disincentive to save than does a flat-rate annual income tax.

In conclusion, besides supporting Vickrey's claim of neutrality of cumulative averaging with respect to the timing of income, we have found a more practical test of neutrality than the present-value invariance rule that Samuelson used in his famous, but misleading, theorem. Briefly, if the tax system is neutral toward all alternative investments for one taxpayer, it is equally neutral for everyone, regardless of tax bracket. Cumulative averaging could be a practical tool in a total package aimed at such neutrality.

References

Bailey, Martin J. "Capital Gains and Income Taxation." In Arnold C. Harberger and Martin J. Bailey (eds.), *The Taxation of Income from Capital.* Washington, D.C.: The Brookings Institution, 1969.

Bailey, Martin J. "Progressivity and Investment Yields under U.S. Income Taxation." *Journal of Political Economy* 82 (1974): 1157.

Samuelson, Paul A. "Tax Deductibility of Economic Depreciation To Insure Invariant Valuations." *Journal of Political Economy* 72 (1964): 604.

Vickrey, William, "Averaging of Income for Income Tax Purposes." *Journal of Political Economy* 47 (1939): 379.

Vickrey, William, *Agenda for Progressive Taxation.* New York: Ronald Press, 1947.

4

Scale Economies, Average Cost, and the Profitability of Marginal Cost Pricing

William J. Baumol

This chapter examines the behavior of costs in the presence of scale economies in a multi-product firm. It discusses the difficult problems of definition of average cost where there is more than one output and the production function is not homothetic. It also characterizes the circumstances in which prices set equal to marginal costs yield a total revenue less than total cost.

1. Economies of Scale and Efficient Expansion

The definition of scale economies can be extended as follows to a multi-product enterprise.[a]

> DEFINITION 4.1. *Economies of Scale. Given a firm producing* $\underline{n}$ *outputs whose quantities are given by the vector* $y = (y_1, \ldots, y_n)$ *and which uses* $\underline{m}$ *inputs whose quantities are* $x = (x_1, \ldots, x_m)$ *if all input quantities are multiplied by the same constant* $\underline{k} > 1$, *then all output quantities can be increased at least* $\underline{k}$ *times, and if in the neighborhood of* $k = 1$, *they are increased by at least* k^r, $r > 1$.

> DEFINITION 4.2. *Strict Economies of scale are said to characterize a production function if a* $\underline{k}$-*fold increase in each input quantity permits at least a* $\underline{k}$-*fold increase in each output quantity with at least one output increased more than* $\underline{k}$-*fold,*[b] *and if in the neighborhood of* $k = 1$, *the increases in output are at least* k^r-*fold,* $r > 1$.

I am grateful to the office of Science Information Services of the National Science Foundation under whose grant for a study on the Economics of Information this chapter was written. I am also most thankful to Elizabeth Bailey, Dietrich Fischer, John Panzar, Janusz Ordover, and Robert Willig for their very helpful suggestions.

[a]This definition is based on Panzar and Willig. The reason for the requirement that outouts increase k^r-fold in the vicinity of $k = 1$ is that otherwise scale economies may permit a zero derivative of average cost for a proportionate increase in all outputs. The definition given in an earlier draft of this chapter was deficient in this respect. I am grateful to Panzar and Willig for pointing out the consequent errors.

[b]If resources are divisible, transferable and have a positive marginal yield in the production of each of the producer's outputs then strict economies can be taken to require that

A production function may have economies of scale which are *global* (the preceding conditions hold for all input and output combinations) or local (they hold only for particular neighborhoods).

As usual, the definitions are expressed in terms of a *proportionate* increase in the usage of all inputs.

Now, as has recently been emphasized, (See C.H. Shami and E.F. Sudit (1974). See also G. Hanoch (1975).) firms do not generally expand their input usage proportionately either in practice or even in theory. It is true that if the production function is homothetic the cost minimizing way to expand all outputs proportionately is to increase inputs proportionately. But there is no reason to expect all production functions to be of this particular type, so that efficiency may, for example, call for an increasing ratio of capital to labor as outputs rise.

In such a case, obviously, a comparison of the input-output combinations along a ray may not yield the same sort of results as a comparison along the efficient expansion path. For example, while a doubling of all inputs may only permit an exact doubling of all outputs, an efficient but disproportionate increase in input quantities may permit a greater rise in outputs at the same total cost. In that case, it would seem that we might have constant returns to scale and yet declining average costs, since the cost function gives the cost of output expansion, not along a ray in input space, but with the utilization of the cost-minimizing combinations of inputs, whatever they may be.

2. Average Costs and Scale Economies
in an *n*-Output Enterprise

The counterparts of economies of scale in terms of cost functions are obviously either marginal or average costs that decline when outputs rise. Declining marginal costs can be expressed simply as:

$$\partial^2 C(w^*, y^*)/\partial y_i^2 < 0, \qquad\qquad (4\text{-}1)$$

where $C(\cdot)$ is the standard cost function of duality theory, with w^* and y^*, respectively, being given vectors of input prices and output quantities.

Unfortunately, there is no such straightforward definition of declining average cost except for the uninteresting case of the single-product enterprise which is almost never found outside the elementary textbooks. The problem is that we normally have no acceptable way either to aggregate outputs or to disaggregate costs, and so it is not generally possible to define the average cost

---

all outputs increase more than k times. For let commodity n be the only output which has gone up more than $k + \Delta$ fold while all other outputs have risen exactly k-fold. Then a small transfer of resources from output n to each of the other outputs of the producer will bring each of them to an amount at least slightly bigger than k times its initial level.

corresponding either to the firm's output taken as a whole or that corresponding to the output of any one of its products by itself. Clearly Σy_i is not defined since outputs are not measured in common units. We cannot use product prices for the purpose because they themselves are likely to be endogenous variables of the problem—variables whose values decline monotonically with output levels, thus introducing a systematic bias into the calculation. We just have no easy way to determine a denominator for the average cost figure.

Nor is it any easier to deal with the numerator in the average cost expression to apportion total cost among the individual outputs of the enterprise, permitting the calculation of a separate average cost, item by item. The firm's total cost includes some outlays attributable directly to particular goods in the firm's product line and some expenditres which are incurred in common for several such outputs simultaneously. Except by arbitrary convention it is therefore impossible in general to divide up the firm's total costs in a unique manner, imputing every part of this cost explicitly to one or another of the supplier's outputs.

There seem only to be available two acceptable ways of getting around these problems. First, we may deal exclusively with *proportionate* changes in the outputs of the firm. In that case we can speak of *ray* average costs and offer two slightly different definitions of the case where these are decreasing:

DEFINITION 4.3a. Ray average costs are strictly and globally declining if

$$\frac{C(w^*, vy^*)}{v} < C(w^*, y^*) \quad \text{for } \underline{v} > 1 \text{ and any } y^*. \tag{4-2a}$$

Or, instead, we can use

DEFINITION 4.3b. Ray average costs are strictly declining at every point if

$$\frac{\partial [C(w^*, vy^*)/v]}{\partial v} < 0 \quad \text{for any } y^*. \tag{4-2b}$$

We can also define[c] an average variable cost of a particular output $\underline{i}$:

DEFINITION 4.4 The supplier's average variable costs for product $\underline{i}$ are declining if

$$\partial(V^i/y_i)/\partial y_i < 0 \tag{4-3}$$

---

[c]It is easy to show that average variable costs and ray average costs need not behave similarly. For example, if all the costs of a firm are fixed then its ray average costs will decline: $C(w^*, vy^*)/v$ will be a rectangular hyperbola; but its average variable costs will all be constant and equal to zero.

where $V^i(w^*, y^*)$ is the total variable cost of output $\underline{i}$; that is, for a given output vector, y^*

$$V^i(w^*, y^*) = C(w^*, y_1^*, \ldots, y_{i-1}^*, y_i^*, y_{i+1}^*, \ldots, y_n^*)$$

$$- C(w^*, y_1^*, \ldots, y_{i-1}^*, 0, y_{i+1}^*, \ldots, y_n^*). \quad\quad\quad (4\text{-}4)$$

Having gotten over these definitional issues we may turn to a more substantive matter: the nature of the relationship between economies of scale and declining average costs. Intuitively it is certainly plausible that the relationship is close. For scale economies imply that the firm can obtain larger outputs "per unit" of input as it expands its operations. The difficulty, as already noted, is that the two concepts do not refer to the same expansion path and so it is not easy to jump from information about the one to conclusions about the other.

We will now argue[d]

> PROPOSITION 4.1. *Strict global economies of scale are sufficient but not necessary to guarantee that* ray average *costs are strictly declining as defined by (4.2.a).*

To show sufficiency let (x^*, y^*) be an initial and efficient input-output bundle, w_i^* be the price of input $\underline{i}$ and let the input bundle $kx_1, \ldots, kx_m$, where $k > 1$, be capable of yielding some output bundle[e] $vy_1^*, \ldots, vy_n^*, v > k$. Then obviously

$$\Sigma w_j^* x_j > \frac{\Sigma w_j^* k x_j}{v} .$$

However, since the proportionate increase in input use is not necessarily cost minimizing, there may exist another bundle of inputs $x_1', \ldots, x_m'$ capable of producing vy at least as cheaply as the input bundle $kx_1, \ldots, kx_m$. Then we must have $\Sigma w_j^* x_j' \leq \Sigma w_j^* k x_j$ so that

$$\frac{\Sigma w_j^* x_j'}{v} \leq \frac{\Sigma w_j^* k x_j}{v} < \Sigma w_j^* x_j . \quad\quad\quad (4\text{-}5)$$

---

[d]The discussion in the next few paragraphs follow an argument put forth by Shami and Sudit (1974).

[e]For a production function with strict global economies of scale, divisibility and transferability of resources it is trivial to show that the output bundle $vy_1^*, \ldots, vy_n^*$ is attainable, provided there is sufficient transferability of inputs among the producer's outputs and free disposal. For with strict economies of scale and resource transferability with a k-fold increase in all inputs we can attain an output bundle $v_1 y_1^*, \ldots v_n y_n^*$ all $v_i > k$. Now set $v = \min v_i$ and by the assumption of free disposal the output bundle of the text can obviously be attained.

That is, the increasing returns condition $\underline{v} > \underline{k}$ is sufficient to guarantee (4-2a) which is the condition of declining *ray* average cost.[f]

That $v > k$ is not necessary for the result follows if the proportionate expansion path is not efficient, so that the first inequality in (4-5) becomes a strict inequality. For suppose then that a v-fold increase in output can just be produced with a v-fold proportional increase in all inputs[g] so that in that neighborhood $\underline{v} = \underline{k}$. Then (4-5) becomes

$$\frac{\Sigma w_j^* x_j'}{v} < \frac{\Sigma w_j^* v x_j}{v} = \Sigma w_j^* x_j . \tag{4-6}$$

Thus, it is still possible (as is shown by comparing the left hand and right hand terms in (4-6) alone) for overall average costs to decline even if returns to scale are locally constant[h] or declining slightly. Obviously that will never be true, if the production function is homothetic throughout, for then the efficient expansion path will always call for proportionate increases in inputs.

However, as we will see presently, this problem can arise only for sub-

---

[f]Since we have defined scale economies to involve an increase in outputs by at least the proportion k^r, $r > 0$ when all inputs increase by the same proportion k and $k \rightarrow 1$, it also follows in the limit that $d[C(w^*, vy^*)/v]/dv < 0$, i.e., that scale economies as defined also imply decreasing average costs as given by (4-2b).

[g]This assumption obviously calls for locally constant returns and does not mean that the production function must be characterized by constant returns to scale for *all* output and input changes. If the latter were true the argument would imply that an efficient path would always involve proportionate changes in all inputs.

[h]For example, consider the function $y = x_1^a + x_1^b x_2^b$, $0 < a < 1$, $0.5 < b < 1$, whose least-cost expansion path (with input prices fixed) must satisfy

$$\frac{w_1}{w_2} = \frac{a x_1^{a-1} + b x_1^{b-1} x_2^b}{b x_1^b x_2^{b-1}} = a x_1^{a-1}/b x_1^b x_2^{b-1} + x_2/x_1 \tag{4-i}$$

and so is not a ray.

Yet it is not difficult to show that for appropriate values of a, b, x_1 and x_2 that

$$ky = (kx_1)^a + (kx_1 kx_2)^b \tag{4-ii}$$

has a positive root of k other than $k = 1$ so that for the corresponding interval there will be constant returns along a ray which will not be an efficient path.

For example, if we set $y = 1$, $a = 0.6$, $b = 0.9$, we have, dividing (4-ii) through by k,

$$1 = k^{-0.4} x_1^{0.6} + k^{0.8} (x_1 x_2)^{0.9} .$$

Setting $x_1^{0.6} = 6/7$ and $(x_1 x_2)^{0.9} = 1/7$ and writing $\lambda = k^{0.4}$

the preceding equation becomes

$$1 = 6/(7\lambda) + (\lambda^2)/7,$$

which is easily verified to have the positive roots $\lambda = 1$ and $\lambda = 2$. Thus with these illustrative values our non-homothetic function exhibits constant returns in the large in the interval $k = 1$ and $k = (2)^{1/0.4}$

stantial increases in output. In a small neighborhood of a point on the efficient path the average costs will decline if and only if there are strict local economies of scale.

3. A Diagrammatic Discussion

The character of the preceding discussion can be made clearer with the aid of a pair of simple diagrams representing, respectively, the production isoquants in input space (figure 4-1) and the production possibility loci (figure 4-2) for a production function $F(x_1, x_2, y_1, y_2) \leqslant 0$ in two inputs and two outputs. This function is not necessarily homthetic either in outputs or in inputs. Hence the production indifference curves (such as X^a and X^b) need not be similar in shape and neither need the production possibility loci (such as Y^A and Y^B) resemble one another.

In all of the discussion in this section we will assume that we start off with input-output combination $(x_{1a}, x_{2a}, y_{1a}, y_{2a})$, i.e., points $\underline{a}$ and $\underline{A}$ in Figures 4-1 and 4-2 respectively. In the first of these diagrams iso-product locus $\underline{X}^a$ represents all combinations of x_1 and x_2 capable of producing output *combination* y_{1a}, y_{2a}, and similarly, in the second figure, production-possibility locus Y^A represents all combinations of outputs y_1, y_2 that can be produced with input combination x_{1a}, x_{2a}.

Now let us see how we test for the presence of economies of scale in such a non-homothetic function. This is done in three steps: First we consider a hypothetical $\underline{k}$-fold increase in all input quantities (the move from point a to b in figure 4-1. That is, we consider some *proportionate* change in input quantities in order to determine the effect of a change in the scale of input usage without any change in relative input use. Second, we determine the corresponding change in the *set* of output combinations that results from the rise in input usage by the producer. This moves us from point $\underline{A}$ in figure 4-2 to any point on production possibility locus Y^B. Any output combination on that locus can now be produced by the firm. Finally, to test for economies of scale, we determine the point of intersection of Y^B with the ray through initial point $\underline{A}$. This gives us point $\underline{B}$, the largest output combination the firm can produce with its new level of input usage *if it were to choose to produce its outputs in the same output proportions as it did at A.*

We now say that there are local economies of scale if in figure 4-2 $\underline{OB/OA} > Ob/Oa$ in figure 4-1, that is, if a given percentage increase in input quanties *permits*   a greater percentage increase in all outputs, should the producer elect such proportionate changes.

Similarly, global economies of scale require the same relationships for every possible initial input-output combination $(y_1^i, y_2^i, x_1^i, x_2^i)$ and for every pro-

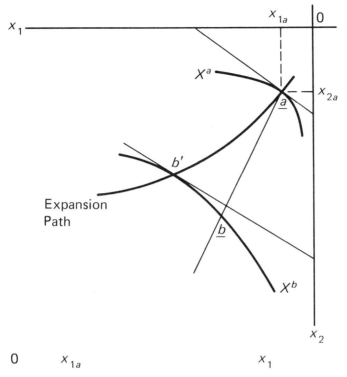

Figure 4-1. Input Space

portionate increase in input quantities from this initial point. Moreover, it requires that $\underline{OB}/\underline{OA} > \underline{Ob}/\underline{Oa}$ for *every* pair of rays in the two figures so that every point on Y^B in figure 4-2 must be more than $k = Ob/Oa$ times as far from the origin as the point on the corresponding ray on curve Y^A.

Now to show that in this case, so long as input prices are given, overall average costs must be declining we proceed in two steps: *Step i.* The coordinates of points b and B are respectively kx_{1a}, kx_{2a} and vy_{1a} and vy_{2a}. Hence, if the firm were to multiply all its input quantities by $\underline{k}$ to produce a proportionate change in outputs, its cost per unit would necessarily fall from $(w_1 x_{1a} + w_2 x_{2a})/y_{1a}$ to $(kw_1 x_{1a} + kw_2 x_{2a})/vy_{1a}$. *Step II.* Since the function is not homothetic, the firm's expansion path need not be a ray. Thus there may be a less expensive combination of inputs capable of producing output combination $\underline{B}$. In figure 4-1 this least-cost input combination is given by point $\underline{b}'$ at which the iso production curve through point $\underline{b}$ is tangent to a budget line parallel to that at the initial point $\underline{a}$. Write $C(b')$ and $C(b) = kw_1 x_{1a} + kw_2 x_{2a}$ for the total input costs at points $\underline{b}'$ and $\underline{b}$ respectively, where necessarily $C(b') \leqslant C(b)$. Hence we must have, from the preceding step,

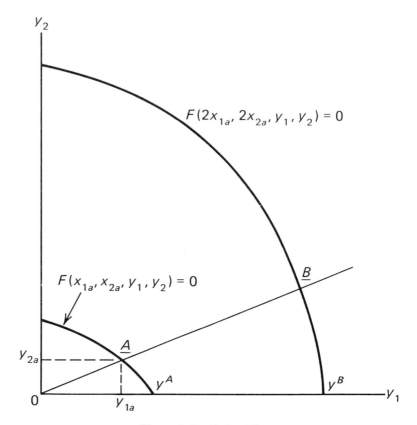

Figure 4-2. Output Space

$$C(a) = w_1 x_{1a} + w_2 x_{2a} > (k w_1 x_{1a} + k w_2 x_{2a})/v = C(b)/v \geqslant C(b')/v$$

$$(4\text{-}7)$$

which proves our result. That is, we have shown that if overall average costs fall with a proportionate increase on all inputs from $\underline{a}$ to $\underline{b}$, (which may not be the most efficient way to expand), overall average costs must certainly fall *a fortiori*, if expansion proceeds along the efficient path (from $\underline{a}$ to $\underline{b}'$) which is certainly at least as cheap as the move from $\underline{a}$ to $\underline{b}$.

Finally, we can see why with a non-homothetic production relationship we may have declining average costs overall *even without scale economies*. For suppose the move from $\underline{a}$ to $\underline{b}$ (a proportionate increase in inputs) actually increases overall average costs slightly because we have slight diseconomies of scale. Then if the move from $\underline{b}$ to the efficient expansion point saves an amount of expenditure more than sufficient to make up for the rise in costs yielded by a proportionate expansion in *inputs* it will lead, on balance, to a reduction in the overall average costs entailed in a proportionate expansion in outputs. This is why scale economies are indeed sufficient but not necessary for a curve of overall average costs to be declining in the large.

4. Two Propositions on Scale Economies in the Small

At this point it is convenient to review two propositions, neither of which is new, though they are not widely discussed. The first reminds us that, given input prices, if we start off from an efficient input-output combination, then a small given increase in the vector of outputs can be achieved at minimum cost via *any* of a wide set of combinations of input expansions. One can achieve a small expansion in outputs at minimum cost by increasing the quantity of any one (initially non-zero) input by itself or by a suitable increase in any combination of such inputs.[i] In sum, there will be no unique expansion path in the small. The second proposition asserts that in particular, if some inputs whose quantities are positive initially also have positive marginal products, and all such marginal products are nonnegative, it will always be possible, starting from an efficient point, to achieve a small output increase at minimum cost through a *proportionate* increase of all inputs, i.e., through a small expansion to scale.

We begin by proving:

PROPOSITION 4.2. Assuming the production function to be everywhere twice differentiable with several inputs having positive marginal products, and all of them nonnegative, then starting from an initial input combination that is efficient, there will be a multiplicity of input combinations capable of achieving a given vector of small output increases $d\dot{y}^* = (dy_1^*, \ldots, dy_n^*)$.

Proof: Given the production function

$$F(y_1, \ldots, y_n, x_1, \ldots, x_m) \leqslant 0 \qquad (4\text{-}8)$$

two necessary conditions for economic efficiency with a set of positive input quantities, are, first, that for any input i

$$w_i = aF_i \qquad (4\text{-}9)$$

---

[i]There is a simple intuitive explanation for this conclusion which may strike some as paradoxical. At any point on the efficient path all non-zero inputs will have an equal ratio of marginal product to price. Hence any such input will yield the same (small) expansion in output per dollar of expenditure upon it.

where $F_i = \partial F/\partial x_i$, w_i is the price of input i and a is a constant and, second, that the given combination of inputs satisfy (4-8) as an equality, i.e.,

$$\underline{F}\,(\cdot) = 0 \tag{4-10}$$

A cost-minimizing *increase* in input quantities $dx_1^0, \ldots, dx_m^0$ must also leave (4-10) satisfied so that we must have

$$\Sigma F_j dy_j^* + \Sigma F_i dx_i^0 = 0. \tag{4-11}$$

Next, consider any of the multiplicity of vectors $dx^* = (dx_i^*, \ldots, dx_m^*)$ satisfying

$$\Sigma F_i dx_i^* = 0. \tag{4-12}$$

Obviously, with all $F_i \geqslant 0$ and several $F_i > 0$, there will be many combinations of dx_i^* (some positive and some negative) which are consistent with (4-12). Now define

$$dx_i = dx_i^0 + dx_i^*.$$

Then these dx_i will also satisfy (4-11) and consequently (4-10) since

$$\Sigma F_j dy_j^* + \Sigma F_i dx_i = \Sigma F_j dy_j^* + \Sigma F_i dx_i^0 + \Sigma F_i dx_i^* = 0$$

by (4-11) and (4-12). That is, these dx_i will also be capable of achieving the given increases in output, dy_j^*.

Moreover, the cost of increasing the output via the dx_i is the same as doing so via the cost minimizing input increases dx_i^0. For the cost of the former is

$$\Sigma w_i dx_i = \Sigma w_i dx_i^0 + \Sigma w_i dx_i^*$$

$$= \Sigma w_i dx_i^0 + \Sigma a F_i dx_i^* = \Sigma w_i dx_i^0 + a \Sigma F_i dx_i^* \text{ [by (4-9)]}$$

$$= \Sigma w_i dx_i^0 + 0 \text{ [by (4-12)]}$$

which is the least cost way to achieve the given increase in outputs.

Next we prove:

PROPOSITION 4.3. Under the conditions of Proposition 2 it is always possible to achieve a small increase in the vector of outputs at minimum cost if, starting from an efficient input combination, all inputs are increased to scale (i.e., proportionately).

Proof: We require a set of dx_i^* which satisfy (4-12) so that by Proposition 2 they achieve the required output increase at minimum cost, and which satisfy the $m - 1$ requirements of proportionate expansion in inputs

$$\frac{dx_i^* + dx_i^0}{x_i} = \frac{dx_m^* + dx_m^0}{x_m} \qquad (i = 1, \ldots, m - 1)$$

that is

$$x_m dx_i^* - x_i dx_m^* = x_i dx_m^0 - x_n dx_i^0 \qquad (i = 1, \ldots, m - 1). \qquad (4\text{-}13)$$

Together (4-12) and (4-13) constitute a system of m linear equations in the m variables $dx_1^*, \ldots, dx_m^*$. Now, this sytem will have a non-trivial solution if the determinant of the system is non-zero. But that determinant is

$$D = \begin{vmatrix} F_1 & F_2 & \cdots & F_{m-1} & F_m \\ x_m & 0 & \cdots & 0 & -x_1 \\ 0 & x_m & \cdots & 0 & -x_2 \\ \cdot & \cdot & \cdot & \cdot & \cdot \\ 0 & 0 & & x_m & -x_{m-1} \end{vmatrix} \qquad (4\text{-}14)$$

Expanding D in terms of the elements of its first row we obtain as a typical term

$$(-1)^{i+1} F_i \begin{vmatrix} x_m & \cdots & 0 & 0 & \cdots & 0 & -x_1 \\ \cdot & \cdot & \cdot & \cdot & \cdot & \cdot & \cdot \\ 0 & \cdots & x_m & 0 & \cdots & 0 & -x_{i-1} \\ 0 & \cdots & 0 & 0 & \cdots & 0 & -x_i \\ 0 & \cdots & 0 & x_m & \cdots & 0 & -x_{i+1} \\ \cdot & \cdot & \cdot & \cdot & \cdot & \cdot & \cdot \\ 0 & \cdots & 0 & 0 & \cdots & x_m & -x_{m-1} \end{vmatrix} = -F_i x_i \begin{vmatrix} x_m & 0 & \cdots & 0 \\ 0 & x_m & \cdots & 0 \\ \cdot & \cdot & \cdot & \cdot \\ 0 & 0 & \cdots & x_m \end{vmatrix}$$

$$= -F_i x_i (x_m)^{m-2}$$

Hence D, the determinant in (4-14), must be given by

$$D = - \sum_{i=1}^{m-1} F_i x_i (x_m)^{m-2}$$

which cannot be zero if the F_i do not vary in sign, as assumed. Q.E.D.

5. On the Profitability of Marginal
   Cost Pricing

One of the policy problems generally taken to follow from economies of scale is the unprofitability of marginal cost pricing.

For the single product firm it is, of course, easy to show that in a firm with declining average cost the sale of its product at a price equal to marginal cost must force it to lose money.

The issue then is whether a similar relationship holds for the multi-product firm. As a matter of fact, it is not difficult to show

PROPOSITION 4.4. *Ray average cost declining at every point, as defined by (4-2b) is necessary and sufficient to assure the unprofitability of marginal cost pricing.*[j]

Proof: Given any vector, y^*, of output levels, if (4-2b), the condition for ray average cost to decline at every point, is satisfied we must have (assuming differentiability)

$$\frac{\partial C(w^*, vy^*)/v}{\partial v} = \frac{\left(\sum \frac{\partial C}{\partial vy_j^*} y_j^* \right) v - C(w^*, vy^*)}{v^2} < 0 \qquad (4\text{-}15)$$

or, setting $v = 1$

$$\sum \frac{\partial C}{\partial y_j^*} y_j^* < C(w^*, y^*). \qquad (4\text{-}16)$$

That is, in this case the sale of each output, j, at a price, p_j, equal to marginal

---

[j]Robert Willig and John Panzar have pointed out an error in my original formulation in which I utilized condition (4-2a) instead of (4-2b) in deriving Proposition 4. But declining average costs of the former variety do not exclude points of inflexion where $dAC/dy = 0$, so that at point $\Sigma C_i y_i = C$. For a further discussion see Panzar and Willig (forthcoming).

cost $\partial C/\partial y_j$ will not bring in enough revenue to cover total cost $C(w^*, y^*)$. This shows the sufficiency of decreasing ray average costs for unprofitability of marginal cost pricing. The necessity also follows from (4–15) and (4–16). For if ray average costs are constant or increasing at some point so that the $<$ in (4–15) is replaced by a $\geqslant$, then in (4–16) the same replacement will be required, i.e., in such cases the revenues derived from marginal cost pricing will at least be sufficient to cover total costs.

Since strict, global economies of scale have been shown in Section 3 to be sufficient but not necessary for declining ray average costs we deduce immediately

> *PROPOSITION 4.5. Strict, global economies of scale are sufficient but not necessary to assure the unprofitability of marginal cost pricing.*

However, the profitability of marginal-cost pricing is a local rather than a global matter, involving the relationship between $C(\cdot)$ and $\Sigma F_j y_j$ at a point in $n + m$ dimensional input-output space. Now we saw in propositions 2 and 3 that, starting from an efficient point, a small output expansion can be achieved by a proportionate increase in inputs at the same cost as it can by a move along the efficient path. We can therefore prove

> *PROPOSITION 4.6. A necessary and sufficient condition for the unprofitability of marginal cost pricing is the presence of strict local scale economies. Moreover if, locally a $1 + k$-fold increase in all inputs can just achieve a $1 + v$-fold increase in outputs, then the ratio of total cost to the total revenues derived from marginal cost pricing must be exactly v/k.*

Proof: The proportionate expansion of all input quantities must satisfy

$$dx_i = kx_i$$

and the proportionate expansion in all inputs, by hypotheses, satisfies

$$dy_j = vy_j .$$

Consequently, we have as the minimum cost of the output expansion

$$dC(\cdot) = \Sigma(\partial C/\partial y_j)\, dy_j = v\, \Sigma(\partial C/\partial y_j)\, y_j . \qquad (4\text{–}17)$$

But since by Proposition 3 the proportionate increase in inputs achieves the output expansion at minimum cost, $dC(\cdot)$, we also have

$$dC(\cdot) = \Sigma(\partial C/\partial x_i)\, dx_i = \Sigma w_i dx_i = k\Sigma w_i x_i = kC. \qquad (4\text{–}18)$$

Equating (4–17) and (4–18) we have our result $C/\Sigma(\partial C/\partial y_j)y_j = v/k$. Finally, comparison of Propositions (4.4) and (4.6) shows at once

PROPOSITION 4.7. Strict local economies of scale are necessary and sufficient for overall average costs to be strictly declining locally.

Concluding Comment

The preceding pages have sought to characterize the relationships among scale economies, decling average costs, and the profitability or unprofitability of marginal cost pricing. We know, of course, that corresponding to any given cost function there is associated an implicit production relationship, and that the characteristics of either of these can be inferred from the other. Yet it seems useful to have laid out explicitly the cost function behavior corresponding to so important a production-function phenomenon as economies of scale. It will perhaps prove helpful in empirical work to have this relationship spelled out so that one can deal with the issue directly in terms of cost functions whose estimation may be less difficult than that of production functions.

Unfortunately, we have dealt with only one of the three policy issues that are generally associated with scale economies—the viability of marginal cost pricing. The other two issues, which are at least equally important, are closely interrelated. The first of these is the desirability, in term of efficiency of resources use, of a multiplicity of producers. Subadditivity of costs, meaning that two can be produced more cheaply than one, is not quite the same thing as economies of scale, but the precise specification of the similarities and differences remains to be spelled out. The final issue is the *sustainability* of a multiplicity of firms even where it is desirable (or the reverse—the sustainability of single-firm production where that is most efficient). It has been shown by Faulhaber (1975) that this issue is not the same as the preceding one. One can, for example, have an industry in which single-firm production is most economical but is not sustainable.

Both of these problems are global in character—they involve the entire production set and not merely its behavior in the immediate neighborhood of a point, as in the case of sustainability of marginal cost pricing. Since this chapter was written, their analysis has been explored in several subsequent papers.

References

Baumol, W.J. "On the Proper Cost Tests for Natural Monopoly in a Multi-Product Industry." (1975, forthcoming).

Baumol, W.J., E.E. Bailey, and R.D. Willig. "Weak Invisible Hand Theorems on the Sustainability of Multi-Product Monopoly." (1975, forthcoming).

Baumol, W.J., D. Fischer, and J.A. Ordover. "On the Existence and Uniqueness of Pareto-Optimal Pricing Under a Budget Constraint." (1975, forthcoming).

Faulhaber, Gerald R. "Cross-Subsidization: Pricing in Public Enterprise." *American Economic Review,* Dec. 1975.

Hanoch, Giora. "The Elasticity of Scale and the Shape of Average Costs." *American Economic Review* 65 (1975): 492–497.

Panzar, J.C. and R.D. Willig. "Economies of Scale and Economies of Scope in Multi-Output Production." Bell Laboratories, (forthcoming).

Shami, C.H. and E.F. Sudit. "Generalized Concepts of Scale and Expansion Effects in Production." (Unpublished manuscript, 1974).

5 Pricing, Spending, and Gambling Rules for Non-Profit Organizations

Jacques H. Dreze
Maurice Marchand

1. Introduction and Conclusions

Questions

During our association with universities in Europe and in the United States, we have encountered many questions apt to challenge economists, for instance:

1. Should prices charged in university hospitals reflect (marginal) costs alone, or include a monopolistic markup?
2. Should faculty salaries be determined by a standard scale, or vary with the alternative opportunities of faculty members? (For instance, should the respective salaries of a medical doctor and of a biologist, doing similar work in a research laboratory, reflect the higher opportunity cost of the medical doctor?)
3. How should a university allocate its resources among alternative uses, like education and research?
4. Should universities enjoying an endowment fund aim at spending income and maintaining capital, or at accumulating part of the income, or at depleting the fund at some optimal rate?
5. What rate of discount should be used by a university for decisions about plant and equipment?
6. What should be the attitude of a university toward portfolio risks? Should universities adopt less conservative investment policies than, say, managers of private trust funds? (This was once intimated by officers of a foundation oriented toward research and development; that foundation has recently reduced its spending, due to a sharp decline in market value of endowment.)

All these questions arise because universities operate under a budget constraint, the level of which is not always set optimally; produce public goods (research); and are sometimes required to sell services below cost (education in state universities).

Similar questions are faced by all non-profit organizations aiming at public service rendered under a budget constraint.

59

Pricing rules for such organizations have been derived from the first-order conditions for (constrained) Pareto-optimality by Boiteux (1956), in a model related to that investigated thirty years earlier by Ramsey (1927). A straightforward extension of that model to the case of public goods provides the natural framework to answer the questions listed above. Various simplifications must be introduced in order to translate the theoretical answers into operational rules. The purpose of the present chapter is to develop these extensions and simplifications, and to draw conclusions for problems of pricing, resource allocation, and risk-bearing in non-profit organizations.

Answers

Within the limitations of the model studied below,[a] we obtain the following answers to the questions listed above:

1.   A university operating under a binding budget constraint should operate, on the markets for private goods and services, like a profit-maximizing monopolist, except that the university should blow up all price elasticities by a constant factor $1/\bar{\gamma}$ (>1); that factor should be such that the budget constraint be satisfied; in particular, the university should engage in price discrimination whenever possible.

2.   A university should adopt the personnel policies of a discriminating monopsonist, except that the university should blow up by the same factor $1/\bar{\gamma}$ the price elasticity of labor supply; outside opportunities are relevant only to the extent that they result in higher price elasticities of supply; for a given type of labor, a lower price elasticity of supply will imply a lower level of employment and a higher excess of marginal productivity over salary.[b]

3.   If the university produces public goods, it should aim at equating (across public goods) the ratios of marginal cost to marginal value, where marginal value is defined by the sum over all consumers of their marginal demand price (willingness to pay) for the public good; this ratio should furthermore be equal to $(1 - \bar{\gamma})$, under the budget constraint; the rules defined under (1) for private goods and under (3) for public goods characterize efficient resource allocation unambiguously.

4.   The same principles apply to intertemporal allocation; intertemporal efficiency will not (except by accident) result in maintaining capital; in

---

[a]One major limitation is the assumption that the rest of the economy behaves competitively.

[b]The authors have discovered that the price elasticity of labor supply was very low in their own case. Accordingly, few details about question 2 are given below.

particular, expenditures might exceed receipts in periods where income from sources other than endowment are abnormally low, and conversely; intertemporal efficiency does not require that endowment income be defined.

5. By further application of the same principles, the internal rate of discount to be used in a University should be equal to the relevant market rate plus $\bar{\gamma}$ times its elasticity; the relevant market rate may be either a borrowing rate or a lending rate, as the case may be.

6. Portfolio choices by a University producing a public good should be guided by a risk aversion function defined as the sum of (i) the elasticity (with respect to quantity) of the marginal value of the public good, and (ii) minus the output elasticity of the marginal cost of the public good; that sum should furthermore be multiplied by the ratio of average to marginal cost in order to obtain the relative risk aversion function, or by output times the reciprocal of marginal cost to obtain the absolute risk aversion function.

We believe that these answers provide theoretically sound approximations to optimal decision rules for non-profit organizations (NPOs). Practical application of these rules still requires a knowledge of cost and demand parameters that is typically not available. We hope that our theoretical analysis may stimulate further work on the measurement problems.

Organization of the Chapter

The chapter is organized as follows. The Ramsey-Boiteux models are extended to the case of public goods in Section 2. The role of income transfers in that model is discussed and illustrated in Section 3, which is in the nature of a digression. The results are applied to problems of pricing and resource allocation in Section 4. In Section 5, the model is simplified and extended, so as to permit a discussion of risk preferences. Section 5 is largely independent of Sections 3 and 4 and may be read after Section 2.

Bibliographical Remark. The idea of extending the models of Ramsey and Boiteux to public goods is not new. Our results in Section 2 parallel those of Diamond-Mirrlees (1971), Stiglitz-Dasgupta (1971) and Atkinson-Stern (1974). Systematic discussions of budget constraints for producers appear in the works of Bronsard (1971) or Kolm (1970). A recent survey of this and related work—e.g., by Baumol-Bradford (1970) or Bergson (1972)—is given by Guesnerie (1975).

2. Pricing and Public Goods Production Under a Budget Constraint

The Model

Following Boiteux (1956), we consider an economy consisting of m individuals, indexed $k = 1, \ldots, m$; v private firms, indexed $h = 1, \ldots, v$; and a public sector. There are n private goods, indexed $i = 1, \ldots, n$, with market prices $p_1 \ldots p_i \ldots p_n$, consumed or supplied by the individuals, the private firms and the public sector, in respective quantities $q_i^k, x_i^h, y_i, i = 1, \ldots, n, k = 1, \ldots, m,$ $h = 1, \ldots, v$; these quantities are also denoted q^k, x^h, y in vector notation. The nth good is used as numeraire ($p_n = 1$). In addition, we introduce ϵ public goods, indexed $j = 1, \ldots, \epsilon$. These goods are produced by the public sector, and consumed by the individuals, in (identical) quantities $z_j, j = 1, \ldots, \epsilon$. For simplicity, we assume that the production possibilities of the private firms are independent of the production of public goods. The more general case presents no special difficulty (see, e.g., Ramsey 1927).

Individual preferences are assumed representable by quasi-concave, twice continuously differentiable utility functions $U^k(q^k, z)$. Each individual is assumed to maximize utility under the budget constraint

$$p \cdot q^k - r^k = 0 \tag{5-1}$$

where r^k denotes the "income" of individual k. Incomes are measured in terms of the numeraire. In the model of this section, we follow Boiteux in assuming that individual incomes are policy variables, which can be redistributed freely under the single constraint that their sum be equal to the net profits of the private and public sector, as per equation (5-6) below.

First-order conditions for consumer equilibrium imply, together with (5-1):

$$\frac{U_i^k}{U_n^k} = \frac{p_i}{p_n}, i = 1, \ldots, n, \sum_i p_i \frac{\partial q_i^k}{\partial r^k} = 1, \sum_i p_i \frac{\partial q_i^k}{\partial p_a} + q_a^k = 0, a = 1, \ldots, n-1;$$

$$\sum_i p_i \frac{\partial q_i^k}{\partial z_j} = 0, j = 1, \ldots, \epsilon, k = 1, \ldots, m, \tag{5-2}$$

where U_i^k denotes the partial derivative of U^k with respect to q_i^k.

The production sets of private firms are assumed representable by concave, continuously differentiable production functions $f^h(x^h)$. Each firm is assumed to maximize its profits $p \cdot x^h$ under the constraint $f^h(x^h) = 0$, taking p as given. The first-order conditions imply

$$\frac{f_i^h}{f_n^h} = \frac{p_i}{p_n}, \, i = 1, \ldots, n, \, \sum_i p_i \frac{\partial x_i^h}{\partial p_a} = 0, \, a = 1, \ldots, n-1, \quad (5\text{-}3)$$

where f_i^h denotes the partial derivative of f^h with respect to x_i^h.

The public sector has a production set in the space of private and public goods, here assumed representable by the twice continuously differentiable production function $g(y, z)$. The budget constraint of the public sector takes the form

$$b - p \cdot y = 0 \quad (5\text{-}4)$$

where b is some given number. Partial derivatives of the production function g with respect to y_i or z_j will be denoted g_i or g_j, a concise notation that should not cause confusion.

The physical constraints, or market clearing conditions, are

$$\sum_k q^k - y - \sum_h x^h = 0. \quad (5\text{-}5)$$

Together, they imply a constraint on the sum of individual incomes

$$p \cdot \sum_k q^k = \sum_k r^k = p \cdot y + p \cdot \sum_h x^h = b + \sum_h (p \cdot x^h). \quad (5\text{-}6)$$

First-order Conditions

The problem of defining a constrained Pareto optimum may be written as

$$\underset{p,r,y,z}{\text{Max}} \, \sum_k \lambda^k U^k [q^k(p, r^k, z), z]$$

subject to

(α) $\sum_k q^k (p, r^k, z) - y - \sum_h x^h (p) = 0$

(β) $g(y, z) = 0$

(γ) $b - p \cdot y = 0$

where the greek letters denote Lagrange multipliers and where the first-order conditions and constraints on the behavior of individuals and private firms are implied by the symbols $q^k(p, r^k, z), x^h(p)$, which denote demand or supply functions.

Remarks

1. The demand and supply functions of individuals and private firms embody the implicit assumption of competitive behavior in the private sector.
2. In this formulation, non-negativity conditions are ignored. A more courageous formulation, using the Kuhn-Tucker condition, would not change the nature of our results.
3. Using both prices (p) and quantities (z) as decision variables—constrained by (α)—is convenient for exposition. If non-negativity conditions were recognized, a number of private goods (not supplied by the public sector) would cease to enter as policy instruments.

The first-order conditions are

$$(p_a)\ \sum_k \sum_i \lambda^k U_i^k \frac{\partial q_i^k}{\partial p_a} - \sum_i \alpha_i \left(\sum_k \frac{\partial q_i^k}{\partial p_a} - \sum_h \frac{\partial x_i^h}{\partial p_a} \right) + \gamma y_a = 0, \quad a = 1, \ldots, n-1.$$

$$(r^k)\ \lambda^k \sum_i U_i^k \frac{\partial q_i^k}{\partial r^k} - \sum_i \alpha_i \frac{\partial q_i^k}{\partial r^k} = 0, \quad k = 1, \ldots, m.$$

$$(y_i)\ \alpha_i - \beta g_i + \gamma p_i = 0, \quad i = 1, \ldots, n$$

$$(z_j)\ \sum_k \lambda^k \left(U_j^k + \sum_i U_i^k \frac{\partial q_i^k}{\partial z_j} \right) - \sum_i \alpha_i \sum_k \frac{\partial q_i^k}{\partial z_j} - \beta g_j = 0, \quad j = 1, \ldots, a.$$

Using (5-2), one may rewrite the conditions (r^k) and then (p_a) as follows:

$$\lambda^k U_n^k / p_n = \sum_i \alpha_i \frac{\partial q_i^k}{\partial r^k} \tag{5-7}$$

$$\sum_i \alpha_i \left[\sum_k \left(\frac{\partial q_i^k}{\partial p_a} + q_a^k \frac{\partial q_i^k}{\partial r^k} \right) - \sum_h \frac{\partial x_i^h}{\partial p_a} \right] = \gamma y_a. \tag{5-8}$$

Because the first-order conditions are homogeneous of degree zero in the Lagrange multipliers, ($\alpha, \beta, \gamma, \lambda$), one may multiply these by an arbitrary non-null scalar. It is convenient to define $\bar\alpha = \alpha p_n / \beta g_n$, $\bar\gamma = \gamma p_n / \beta g_n$, $\bar\lambda = \lambda p_n / \beta g_n$. After this transformation, conditions (y_i) become

$$\bar\alpha_n + \bar\gamma p_n = p_n, \qquad \bar\alpha_i = \frac{g_i}{g_n} p_n - \bar\gamma p_i, \quad i = 1, \ldots, n. \tag{5-9}$$

Let n be the index of an input (to the public sector), in terms of which costs and productivities will be measured. When i is the index of an output, $g_i/g_n\, p_n$ defines the marginal cost of good i. When i is the index of an input, $g_i/g_n\, p_n$ defines the marginal value productivity of factor i. We find it convenient to write $Cm_i = \text{def}\ g_i/g_n\, p_n$, and to phrase our interpretation for the case where Cm_i is the marginal cost of output i. We leave to the reader the appropriate rephrasing needed when Cm_i is the marginal productivity of input i.

The terms in brackets in (5–8) are the partial derivatives, with respect to p_a, of the compensated market demand functions for y_i, $i = 1, \ldots , n$. Denote these terms by $\partial \hat{y}_i/\partial p_a$, where the symbol $\hat{\ }$ indicates that the demand function is compensated. By conditions (5–2) and (5–3),

$$\sum_i p_i \frac{\partial \hat{y}_i}{\partial p_a} = 0.$$

Multiplying (5–8) by

$$\frac{p_n}{\beta g_n}, \text{ adding } (\bar{\gamma} - 1) \sum_i p_i \frac{\partial \hat{y}_i}{\partial p_a}$$

to the left-hand side and using (5–9), we obtain

$$\sum_i (Cm_i - p_i) \frac{\partial \hat{y}_i}{\partial p_a} = \bar{\gamma} y_a. \tag{5-10}$$

These are precisely the "Ramsey-Boiteux conditions" for optimal pricing under a budget constraint. In the absence of public goods, $\bar{\gamma}$ should be such that $p \cdot y = b$. With public goods, we go back to conditions (z_j) and rewrite them successively as follows, using (5–2), (5–7), and (5–9):

$$\sum_k \frac{U_j^k}{U_n^k} (\lambda^k U_n^k) = \beta g_j + \sum_i \alpha_i \sum \frac{\partial q_i^k}{\partial z_j}$$

$$p_n \sum_k \frac{U_j^k}{U_n^k} \left[\sum_i \bar{\alpha}_i \frac{\partial q_i^k}{\partial r^k} \right] = \frac{g_j}{g_n} p_n + \sum_i \bar{\alpha}_i \sum_k \frac{\partial q_i^k}{\partial z_j} \tag{5-11}$$

$$p_n \sum_k \frac{U_j^k}{U_n^k} \left[1 - \bar{\gamma} + \sum_i (Cm_i - p_i) \frac{\partial q_i^k}{\partial r^k} \right] = Cm_j - \sum_i (p_i - Cm_i) \sum_k \frac{\partial q_i^k}{\partial z_j}.$$

Following standard notation in the literature on public goods, we will denote the amount of numeraire that individual k would be just willing to pay for one additional unit of public good j by

$$\pi \frac{k}{j} = P_n \frac{U_j^k}{U_n^k}.$$

We will also denote by $\partial \hat{y}_i / \partial z_j$ the partial derivative, with respect to z_j, of the compensated market demand function for y_i:

$$\frac{\partial \hat{y}_i}{\partial z_j} = \sum_k \left(\frac{\partial q_i^k}{\partial z_j} - \pi_j^k \frac{\partial q_i^k}{\partial r^k} \right). \tag{5-12}$$

Indeed, $-\pi\, k/j$ is the income adjustment that would exactly compensate individual k for a unit increase in z_j.

With this notation, (5-11) may be written as

$$\sum_k \pi_j^k = \frac{1}{1 - \bar{\gamma}} \left[Cm_j - \sum_i (p_i - Cm_i) \frac{\partial \hat{y}_i}{\partial z_j} \right]. \tag{5-13}$$

Together, conditions (5-4), (5-10), and (5-13) define the rules for pricing and public goods production that should be followed in the public sector.

Interpretation

In the absence of a budget constraint, optimal production of public goods would be defined by the "Samuelson conditions":

$$\sum_k \pi_j^k = Cm_j.$$

This result would coincide with (5-13) if $\bar{\gamma}$ (hence γ, the Lagrange multiplier associated with the budget constraint) were equal to zero, in which case (5-10) would also hold with $p_i = Cm_i$, $i = 1, \ldots, n$. In general, however, this solution will not be consistent with (5-4), calling for $\bar{\gamma} \neq 0$, prices different from marginal costs, and

$$\sum_k \pi_j^k \neq Cm_j.$$

Furthermore, $0 < \bar{\gamma} < 1$ under the plausible assumption that b exceeds the (probably negative) profits that the public sector would make if no budget constraint were imposed (first-best optimum).[c] In terms of (5-13), the impact of the budget constraint on production rules for public goods is twofold:

1. The marginal cost of public good j is corrected by a term reflecting the difference in net profits from private goods production that would accrue to the public sector if output of z_j were increased by one unit; these profits are evaluated by means of the compensated demand functions, for reasons valid in connection with (5-10) and (5-13) alike, and discussed in the next section; the signs of these adjustments to marginal costs are a priori indeterminate.

2. Denote by Cm_j the marginal cost of public good j adjusted for the difference in profits; then

$$\sum_k \pi_j^k = \frac{Cm_j}{1 - \gamma} > Cm_j$$

(since $\bar{\gamma} > 0$). The cost at market prices is inflated by a factor $(1 - \bar{\gamma})^{-1}$ to reflect the fact that production of public good j (a) uses real resources, in an amount measured by CM_j, and (b) uses resources from the public sector, whose social opportunity cost is higher than if they were used in the private sector (because of the budget constraint).

If all cross-elasticities are negligible, the analogy between conditions (5-10) and (5-13) can be made more apparent by rewriting them as:

$$\bar{\gamma} = \frac{p_i - CM_i}{p_i} \left| \hat{n}_{y_i p_i} \right| \qquad (5-14)$$

$$\bar{\gamma} = \frac{\sum_k \pi_j^k - Cm_j}{\sum_k \pi_j^k} \left| \hat{n}_{z_j z_j} \right| \qquad (5-15)$$

---

[c]Under this assumption, $dL/db = -\gamma < 0$, where L stands for the Lagrangian of our maximization problem. From the signs of the derivatives of L with respect to initial endowments of the nth good given respectively to the private and public sectors, one also infers that $\alpha_n > 0$ and $\beta g_n > 0$. Since

$$\bar{\gamma} = \frac{\gamma}{\beta g_n} = 1 - \frac{\alpha_n}{\beta g_n}$$

it then follows that $0 < \bar{\gamma} < 1$.

where $\hat{n}$ stands for the compensated demand elasticity

$$(\hat{n}_{z_j z_j} = 1).$$

3. Role of the Income Transfers

Comments

In the preceding section, it was assumed that individual incomes could be redistributed freely, subject to condition (5-6). The income transfers, governed by conditions (5-7), have a natural interpretation, familiar in related contexts. (5-7) implies

$$\frac{\lambda^k U_n^k}{\lambda^m U_n^m} = \frac{1 - \dfrac{1}{1 - \bar{\gamma}} \sum_i (p_i - Cm_i) \dfrac{\partial q_i^k}{\partial r^k}}{1 - \dfrac{1}{1 - \bar{\gamma}} \sum_i (p_i - Cm_i) \dfrac{\partial q_i^m}{\partial r^m}} \qquad (5\text{-}16)$$

The left-hand side of (5-16) may be interpreted as the implicit ratio of redistributive weights attributed to marginal income transfers in favor of individuals k and m, respectively. The right-hand side is the ratio of social costs associated with these marginal transfers.

Under unconstrained Pareto optimality, this ratio would be equal to one. In the present case the scales of equity are tilted in favor of those individuals who concentrate their marginal spending on commodities whose contribution to the net revenues of the public sector is highest (see Marchand 1968).

These income transfers call for the following comments:

1. The transfers account for the compensated nature of the demand functions used in conditions (5-10) and (5-13); as will be seen below, the same formulae based on uncompensated demand functions are sometimes relevant, in the absence of transfers.
2. The assumption that incomes are redistributed freely by the public sector is not very realistic. When we turn to a specific NPO (like a university, a foundation or a charitable organization), the assumption becomes entirely unrealistic; it will be abandoned in this section.
3. The rules governing income transfers in Section 2 are quite sophisticated, on the cost side, and hence difficult to apply. Two individuals with different marginal propensities to consume specific commodities

$$\left(\frac{\partial q^k}{\partial r^k} \neq \frac{\partial q^m}{\partial r^m} \right)$$

should get different incomes, even though society would like to treat them symmetrically on the "merit" side.

4. The possibility of income transfers matters not only from the viewpoint of distribution but also from the viewpoint of efficiency.

This last comment is perhaps less widely appreciated than the previous ones. Before turning to the derivation of managerial rules in the absence of transfers, we will elaborate briefly on the role of transfers from the efficiency viewpoint.

In general, the budget constraint imposed on the public sector (or on a specific NPO) entails a loss of efficiency. For instance, marginal cost pricing is inapplicable under increasing returns to scale because it would entail a deficit, or public goods production is kept too low due to an inadequate budgetary appropriation. In the absence of the constraint, a more efficient production could be planned, and financed by means of lump sum taxes adding up to a negative amount.[d]

Consider now conditions (5-10), and assume that a particular good a is consumed only by individual m, whose *compensated* demand elasticity for a good a is *zero* (right-angle indifference curve). It is then possible to satisfy conditions (5-10) with $\bar{\gamma} = 0$, $Cm_i = p_i$ for all $i \neq a$ and p_a such that (5-4) holds. All that is required to that effect is to raise r^m so as to enable individual m to pay the price p_a—the incomes of all other individuals being appropriately lowered. In this way, the full set of Pareto optima attainable in the absence of the budget constraint becomes accessible. Instead of taxing individuals to cover the deficit of the public sector, one taxes the individuals $k = 1, \ldots, m - 1$ to subsidize individual m, and the public sector collects back that subsidy through monopolistic pricing of good a (consumed by m alone). This indirect solution is achieved at no welfare cost, because the compensated demand elasticity for $q_a^m = y_a$ is zero. Income transfers operate here as a perfect substitute for lump sum taxes levied on behalf of the public sector. Clearly, this solution rests crucially on the possibility of transfers. An example in the section on "income transfers" below illustrates this point.

First-Order Conditions Without Transfers

In the absence of income transfers, it is imperative that we consider explicitly how the profits of private firms are distributed among individuals, i.e., that we specify consistent rules of income formation. The simplest specification is that of a private ownership economy, where each individual k owns a given fraction θ_h^k of the profits $p \cdot x^h$ of firm h, with $\Sigma_h \theta_h^k = 1$. Allowing in addition for predetermined transfers r_0^k adding up to b, we have

---

[d]If the only available taxes are distortionary, the deficit of the public has to be set optimally. See Stiglitz and Dasgupta (1971).

$$r^k = r_0^k + \sum_h \theta_h^k p \cdot x^h, \; k = 1, \ldots, m \qquad (5\text{-}17)$$

The problem now is to maximize

$$\sum_k \lambda^k U^k [q^k(p, r_0^k + \sum_h \theta_h^k p \cdot x^h, z), z]$$

with respect to p, y, and z and subject to the constraints (α), (β) and (γ). The first-order conditions for this problem are (y_i), (z_j) and

$$\sum_i \sum_k (\lambda^k U_i^k - \alpha_i) \left\{ \frac{\partial q_i^k}{\partial p_a} + \frac{\partial q_i^k}{\partial r^k} \sum_h \theta_h^k \left(x_a^h + \sum_c p_c \frac{\partial x_i^h}{\partial p_a} \right) \right\}$$

$$+ \sum_i \alpha_i \sum_h \frac{\partial x_i^h}{\partial p_a} + \gamma y_a = 0, \; a = 1, \ldots, n = 1. \qquad (5\text{-}18)$$

Using (5-2)-(5-3) and (5-9), (5-18) may be rewritten as:

$$\sum_k \frac{\bar{\lambda}^k U_n^k}{p_n} \left(-q_a^k + \sum_h \theta_h^k x_a^h \right) - \sum_i Cm_i \left[\sum_k \left(\frac{\partial q_i^k}{\partial p_a} + \frac{\partial q_i^k}{\partial r^k} \sum_h \theta_h^k x_a^h \right) \right.$$

$$\left. - \sum_h \frac{\partial x_i^h}{\partial p_a} \right] = 0. \qquad (5\text{-}19)$$

$$\sum_i (Cm_i - p_i) \left\{ \sum_k \left(\frac{\partial q_i^k}{\partial p_a} + \frac{\partial q_i^k}{\partial r^k} \sum_h \theta_h^k x_a^h \right) - \sum_h \frac{\partial x_i^h}{\partial p_a} \right\} = \sum_k q_a^k - \sum_h x_a^h$$

$$- \sum_h x_a^h - \sum_k \frac{\bar{\lambda}^k U_n^k}{p_n} \left(q_a^k - \sum_h \theta_h^k x_a^h \right) = \sum_k \left(1 - \frac{\bar{\lambda}^k U_n^k}{p_n} \right) \left(q_a^k - \sum_h \theta_h^k x_a^h \right)$$

$$= \sum_k \left(1 - \frac{\bar{\lambda}^m U_n^m}{p_n} \frac{\bar{\lambda}^k U_n^k}{\bar{\lambda}^m U_n^m} \right) \left(q_a^k - \sum_h \theta_h^k x_a^h \right). \qquad (5\text{-}20)$$

The terms in brackets in (5-20) are the partial derivatives, with respect to p_a, of the market demand functions for y_i, taking into account the income effects associated with the increases x_a^h in profits of the private firms. Denote these terms by $\partial \tilde{y}_i / \partial p_a$, where the symbol $\sim$ indicates that business profits are taken into account. Let furthermore ζ denote

$$\frac{\bar{\lambda}^m U_n^m}{p_n} = \frac{\lambda^m U_n^m}{\beta g_n}$$

so that (5-20) becomes:

$$\sum_i (Cm_i - p_i) \frac{\partial \tilde{y}_i}{\partial p_a} = \sum_k \left(1 - \zeta \frac{\lambda^k U_n^k}{\lambda^m U_n^m} \right) \left(q_a^k - \sum_h \theta_h^k x_a^h \right). \tag{5-21}$$

Following (5-11), we also rewrite the conditions (z_j) as:

$$\sum_k \pi_j^k \frac{\bar{\lambda}^k U_n^k}{p_n} = Cm_j - \sum_i (p_i - Cm_i) \frac{\partial y_i}{\partial z_j}$$

$$\sum_k \pi_j^k \frac{\lambda^k U_n^k}{\lambda^m U_n^m} = \frac{1}{\zeta} \left[Cm_j - \sum_i (p_i - Cm_i) \frac{\partial y_i}{\partial z_j} \right]. \tag{5-22}$$

In (5-21)-(5-22), the terms $\lambda^k U_n^k / \lambda^m U_n^m$ are explicit ratios of redistributive weights attributed (by the public sector or NPO) to marginal income transfers in favor of individuals k and m respectively. The public sector or NPO would view with favor, with indifference or with disfavor a transfer of income from k to m according as $\lambda^k U_n^k / \lambda^m U_n^m$ is less than, equal to or larger than one. Ratios equal to one for all k's may be interpreted as acceptance of the prevailing income distribution. In that case formulae (5-21)-(5-22) simplify to:

$$\sum_i (Cm_i - p_i) \frac{\partial \tilde{y}_i}{\partial p_a} = \bar{\zeta} y_a \tag{5-23}$$

$$\sum_k \pi_j^k = \frac{1}{1 - \bar{\zeta}} \left[Cm_j - \sum_i (p_i - Cm_i) \frac{\partial y_i}{\partial z_j} \right], \tag{5-24}$$

where $\bar{\zeta} = 1 - \zeta$. These are the exact counterparts of conditions (5-10) and (5-13), in terms of uncompensated demand functions. The multiplier $\bar{\zeta}$ plays the same role as $\bar{\gamma}$ and should be determined so that (5-4) holds.[e] More generally, if the NPO wishes to make explicit interpersonal comparisons, ζ should be determined so that (5-4) holds simultaneously with (5-21) and (5-22). Note however that strict application of (5-21) would, in that case, require knowledge of the individual terms $(q_a^k - \sum_h \theta_h^k x_a^h)$. It is difficult to conceive of circumstances where such knowledge would be available.

---

[e]Different symbols are retained, because the value of $\bar{\zeta}$ under which (5-4) holds without transfers will not be the same as the value of $\bar{\gamma}$ under which (5-4) holds with transfers. The symbol $\bar{\gamma}$ in the section "Answers" should be replaced there by $\bar{\zeta}$ when no income transfers are possible.

Income Transfers and Efficiency: An Example

We conclude this section with an example illustrating the relevance of income transfers for efficiency.

Consider an economy with only two consumers and two private goods (no public good). Individual preferences are assumed representable by the utility functions

$$U^1 = \sqrt{Min(q_1^1, q_2^1)} \text{ and } U^2 = (q_1^2, q_2^2)^{1/4} \tag{5-25}$$

where U^1 exhibits absolute complementarity between the two goods so that the compensated demand functions q_i display zero price elasticity.

We use the first good as numeraire and assume that individuals can be charged different prices, p_2^1 and p_2^2, for the second good. The individual demand functions are

$$q_1^1 = q_2^1 = \frac{r^1}{1 + p_2^1} ; q_1^2 = \frac{r^2}{2p_2^2} \text{ and } q_2^2 = \frac{r^2}{2}. \tag{5-26}$$

The economy is initially endowed with twenty units of the first good and zero unit of the second good. The first good can however be used as input to produce the second good. A fixed cost of eight units is incurred whenever a positive amount of the second good is produced, and one further unit of input is required per unit of output.

It is easy to see that Pareto optimality requires that the two goods be consumed in a one-to-one ratio by each individual. The Pareto frontier of utility possibilities is represented in figure 5–1. It can be reached by charging unit prices for both goods and distributing incomes adding up to twelve. But the production sector runs a deficit of eight.

To study the case where the production sector is required to balance its budget, suppose first that the two individuals share the initial endowment of the first good, and the incomes so obtained can be redistributed freely, keeping their sum unchanged. From condition (5–10), the first-order conditions on p_2^1 and p_2^2 are

$$(1 - p_2^i) \frac{\partial \hat{q}_2^i}{\partial p_2^i} = \bar{\gamma} q_2^i, \quad i = 1, 2 \tag{5-27}$$

where $\bar{\gamma}$ is chosen so that the budget constraint on the production sector is met. These conditions hold if income transfers are performed according to condition (5–16).

The first individual's preferences being such that the derivative of his

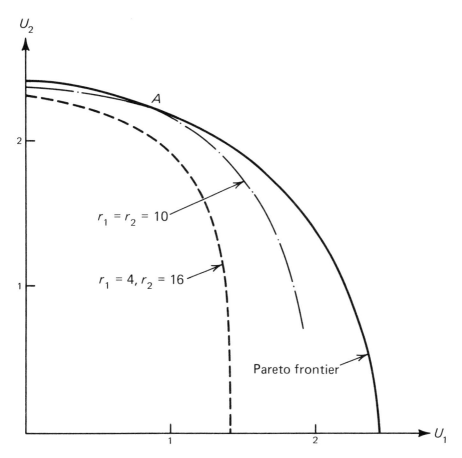

Figure 5-1. Pareto Frontier of Utility Possibilities

compensated demand $\partial q_2^1/\partial p_2^1$ is zero, condition (5-12) implies $\gamma = 0$, from which it follows that $p_2^2 = 1$. The two goods will then be consumed by each individual in a one-to-one ratio. As noted above, this consumption pattern co-incides with a Pareto-optimal allocation. This solution is obtained by raising the price paid by the first individual and giving him income compensation until the budget constraint is met. However high may be the price of the second good, he will keep consuming equal amounts of the two goods. So no welfare cost results from the budget constraint.

Suppose next that no income transfers are possible, with $r_1 = r_2 = 10$. The frontier of utility possibilities is now interior to the Pareto frontier (see Figure 5-1), but there is a point where they are tangent (point A). This point of tangency corresponds to the Pareto-optimal allocation reached in the previous case when both incomes (after transfers) are equal to 10. On the other hand, no point of tangency between the two frontiers appears when $r_1 = 4$ and $r_2 = 16$. It comes from the fact that the income after transfer of the first individual was always higher than eight in the previous case. An income r^1 equal to four is not high enough to eliminate the misallocation caused by the budget constraint imposed on a producer operating under constant marginal costs and a fixed cost equal to eight.

4. Application to Universities and Other NPO's

Atemporal Problems: Pricing and Spending Decisions

It is still a far cry from the theoretical formulae of Sections 2 and 3 to operational rules for pricing and resource allocation in NPO's. Yet, we remember that the paper by Boiteux (1956) was directly inspired by the controversy over pricing rules for the French railroads (see Drèze 1964, pp. 27–28). And we know from other examples like the work of Vickrey on the pricing of urban transportation (1955), that theoretical analysis can inspire ingenious applications.

In order to discuss applications in concrete terms, within reasonable space, we shall treat selected cases only, inviting the reader to approach other cases along the same lines.[f] We shall use the questions raised in the introduction as examples, dealing with the first three in the first two subsections and with the next two in the last subsection. The last question will be considered in Section 6.

To set a very simple stage, consider a medical school, whose faculty simultaneously operates a university hospital and produces television programs designed for medical practitioners. The television programs are public goods. The services rendered in the hospital are private goods, supplied and priced by the university. They have the further property of being perfectly "individualized": each service is consumed by a single individual who cannot transfer his consumption to others (try with an appendectomy!). This has important implications for demand elasticities. In particular, it would seem reasonable in this case to index private goods by the individuality of the beneficiary ($y_i \equiv q_i^i$) and to assume (as an approximation) that

$$\frac{\partial y_i}{\partial z_j} = 0, \forall i, j$$

---

[f] The case of most general interest to universities is probably the allocation of resources between teaching and research. The authors were debating whether further research on that topic could, logically, be justified before knowing the conclusions of such research. The debate was interrupted when one of the authors had to leave for a class. The main practical difficulty lies always with the evaluation of the value of the research output. . . .

and that

$$\frac{\partial y_i}{\partial p_i} < 0, \frac{\partial y_i}{\partial p_a} = 0 \ \forall a \neq i, \forall i.$$

Also, it seems reasonable to assume that no income transfers are possible, and that all income effects $\theta_h^k x_a^h$ are zero. Conditions (5-21)–(5-22) then simplify to:

$$(Cm_k - p_k) \frac{\partial y_k}{\partial p_k} = q_k^k \left(1 - \zeta \frac{\lambda^k U_n^k}{\lambda^m U_n^m} \right), k = 1, \ldots, m \qquad (5\text{-}28)$$

$$\sum_k \pi_j^k \frac{\lambda^k U_n^k}{\lambda^m U_m^k} = \frac{Cm_j}{\zeta}, j = 1, \ldots, \epsilon. \qquad (5\text{-}29)$$

For an individual k such that $\lambda^k U_n^k = \lambda^m U_n^m$, (5-28) may be written as

$$\frac{Cm_k - p_k}{p_k} = \bar{\zeta} \frac{y_k}{p_k} \left(\frac{\partial y_k}{\partial p_k} \right)^{-1} = \frac{\bar{\zeta}}{\eta_{y_k p_k}} \qquad (5\text{-}30)$$

where $\eta_{y_k p_k}$ is the price elasticity of individual k's demand for medical services at the university hospital.[g] We thus verify the standard interpretation of the Boiteux conditions: the hospital should behave as a discriminating, price setting monopolist who inflates all demand elasticities by a factor $1/\bar{\zeta} \geq 1$.

In order to see how $\bar{\zeta}$ is to be determined, we turn to conditions (5-29). To simplify the notation, write the left-hand side as

$$\sum_k \hat{\pi}_j^k$$

and note that it would be equal to

$$\sum_k \hat{\pi}_j^k$$

if the covariance between π_j^k and $\lambda^k U_n^k / \lambda^m U_n^m$ were zero. The left-hand side is a measure of willingness to pay for the public good (possibly adjusted by distributional preferences). There is clearly a serious problem of measurement here. The only approach that comes to mind, in the example under discussion, is to attempt eliciting preferences through a sample survey. But it is hard to avoid the

---

[g]We must assume here that services received at the university hospital are different from services received elsewhere—or else that the hospital acts as a price leader.

"free rider" problem (see, however, Dreze 1971 and Kurz 1974). Of course, some evaluation of

$$\sum_k \hat{\pi}_j^k$$

must have been part of the decision to produce the television programs. Taking difficulties one at a time, we assume that some estimate of

$$\sum_k \hat{\pi}_j^k$$

is available. Then conditions (5-29) may first be verified in the form:

$$\frac{\sum_k \hat{\pi}_j^k}{\sum_k \hat{\pi}_\epsilon^k} = \frac{Cm_j}{Cm_\epsilon}. \tag{5-31}$$

This formulation is geared to verification of the quality of resource allocation among the various public goods. Once (5-31) holds, then $\bar{\zeta}$ is directly measured by

$$\bar{\zeta} = 1 - \frac{Cm_j}{\sum_k \hat{\pi}_j^k} = \frac{\sum_k \hat{\pi}_j^k - Cm_j}{\sum_k \hat{\pi}_j^k}. \tag{5-32}$$

The value of $\bar{\zeta}$ so defined may then be plugged into (5-30) to determine p_k, given Cm_k and some estimate of $\eta_{y_k p_k}$. (Of course, all the prices p_k and production levels z_j must be determined simultaneously. But iterating through $\bar{\zeta}$ in the manner just described should define a converging process, under standard assumptions and precautions.)

To sum up, application of formulae (5-28)–(5-29) requires information that would be needed anyhow, namely marginal costs Cm and willingness to pay for the public goods,

$$\sum_k \pi^k.$$

In addition, it requires an evaluation of the price elasticities of demands, and a simultaneous (or iterative) computation of the various decisions. Clearly, these last two requirements limit the practical applicability to a few goods, i.e., to a limited extent of price discrimination. But the logic of the solution is straightforward.

Interpersonal Discrimination

It is of some interest to compare the attitude of the university toward its patients, its students, and its faculty. Formulae (5-28)-(5-29) permit such a comparison. In these formulae, each individual k may be given more or less weight, by autonomous choice of the parameter λ^k - or $\lambda^k U_n^k / \lambda^m U_n^m$. However, once these parameters have been chosen, the production and pricing rules are fully determined. For those individuals k who receive high weight—say

$$\frac{\lambda^k U_n^k}{\lambda^m U_n^m} \underset{\text{def}}{=} w^k > \bar{w}$$

—formula (5-28) implies a relatively high coefficient for blowing up the demand elasticity, namely

$$(1 - w^k \zeta)^{-1} > (1 - \bar{w}\, \bar{\zeta})^{-1}.$$

Thus, prices will be closer to marginal costs, and wages will be closer to marginal productivity, for those individuals who the NPO wishes to favor. The same individuals will carry more than proportional weight in the computation of the marginal value of public goods. Note however that the spread between price and marginal cost (productivity) still depends upon the price elasticity of demand (labor supply). Thus, if w^k is slightly larger than w^m, but $\eta_{y_k p_k}$ is much smaller (in absolute value) than $\eta_{y_m p_m}$, then it will still be true that $Cm_k - p_k/p_k$ is larger (in absolute value) than $Cm_m - p_m/p_m$. There will be more "price exploitation" of individual k than of individual m, in spite of the desire of the NPO to favor individual k over individual m, because it is still less costly (in welfare terms) to "exploit" the individual whose behavior is less elastic with respect to price.[h]

For some goods, especially for medical services, one might expect the price elasticity of demand to be very low at high incomes. If the NPO adopted weights w^k inversely related to income, the "price exploitation" of the richer patients would reflect both efficiency preoccupations and distributional preferences.[i]

---

[h]Conflicts between efficiency and equity considerations are not uncommon, especially when a budget constraint is involved. A student was once denied a fellowship by the law school of an Ivy League college because his answer to the question "Do you have other means of support" read "I have half-a-million dollars tied up in growth stocks that I cannot afford to sell now." He received a fellowship from a midwestern business school with an aggressive Alumni Association.

[i]No university that we know would admit that it produces inferior goods, so we refrain from spelling out the implications of extreme cases where demand responds positively to price at low incomes.

Conversely, faculty members with higher outside opportunities for professional earnings might be expected to display a higher price elasticity of labor supply. This would lead to salaries closer to marginal productivity. The resulting pressure toward higher salaries might be partly compensated by a lower weight w^k, if the university is egalitarian.[j]

Intertemporal Problems

In a deterministic framework, intertemporal problems are not logically different from atemporal problems. The analysis in the preceding sections may be specialized, with the former index i or j replaced by a double index (i, t) or (j, t), where t denotes the time period. It is then an easy exercise to indicate how endowment resources should be distributed among expenditures at successive time periods. The basic answer is provided by the formulae developed above.

To remain concrete, take the case of television programs considered in the previous subsections, and assume that they are to be financed out of an endowment fund. Let (j, t) stand for programs produced at time t and $(n, 1)$ for some input available at time 1, still used as numeraire ($p_{n,1} = 1$). The same input available at time t will be denoted by (n, t), with $p_{n,t} = (1 + r_t)^{-1}$, where r_t is the rate of interest at which the numeraire is discounted from time t to time 1.

With the notation just introduced, the marginal cost of television programs at time t, expressed in terms of the input available at time 1, is

$$Cm_{j,t} = \frac{g_{j,t}}{g_{n,1}} p_{n,1} = \frac{g_{j,t}}{g_{n,1}}.$$

This marginal cost, expressed in terms of the same input available at time t, is

$$\frac{g_{j,t}}{g_{n,t}} = _{\text{def}} \overline{Cm}_{j,t}.$$

Likewise, $\pi_{j,t}^k$ is defined as the willingness to pay in terms of the numeraire $(n, 1)$. It can be expressed in terms of (n, t),

$$\frac{U_{j,t}^k}{U_{n,t}^k} = _{\text{def}} \overline{\pi}_{j,t}^k.$$

---

[j]Salaries of university presidents or deans may thus be rationalized in three ways, listed here in the order of the authors' subjective plausibilities: (i) a high weight w^k; (ii) a high price elasticity of labor supply; (iii) a high marginal productivity (usually *assumed* positive).

For purpose of simplification, let us assume that $\lambda^k U^k_{n,1} = \lambda^m U^m_{n,1}$. Using the above notation, we can rewrite condition (5-24) as

$$\sum_k \bar{\pi}^k_{j,t} \frac{1}{1+r_t} = \frac{1}{1-\bar{\zeta}} \overline{Cm}_{j,t} \frac{g_{n,t}}{g_{n,1}} \tag{5-33}$$

where we neglect the terms correcting Cm_j on the right-hand side. We can interpret $g_{n,t}/g_{n,1}$ as the discount factor to be used for $Cm_{j,t}$ and define the internal rate of discount ρ_t by means of:

$$\frac{g_{n,t}}{g_{n,1}} = _{\text{def}} (1 + \rho_t)^{-1}. \tag{5-34}$$

To determine how the internal rate of discount is related to the market rate of interest, we start from condition (5-23):

$$\sum_i \sum_s (Cm_{i,s} - p_{i,s}) \frac{\partial \tilde{y}_{i,s}}{\partial p_{n,t}} = \bar{\zeta} y_{n,t}. \tag{5-35}$$

Neglecting all cross-elasticities, it can be rewritten as follows:

$$\frac{g_{n,t}}{g_{n,1}} = p_{n,t} \left[1 + \bar{\zeta} \frac{y_{n,t}}{p_{n,t}} \left(\frac{\partial y_{n,t}}{\partial p_{n,t}} \right)^{-1} \right]$$

$$= p_{n,t} \left[1 - \bar{\zeta} \frac{y_{n,t}}{1+r_t} \left(\frac{\partial \hat{y}_{n,t}}{\partial r_t} \right)^{-1} \right]$$

$$= p_{n,t} \left(1 - \bar{\zeta} \frac{r_t}{1+r_t} \eta^{-1}_{y_{n,t}r_t} \right). \tag{5-36}$$

If the elasticity is small enough, this condition reduces to:

$$\frac{g_{n,t}}{g_{n,1}} = p_{n,t} \left(1 + \bar{\zeta} \frac{r_t}{1+r_t} \eta^{-1}_{y_{n,t}r_t} \right)^{-1}$$

$$= [1 + r_t (1 + \bar{\zeta} \eta^{-1}_{y_{n,t}r_t})]^{-1}. \tag{5-37}$$

The internal rate of discount is then given by:

$$\rho_t = r_t (1 + \bar{\zeta} \eta_{y_{n,t}r_t}). \tag{5-38}$$

which enables us to answer the fifth question raised in the introduction. The elasticity will normally be negative for a net lender, resulting in $\rho_t < r_t$, and positive for a net borrower, resulting in $\rho_t > r_t$.

If a binding borrowing constraint is imposed on the NPO or the public sector, the internal rate of return should be chosen such that the constraint be satisfied.

Assuming that the NPO is confronted with a competitive market ($\eta_{y_{n,t}r_t}^{-1} = 0$). the rates at which the NPO should discount its future costs and benefits are both given by the market rate of interest. Condition (5-33) then yields:

$$\sum_k \bar{\pi}_{j,t}^k = \frac{1}{1 - \bar{\zeta}} \ \overline{Cm}_{j,t} , \qquad\qquad (5\text{-}39)$$

by means of which we can answer the fourth question raised in the introduction. In the special case of stationary costs and preferences, equation (5-39) would be satisfied with the same production level in every period. With an infinite horizon, this would imply a systematic policy of spending income and maintaining capital. Outside of this extreme case, such a policy would not be optimal. Universities should be concerned with the intertemporal efficiency of the use of their endowment. This may require that capital be accumulated, or reduced, at some times.

For instance, when televised education is introduced for the first time, its marginal value to practitioners may be very high, calling for a substantial output and a temporary depletion of capital. Conversely, if the marginal value of the programs were to increase over time (through accumulated experience, for instance), it would be better to accumulate capital now and spend it in the future.

5. Risk Preferences and Portfolio Selection in NPO's[k]

Approach

Until now, we have used a deterministic approach. This was a natural starting point and a satisfactory framework to study pricing rules and some resource allocation problems. However, intertemporal decisions usually involve uncertainty in an essential way. This is particularly true for decisions relating to capital assets, like portfolio choices.

The theory of general equilibrium has been extended to uncertainty by the

---

[k]The authors wish to thank Kåre Hagen for a helpful discussion of the material in this section. Work on this problem was started at the University of Chicago in 1968 by one of the authors, who benefited greatly from discussions with Merton Miller.

introduction of "states of the world" in the definition of commodities (see Arrow 1963-64). If there existed markets and prices for all commodities contingent on all states, the analysis in the foregoing sections would be complete and would not call for a specific extension to uncertainty. Our rules (5-21)-(5-22) could govern pricing and spending on all commodities (including assets) contingent on all states.

When there are no markets for contingent commodities but markets for (some) assets, an analysis of constrained Pareto optimality is still possible (see, e.g., Dreze 1974). One could insert NPO's in a "state model with incomplete markets" and deal explicitly with issues of risky physical investments, portfolio choices, participation of NPOs in control by stockholders, a.s.o.. We feel that an analysis of that kind would be very much worth conducting, but it lies beyond the scope of the present chapter.

There is a more pedestrian, but more operational, approach to some problems of choice under uncertainty, which has been found particularly useful to study portfolio decisions; namely, the analysis of risk preferences in terms of a utility function U and the absolute risk aversion function U''/U' (or the corresponding relative risk aversion function; (see Pratt 1964). This approach is quite satisfactory for analysis of individual decisions, especially in two-assets models. It is not directly applicable to firms, whose preferences should be inferred from those of the individuals ultimately concerned (as workers or stockholders). We will now show how it can be applied to NPOs, in a reasonably operational and rigorous way, but at the cost of severe simplifications.

The derivation of risk aversion functions for NPOs serves two purposes. First, it provides an adequate tool to study those questions which can be answered in terms of a risk aversion function (like portfolio decisions in a world with two assets, or equivalently in a world where the separation theorem holds (see Merton 1971). Second, the analysis of a relatively simple case might serve as a guide for more difficult cases.

In order to place the specific elements of risk bearing by NPOs in proper perspective, we shall first recall the interpretation of the absolute risk aversion function. We return next to the model of Sections 2 and 3, simplify it, extend it to uncertainty, and derive risk aversion functions for NPOs.

Risk Aversion and Portfolio Selection

The interpretation of the risk aversion functions is most easily perceived in terms of a simple portfolio (or asset management) problem. Consider an individual, whose preferences among risky prospects are defined by a cardinal utility function for wealth $U(w)$, and who has the option of purchasing, at price p, an asset with random return ξ, satisfying $E(\xi) = \mu$ and $V(\xi) = \sigma^2$. Denote by r his initial wealth and by θ the number of units of the risky asset bought. Then:

$U(w) = U[r + \theta \ (\xi - p)]$. Let

$$\bar{U} = \underset{\text{def}}{} U[r + \theta \ (\mu - p)] . \tag{5-40}$$

Using a Taylor-series expansion, we may write:

$$\underset{\xi}{E U} \ [r + \theta \ (\xi - p)] = \bar{U} + E(\xi - \mu)\bar{U}'\theta + \frac{E(\xi - \mu)^2}{2} \ \bar{U}''\theta^2 + \text{Rem.}$$

$$\cong \bar{U} + \frac{\sigma^2}{2} \ \bar{U}''\theta^2 . \tag{5-41}$$

The first order condition for a maximum of EU with respect to θ, as obtained from (5-41), is:

$$\bar{U}' \ (\mu - p) + \sigma^2 \ \bar{U}''\theta = 0, \frac{\mu - p}{\sigma^2\theta} = - \frac{U''}{U'} , \tag{5-42}$$

up to third-order terms. Thus, the absolute investment θp in the risky asset is inversely proportional to the absolute risk aversion $-\bar{U}''/U'$ and the relative investment $\theta p/r$ is inversely proportional to the relative risk aversion function $-r \ \bar{U}''/U'$. In both cases, the proportionality factor is the reciprocal of the coefficient of variation per unit of investment, $(\sigma^2/\mu - p) \ 1/p$.

Furthermore, if the price paid for the risky asset varies with the number of units bought, so that $p = p(\theta)$, then (5-42) becomes

$$\bar{U}'\left(\mu - p - \theta \ \frac{dp}{d\theta}\right) + \sigma^2\bar{U}''\theta = 0, \frac{\mu - p \ (1 + \eta_{p\theta})}{\sigma^2\theta} = \frac{-\bar{U}''}{\bar{U}'} . \tag{5-43}$$

This generalization admits of the usual economic interpretation.

Finally, if utility is not a function of wealth, but rather of some commodity z produced by means of the production function g using wealth as input, $z = g(w)$, then $V(w) = U[g(w)]$. Let define: $\bar{V}(r, \theta) = U[g(r + \theta \ (\mu - p))]$. It is then readily verified that:

$$\bar{V}_r = \bar{U}_z g', \ \bar{V}_{rr} = \bar{U}_{zz} (g')^2 + \bar{U}_z g''$$

$$\frac{\bar{V}_{rr}}{\bar{V}_r} = \frac{\bar{U}_{zz}}{\bar{U}_z} g' - \frac{g''}{g'} , \tag{5-44}$$

where all derivatives of g are taken at $w = r + \theta \ (\mu - p)$ and those of U at $z = g(r + \theta \ (\mu - p))$.

Thus, the absolute risk aversion function for the input (wealth) is the sum of two terms: (i) the absolute risk aversion function (utility-wise) for the produced commodity (divided by marginal cost, for scaling); (ii) the logarithmic derivative of the marginal productivity of the input, which has the same interpretation as an absolute risk aversion function (production-wise) for the input. This additive decomposition will be used in the sequel.

We also note for further reference that

$$\bar{V}_{rrr} = \bar{U}_{zzz}(g')^3 + 3\,\bar{U}_{zz}g'g'' + \bar{U}_z g''', \qquad\qquad (5\text{-}45)$$

thereby establishing the "third-order" nature of the term $U_{zz}g'g''$.

A Model of Portfolio Selection by NPOs

We now introduce a simplified version of the model of sections 2 and 3, and generalize to public goods the analysis in the preceding subsection.

Consider the model of Section 2 with *a single private good,* hence no private firms, *a single public good* and *no transfers.* We may identify the private good with the individual incomes $(q^k = r^k)$ and with the budget constraint of the NPO $(y = b)$; and we may express the amount of public good z as an explicit function of the input level b, $z = g(b)$. Then, $U^k(q^k, z) = U^k[r^k, g(b)]$.

We now introduce the possibility, for each individual *and* for the NPO, to acquire a risky asset with random return ξ, satisfying $E(\xi) = \mu$ and $V(\xi) = \sigma^2$.[1] Let the number of units of this asset acquired by individual k be θ^k, the number acquired by the NPO be θ; the total "investment" in the risky asset is then

$$\theta + \sum_k \theta^k.$$

As a convenient shortcut to the more explicit analysis that was recommended in the section "Approach," we assume that the risky asset is acquired at a price

$$p = p(\theta + \sum_k \theta^k)$$

expressed in the same units as r^k and b. For an open economy, p may be interpreted as a price prevailing on an international capital market. In a closed economy, p may be interpreted as the cost (in terms of r^k or b) of producing the risky asset.[m]

---

[1]Following standard practice in portfolio analysis, we assume unanimous agreement about $E(\xi)$ and $V(\xi)$.

[m]An average cost interpretation is natural if the risky asset is incorporated as a new business venture (with the individuals and the NPO supplying the equity capital); a marginal

Taking the risky investments into account, we obtain "ex post incomes" $q^k = r^k + \theta^k(\xi - p)$ and ex post output of the public good $z = g(b + \theta(\xi - p))$, yielding the utility levels $U^k[r^k + \theta^k(\xi - p), g(b + \theta(\xi - p))]$, where

$$p = p(\theta + \sum_k \theta^k).$$

We denote again $U^k[r^k + \theta^k(\mu - p), g(b + \theta(\mu - p))]$ by $\bar{U}^k$ and obtain from a Taylor-series expansion

$$\underset{\xi}{E} U^k = \bar{U}^k + \frac{\sigma^2}{2}[\bar{U}^k_{rr}(\theta^k)^2 + 2\bar{U}^k_{rz}\theta^k\theta g' + \bar{U}^k_{zz}(g')^2 + \bar{U}^k_z g'' \; \theta^2]$$

$$+ \text{Rem.} \tag{5-46}$$

Our analysis will be greatly simplified, both conceptually and exposition-ally, by the assumption that $\bar{U}^k_{rz} = 0 \; \forall k$, meaning that $-\bar{U}^k_{rr}/\bar{U}^k_r$ is independent of z. This assumption is far from innocuous, considering that U^k is defined to a *linear* transformation (our assumption is more restrictive than additive *ordinal* preferences). But it may be argued that in the real world:

1. $\theta^k = 0$ for most beneficiaries of the public goods produced by a specific NPO; $\bar{U}^k_{rz}$ then drops out of (5-46);
2. portfolio diversification would anyhow enable an NPO to hold assets with returns only mildly correlated with those of assets held by the said bene-ficiaries, a feature not recognized in our simplified model; the terms $\bar{U}^k_{rz}$ would then be multiplied by covariances, not by variances; and
3. the cross derivatives U^k_{rz} could not be measured empirically, so that a more general analysis would have academic interest only.

A Risk Aversion Function of NPOs

A gambling rule for the NPO will now be defined by solving the problem

$$\underset{\theta}{\text{Max}} \; \sum_k \lambda^k \underset{\xi}{E} U^k \text{ subject to } p = p \; \theta + \sum_k \theta^k \;, \frac{\partial EU^k}{\partial \theta^k} = 0. \tag{P}$$

---

cost interpretation could easily be formalized, with the added complication of an explicit assignment (among individuals and the NPO) of the initial ownership and profits; that com-plication is of no immediate interest for our purpose in this section.

The first-order condition for a maximum is

$$0 = \frac{d\sum_k \lambda^k EU^k}{d\theta} = \frac{\partial \sum_k \lambda^k EU^k}{\partial \theta} + \frac{\partial \sum_k \lambda^k EU^k}{\partial p}\frac{dp}{d\theta} \tag{5-47}$$

where

$$\frac{\partial EU^k}{\partial \theta} = \bar{U}_z^k g'(\mu - p) + \sigma^2[\{\bar{U}_{zz}^k (g')^2 + \bar{U}_z^k g''\}\theta + \frac{3}{2}\bar{U}_{zz}^k g' g''(\mu - p)\theta^2$$

$$+ \bar{U}_{rz}^k \theta^k \{g' + g''\theta(\mu - p)\}] \tag{5-48}$$

$$\frac{\partial EU^k}{\partial p} = -\bar{U}_r^k \theta^k - \bar{U}_z^k g'\theta - \sigma^2\left[\frac{3}{2}\bar{U}_{zz}^k g' g''\theta^3 + \bar{U}_{rz}^k \theta^k \theta^2 g''\right]$$

$$+ \frac{\partial EU^k}{\partial \theta^k}\frac{d\theta^k}{dp}. \tag{5-49}$$

Upon using our assumption $\bar{U}_{rz}^k = 0$ and the conditions $\partial EU^k/\partial \theta^k = 0$, neglecting the third-order terms $\bar{U}_{zz}^k g' g''$, writing once more π^k for $\bar{U}_z^k/\bar{U}_r^k$ and inserting (5-48)–(5-49) into (5-47), we obtain:

$$0 = \sum_k \lambda^k \bar{U}_r^k \left\{\pi^k g'\left(\mu - p - \theta\frac{dp}{d\theta}\right) - \theta^k\frac{dp}{d\theta} + \sigma^2\theta g'\left[\frac{\bar{U}_{zz}^k}{\bar{U}_r^k} + \frac{g''}{g'}\pi^k\right]\right\}. \tag{5-50}$$

If the NPO views with indifference transfers of income among individuals; more generally, if the NPO assigns weights

$$\frac{\lambda^k \bar{U}_r^k}{\lambda^m \bar{U}_r^m}$$

to marginal income transfers that are uncorrelated (over individuals) with the terms inside the curly brackets, then a final form of the first-order condition (5-47), or (5-50), is:

$$\frac{\mu - p - \theta\dfrac{dp}{d\theta}\dfrac{\sum_k \theta^k}{g'\sum_k \pi^k}\dfrac{dp}{d\theta}}{\sigma^2\theta} = \frac{-g'}{\sum_k \pi^k}\sum_k\frac{\bar{U}_{zz}^k}{\bar{U}_r^k} - \frac{g''}{g'}$$

$$\frac{\mu - p(1 + \eta^\tau_{p\theta})}{\sigma^2 \theta} = \frac{-1}{Cm}\left(\frac{1}{\sum_k \pi^k}\frac{\partial \sum_k \pi^k}{\partial z} - \frac{1}{Cm}\frac{dCm}{dz}\right) \qquad (5\text{-}51)$$

where: $Cm = 1/g'$ is the marginal cost of the public good

$$\frac{dCm}{dz} = \frac{d(1/g')}{dz} = \frac{-1}{(g')^2}\frac{dg'}{dz} = \frac{-1}{(g')^2}\frac{dg'}{dr}\frac{dr}{dz} = \frac{-g''}{(g')^3}$$

$$\eta^\tau_{p\theta} = \frac{\theta^\tau}{p}\frac{dp}{d\theta}, \quad \theta^\tau = \theta + \frac{\sum_k \theta^k}{g' \sum_k \pi^k} = \theta + \frac{Cm}{\sum_k \pi^k}\sum_k \theta^k$$

and where use has been made of $\bar{U}^k_{rz} = 0$ to write

$$\frac{\bar{U}^k_{zz}}{\bar{U}^k_r} = \frac{\partial \pi^k}{\partial z}.$$

According to formula (5-51), the absolute risk aversion function for the NPO is obtained as a sum of two terms, that are directly comparable to the two terms in formula (5-44). The output elasticity of marginal cost is directly measurable within the NPO; the elasticity of willingness to pay for the public good is less directly measurable but the information required for that measurement is not so different from that required to evaluate

$$\sum_k \pi^k.$$

The corresponding relative risk aversion function is obtained upon multiplying by the input level b. By definition, b is also equal to output z times average cost Ca. The relative risk aversion function is then

$$-\frac{zCa}{Cm}\left(\frac{1}{\sum_k \pi^k}\frac{\partial \sum_k \pi^k}{\partial z} - \frac{1}{Cm}\frac{\partial Cm}{\partial z}\right) = \frac{-Ca}{Cm}(\eta_{\sum \pi^k \cdot z} - \eta_{Cm \cdot z})$$

where the η's are elasticities.

When $dp/d\theta = 0$, then the absolute risk aversion of the NPO is simply equated to $\mu - p/\sigma^2\theta$ as in (5-42). When $dp/d\theta \neq 0$, the elasticity of supply of the risky investment comes in—as in (5-43). The elasticity formula $\eta^\tau_{p\theta}$ takes into account the difference in relative valuation between resources used in the public and private sector, namely

$$\sum_{k} \pi^{k} / Cm.$$

As before, individual price elasticities are deflated by the ratio of marginal cost to marginal valuation of the public good. This refinement is not likely to make an essential difference in possible applications of formula (5-51).

In spite of the numerous simplifications made in this section, we regard the r.h.s. of formula (5-51) as the most useful approximation to a risk aversion function for NPOs that we could suggest. We note that, under increasing returns to scale in production, an NPO could conceivably display a positive risk preference.

As a further hint toward interpretation, we mention the case of a single individual (or identical individuals) who regards the private and public goods as perfect substitutes. His risk aversion function for gambles with the resources of the public sector would differ from his risk aversion for gambles with his private resources by the term $\eta_{Cm \cdot z}$ (output elasticity of marginal cost). The public sector would thus be more, or less, risk averse than the individual according as diminishing, or increasing, returns prevailed in production.

We conclude with the remark that further work on this subject is much needed. Indeed, we find in (5-51) that the absolute risk aversion function of an NPO is given by the logarithmic derivative of

$$\frac{\sum_{k} \pi^{k}}{Cm}$$

with respect to b. Going back to formulae (5-9) and (5-13), we find that (in the absence of adjustments to marginal costs for a difference in net profits)

$$\frac{\sum_{k} \pi_{j}^{k}}{Cm_{j}}$$

is equal to

$$\frac{\alpha_{n} + \gamma p_{n}}{\alpha_{n}},$$

where α_{n} and γ are the Lagrange multipliers associated respectively with the market clearing constraint on good n and with the budget constraint. Indeed,

$$\frac{\sum_{k} \pi_{j}^{k}}{Cm_{j}}$$

is a measure of the relative value of inputs inside and outside the public sector. And a transfer of risks between the NPO and the private sector is a gamble about a transfer of inputs between the NPO and the private sector. The assumptions made in this section enable us to write

$$\frac{d}{db} \log \left(\sum_k \pi_j^k / Cm \right)$$

as

$$\frac{1}{Cm} \frac{d}{dz} \log \left(\sum_k \pi_j^k / Cm \right).$$

In the more general model of Sections 2 and 3, a change in b would result in a vector of changes in p, r, y, and z, so that

$$\frac{d}{db} = \frac{\partial}{\partial p} \cdot \frac{dp}{db} + \frac{\partial}{\partial r} \cdot \frac{dr}{db} + \frac{\partial}{\partial y} \cdot \frac{dy}{db} + \frac{\partial}{\partial z} \cdot \frac{dz}{db}.$$

In order to take into account all these effects, one should analyze the differential of the system formed (say, in Section 2) by conditions (α), (β), (γ), (p_a), (r^k), (y_i) and (z_j), and try to obtain a formula for the logarithmic derivative of

$$\frac{\alpha_n + \gamma p_n}{\alpha_n}$$

with respect to b. Research on such technical problems could, in our opinion, be pursued under foundation support.

References

Arrow, K.J. "The Role of Securities in the Optimal Allocation of Risk-Bearing." *Review of Economic Studies* 31 (1963–64): 91–96.

Atkinson, A. and N. Stern. "Pigou, Taxation and Public Goods." *Review of Economic Studies* 41 (1974): 119–128.

Baumol, W. and D. Bradford. "Optimal Departures from Marginal Cost Pricing." *American Economic Review* 60 (1970): 265–283.

Bergson, A. "Optimal Pricing for a Public Enterprise." *Quarterly Journal of Economics* 36 (1972): 518–541.

Boiteux, M. "Sur la gestion des monopoles publics astreint l'équilibre budgétaire." *Econometrica* 24 (1956): 22–40.

Bronsard, C. *Dualité microéconomique et théorie du second-best.* Louvain, Vander, 1971.

Diamond, P. and J. Mirrlees. "Optimal Taxation and Public Production." *American Economic Review* 61 (1971): 8–27 and 261–278.

Drèze, J.H. "Some Postwar Contributions of French Economists to Theory and Public Policy." *American Economic Review* 54 Supplement 4, 2 (1964): 1–64.

Drèze, J.H. and D. de la Vallée Poussin. "A Tatonnement Process for Public Goods." *Review of Economic Studies* 38 (1971): 133–150.

Drèze, J.H. "Investment under Private Ownership: Optimality, Equilibrium and Stability." In J.H. Drèze (ed.), *Allocation under Uncertainty: Equilibrium and Optimality*. McMillan, 1974. Pp. 129–166.

Guesnerie, R. "On Second Best Pareto Optimality in a Class of Models." CEPREMAP, unpublished (1975).

Kolm, C. *Théorie des contraintes de valeur*. Paris: Dunod, 1970.

Kurz, M. "Experimental Approach to the Determination of the Demand for Public Goods." *Journal of Public Economics* 3 (1974): 329–348.

Marchand, M. "A Note on Optimal Tolls in an Imperfect Environment." *Econometrica* 36 (1968): 575–581.

Merton, R.C. "Optimum Consumption and Portfolio Rules in a Continuous Time Model." *Journal of Economic Theory* 3 (1971): 373–413.

Pratt, J.W. "Risk Aversion in the Small and in the Large." *Econometrica* 32 (1964): 122–136.

Ramsey, F.R. "A Contribution to the Theory of Taxation." *Economic Journal* 37 (1927): 47–61.

Sandmo, A. "Optimality Rules for the Provision of Collective Factors of Production." *Journal of Public Economics* 1 (1972): 149–157.

Stiglitz, J. and P. Dasgupta. "Differential Taxation, Public Goods and Economic Efficiency." *Review of Economic Studies* 38 (1971): 151–174.

Vickrey, W.S. "A Proposal for Revising New York's Subway Fare Structure." *Journal of the Operations Research Society of America* 3 (1955): 38–69.

6 Charitable Bequests, Estate Taxation, and Intergenerational Wealth Transfers

Martin Feldstein

The first fundamental study of the economics of charity was Bill Vickrey's "One Economist's View of Philanthropy" (1962). In a recent paper, "Private Philanthropy and Public Finance" (1973), Vickrey returned to examine this subject with special emphasis on the current income tax treatment of charitable gifts and possible alternative tax policies. Vickrey's papers have shown that the appropriate tax treatment of such gifts involves a complex series of economic issues.

The tax treatment of charitable bequests raises similar empirical and philosophical issues. Charitable bequests are an important source of support for non-profit organizations and a significant factor in the dispersion of personal fortunes. In 1970, charitable bequests exceeded $2 billion or 10 percent of the total philanthropic gifts made by individuals.[1] Such bequests are particularly important for educational institutions, accounting for approximately 24 percent of all individual gifts.[2] A very substantial portion of the net value of large estates is contributed to charity. Among estates with a gross value in excess of $1 million in 1970, gifts to charitable organizations were more than 33 percent of the value of gifts to individuals. Among estates with gross value in excess of $5 million, charitable bequests were more than 125 percent of the value of gifts to individuals.

The current estate tax law excludes from the taxable estate all such charitable bequests. The tax law thus makes the "price" of charitable bequests less than the price of bequests to individuals.[a] More specifically, an individual with a marginal estate tax rate of 60 percent can bequeath $100 to charity by foregoing a bequest of $40 to his personal heirs; for him (or them), the net price of charitable bequests is only 0.4. Because the estate tax is very progressive, the net price of charitable bequests falls sharply as estate size increases.

I am grateful to Daniel Frisch for assistance with this research, to the Commission on Private Philanthropy and Public Needs for financial support, and to M. Boskin for useful discussions. A previous version of this paper was prepared as a technical report to the Commission on Private Philanthropy and Public Needs.

[a]Because of the special marital deduction, an individual can give half of his estate to his wife and deduct that amount in computing the taxable estate. The deduction of charitable bequests lowers the price of charity relative to the price of bequests to individuals other than the decedent's spouse and bequests to the spouse in excess of the marital deduction.

This feature of the estate tax law raises three related questions. (1) Does the deduction of charitable bequests increase the total amount of such bequests or does it merely lower the taxes paid by the estates that make such bequests and thus increase the amount that is available for distribution to individual heirs? (2) If the deduction does increase total charitable bequests, are the extra bequests that are induced larger than the estate tax revenue that the Treasury foregoes because of the deduction?[b] That is, what is the efficiency of the charitable bequest deduction, the number of dollars of additional bequests induced per dollar of foregone revenue? (3) What is the effect of the deduction of charitable bequests on the net estates received by individual heirs? If the induced increase in charitable bequests is greater than the foregone revenue, individual heirs receive less than they would if the deduction were eliminated. But if the induced increase in charitable bequests is less than the foregone revenue, individual heirs are better off than they would be if the current deduction were eliminated.

The answer to all three questions depends on the elasticity of charitable bequests with respect to price. The primary focus of this chapter will be on the estimation of this price elasticity. An estimated price elasticity that is not significantly different from zero implies that the current deduction does not increase charitable giving. In contrast, a significant negative price elasticity implies that charitable organizations do receive more than they would if the deduction were eliminated. If the absolute price elasticity is greater than one (i.e., if the price elasticity is algebraically less than minus one), charitable organizations receive more in additional contributions than the Treasury foregoes in revenue. The absolute elasticity is itself a measure of the efficiency of the deduction, i.e., the ratio of additional charitable bequests to lost tax revenue.[c] It is also clear that an elasticity greater than one implies that the current deduction reduces the size of the net estate received by individual heirs; although the deduction reduces the taxes paid, charitable gifts are increased by more than taxes are reduced so that the net estate after taxes and charitable gifts is reduced. Obviously, a price elasticity less than one implies that the deduction increases the size of the net estate available for individual heirs.

The evidence presented in this chapter suggests that the price elasticity of charitable bequests is significantly negative and probably between minus one and minus three. This result is therefore quite consistent with Boskin's

---

[b]In 1970, additional federal estate tax liabilities would have been $1.0 billion if charitable bequests were not deducted in calculating taxable estates and if total estates nevertheless remained the same. Total estate tax collections in 1970 were $3.4 billion. This calculation ignores state inheritance and death taxes.

[c]This is exactly true only if the price is close to one or the elasticity is close to true. It remains a reasonable approximation over a much wider range.

(1974) estimate that the price elasticity is between minus one and minus two. This agreement is particularly reassuring because Boskin used a very different type of data and estimation method.

The current chapter examines the sensitivity of the estimated price elasticity to alternative definitions of price and to alternative functional forms. Changing the measure of price has little effect on the estimated price elasticity. In contrast, the price elasticity is quite sensitive to the choice of functional form relating charitable bequests to price and estate size. In particular, a number of functional forms imply positive price elasticities over the entire range of estate sizes or a large part of that range. These unstable and unacceptable price elasticities must be borne in mind and regarded as a warning that these results may be subject to serious potential error. The evidence here is clearly not as strong as it was in previous studies of the effect of taxation on charitable gifts by living individuals.[3]

The data and the measurement of variables are discussed in the next section. The basic parameter estimates are presented in Section 2. Separate estimates for large estates are developed in the third section. In Section 4, gifts to different types of donees are studied. There is a brief concluding section.

1. Data and Measurement

At irregular intervals the Internal Revenue Service published the value of charitable contributions in each gross estate class during a single recent year.[4] The current study uses a time series of these cross-sections for the available years from 1948 through 1963.[d] With 15 gross estate classes,[e] the sample has 135 aggregate observations. Although there was no change in the estate tax rates during the sample period, the tax rate at every *real* level of gross estate has been increasing because of inflation. This source of variation reduces somewhat the collinearity between price and estate size that exists within a single year.

A variety of functional specifications relating charitable giving (G) to estate size (E) and a price (P) have been investigated. The most basic specification is the equation:

$$\frac{G_{it}}{E_{it}} = \alpha + \beta P_{it} + \gamma E_{it} + \epsilon_{it}. \tag{6.1}$$

---

[d]For estates after 1963 the Internal Revenue Service published bequests by "economic estate class" rather than "gross estate class" so that the data are no longer comparable.

[e]The gross estate class lower limits are (in $1000 units): 60, 70, 80, 90, 100, 120, 150, 200, 300, 500, 1000, 2000, 3000, 5000, 10,000.

The subscript i denotes the gross estate size class and the subscript t denotes the year. The variable ϵ_{it} is an unobservable residual that reflects random disturbances and specification errors. The more general specifications described below allow the effects of estate size and price to vary with the levels of estate size and price.

The variable G_{it} is the average charitable bequest per return in gross estate class i and year t. The bequest is defined as the *gross* amount given by the individual estate to charity and not as the *net* cost of that contribution to the individual heirs. These amounts include the value of donated assets as well as gifts of money. Bequests are measured in constant 1957–59 dollars by deflating with the consumer price index. Of course, only those estates that file estate tax returns, i.e., those with gross estates in excess of $60,000, are included in the sample.

The basic measure of estate size (E) used in this study has been gross estate minus all noncharitable deductions except the marital deduction. This measure assumes that the marital deduction takes priority in the individual's estate planning. Fortunately, a variety of other definitions of estate size, including gross estate minus noncharitable deductions, gross estate minus the tax liability if no charitable bequests were made, and gross estate itself yielded very similar estimates for the key price elasticity. In practice, the value of E_{it} is the average real value of the estate per return in gross estate class i and year t, measured in constant 1957–59 dollars. Although the results are not sensitive to the available measures of estate size, it is clear that none of the available variables is an ideal measure of the decedent's economic situation. The value of previously created trusts and of gifts inter vivos, as well as the number and financial positions of the decedent's potential heirs, should all influence charitable giving.

The price variable (P) measures the estate's opportunity cost per dollar of charitable bequest in terms of foregone personal bequests to individual heirs. An estate with marginal tax rate $\underline{m}$ can choose between (1) contributing one dollar to charity and (2) having $1 - \underline{m}$ dollars for additional personal bequests to individual heirs. We therefore define the individual's price of charitable giving by $P = 1 - m$. In practice, P_{it} is measured by using the marginal tax rate for an estate with the average "taxable estate" in gross estate class i and year t. Two different measures of "taxable estate" and therefore of price have been used: $P1$ is based on the actual taxable estate plus charitable bequests and $P2$ on the actual taxable estate plus both charitable bequests and the marital deduction. Both measures yield the marginal tax rate for the first dollar of charitable bequest. This makes the price variable exogenous; using actual taxable estate would make the price variable depend upon the charitable bequest itself. The first measure of price assumes that the decedents choose their marital bequests before they decide on their charitable gifts while the second measure assumes that both decisions are made jointly.[f] Fortunately, there is little difference in the results corresponding to these different measures of price.

Contributions of appreciated assets create no special problem for measuring the price of charitable bequests. When an asset is bequeathed, either to an individual or to a charitable organization, its full value can be deducted from the donor's taxable estate and there is no constructive realization and therefore no income tax to be paid by the decedent or by the recipient. Asset gifts have the same price as cash gifts.

Estates are subject not only to federal estate tax but also to taxes levied by individual states. Because the federal government gives a direct tax credit for a portion of the state taxes paid, the two rates do not fully cumulate. To assess the importance of the state tax rates, the following calculation was performed for 1963. For each of the fifteen published gross estate classes, an estate at the midpoint of the class was chosen. On the assumption that the full marital deduction is used and that the remainder is given to the decedent's minor children, the inheritance tax in each state for each size estate was calculated. The excess of this inheritance tax over the federal tax credit is the "excess state tax." Weighting the excess state rates by the number of estates in each size class and state yields the average excess state rate by size of estate. In every case, this average excess state rate was less than one percent. On the basis of this it was decided to ignore the state inheritance taxes.[g]

Table 6-1 presents the values of G_{it}, E_{it}, and Pl_{it} for each gross estate class for 1963, the most recent year in the sample. For each estate class, the table also shows the ratio of gifts to the estate after all noncharitable deductions (column 5).

Each of the observations represented a different number of estate tax returns. In the very highest estate size classes, there are relatively few returns each year and substantial year to year variation in the ratio of bequests to estate size. Although the available data are not a sample but a report of all estates, one can regard each year's actual observation as a sample from the population of possible decedents. If the underlying microeconomic relations have constant variance, the process of averaging implies that the error variance will be larger for the observations based on a small number of returns. We have therefore weighted each of the observations by the square root of the number of returns represented by that observation.

---

[f]The individual faces two prices when making the joint decision: the price of charity and the price of gifts to a spouse. Both first dollar prices are the same since neither gift is taxed.

[g]The assumption that the heirs are a spouse and minor children lowers the state inheritance tax. It would in principle be desirable to examine this in greater detail but the current results suggest that such effort may not be worth while.

Table 6-1
Charitable Bequests by Estate Size, 1963

Gross Estate Size Class (in $1,000)	Average Charitable Bequests (in $1,000)	Average Net Estate* (in $1,000)	P1	Charity as Percentage of Net Estate*
(1)	(2)	(3)	(4)	(5)
60–69	1.02	55.89	1.00	2.15
70–79	1.10	63.88	1.00	2.10
80–89	1.35	72.14	0.97	2.32
90–99	1.49	80.46	0.93	2.35
100–119	1.80	93.16	0.89	2.50
120–149	2.68	113.07	0.82	3.10
150–199	4.00	145.49	0.75	3.58
200–299	6.53	203.42	0.70	4.15
300–499	14.19	322.23	0.70	5.60
500–999	36.23	580.47	0.68	7.77
1,000–1,999	112.69	1,169.99	0.63	11.63
2,000–2,999	190.23	2,053.78	0.55	11.14
3,000–4,999	378.66	3,207.53	0.47	14.60
5,000–9,999	828.04	5,568.44	0.37	17.84
10,000+	3,409.98	15,582.48	0.23	27.99

*Estate value is measured by gross estate minus all noncharitable deductions. P1 is based on taxable estate plus charitable bequests.

2. Effects of Price and Estate Size

Equation 6-2 presents the estimated parameters for a simple specification:

$$\frac{G_{it}}{E_{it}} = 0.118 - \underset{(0.010)}{0.107}\ P1_{it} + \underset{(0.083)}{0.994} \cdot 10^{-8}\ E_{it} \ . \tag{6-2}$$

$R^2 = 0.82$

$N = 135$

The value of the estate is measured by the gross estate minus all deductions except charitable bequests and the marital deduction. The price P1 is based on the taxable estate plus charitable bequests. The ratio of charitable bequests to estate value is significantly related to both price and estate size. The equation provides a quite good explanation of the overall variation in the bequest ratio: $R^2 = 0.82$. Despite the potential problem of collinearity between estate value and price, the standard errors of the estimated coefficients are very small.

The specification of equation (6-2) implies that the price elasticity of charitable bequests varies with price:

$$\frac{dG}{dP}\frac{P}{G} = \frac{d(G/E)}{dP}\frac{P}{(G/E)} = -0.107\frac{P}{(G/E)}. \tag{6-3}$$

The price elasticity has been evaluated for the average value of P and the corresponding value of G/E at four different sizes of the taxable estate. For taxable estates of $80,000, the average price in 1963 was 0.89 and the predicted ratio of charitable gifts to estate value was 0.022. This implies a local price elasticity of −4.04. By a similar calculation the price elasticity at $120,000 is −2.06, at $500,000 is −1.45 and at $5,000,000 is −0.31.

The very substantial changes in estimated elasticity may represent true behavioral differences but may also reflect only the restricted functional form. As table 6-1 showed, the ratio of gifts to estate size rises very rapidly for large estates. The specification of equation (6-2) imposes a linear relationship which may distort the implied elasticities. As an alternative, equation (6-3) transforms the dependent variable so that changes in price and estate size cause proportional changes in the ratio of gifts to estate size:

$$\ln\frac{G_{it}}{E_{it}} = -0.989 - \underset{(0.16)}{3.18} \ P1_{it} + \underset{(0.14)}{0.38} \cdot 10^{-7} \ E_{it}. \tag{6-4}$$

$$R^2 = 0.83$$

$$N = 135$$

The coefficients are again very significant and the overall explanatory power is quite high.[h] The corresponding elasticities are derived from:

$$\frac{dG}{dP} \cdot \frac{P}{G} = \frac{d(G/E)}{dP} \cdot \frac{P}{(G/E)}$$

$$= \frac{d\ln(G/E)}{dP} \cdot P$$

$$= -3.18 \ P. \tag{6-5}$$

The specific elasticities are now −2.83 for a gross estate of $80,000, −2.39 for an estate of $120,000, −2.16 for an estate of $500,000 and −1.18 for an estate of $5,000,000.

There are of course other ways to generalize the specification of equation (6-2). Of particular importance is the potential nonlinearity in the effect of

---

[h]The R^2 values for the two equations cannot be compared directly because the dependent variables are different.

estate size. It seems reasonable to expect that an extra $1,000 of estate value will have a larger effect in small estates than in very large estates. This is confirmed by the estimates of equation (6-6).

$$\frac{G_{it}}{E_{it}} = 0.138 - \underset{(0.21)}{0.20} \ P1_{it} + \underset{(0.118)}{0.076} \ (P1)^2_{it}$$

$$+ \ \underset{(0.06)}{0.20} \cdot 10^{-7} \ E_{it} - \underset{(0.16)}{0.53} \cdot 10^{-15} \ E^2_{it} \ . \tag{6-6}$$

$$R^2 = 0.88$$

$$N = 135$$

The price elasticity is now derived, by an extension of equation (6-3) from

$$\frac{dG}{dP} \cdot \frac{P}{G} = (-0.20 + 0.15 \ P) \frac{P}{(G/E)} \ . \tag{6-7}$$

The implied price elasticities vary substantially but at a lower level than in the simpler specification of equation (6-2): -1.96 at $80,000, -1.09 at $120,000, -0.69 at $500,000 and -0.11 at $5,000,000.

Unfortunately, other generalizations have conflicting implications. Equation (6-8) extends the previous specification by introducing a cross-product term between price and estate size. To prevent this term from being dominated by the very largest estates, the logarithm of estate size is used.

$$\frac{G_{it}}{E_{it}} = 0.096 - \underset{(0.18)}{0.56} \ P1_{it} + \underset{(0.10)}{0.16} \ (P1_{it})^2$$

$$+ \ \underset{(0.05)}{0.17} \cdot 10^{-7} \ E_{it} - \underset{(0.14)}{0.36} \cdot 10^{-15} \ E^2_{it}$$

$$+ \ \underset{(0.004)}{0.029} \ P1_{it} \cdot 1n(E_{it}). \tag{6-8}$$

$$R^2 = 0.91$$

$$N = 135$$

Each of the terms in this new specification is statistically significant but the elasticities, calculated from

$$\frac{dG}{dP}\frac{P}{G} = [-0.56 + + 0.32\,P + 0.32\,P + 0.03\,1n(E)]\,\frac{P}{G/E}, \qquad (6\text{-}9)$$

now have the wrong sign for all size estates: +1.50 at $80,000, +0.70 at $120,000, +0.54 at $500,000 and +0.18 at $5,000,000. Although these results are clearly unacceptable, they serve as a warning that the previous estimates may be more uncertain than their standard errors imply.

A specification similar to equation (6-8) but in semilogarithmic form also shows the importance of nonlinearities and of the interaction of price and estate size:

$$1n\,\frac{G_{it}}{E_{it}} = 1.75 - \underset{(2.55)}{22.12}\;P1_{it} + \underset{(1.43)}{7.90}\;(P1)^2_{it}$$

$$- \underset{(0.07)}{0.16}\cdot 10^{-6}\,E_{it} + \underset{(0.19)}{0.42}\;10^{-14}\,E^2_{it}$$

$$+ \underset{(0.06)}{0.76}\;P1_{it}\;1n(E_{it}). \qquad (6\text{-}10)$$

$$R^2 = 0.94$$

$$N = 135$$

Again, the elasticities implied by

$$\frac{dG}{dP}\frac{P}{G} = [-22.12 + 15.80\,P1 + 0.76\,1n(E)]\,P \qquad (6\text{-}11)$$

are positive and unacceptable: +2.01 at $80,000 but +1.92 at $120,000, +2.48 at $500,000 and +2.00 at $5,000,000.

The final specification to be considered is the simple constant elasticity relationship:

$$1n\,G_{it} = -10.28 + \underset{(0.04)}{1.56}\;1n(E_{it}) + \underset{(0.18)}{0.19}\;1nP1_{it}. \qquad (6\text{-}12)$$

$$R^2 = 0.99$$

$$N = 135$$

The price elasticity is insignificant and has the wrong sign, a further warning about the reliability of the semilogarithm elasticities. All attempts to generalize this specification by adding the squares and cross-product of $\ln P1$ and $\ln E$ always resulted in the insignificance of all price terms and no improvement in the explanatory power of the equation.

Table 6-2 summarizes the parameter estimates for the linear and semi-logarithmic equations. The corresponding elasticities are pesented in table 6-3. In general the results are less volatile and more plausible for the second form.

Each of the specifications has been reestimated using the alternative definition of price $(P2)$, which is based on taxable income plus both charitable bequests and the marital deduction. The parameter estimates are presented in table 6-4 and the corresponding price elasticities in table 6-5. Comparing the R^2 values in table 6-2 and 6-4 shows that $P1$ has a greater explanatory power, i.e., charitable bequests are generally determined after allowing for the marital deduction. The elasticities are similar in tables 6-3 and 6-5 but the original values based on $P1$ are generally more reasonable.

3. Behavior of Large Estates

The assumption that a single behavioral equation can represent both the small estates and the very large estates is of course a great simplification. Moreover, because of the weighting of observations the parameter estimates of Section 2 are heavily influenced by the behavior of the smaller estates. The current section focuses on the observations corresponding to estates with real net values (i.e., gross estate minus charitable and marital deductions) of at least $500,000.[i] These estates accounted for 78 percent of all charitable bequests in 1963. This reduces the sample to only 54 observations and makes precise estimation even more difficult. Nevertheless, the results are quite interesting and nearly all of the calculated price elasticities imply a substantial price sensitivity.

Table 6-6 presents the estimated parameters for the same specifications as in table 6-2. The price variable is again $P1$. With the exception of equations (6-6.3) and (6-6.6), the price variable has a significant effect on the ratio of giving to estate size. Table 6-7 shows the price elasticities corresponding to these equations.[j]

---

[i]More specifically, an observation is included if the mean net value in 1957–59 dollars is at least $500,000.

[j]It remains impossible to obtain valid estimates of the constant elasticity logarithmic equation or its generalizations. The coefficient of the price variables are generally positive and always smaller than their standard errors. The tax schedule is apparently such that the correlation between $\ln P$ and $\ln E$ is too high to permit meaningful estimation.

Table 6–2
Effects of Price and Estate Size on Charitable Bequests: Price Measured by $P1$

Equation	Dependent Variable	Constant	$P1$	$(P1)^2$	E	E^2	$P1 \cdot ln(E)$	R^2
2.6.1	G/E	0.118 (0.008)	−0.107 (0.010)		0.994×10^{-8} (0.083)			0.82
2.6.2	G/E	0.138 (0.088)	−0.200 (0.205)	0.076 (0.118)	0.201×10^{-7} (0.057)	-0.527×10^{-15} (0.159)		0.88
2.6.3	G/E	0.096 (0.075)	−0.563 (0.180)	0.161 (0.100)	0.166×10^{-7} (0.048)	-0.364×10^{-15} (0.136)	0.029 (0.004)	0.91
2.6.4	$ln(G/E)$	−0.989 (0.141)	−3.182 (0.164)		0.375×10^{-7} (1.106)			0.83
2.6.5	$ln(G/E)$	2.831 (1.64)	−12.59 (3.81)	5.685 (2.201)	-0.731×10^{-7} (1.106)	-0.518×10^{-16} (29.60)		0.86
2.6.6	$ln(G/E)$	1.745 (1.06)	−22.12 (2.55)	7.904 (1.425)	-0.163×10^{-6} (0.068)	0.422×10^{-14} (0.193)	0.759 (0.056)	0.94

NOTES:
1. Price variable $P1$ is based on the taxable estates plus charitable bequests.
2. Standard errors are shown in parentheses.
3. All estimates refer to 135 observations from the period 1948 through 1963.

Table 6–3
Price Elasticities of Charitable Giving: Price Measured by $P1$

Equation	Estate Size			
	$80,000	$120,000	$500,000	$5,000,000
2.6.1	−4.04	−2.06	−1.45	−0.31
2.6.2	−1.96	−1.09	−0.69	−0.11
2.6.3	1.50	0.70	0.54	0.18
2.6.4	−2.83	−2.39	−2.16	−1.18
2.6.5	−1.09	−0.92	−0.83	−0.45
2.6.6	2.01	1.92	2.48	2.00

4. Bequests by Major Types of Donees

In six of the nine sample years, the Internal Revenue Service published separate estimates of charitable bequests made to three major types of donees: private educational institutions, public educational institutions, and religious organizations. These disaggregated data are analyzed briefly in this section.

Unfortunately, the gifts identified as going to these three categories of donees account for a relatively small proportion of total bequests. Table 6-8 presents data by estate size for 1961, the last year of the sample with disaggregated information. The residual category of "other" donees received some 50 percent of charitable bequests from small estates and more than 70 percent from estates of more than $500,000. It is not clear whether this large residual category actually reflects gifts to other types of donees, especially to private family foundations that will later distribute these funds to particular institutions, or merely the problems of identifying particular types of donees from available records. In either case, the disaggregated data and its implications must be regarded with substantial caution.

Table 6-8 implies that the gifts recorded as going to religious organizations received an almost constant share of total giving and of total estates for all size estates up to $1 million. These gifts were about 0.7 percent of total estates between $60,000 and $1,000,000 and rose only to about one percent for estates between $1 million and $5 million. By contrast, gifts to private and public education rose rapidly as a percentage of total estates.

Because of the obvious inadequacy of the disaggregated data, only a cursory analysis has been performed. Table 6-9 presents the estimated price and estate size coefficients for the basic specification of equation (6-1) and the corresponding price elasticities.

The parameter estimates indicate that the share of the estate recorded as

Table 6-4
Effects of Price and Estate Size on Charitable Bequests: Price Measured by P2

Equation	Dependent Variable	Constant	P2	(P2)²	E	E²	P2 · ln(E)	R²
4.6.1	G/E	0.115 (0.009)	-0.110 (0.011)		0.101×10^{-7} (0.009)			0.80
4.6.2	G/E	0.217 (0.078)	-0.402 (0.185)	0.199 (0.109)	0.150×10^{-7} (0.054)	-0.391×10^{-15} (0.109)		0.87
4.6.3	G/E	0.106 (0.065)	-0.582 (0.153)	0.179 (0.090)	0.162×10^{-7} (0.045)	-0.354×10^{-15} (0.131)	0.030 (0.004)	0.91
4.6.4	ln(G/E)	-1.107 (0.163)	-3.208 (0.200)		0.461×10^{-7} (0.160)			0.78
4.6.5	ln(G/E)	4.063 (1.58)	-16.15 (3.77)	7.980 (2.229)	-0.153×10^{-6} (0.111)	0.229×10^{-14} (0.324)		0.82
4.6.6	ln(G/E)	0.799 (0.905)	-21.43 (2.13)	7.404 (1.245)	-0.120×10^{-6} (0.062)	0.338×10^{-14} (0.181)	0.849 (0.068)	0.97

NOTES:
1. Price variable P2 is based on the taxable estate plus both charitable bequests and the marital deduction.
2. Standard errors are shown in parentheses.
3. All estimates refer to 135 observations in the period 1948 through 1963.

Table 6–5
Price Elasticities of Charitable Giving: Price Measured by $P2$

Equation	Estate Size			
	$80,000	$120,000	$500,000	$5,000,000
4.6.1	−5.47	−2.45	−1.65	−0.33
4.6.2	−0.20	−0.10	−0.06	−0.01
4.6.3	1.46	0.77	0.59	0.20
4.6.4	−2.86	−2.41	−2.18	−1.19
4.6.5	−0.17	−0.14	−0.13	−0.07
4.6.6	2.64	2.48	3.07	2.40

going to private education is quite sensitive to price, except perhaps for the largest size estates. Gifts to public educational institutions show approximately equal sensitivity while gifts to religious organizations are least sensitive.

It should again be emphasized that most of the charitable bequests were not allocated to any one of these three categories and that the analysis therefore may substantially misrepresent the effect of taxes on individual types of donees. The current results are put forward as preliminary estimates based on the only available data. A more careful classification of charitable bequests by the Internal Revenue Service would provide an opportunity to provide a much better analysis of the effect of the estate tax on different types of donees.

5. Concluding Remarks

This study has analyzed the only available time series data on charitable bequests by estates of different size. The evidence generally implies that charitable bequests are quite sensitive to the price of such bequests that is implied by the current deductibility of charitable bequests for estate tax purposes. Most of the functional specifications that yield negative price elasticities over the entire range indicate high price elasticities, almost always greater than one and often substantially greater. These results are strengthened by separate estimates for large estates that indicate even higher price elasticities for these bequests.

The implications of such high price elasticities are clear and important. (1) The current deductibility feature of the estate tax law induces a substantial increase in charitable bequests. (2) The charitable organizations receive more in additional bequests than the Treasury foregoes in potential estate tax revenue. (3) Private intergenerational transfers of wealth to individuals are therefore reduced; because charitable gifts are increased by more than taxes are reduced, the personal heirs now receive less than they would if the current deduction were eliminated.

Table 6-6
Effects of Price and Estate Size on Charitable Bequests by Large Estates

Equation	Dependent Variable	Constant	P1	$(P1)^2$	E	E^2	$P1 \cdot ln(E)$	R^2
6.6.1	G/E	0.235 (0.034)	−0.255 (0.052)		0.416×10^{-8} (0.155)			0.78
6.6.2	G/E	−0.371 (0.234)	1.309 (0.604)	−1.042 (0.420)	0.368×10^{-7} (0.136)	-0.813×10^{-15} (0.357)		0.81
6.6.3	G/E	−0.421 (0.361)	1.642 (1.914)	−1.226 (1.085)	0.389×10^{-7} (0.181)	-0.862×10^{-15} (0.448)	0.010 (0.056)	0.81
6.6.4	$ln(G/E)$	−0.594 (0.273)	−3.157 (0.417)		-0.375×10^{-8} (1.240)			0.78
6.6.5	$ln(G/E)$	−6.366 (1.72)	13.519 (4.446)	−12.510 (3.095)	0.237×10^{-6} (0.100)	-0.524×10^{-14} (0.263)		0.84
6.6.6	$ln(G/E)$	−3.482 (2.60)	−5.652 (13.79)	−1.962 (7.815)	0.112×10^{-6} (0.130)	-0.244×10^{-14} (0.323)	0.588 (0.401)	0.85

NOTES:

1. Price variable P1 is based on the taxable estate plus charitable bequests.
2. Observations refer to estates with real 1957–59 values of at least $500,000.
3. All estimates are for 54 observations in the period 1948 through 1963.

Table 6–7
Price Elasticities of Charitable Giving for Large Estates

	Estate Size		
Equation	$500,000	$1,000,000	$5,000,000
6.6.1	−2.72	−2.05	−0.58
6.6.2	−9.50	−6.42	−2.13
6.6.3	−1.65	−1.40	−0.70
6.6.4	−2.15	−1.99	−1.17
6.6.5	−7.82	−7.25	−4.26
6.6.6	−1.27	−0.92	−0.19

Nevertheless it is important in concluding this chapter to emphasize that the specific estimates of the price elasticity of charitable bequests are quite sensitive to the particular specification of the equation. The equations that best explain the data for the entire sample imply·positive price elasticities. Similarly, the simple constant elasticity specification also has a positive price elasticity. Even the specifications that imply negative price elasticities often have implausibly large elasticities. Finally, the data for disaggregated analysis by type of donee was quite inadequate because of the very large unallocated fraction of charitable bequests.

What interpretation should therefore be given to this study as a whole? Some readers will undoubtedly conclude from the instability of the parameter estimates and the frequency of implausible estimates that the current evidence is without value. Others however will stress that nearly all of the acceptable specifications imply substantial price elasticities and that this result supports the conclusion reached by Boskin with individual cross-section data. I prefer to leave each reader to decide for himself how the current evidence should modify his own prior beliefs.

References

American Association of Fund-Raising Counsel, Inc. *Giving USA*. New York: American Association of Fund-Raising Counsel, 1974.

Boskin, Michael. "Estate Taxation and Charitable Bequests." *Journal of Public Economics* (forthcoming), 1976.

Boskin, Michael and Martin Feldstein. "Effects of the Charitable Deduction on Contributions by Low Income and Middle Income Households." Mimeo, 1975.

Council for Financial Aid to Education. *Voluntary Support of Education 1971–1972*. New York: Council for Financial Aid to Education, 1973.

Feldstein, Martin. "The Income Tax and Charitable Contributions: Part I—Aggregate and Distributional Effects." *National Tax Journal* 28, 1 (March 1975a): 81–99.

Table 6–8
Charitable Bequests to Major Types of Donees, 1960

Estate Size Class (in $1,000)	Charitable Bequests as Percentage of Net Estate				Gifts by Donee as Percentage of Total Charitable Bequests			
	All Gifts	Private Education	Public Education	Religion	Private Education	Public Education	Religion	Other
60–69	1.91	0.07	0.05	0.68	3.91	2.75	35.32	58.02
70–79	1.60	0.16	0.06	0.57	9.88	3.48	35.48	51.16
80–89	1.93	0.13	0.08	0.66	6.78	4.27	33.93	54.92
90–99	1.78	0.06	0.04	0.62	3.21	2.47	35.20	59.13
100–119	1.99	0.09	0.05	0.65	4.75	2.65	32.49	60.11
120–149	2.18	0.16	0.05	0.65	7.43	2.32	29.81	60.44
150–199	2.66	0.16	0.06	0.66	6.00	2.38	24.82	66.81
200–299	3.50	0.29	0.14	0.77	8.40	3.88	21.95	65.78
300–499	4.41	0.39	0.16	0.80	8.94	3.59	18.20	69.27
500–999	5.84	0.65	0.30	0.65	11.18	5.09	11.13	72.59
1,000–1,999	8.49	0.66	0.19	0.71	7.80	2.26	8.36	81.58
2,000–2,999	12.74	1.24	1.07	1.07	9.72	8.39	8.37	73.53
3,000–4,999	11.27	0.91	0.26	1.23	8.12	2.33	10.90	78.65
5,000–9,999	16.81	4.26	0.48	0.19	25.36	2.86	1.13	70.65
10,000+	31.12	1.46	0.84	0.11	4.70	2.69	0.36	92.24

Table 6-9
Effects of Price and Estate Size on Charitable Bequests by Major Type of Donee

Equation	Donee	Sample	Constant	P1	Estate	R^2	Price Elasticities by Estate Size			
							$80,000	$120,000	$500,000	$5,000,000
9.6.1	Private Education	All	0.021 (0.005)	-0.021 (0.006)	0.262×10^{-8} (0.049)	.50	-7.42	-2.83	-1.78	-0.30
9.6.2	Public Education	All	0.011 (0.002)	-0.011 (0.002)	0.393×10^{-10} (1.723)	.31	-8.07	-2.99	-2.11	-0.57
9.6.3	Religious Organizations	All	0.010 (0.001)	-0.005 (0.002)	-0.190×10^{-9} (0.142)	.09	-0.80	-0.60	-0.52	-0.26
9.6.4	Private Education	≥ $500,000	0.085 (0.028)	-0.116 (0.043)	0.616×10^{-10} (12.22)	.43	—	—	-12.82	-1.01
9.6.5	Public Education	≥ $500,000	0.023 (0.010)	-0.026 (0.015)	-0.528×10^{-9} (0.417)	.09	—	—	-3.50	-0.90
9.6.6	Religious Organizations	≥ $500,000	0.007 (0.007)	0.001 (0.010)	-0.811×10^{-10} (2.982)	.01	—	—	0.09	0.05

Feldstein, Martin. "The Income Tax and Charitable Contributions: Part II—The Impact on Religious, Educational and Other Organizations." *National Tax Journal* 28, 1 (June 1975b): 209–226.

Feldstein, Martin and Charles Clotfelter. "Tax Incentives and Charitable Contributions in the United States: A Microeconometric Analysis." *Journal of Public Economics* (forthcoming), 1976.

Feldstein, Martin and Amy Taylor. "The Income Tax and Charitable Contributions: Estimates and Simulations with the Treasury Tax Files." Mimeo, 1975.

Internal Revenue Service, U.S. Treasury Department. *Statistics of Income 1965, Fiduciary, Gift and Estate Tax Returns.* Publication No. 406 (11–67). Washington, D.C.: U.S. Government Printing Office, 1967.

Vickrey, William. "One Economist's View of Philanthropy." In Frank Dickinson (ed.), *Philanthropy and Public Policy.* New York: Columbia University Press, 1962, pp. 31–56.

Vickrey, William. "Private Philanthropy and Public Finance." Mimeo, 1973.

Notes

1. See American Association of Fund Raising Counsel (1974).
2. Council for Financial Aid to Education (1973).
3. The studies of the effects of taxation on charitable giving by living individuals are presented in Feldstein (1975a, 1975b), Feldstein and Clotfelter (1974), Feldstein and Taylor (1975), and Boskin and Feldstein (1975).
4. See for example Internal Revenue Service (1965), p. 62.

7 Philanthropy: Thoughts on the Role of Corporations

C. Lowell Harriss

Introduction

The term "philanthropy" may be misleading as applied to business giving. Although no *quid pro quo* will ordinarily exist, corporate donations should flow from belief that in some way, at some time, the company will benefit.

Philanthropy has long been one of William Vickrey's many interests. In 1938 he and I discussed what seemed to us surprisingly small deductions taken for personal income tax purposes by individuals subject to high marginal tax rates. Since then contributions have risen manyfold. The economy has prospered to a degree none of us imagined. Yet persuasive appeals from worthy organizations reach us with, it seems, increasing frequency.

Those of us familiar with the affairs of non-governmental universities and other non-profit organizations know that financial problems are terribly difficult —and getting more so. Institutions which perhaps most of us believe are of enormous value for the good society need more contributions to continue their essential functions. Perhaps hope for aid in meaningful amounts lies in a growth of corporation giving.

Will business payments outside of the normal processes of the market— contributions to non-profit institutions—rise significantly? A key to the answer lies, I believe, in management perception of whether or not companies stand to benefit from such uses of funds. That is, will shareholders, employees, and customers—those who constitute the firm as an entity—be served by corporate contributions?

Will conditions in the community be better because of contributions and thus permit lower-cost production—perhaps as the health, recreational, security, educational, and cultural environment for employees and operations are better? Perhaps the image of the company can benefit with advantages to the enterprise. Ill-considered and harmful governmental policies may be less of a danger if the company, and others, have demonstrated effort to help deal with problems outside the more restricted, traditional range of business activities. The belief that well considered corporate gifts can advance the long-run interests of the enter-

---

This chapter grows out of a much longer study made for the (Filer) Commission on Private Philanthropy and Public Needs. The Commission has not made its recommendations, if any, on the topics dealt with here, or on the others examined in my report. Views are my own and not necessarily those of any organization with which I am associated.

prise is by no means new, but its acceptance has been expanding. Difficult challenges face management in designing and executing a corporate contributions program which offers good prospects of realizing the potentials for the enterprise.

Corporations, on the one hand, and recipient agencies, on the other, should, I believe, continue efforts to make this aspect of American life increasingly effective. Thoughtful leaders are trying to do so. Dozens of the corporate contributions' officers do meet periodically to discuss issues of general goals and implementation of specific programs. My few observations on what companies are doing would be anecdotal and inadequate for generalization. But I venture some impressions about aspects of broader public policy.

The Recent Record

If profits rise, contributions seem certain to increase, though with some lag. Beyond that, will donations as a percentage of profit increase from the annual average of slightly over one percent of pre-tax income? Some such trend seems probable. If the leadership of the business world becomes more convinced of the merits of research and higher education, of civic projects and the United Way, of the many art and other cultural agencies, and of innumerable other organizations supported by donations, then corporate giving will rise relatively more than profit.

State laws and judicial interpretations have removed doubts and restrictions about legality.[1] Within the business world, discussions of "social responsibility," an imprecise but influential term, support an expansion of contributions. The federal tax law permits corporations in computing taxable income to deduct contributions of up to 5 percent of net earnings, but few do so.

Most profitable corporations, it seems, contribute little or nothing—at least a special Treasury tabulation of 1970 tax returns showed that four out of five corporations with profit took no contribution deductions at all. And 69 percent of those reporting gifts deducted less than $500. These figures strike me as improbable. Many companies, I suspect, deduct payments to United Funds and some other non-profit organizations as business expenses. For tax purposes neither the Treasury nor the corporation will have any concern about the deduction classification of many donations. For the company's own purposes, aid to community affairs projects may not inappropriately be included in one or another account.

Be that as it may, although deductions of contributions have been rising— from $252 million in 1950 to around $1,200 million in 1973—the total seems less than recipient agencies might hope for. Why do not more companies equal, say, half the percentages of others? The detailed tabulations show, not only that in 1970 many deducted nothing, but that among the givers some corporations donated very much more than others. For example, 26 percent of contributions deducted came from corporations utilizing the full 5 percent. One explanation, I believe, is that some corporations set dollar amounts for many specific agencies and change only slowly. Companies with this policy, but which had relatively poor earnings in 1970, would have kept donations at a level which as a percentage of that year's income was above average for a period of years.

Donations probably depend to a greater extent than most other management choices on attitudes, on conceptions of what "must" be done, of what is acceptable, and of what is not. The views of peers in the business world (and the amounts given by other companies) and public opinion can exert influence of a discretionary nature not found in most business transactions. Some beliefs, e.g., the desirability of supporting community funds, may reflect long-standing tradition; others, e.g., concern for colleges, the arts, and ghetto conditions, are newer.

Types of aid and the types of help which businesses give include not only direct gifts of funds but also the use of property and the time of personnel. The last two, especially staff time, would if priced sometimes mount to totals that might surprise all concerned. Part of the time devoted may be during working hours and thus a corporate contribution; other hours may be the employee's freely given time from his leisure; some may be a mixture.[a]

When a company makes an auditorium or athletic facilities available to a community group, the out-of-pocket cost may be modest compared with a commercial charge. Crews to help put up Christmas decorations, or a company's gift of computer time for a research project or some job of a non-profit organization, may never be costed as contributions and yet worth something to the recipient.

Purchases and loans are sometimes made on terms representing concessions from what would be available in the market. In such cases the company's accounts may, or may not, identify what it sacrifices. Sometimes, as in the special (1968) $2 billion Life Insurance Industry loans for urban aid, an effort may be made to inform the public of what has been done.

The reasons for non-monetary assistance are varied. My contacts have revealed marked differences from one company to another—in goals, long- and short-run, content, size, direction, and other respects. Some corporations seem to concentrate on financial aid to established organizations, such as colleges and United Funds, without staff involvement in execution of programs. Some are trying to be innovative—in quite new undertakings or in direct influence on one or more activities.

---

[a]For 1973 a report of 152 life insurance companies counted 65,000 manhours of persons loaned to government and community agencies. Employees released during normal business hours gave 143,000 hours to volunteer work. One-fourth of the work force participated in some way in community and similar efforts. Clearinghouse on Social Responsibility (Life Insurance Industry, 277 Park Ave., New York City), *Report, 1974,* p. 25. This document also identified investments made for fifteen types of "socially desirable purposes."

Tax Considerations

The role of taxation in corporate giving is more generally permissive than seriously restrictive or positively encouraging. On the one hand, tax rates around 50 percent reduce net incomes and thus the ability of business to help philanthropies or support other purposes—the "income" effect. On the other hand, deduction where marginal rates are 50 percent or more has a "price" effect—reduction in the deprivation resulting from a deductible contribution.

The "Tax Expenditure" Concept

What government does not take, we are being told, is a "tax expenditure." Corporate contributions are said to constitute one example. This interpretation seems to me misleading.

The president, in submitting the budget for 1976, was required to provide estimates of the magnitudes of "tax expenditures." The staff in doing so assumed that business donations would be the same regardless of tax treatment (an assumption which quite clearly is *not* valid). Then it estimated that because of deductibility of corporate gifts, the Treasury will not receive $440 million. We are not told—the law requires no such statement—that (*the beneficiaries of*) universities, hospitals, art institutions and other non-profit recipient organizations will receive around twice as much.

An aspect more fundamental even than this omission is likely to mislead. When government takes as much from businesses as it does now, a willingness to refrain from taking more may hardly qualify as a "tax expenditure" or a "subsidy" for companies aiding non-profit institutions. Government does not provide anything to the company or to the beneficiaries of philanthropies.[b]

Advocates of treating the "non-taking" (when a corporation aids a non-profit program) as in effect "expenditure making" point to the effect of the tax provisions on relations among alternatives—the extent to which the company can influence the use of funds. If it did not make the contribution, it would have to pay more to government. When some uses of funds do not involve tax that would be required with other uses, more choice remains to businesses (and to other voluntary associations), as distinguished from collective action through government. To the extent that contributions reduce tax receipts, the decisions of political authorities have less influence on the use of resources.

Nevertheless, the amounts which governments, federal and state, do not

---

[b]Others take from the company—employees and providers of supplies and capital equipment—but for values supplied to the company. What government takes is not necessarily matched by positive services it renders which enable the firm to produce more cheaply or sell on better terms.

take from corporations scarcely fit into a "normal" definition of "expenditure."[c] "Not taking" does differ from "making an outlay." Government is not refraining from taking something which "belongs" to it in any sense I can recognize. The dollars which would be the tax if a contribution had not been made are not dollars which political processes (government) created. And must not creativity be one source of "belonging"? Perhaps *creating* in the sense of producing is *the* origin of the legitimacy of acquisition.

The fact that government could insist upon absorbing more of what a business produces does not mean that government has originated what it takes or does not take. In any case, is it not ridiculous to assert that everything a business deducts in computing tax (e.g., wages) is an expenditure of government to the amount of the marginal tax rate?

Benefits from philanthropy, of course, go to the *recipients*. Beyond the beneficiaries, however, an *individual* making a contribution presumably gets some feeling that the funds will do something he approves. Any such satisfactions will be intangible, psychic, and not quantifiable. Any such benefits to a contributor are not a *quid pro quo* from the recipient. The individual donor would not ordinarily expect a benefit in the form of (1) larger income or (2) lower expenses of getting income.

For a *corporation,* however, matters differ. If a company's officers do decide wisely in making contributions, the business will benefit—sometime, in some way. Despite tremendous difficulties of ever learning what results do flow from donations, only uses of corporate funds which offer prospects of aiding the business seem to me justified and consistent with state corporate law. Eventually, therefore, income on which corporate tax is to be payable will be greater than if the contributions had not been made. The tax deduction of the business gifts that made the eventual benefit possible is not only appropriate. It is necessary— just as is the deduction of wages or the cost of materials—to compute accurately the expenses incurred in getting a figure of *net* income.

Whatever one may feel about personal philanthropy, deductibility for business is not a concession. It is not a matter of grace. Deduction is an element which is essential for an accurate measurement of business net earnings over time.

Nor is there logic in restricting the deductions to 5 percent of net income. Deduction of wages, interest, and the other outlays that make possible the total results of a company's operations are not limited (to the extent that they are "ordinary and necessary"). Of course, not all business contributions will be suc-

---

[c]The fact that standard dictionary definitions do not embrace a proposed usage of a term does not preclude benefiting from such usage. Language changes. I would by no means want to impede enrichment of the English language. Not every proposal, however, would yield progress as against fuzziness and misrepresentation. To include corporate contributions along with other proposed applications of "tax expenditure" would, I submit, produce misunderstanding as against sharpening our tools for learning.

cessful as judged by either well-defined or quite imprecise criteria. Some, however, may be more rewarding per dollar than are some dollars spent on wages, interest, or other clearly deductible expenses. No one will know in advance which will be which. No tax law could possibly identify degrees of accomplishment of widely different non-profit activities.

Advocates of business giving quite properly stress *enlightened self-interest.* The self-interest will presumably be some eventual benefit to the company which, probably indirectly, not identifiably, and often long-delayed, takes the form of larger receipts or lower costs. For example, business leaders who support gifts to colleges hope that the funds will help to improve the capacities of future employees—managers, technicians, and so on. The larger the country's or the area's pool of better as against less well trained personnel, the better will be a company's prospects of success. Another example: A healthier and more attractive community environment can improve labor productivity. The better the cultural and general community facilities, it is argued, the better the quality of employee and the output obtainable (for the same wage outlay). Another example: Life insurance company programs for health, some of which go back for decades, have a direct relation to the business of the company.

In considering corporate philanthropy, some commentators may disparage motives which have overtones of self-interest.[d] Yet for such outlays, the appropriateness of allowing the deduction must be even clearer than if pure altruism were involved.

Cost of Giving

The fact that contributions are deductible leads, of course, to the familiar conclusion that the "cost" to the corporation per dollar given is the dollar minus the marginal tax rate. Deductibility gives a company a kind of freedom in deciding on the use of some of its earnings. For the typical large corporation the *marginal* rate will be around 50 percent—48 percent of federal tax plus a few percentage points representing the net effect of state taxes. A contribution of $100 reduces the net remaining for shareholders by $50.

Most corporations, of course, are small. For them the marginal rate will be nearer the 20 percent which the federal government now (1975) imposes on the first $25,000 of earnings or the 22 percent on amounts from $25,000 to $50,000.[e]

---

[d]College faculties may include members who tend to have a low opinion of the worthiness of self-interest in business and yet who would not reject salaries paid in part from corporate contributions.

[e]Before 1975 the federal tax was 22 percent on the first $25,000 of earnings and 48 percent above the amount. Significantly different conditions existed during World War II and again during the Korean conflict. *Excess profits taxes* imposed exceedingly high margi-

What must the corporation do to be able to contribute a dollar? It must earn a full dollar. In one sense, what it gives up is not 50 cents for shareholders but whatever was required to get $1 of income. Having succeeded in earning the dollar, it can choose whether governments will get 50 cents or philanthropies $1. But to replace that 50 cents, i.e., to make it up to the shareholders, the corporation must earn, not another 50 cents, but another $1. Hopefully, the contributions will eventually enable the company to benefit enough to offset what it has given.

Some life insurance companies in fact get no deduction for contributions because they are taxed under special income tax rules. For them the cost of donations is the amount of the gift.

Is There a "Tax Incentive"?

Although deductibility is frequently said to grant a "tax incentive," there is no more incentive than is the deductibility of wages or other expenses. A denial of deduction for contributions or for any other (legal) outlays which management believes appropriate would depart from what is essential to compute net income.

Obviously, business giving would be more difficult if deduction were not allowed. Just as obviously, giving would be easier if deduction were allowed on more than a dollar-for-dollar basis—if $100 of donation were treated as $150 of deduction. If such were the case, the term "incentive" would be appropriate.

Closely-Owned Contrasted with
Large Corporations

Owners of the great majority of "small" corporations—though some may have operations of considerable size—will at times have choice as to whether contributions will be made by the corporation or by about the same persons as

---

nal tax rates on some corporations. The cost of giving as ordinarily conceived dropped markedly, sometimes to only a few cents on the dollar. Under these exceptional conditions contributions rose. The excess profits taxes, of course, also made the retention for shareholders of marginal earnings more difficult; to keep $1 for shareholders, corporations had to earn many times as much as $1.

The taxes, however, were expected to be temporary. It became sensible to use funds in some ways which were deductible currently, but which could yield benefits over the longer run when marginal tax rates would be much lower. In the short run, therefore, some contributions, i.e., to company foundations, were governed by considerations quite different from those which apply normally. Calculations then applicable had validity, in large part because the tax conditions were assumed to be *temporary*.

shareholders out of dividend (or salary) income. The considerations can be complex; one element will be the marginal income tax brackets applicable, and another will be the percentage limits on amounts deductible.

Owner-shareholders of "small" corporations may consider some giving in their personal capacity to be the same as they would desire for the company, and vice versa. Personal and business affairs can be closely intertwined. As to taxes, marginal corporate rates on income will frequently be lower than the personal rate.

In contrast, most shareholders of large corporations will be subject to lower personal income tax rates than the corporations will pay. I doubt that such considerations exert any influence on decisions of largest corporations, but of course, I have no way of knowing. The argument would be for a "tilt" toward corporate rather than personal contributions on the basis of judgments about the prospective benefits for the enterprise.

Issues of Corporate Giving

The issues deserving attention greatly exceed my space limits and, of course, my competence. Some observations, however, may help to understand the modern American economy.

Why Not Leave Philanthropy to Stockholders?

Corporations, it is sometimes said, should avoid philanthropy—shareholders ought to decide how, if at all, "their" money is to be given away. Let the corporation stick to its normal job of earning income, not trying to go beyond by helping non-profit agencies. Then dividends can be larger and stockholders will be free to contribute as they wish.

This argument fails to recognize what seems to me the fundamental reason for corporate aid to non-profit organizations—the benefit to the business. Shareholders cannot be expected to know what of many philanthropic activities will best serve the company, in some way, at some time, perhaps as a supplement to employee benefits or public relations or advertising. How could the thousands or tens of thousands of stockholders possibly be expected to finance the non-profit programs *of benefit to the corporation?* Shareholders cannot know which philanthropies would be of greatest potential for the corporation; individuals would not give personal funds to advance their fractional interest—one hundred-thousandth, one millionth—in a corporation.

Stockholder Support and Opposition

Contributions have been a topic of some stockholder comment at annual meetings. Advocates of more direct shareholder participation in company affairs have sometimes criticized "giving away stockholders' money."

The Conference Board surveys of corporate contributions have found that actual cases of shareholder influence have been few. The recent (1974) survey found that among the 417 corporate chairmen and presidents responding, 88 percent reported that stockholder reactions had had no real influence; among the 33 in which there was some influence, it led to less giving in 25 cases and more giving in 8 cases. Where stockholders have indicated reactions, the "mainly favorable" were more (seven times) numerous than the "mainly unfavorable."

Sophisticated shareholders might see in corporate giving some slight solution of the "free rider" problem. All stockholders, it may be argued, contribute; none can get benefits from the programs of non-profit agencies and yet fail to join in sharing the cost.

Management, of course, will have great difficulties deciding how best to allocate a contribution. But executives can make an effort to judge which programs ought to get how much—from each year's appeals in localities with company personnel to universities training for what may be advances in basic knowledge decades in the future.

Let no one conclude that I believe that managements can always know what contributions will best serve the long-run interests of the company—or that many contributions do not follow prejudice and the less laudable propensities of mortals. Wherever market tests do not direct decisions and are not present to correct mistakes—and corporate philanthropy obviously offers examples—errors will be made and repetition can continue.

Yet a fundamental remains: Some things of concern to the enterprise as such lie outside the normal processes of the market. Individual gifts of money and leadership cannot be counted upon to serve business needs adequately.

*Preserving the Conditions for Businesses to
Perform Their Essential Functions*

Perhaps the clearest example of corporate purposes which shareholders cannot be expected to support as fully as is in the interests of business can be called "preserving the conditions for businesses to perform their essential functions." Company funds for trade association activities, lobbying, the programs of such general business associations as chambers of commerce, influencing public opinion, and so on, may, or may not, come from the contributions budget. Some purposes would not ordinarily be thought of as philanthropic; at times dividing lines between ordinary business expenses and donations will be vague.

Company practices differ. But a general condition can be indicated: A corporation is limited in the amounts it can use for purposes other than those for rather direct benefit to it. Yet one management responsibility, not always recognized, should be to protect what is favorable to the enterprise and to oppose those things which would hurt it.[f] The public relations aspects of business giving relate to the development of attitudes which can help ward off actions that would harm the company's customers, employees, and suppliers of capital.

Actions may be required outside the scope of any one firm's capacity—for example, trying to alter federal, state, or local law, or warding off anti-business proposals. Legislative bodies get suggestions for tax and other laws that would raise business costs. Proposals that would restrain operations may be advanced with good intentions but without full awareness of the effects. Corporations cannot vote. Laws forbid them from making political contributions even though one candidate might seem likely to sponsor harmful government policies while another would seem to be neutral (or favor) the company.

Who stands equipped and willing to present the positions of those companies which would be hurt? Individually, the great majority of businesses will not have capacity to do a fully effective job. Shareholders as individuals will not themselves often intervene in politics to speak and work for business or, more generally, try to create a more favorable public opinion of the corporation. Individuals will not finance adequately the organizations to perform such services.

*Externalities: Encouraging More
Company Actions*[2]

Business outlays on art, health, civic affairs, and other non-profit activities yield results which spread widely through the community. Typically, much of the benefit from corporate philanthropy will not become the property of the companies making the contributions possible. Most of the fruits of a corporation's gifts to specific colleges or youth clubs or other non-profit organizations remain outside—external to—the corporation, as distinguished from the "internalized" benefits which a company gets from the sale of a product or service. Economists do not need an explanation of "public goods" and "excludability" and "free

---

[f]In asserting that businesses have a responsibility to try to protect themselves in the world of politics and elsewhere, I do not imply that everything businesses will try to do will advance the good society (as I see it). But politics does not always call out the best of human actions—and most decidedly not to correct errors with desirable dispatch and thoroughness. One result of the expansion of the role of government has been an enlargement of the need for businesses to act beyond the normal boundaries of the market place.

riders" and "externalities," but brief comment on the application to business giving will be useful.

Market forces in a competitive, enterprise economy will provide most things that people want enough to cover the full costs of supplying them. But there are exceptions. The difference between a better and a poorer quality of life depends in part upon elements beyond those yielded by market forces plus the philanthropy of individuals. Some of the additional benefits that are attainable would be worth more than they would cost. Yet no single company may feel that it will harvest enough of these positive results to justify incurring much of the expense.

If many companies, perhaps fifty, were to provide more aid to university research or educational broadcasting or recreational programs, perhaps $500 more by each company, the advantages resulting from the use of the $25,000 might benefit each company by an amount greater than the $500 of its outlays.

If any one firm were to provide $500 and the others did nothing, the gain would be too slight to justify the gift. No one company alone can make possible what each one can get if they act together. And for the corporations the additional benefits, not measured and probably not measurable, would add to the worth of the businesses as such. No one can be certain, but more than wishful thinking seems to me to support the conclusion.

Companies acting on their own individually will not pay for as much activity of sorts with external benefits as would be to the advantage of business as a whole—and to the community in general. The failure of men and women of goodwill to finance "socially" desirable activities on an "adequate" scale can be understood as one recognizes that too much of the total of benefits is external to those who would bear the cost. It follows that academicians or someone else thinking of the "broad picture" can be enticed by the potentials of reaping the fruits of going beyond market achievements (and personal philanthropy).

One possible method is to use political processes and compulsion. Governments can force people to pay. No one can be a "free rider," sharing in benefits without carrying some of the cost. But political processes and bureaucracy have their own deficiencies; evidence of inability to "deliver" adequately is plentiful. The hopes underlying proposals to let "government" "do" something have too often been disappointed when accomplishments are set over against costs.

Special Interests of Academicians

Non-governmental means—private, voluntary agencies—also exist. Joint efforts arranged voluntarily offer an opportunity for cooperative effort and cost sharing. Academicians have more interest than most of us realize in the efforts of some business leaders to get corporate support for us.[g] They argue that the training of scientific and managerial personnel will eventually benefit the business world. Of course, any one company contributing to one college or to a group of universities cannot count upon obtaining as employees the persons who are trained as a result. Competitors may get them. Most students who benefit from the gifts may not in any discernable way be suitable for the future needs of the donating companies as against firms in quite different industries.[h]

Graduate education presents special difficulties of financing. Costs are high, often very high per student. The benefits in the advance of knowledge are inevitably spread over a long future. Popular support among alumni and in legislatures will probably be small relative to that for undergraduate programs. Corporate leaders, however, ought to be able to take a broader view of the long-run interest of business. Perhaps they will deliberately recognize such conditions in allocating funds.

Corporate aid for private colleges and universities is reenforced by an additional consideration. Our system consists of some institutions which are supported predominantly by tax funds and some that are private. Corporate taxes help to pay for the first group. Contributions to non-governmental colleges will help to meet their needs, to balance somewhat the amounts going through taxes, and to reduce the pressure for more governmental colleges and higher taxes on business. Inflation has added to the need to private institutions which cannot look to annual appropriations of tax funds. Endowments have rarely, I expect, risen enough so that yields have maintained the real per student purchasing power of endowment income.

Corporate Help in Planning and Supervising;
Diversity and Creativity in Service
Delivery Systems

The growth of both governmental and private "social" programs testifies, among other things, to the desire to achieve results which are at times elusive,

---

[g]From the point of view of one or another academic economist—or the majority of the public if anyone could discern what the majority would prefer if it knew its interest— managements may be right, or wrong, in advancing or opposing certain policies. Majority rule is not, of course, always to be endorsed. The Bill of Rights sets Constitutional limits. And other aspects of life are scarcely appropriate for determination. But so much of concern to everyone hinges upon the production system that its protection and encouragement do have far-reaching significance. Part of business action to protect its interests will be through organizations supported by contributions.

[h]Two years ago, Mr. David Packard urged corporate executives to direct gifts for higher education to programs friendly to business rather than to those antagonistic. Why support persons who are, or are likely to be, anti-business? Doing so does seem less than the epitome of wisdom. If there are friends in universities, aid for them can be justified. Since funds are limited, efficient allocation, his argument ran, should take account of probable results.

intangible, and hard to attain. Costs in relation to accomplishments are difficult to judge. Development of information about potentials and realities, and making the knowledge broadly useful, often requires methods not yet fully developed. One aspect of some corporate participation deserves note.

Corporations are supplying assistance beyond dollars–monitoring and guidance, direction and redirection, evaluation and more or less direct oversight. Supplying them well, however, is by no means a matter of routine. Competent outsiders can contribute to the effectiveness of non-profit organizations, and to some governmental programs; governments do not always supply the full range of skills, plus the freedom, flexibility, independence, and other conditions needed for successful accomplishment.[i]

Supplying dollars, we hear, cannot be counted upon always to "solve" problems. Both major matters of program selection, i.e., broad policy choices, and concrete aspects of management, i.e., efficiency in operation, can benefit from assistance from corporations. "Entrepreneurship" in devising and promoting programs with new undertakings and approaches, and management in the execution of projects, do come from corporate personnel.[j]

Corporate contributions–of money and leadership–aid the maintenance of diversity in the structure of systems for delivering services, including, among other things, the programs of agencies concerned with beauty, the advance of knowledge, the healing arts, and understanding of public policy issues affecting business. As contrasted with corporation tax payments to support governmental projects, the opportunity for both voluntary financing and provision of leadership provides more "points of entry"–and, in practice, more influence on accomplishment. Private, non-profit programs offer opportunities for evolving new methods to meet needs, old and new. Experimental innovation can be undertaken at more points than if government were a near-monopolist.[k]

Most *individual* donors, of course, cannot devote time to meaningful evaluation of non-profit agencies. Which programs are most promising? How can functioning and service delivery be improved? (Large) *companies,* however, can provide personnel to screen applications, monitor activities already in process, and assist in improving performance. Different corporations with different direct

---

[i]The Economic Development Council of New York, using funds and personnel supplied by corporations, has helped to improve the operations of city agencies–courts, schools, and the administration of public assistance. No one, I imagine, knows how much help, and of what kinds, businesses give over the country to governmental activities. A forthcoming Conference Board report based on a 1974 survey will show that 378 chairmen and presidents of leading corporations spend on the average (mean) 6.8 hours a week on "public service activities." The median is 6.0 hours.

[j]The aid discussed here, though not always clearly distinguishable, goes beyond that from service on boards of trustees.

[k]One merit of the market process is that activities not worth their cost are eliminated. For non-profit undertakings, of course, matters are much more complex. Corporate support may sustain programs which (by some criteria) ought not to survive.

contacts can help each other in allocating funds. As agencies and programs benefit, the effectiveness of *personal,* as well as business, contribution will increase.

The freedom of private donors as distinguished from what they pay in taxes permits flexibility. One can hope that as concerned corporations obtain and evaluate information from year to year, small-stage adjustments will cumulate to significant totals over time. The corporate sector by this process can, among other things, offset some of the lack of flexibility and inertia of government (legislatures and the civil service) and the various limitations of philanthropic organizations themselves.

To date, I expect, constructuve results of this general nature are scattered and often more experimental and exploratory than thorough and sustained. But through corporations the United States is developing—informally, somewhat tentatively, and incompletely—various procedures for enhancing the effectiveness of non-profit activities.

Not all such assistance, of course, will be productive. Executive effort may be diverted from activities of greater worth; time allocated to philanthropy can have high cost in terms of sacrificed alternatives. And questions of importance but which I cannot answer do arise. Will persons controlling corporate gifts thereby exert "undue" power? Will the personnel of corporations be really competent? What will likely be the results on non-profit sectors of more influence originating in business?

Voluntarism Aided by Corporate Giving

Today should we not be aware of a tendency, in fact even though not stated, to argue that all *group* action should be coercive, i.e., governmental? Such an attitude seems to me to be implied in some "tax reform" argumentation. The attitude rests, I submit, not on conviction growing out of experience that people perform well in politics or a conviction that the successes of governmental bureaucracy call for its extension as a way for improving the human condition. No. Support for the enlargement of government seems to me to grow out of dreamy, wishful thinking that power and wisdom and goodwill ought to go together.[1] Moreover, some things that ought to be done are too small or too temporary or too limited geographically to expect people to deal with them effactually through politics.

Preservation and expansion of voluntarism will, I am convinced, make for a

---

[1]Prof. Frank Knight, who used to explain to us his understanding of the reasons underlying advocacy of transfer of activity from the market place to government, might say something like, "The 'bigger government' fellow expects to be sure that his views will dominate, but he assumes that the costs are to be paid with the 'other fellow's' money."

country which is better than if compulsion were to operate more broadly. Plural-
ism and freedom are valuable, not only as ends of humane life but also as means
for attaining many other goals. Business—enterprise—has an interest in preserving
voluntarism. Corporate gifts can help to preserve—and, I should hope, to en-
large—the effective roles of freedom and diversity.

The expansion of government involves added restrictions, regulations, and
taxes. Businesses can suffer from the expansion of governmental coercion, including taxes, for purposes which do not in fact achieve reasonably satisfying results.
The private instruments of a pluralistic society can serve. Corporate contributions
can aid in the preservation of the diversity, flexibility, adaptability, freedom,
efficiency, opportunity, and humanity of pluralistic society.

"But," we hear, "if the dollars could go in taxes, they are 'government
funds' and should be allocated by politics." In returning to this point, I call
attention to the Founding Fathers. Although never imagining the details of life
today, they laid down general rules for government, one of which, now generally
ignored, directly supports voluntarism.

". . . or to the People": The Bill of Rights
and Voluntarism

The Tenth Amendment reads, in full, "The powers not delegated to the
United States by the Constitution, nor prohibited by it to the States, are reserved
to the States respectively, *or to the people*." [Italics supplied.] In using these
words, the framers of the Bill of Rights did more than merely suggest that neither
the national government nor the states (and localities as creatures of states) are
to try to do everything that people want.

Here the Constitution assigns wide scope to "the people" in their private,
non-governmental, capacities. Does it not call for government to do less, rather
than more, to hamper voluntary and dispersed action as "the people" wish? The
desires of minorities, the preferences of groups formed and acting voluntarily,
are not merely to be tolerated. People deserve protection from governmentally
created impediments—not only as provided in the first nine amendments but the
last one as well.

The objectives which groupings of people try to achieve by using non-
political agencies will have many features. Some will have narrow, others broad,
aims. Most individuals have affinities with many groups; the compositions of
these groups will differ widely. In reserving "power to the people," the Constitution, it seems to me, asserts that government—at all levels combined—is not to be
all-embracing. Nor does political action have some claim to moral superiority
over voluntary group action.

The Constitution does not imply that all approvable group actions are
governmental. Quite the contrary. A tax law which refrains from imposing

obstacles to voluntary group action for philanthropy is not "doing a favor." It respects the Bill of Rights. No corporation, no industry, no existing organization of companies by giving aid to non-profit activities can assure us protection against harmful expansion of compulsion (government). We should not expect business to do all of this job. But two conclusions do seem to me correct. (1) Businessmen can include the assistance to voluntarism as one element in their decisions. (2) Any legislative proposals to restrict (or perhaps to encourage) business contributions should explicitly recognize the Bill of Rights.

Concluding Comment

The world of corporate philanthropy has far more diversity than I had imagined. Much is being done on many fronts and in many ways. The range of developments far exceeds what most of us in the "ivory tower" of academe will encounter.

This chapter has not attempted to explain why corporations do not provide more support for non-profit activities. Space limits have kept me from examining the reasons sometimes cited for businesses to refrain from participation beyond the traditional limits of business activity.

Colleges and research agencies, health and art organizations, civic and youth groups, and others pressed for funds may well ask, "How might governmental policy be tilted to encourage more corporate giving?" An obvious means would be to alter tax laws so that in effect a dollar contributed would count as more than a dollar of wage or other expense in computing taxable earnings.[m] If positive externalities result to the extent that I believe probable, then the case for deliberate, governmental encouragement of business aid to non-profit institutions does seem persuasive. At least for the present, however, I would not urge departure from the present neutrality.

Notes

1. For a discussion of legal aspects see Phillip I. Blumberg, "Corporate Responsibility and the Social Crisis," *Boston University Law Review* 50 (1970): 157. A report prepared for the Commission on Private Philanthropy and Public Needs provides an up-to-date analysis; my observations here rest on its conclusions.
2. For a more systematic discussion see William J. Baumol "Enlightened Self-Interest and Corporate Philanthropy," in Baumol et al., *A New Rationale for Corporate Social Policy* (New York: Committee for Economic Development, 1970), pp. 3–19.

---

[m]Special situations do call for reexamination—and reform. Raising, or lifting entirely, the 5 percent ceiling would be sensible. Public utilities in some cases are not allowed to treat contributions as expense in determining rates to be allowed. Some insurnace companies do not in fact get a deduction for contributions.

8 The Pure Theory of Impure Public Goods

Kelvin Lancaster

The pure theory of pure public goods[1] is a beautiful piece of analysis, the practicality of which is severely reduced by, among other things, the elusiveness of the "pure" public good. The good old lighthouse is localized, so it is at best a local public good; its benefits accrue to a specific section of the community, making it more of a club good; and finally it is not impossible to devise some technique of exclusion, making it potentially marketable. "Defense," in some abstract sense, is probably a true public good (provided everyone agrees as to who is the enemy), but any specific activity in furtherance of defense almost always has some local or special interest property. A ring of ABMs around Washington, D.C., may or may not increase total defense of the United States, but it might well reduce welfare in some other major cities, which now become more likely targets because of the elimination of Washington. Similar arguments hold for police protection but not, presumably, for fire protection unless most fires are set by arsonists.

Among other candidates that have been nominated for public good status are weather forecasting, the space program, the system of courts and other aspects of the administration of justice, clean air, an attractive environment, the basic structure of governmental administration and, most recently, a just distribution of income. In some of these, there is an abstract notion which represents the public good aspect, but any specific measure will involve local effects, special group effects, special group effects, or clear possibilities of exclusion.

The unwillingness of economists to give up on the public good idea[a] has not been due to pure stubbornness or to any real faith that the pure public good will one day be found, but rather to a firm conviction that "publicness" is a crucial property of certain types of goods, even though it may not be the only property to be considered.

It is the purpose of the present chapter to provide a potentially more practical alternative to the theory of the "pure" public good by considering instead the "impure" public good, a good which has some properties like those of the pure public good, and others like an ordinary private good.

---

[a]Some economists *have* given up on the "pure" public good, of course, but not the economics profession in general.

Goods with Public and
Private Characteristics

We shall build our theory of impure public goods (or "mixed" goods) on the basis of the characteristics analysis of goods which the author has developed elsewhere.[2] The essential feature of this analysis is that each good possesses properties or characteristics that are technically determined by the nature of the good, that individuals' preferences, utility, and welfare are based only on the characteristics they obtain, and that goods are regarded only as vehicles for supplying characteristics.

In the present context, we shall concentrate on the broad division of characteristics into "private" and "public." The private characteristics have the properties assumed in the standard characteristics analysis, namely that they are obtainable only by direct consumption of the goods containing them and have no effect on other individuals. Public characteristics, on the other hand, are assumed to have the essential property of the pure public good, that the effect on each individual is determined only by the total amount of that characteristic over the economy as a whole. There will, in general, be a variety of different private and public characteristics, each related to both preferences and to goods in a particular way.

Any good will typically possess a number of characteristics, all of which might be private (giving a standard private good), all public (a pure public good, if such exists), or some private and some public, giving the mixed good, or impure public good, in which we are interested here.

Most, if not all, of the standard list of public goods are better described as mixed goods, while many goods which are not considered as true public goods but which possess enough "publicness" to have historically resulted in their removal from the free market (such as education) can also be considered as mixed goods. Many goods commonly treated as pure private goods may possess some public characteristics and also qualify for mixed good treatment. Housing, for example, may fall into this category if consumers in general are morally or aesthetically disturbed by the existence of substandard housing.

We can consider education a mixed good by noting that the existence of universal literacy can be treated as a public characteristic, while the education of a specific person has a high private content,[b] so that an individual gains both from his own education and also from the general education level. Education of one person, therefore, gives rise both to a private characteristic and to a contribution toward the society total of a public characteristic. Somewhat less obviously, we might make a similar kind of argument with respect to public transport, that the existence of a well traveled transport network benefits even those not

---

[b]We are ignoring here both the "merit" argument (see Musgrave 1959) and the "human capital" analysis in which education as a consumption good appears in a minor role.

using it at a particular time, so that each user provides himself with an immediate private benefit and also makes a contribution towards a public benefit.[c] The same considerations would apply to communication, to both the telephone and postal networks, and even to housing if the general level of housing impinges on the sensibilities of each individual. Health services may be an even better example than any of these, providing a public characteristic (general health level of the population) and a private characteristic (treatment of the individual for a specific health problem).

Thus the mixed good concept can be considered to cover a wide range of goods, from those generally considered to be public goods of a kind to others not generally included in the same class as public goods, and covering goods generally supplied through the market as well as goods generally supplied directly by government.

The mixed good is, of course, similar to the private good plus externalities. The main differences between the analysis here and the general analysis of externalities lie in two special features:

1. The externalities are, so to speak, "externalized" by being treated as objective characteristics of the goods rather than as properties of individual preferences. This permits us to separate the technical specification of how much of this externality-characteristic is inherent in the good (different automobiles pollute the air to different degrees) from the subjective aspect of how much this particular characteristic affects the specific individual.

2. We are concerned here with only one class of externalities, those that can be classified as true public characteristics. It is obvious that there are other situations for which it would be appropriate to introduce the concept of a characteristic which impinges on individuals other than the direct consumer of the good possessing it, but in which the externality is too restricted to be considered a public characteristic.[3]

The Two Good Analysis

The simplest model incorporating the essential features of the mixed good analysis is one involving two goods, one of which is taken to be a private good, the other a mixed good. This is then comparable with the standard public good analysis which is carried out in terms of one private good and one public good. We assume two characteristics only, one private characteristic and one public characteristic.

The private good possesses only the private characteristic, while the mixed good possesses both private and public characteristics. The amounts of the

---

[c]This assumes there are no congestion problems. It seems a pity to ignore one of Vickrey's favorite problems in an essay written in his honor, but it cannot be helped!

private and public characteristics per unit of mixed good are taken to be constant, technologically given, and the same for all individuals.

Formal specification of the model is then as follows:

$$u^i = u^i(z_i, Z) \qquad i = 1, \ldots, n \tag{8-1}$$

$$z_i = x_i + aX_i \qquad i = 1, \ldots, n \tag{8-2}$$

$$Z = \sum_1^n X_i + X_G \tag{8-3}$$

$$V = T\left(\sum_1^n x_i, \sum_1^n X_i + X_G\right) \tag{8-4}$$

For the ith individual, u^i is his utility function, z_i the amount he obtains of the private characteristic, x_i his consumption of the private good, and x_i his consumption of the mixed good. Z is the total amount of the public characteristic, X_G the amount of the mixed good supplied by the government as a public good, and V the total amount of the resource mix required to produce the specified quantities of the two goods.

Units have been normalized so that one unit of private good contains one unit of private characteristic, and one unit of mixed good contains one unit of public characteristic. The technical relationship in consumption between the two goods is then reduced to the single parameter a, representing the amount of private characteristic per unit of mixed good. The private characteristic is obtained from the mixed good only to the extent that the individual in question consumes that good directly, while the amount of the public characteristic is the same for all individuals and equal to the amount contained in the aggregate supply of the mixed good.

Any socially efficient configuration of the economy must be a solution of the problem.

Min V, subject to $u^i = \bar{u}^i, i = 1, \ldots, n$

given the above structure and the implied non-negativity constraints.

Necessary conditions for an optimum are then given by:

$$T_1 \geqslant \lambda_i u_1^i \qquad (i = 1, \ldots, n) \tag{8-5}$$

$$T_2 \geqslant a \lambda_i u_1^i + \Sigma_j \lambda_j u_2^j \qquad (i = 1, \ldots, n) \tag{8-6}$$

$$T_2 \geqslant \Sigma \lambda_j u_2^j \qquad\qquad (8\text{-}7)$$

where $x_i = 0$ if the strict inequality holds in (8-5), $X_i = 0$ if it holds in (8-6), and $X_G = 0$ if it holds in (8-7). All summations are for $j = 1$ to n, and u_1^i, u_2^i are the partial derivatives of u^i with respect to the natural arguments, that is to the characteristics Z_i, Z. T_1, T_2 are the partial derivatives of V with respect to the private and mixed goods, respectively.

It is obvious that (8-6) and (8-7) can both be satisfied only by a strict inequality in (8-7) and thus with $X_G = 0$.[d] Thus we can, in general, expect to find non-zero solutions for x_i, X_i by taking (8-5) and (8-6) as equations and ignoring (8-7).

By taking any of the equations (8-6) in combination with all of the equations (8-5), we then obtain[e]

$$T_2/T_1 = a + \Sigma\, MRSC_j \qquad\qquad (8\text{-}8)$$

where $MRSC_j$ $(= u_2^j/u_1^j)$ is the marginal rate of substitution between *characteristics* for the jth individual.

Comparison with Other Solutions

The optimal solution for the mixed good case bears some resemblance to the standard Samuelson solution for the pure public good case, in that the sum of marginal rates of substitution appears rather than a single marginal rate of substitution. The mixed good solution differs, however, in the appearance of the parameter a and in the fact that the marginal rates of substitution are those for characteristics rather than goods.

It is easier to compare the mixed good solution with other cases if we recast it in terms of marginal rates of substitution between goods rather than between characteristics. From (8-1), (8-2), and (8-3) we have

$$\frac{\partial u^i}{\partial x_i} = u_1^i \qquad\qquad (8\text{-}9)$$

---

[d]Since private consumption of the mixed good gives both private and public characteristics, it is to be expected that the optimal solution will rule out allocations that eliminate this private characteristic while providing no more of the public.

[e]This assumes that none of the individuals will be at a boundary optimum with strict inequality in either (8-5) or (8-6). If preferences are widely dispersed, some individuals with preferences strongly biased toward either private or public characteristics may be on the boundary.

$$\frac{\partial u^i}{\partial X_i} = au_1^i + u_2^i \tag{8-10}$$

$$\frac{\partial u^i}{\partial X_G} = u_2^i \tag{8-11}$$

Thus the marginal rate of substitution between X_i and x_i, which we shall write as $MRSG$, is given by

$$MRSG_i = a + MRSC_i. \tag{8-12}$$

On the other hand, the marginal rate of substitution between X_G and x_i, to which we will give no special symbol, is simply equal to $MRSC$.

We are now in a position to compare the optimal mixed good solution, which we shall refer to as OPT, with two suboptimal solutions of particular significance, one in which both goods are treated as pure private goods (PRIV), the other in which the mixed good is treated as a pure public good (solution PUB).

If the goods are treated simply as private goods, the apparently "efficient" solution, and the solution under perfect competition, will equate the marginal rate of transformation between X_i and x_i with the marginal rate of substitution of goods in consumption which will necessarily be the same for all individuals. Thus we have

Solution PRIV $T_2/T_1 = MRSG_i = MRSG_j$, all i, j. $\tag{8-13}$

Treating X as a pure public good implies supplying it as X_G rather than X_i, and we obtain the standard condition that the marginal rate of transformation between X and x should be equal to the sum of the marginal rates of substitution between X_G and x_i (*not* X_i and x_i). This gives us

Solution PUB $T_2/T_1 = \Sigma MRSC_j.$ $\tag{8-14}$

Finally, we can use (8-12) to rewrite the optimal solution in terms of $MRSG$, giving two forms for this solution

Solution OPT $T_2/T_1 = a + \Sigma MRSC_j$ (from (8-8)) $\tag{8-15}$

Solution OPT $T_2/T_1 = \Sigma MRSG_j - (n-1)a$ (using (8-12)). $\tag{8-15a}$

Suppose initially that there is a linear transformation curve between x and X, so that T_2/T_1 is the same for all solutions. Then, if we compare solutions OPT and PRI, using the $MRSG$ version of the latter, we have the following relationship:

$$MRSG_i \text{ (PRI)} = \sum_j MRSG_j \text{ (OPT)} - (n-1)a \qquad \text{(all } i) \qquad (8\text{-}16)$$

Now $MRSG = a + MRSC$, so that $MRSG_j > a$ for all j. Thus the right-hand side of (8-16) is necessarily greater than any $MRSG_j$.
Thus

$$MRSG_i \text{ (PRI)} > \text{Max}_j MRSG_j \text{ (OPT)}. \qquad (8\text{-}17)$$

This implies that the private good solution will have *every* individual consuming more of the private, and less of the mixed, good than at the optimum.

Comparing the public good solution with the optimum, using (8-14) and (8-15), we have

$$\sum MRSC_j \text{ (PUB)} = a + \sum MRSC_j \text{ (OPT)} \qquad (8\text{-}18)$$

so that

$$\sum MRSC_j \text{ (PUB)} > \sum MRSC_j \text{ (OPT)}. \qquad (8\text{-}19)$$

The implication of (8-19), which is initially surprising, is that the public good solution will provide the average individual with *less* of the public characteristic than will the optimal solution. The reason for this is that, in the optimal solution where individuals obtain private as well as public characteristics, part of their supply of the private characteristic is obtained from the mixed good which supplies public characteristic at the same time. In the public good solution, on the other hand, all of the private characteristic must be obtained from the private good, partly at the expense of the public good and thus of the public characteristic.

A Numerical Example

Since the relationship between the optimal solution and the public good solution is surprising, it seems worthwhile to illustrate with a simple example. We shall assume identical utility functions of the form $u = z_i^{\frac{1}{2}} Z^{\frac{1}{2}}$, a population of 10, a transformation relationship of the form $V = \sum_i x_i + \sum_i X_i + X_G$, a value of 0.2 for the parameter a, and work with utility levels in each case that require a resource level of $V = 100$ and give equal welfare to all individuals.

It is obvious that all three solutions will result in x_i and X_i being the same for all individuals, so we can drop the subscript i and sum by multiplying by n. All consumers will have the same value for $MRSC$ which will be given by

$$MRSC = \frac{x + aX}{nX} \qquad \text{for OPT and PRIV solutions}$$

$$MRSC = \frac{x}{X_G} \qquad \text{for PUB solution.}$$

We have T_2/T_1 constant and equal to unity.

The solutions for all three cases are set out in table 8–1 for the numerical values chosen.

In this particular case, the amount of private characteristic per individual is the same in both the optimal and public good solutions, but in the public good solution this requires relatively more of the private good, leaving less resources available for the mixed good (here a public good) and thus a smaller amount of public characteristic.

Although we initially assumed a constant marginal rate of transformation in order to simplify the comparison of the solutions in the three cases, the relative ordering of these solutions is not changed if the transformation relationship is of the usual nonlinear form, with the transformation curve for given V concave toward the origin. Such curvature brings the solutions closer together (in terms of quantities of goods), but it remains true that the largest ratio of public characteristic to private characteristic will be in the optimal (mixed good) solution, the next largest in the public good solution, and the smallest in the private good solution.

Policy Implications

Since it is not optimal to treat both goods as private goods and rely on the operation of the competitive market, and since it not optimal to supply the mixed good as if it were a public good (because then the potential private characteristic content is lost), it is obvious that the optimal solution requires that individuals actually purchase the mixed good themselves, but not at the relative prices corresponding to marginal production costs. Optimal policy requires some form of subsidy on the mixed good, tax on the private good, or a combination of both.

If both goods are sold through the market, the individual purchaser will buy the two goods in proportions which equate the marginal rate of substitution between the goods to the buyer price ratio. Denote the buyer price ratio for the

Table 8–1
Value for Numerical Example

Solution	Σx_i	ΣX_i	X_G	z_i	Z	u^i
OPT	37.5	62.5	—	5.00	62.5	312.5
PRIV	88.64	11.36	—	9.09	11.36	103.3
PUB	50.0	—	50.0	5.00	50.0	250.0

jth consumer by R_j, and the producer price ratio (T_2/T_1) by r. Then the optimum condition requires that

$$r = T_2/T_1 = \Sigma \, MRSG_j - (n - 1)a \qquad \text{(from (8-15a))}$$

$$= \Sigma \, R_j - (n - 1)a. \qquad (8\text{-}20)$$

Noting that $R_j = MRSG_j > a$, for all j, it follows that

$$r > \underset{j}{\text{Max}} \, R_j \qquad (8\text{-}21)$$

so that a subsidy-tax combination in favor of the mixed good will be required for every individual. In general, the optimum will require a different value of R_j, and thus of the subsidy-tax combination, for every different individual.

Let us remove the complication of individually tailored subsidy-tax combinations by assuming all individuals have identical homothetic preferences, so that $R_i = R_j = R$, all i, j.

The subsidy-tax formula takes a simple form in the case of identical preferences. We have

$$r = nR - (n - 1)a$$

$$R - a = \frac{1}{n}(r - a). \qquad (8\text{-}22)$$

That is, the difference between R and a is always less than the difference between r and a, with R becoming closer and closer to a as n increases. Note that R is always strictly greater than a (as indicated above), but is very close to a for a large population. For the numerical example given in the last section we have $a = 0.2$ and $R = 0.28$. If the population were 100 instead of 10, the value of R would be 0.208.

Thus the optimal solution for the mixed good case can be attained by sale of both goods in the market, but with policy intervention in the form of a subsidy tax arrangement (always in the direction of reducing the buyer price of the mixed good in terms of the private good relative to the producer price ratio). If consumers have identical preferences or can be represented by a "typical" consumer, the required difference between producer and buyer price ratios is given from (8-22) above. Whatever the producer price ratio, the optimal buyer price ratio will be very close to a (but on the "up" side) when the population is large.

Note that in the mixed good analysis through characteristics, the crucial quantitative information for policy purposes is that concerning the value of the parameter a. This is a technical parameter which has been taken above to be constant over the economy, although we shall drop this assumption of constancy in the next section. Whatever the conceptual or measurement problems associated with the parameter a, they are insignificant compared with the problem of extimating the $\Sigma\ MRS$ required for the pure public good case. In this mixed case, if we knew only the technical parameter a we could expect to move from an arbitrary initial position towards the optimum by a convergence process of the following kind:

Step 1. Given the initial producer price ratio r_0, determine a buyer price ratio R_1 from the formula $R_1 - a = k(r_0 - a)$, where k is an arbitrary number less than unity (say ½), and set the subsidy-tax combination to give the appropriate divergence between r_0 and R_1.

Step 2. As a result of step 1, quantities of the goods produced and consumed will change from the initial situation, resulting in a new producer price ratio r_1. A new buyer price ratio R_2 is then obtained by applying the same formula as in step 1.

Step 3, etc. Continue the process.

We cannot find out *exactly* where to stop without an estimate of marginal rates of substitution, but a few steps of the above kind can be expected to put the economy into the ballpark neighborhood of the optimum. This in itself is a very strong result relative to what we usually obtain from the analysis of public goods or externalities.

Technical Variations

It is possible that the ratio of private to public characteristic in the mixed good may differ between groups because of local or other *objectively* identifiable causes. To a rural dweller, the existence of a well-developed urban transport network may still represent a public characteristic to him (as a guarantee he will be able easily to move around if and when he goes to the city), but the private characteristic content to him is small. To a family with grown up children, the public characteristic content of an education system may be important, the private characteristic content small or zero.

We must be careful to distinguish between the *subjective* preferences of an individual for private versus publich characteristics (expressed in preference orderings or utility functions) and *objective* differences between groups as to the extent to which a private characteristic can be obtained from a specific mixed good (expressed in the parameter a). An individual may have a small interest in the public characteristic relative to the private, but be able to obtain a high ratio of private to public characteristic from the mixed good.

It will be assumed that there are three homogeneous groups in the economy, each facing a different value of the parameter a. Denote the values of a for the three groups by a_1, a_2, a_3, with $a_3 > a_2 > a_1$ so that the least amount of private characteristic per unit of the mixed good is obtained by persons of the first group, the greatest by persons of group three. In spite of the different values of a, we identify the mixed goods as being the same good no matter to which group they are allocated, because they are either physically identical or are perfect substitutes in production under all circumstances.

Formal specification and optimization of the model follows the same lines as before, modified to account of the different values of a for the three groups. Inequalities (8-5) will be unchanged, but the inequalities (8-6) will be divided into three different inequalities

$$T_2 \geqslant a_1 \lambda_i u_1^i + \Sigma \lambda_j u_2^j \qquad (i \in G_1) \qquad (8\text{-}23)$$

$$T_2 \geqslant a_2 \lambda_i u_1^i + \Sigma \lambda_j u_2^j \qquad (i \in G_2) \qquad (8\text{-}24)$$

$$T_2 \geqslant a_3 \lambda_i u_1^i + \Sigma \lambda_j u_2^j \qquad (i \in G_3) \qquad (8\text{-}25)$$

where G_1, G_2, G_3 are the three groups, but summations over j are over the whole population.

It is immediately obvious that the inequalities $T_1 \geqslant \lambda_i u_1^i$ and the inequalities (8-23)–(8-25) cannot all be satisfied as equations. What we can consider to be the typical solution will have the following form

$$T_1 = \lambda_i u_1^i, i \in G_1, G_2; T_1 > \lambda_i u_1^i \text{ and } x_i = 0; i \in G_3. \qquad (8\text{-}26)$$

$$T_2 > a_1 \lambda_i u_1^i + \Sigma \lambda_j u_2^j \text{ and } X_i = 0; i \in G_1. \qquad (8\text{-}27)$$

$$T_2 = a_s \lambda_i u_1^i + \Sigma \lambda_j u_2^j; s = 2, 3; i \in G_2, G_3. \qquad (8\text{-}28)$$

Individuals in G_1 will receive none of the mixed good but will obtain all their public characteristic from the mixed good consumed from the other groups. Individuals in G_3 will receive none of the private good, but will obtain the private characteristic from consumption of the mixed good. Only the individuals in G_2 will consume both goods.

From (8-26), (8-27), and (8-28), we obtain our basic optimum condition

$$T_2/T_1 = a_2 + \overset{G_1, G_2}{\underset{}{\sum}} MRSC_j + (a_2/a_3) \overset{G_3}{\underset{}{\sum}} MRSC_k \qquad (8\text{-}29)$$

where the first summation is over members of G_1, G_2, the second over members of G_3.

The solution in (8-29) has a generic similarity to the solution (8-8) for the fixed parameter case, with the "average" parameter a_2 playing the role of the former single parameter. It differs in that the marginal rates of substitution for G_3 individuals are added in with less than unit weights.

In this case, assuming all consumers have identical preferences does not lead

PUBLIC ECONOMICS

to so direct a simplification as in the case with a single value for the parameter a. Here, even if all consumers are identical, the consumers from different groups face different properties of the consumption technology (represented by the three values a_1, a_2, a_3), and will have differing marginal rates of substitution between characteristics. We can show, in fact, that the marginal rates of substitution will necessarily differ between the groups, being highest for the individuals in G_1, lowest for individuals in G_3, and intermediate for individuals in G_2.

Let us assume that all individuals in a group have identical preferences, and denote the marginal rate of substitution between characteristics (at the optimum) by $MRSC$ for members of G_2. Then, if the total population is n, we can write (8-29) as

$$T_2/T_1 = a_2 + nK \cdot MRSC \qquad (8\text{-}30)$$

where K is the ratio of the average of the terms to the right of a_2 in (8-29) to $MRSC$ (for G_2). Note that $MRSC_j$ for individuals in G_1 will be less than $MRSC$, while $MRSC_k$ for individuals in G_3 will be greater than $MRSC$ but is given a weight of less than unity. We cannot be certain, therefore, whether K is greater or less than unity but we do not expect it to differ from unity to a very large extent. The value of K depends on the proportions of the population in each of the groups, given the preferences. Due to the public characteristic effect, a change in the population size will change *all* marginal rates of substitution but we can suppose that it causes only second-order changes in the relationship between those rates in different groups. Thus, if we take the proportions of the population in the different groups as fixed, and preferences as identical between group members and fixed, we can consider K to be a parameter of the population *structure* and substantially independent of n.

We are now in a position to consider optimal policy. Since only members of G_2 buy both goods, the appropriate buyer price ratio is equal to the marginal rate of substitution between goods in G_2. Denoting this optimal buyer price ratio by R, we have (using (8-12))

$$R - a_2 = MRSC \qquad (8\text{-}31)$$

Let r be the producer price ratio $(= T_2/T_1)$. Then, from (8-30) and (8-31) we have

$$R - a_2 = \frac{1}{nK}(r - a_2). \qquad (8\text{-}32)$$

This differs from the subsidy-tax formula for the single parameter case (once a_2 is used for the parameter) only in the presence of K. Since we have argued that K is substantially independent of n, we reach the same conclusion as in the earlier case, that R will be close to, but above, a_2 when the population is large.

Thus, since practical policy measures can be approximate at best, we can argue that the existence of multiple values of the parameter a will not substantially affect the policy prescriptions, provided the parameter value used is that appropriate to the middle group.

Conclusion

By analyzing "impure" public goods as mixed goods possessing both public and private *characteristics* in technically determined proportions, we have been able to reach an important conclusion, that treating such goods as if they were pure public goods will not only be suboptimal, but suboptimal in the particular and surprising sense that the pure public good solution will provide *too little* of the specifically public content. In other words, within the confines of our simple model, supply of, say, health services, education, communication as public goods would provide too little "general health" relative to specific treatment, with equivalent deficiencies in other cases.

Optimality in the mixed good case requires supply through the market, not supply as a public good. But it cannot be reached by the free market (treating the mixed good as a pure private good will, in general, be even more suboptimal than treating it as a public good), and a subsidy-tax mix is required. This will always be one that reduces the price of the mixed good to the buyer, relative to the private good, as compared with the producer price ratio.

The analysis provides a formula for the required subsidy-tax combination which, for population sizes of a realistically large order, can be closely approximated from a knowledge only of the single technical parameter which gives the ratio of the private to public characteristic content of the mixed good.

Notes

1. The classic statement of which is Samuelson's (1964) paper.
2. See Lancaster (1966, 1971).
3. A classification of most of the possible externality combinations is given by Shoup (1969). For a discussion of externalities that can be considered as mini-public characteristics within the household, see Lancaster (1975).

References

Lancaster, K. "A New Approach to Consumer Theory." *Journal of Political Economy* 74 (1966): 132–57.

Lancaster, K. *Consumer Demand: A New Approach.* Columbia University Press, 1971.

Lancaster, K. "The Theory of Household Behavior: Some Foundations." *Annals of Economic and Social Measurement* 4 (1975): 1–17.

Musgrave, R. *The Theory of Public Finance.* New York: McGraw-Hill, 1959.

Samuelson, P. "The Pure Theory of Public Expenditure." *Review of Economics and Statistics* 36 (1964): 387–89.

Shoup, C. *Public Finance.* Aldine, 1969.

Dynamics and Land Use: The Case of Forestry

John Ledyard
Leon N. Moses

In 1836 Thunen published the classic volume in which he developed his theory of agricultural rent and land use.[1] He assumed a plane in which transport was a ubiquity and all land was of uniform quality. In the middle of this plane was a town or marketing center where the agricultural products that could be grown in the region were sold. The town and its agricultural hinterland were taken to be isolated from all other areas and surrounded by an uncultivated wilderness. Thunen formulated a model that determined a rational allocation of land to the alternative crops and the economic limit of cultivation beyond which the wilderness began. This model treated prices for products in the marketing center and the costs of transporting them from farms to the center as given. These costs were functions of distance. They also varied by product, some crops being more difficult to transport than others because of their greater bulk or perishability. Thunen assumed a fixed coefficient production function with a fixed yield per unit of land and fixed requirements of capital and labor for each crop. Finally, he assumed a wage rate, which he thought might decline with distance from the town, and a uniform return on capital.

With the structure of his model thus established, Thunen was able to derive what have become known as bid-rent functions. Each function pertains to a given crop. It shows the rent that land located at varying distances from the town would yield if devoted to that crop. This rent is the difference between on-the-farm gross revenue, which is the product of price at the town and yield, and the sum of labor, capital, and transport cost. With perfect foresight and competition, or perfect planning, each parcel of land is allocated to the use in which it yields the maximum rent and all land is thereby allocated in an optimal fashion. The wilderness area begins at that distance where land yields a zero rent.

Figures 9-1 (a) and 9-1 (b) illustrate the workings of the model for a three-crop system. Three bid rent functions are shown in 9-1(a). In order, AB, CD, and EF show the rent that would be yielded by land at varying distances from the center when devoted to garden crops, milk or pasture, and grain. The intersections of the bid rent functions determine the distances from the town at

This paper is based on a talk presented at a symposium, *The Economics of Sustained Yield Forestry,* College of Forest Resources, University of Washington, November 1974. The authors wish to acknowledge the very considerable benefit they have derived from a second paper presented at this symposium: Paul A. Samuelson, "Economics of Forestry in an Evolving Society."

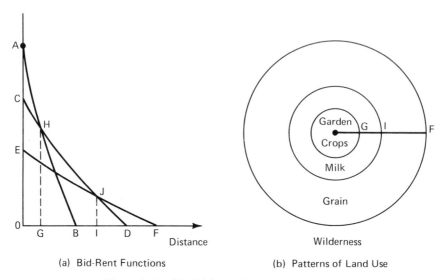

(a) Bid-Rent Functions   (b) Patterns of Land Use

Figure 9-1. Model for a Three-Crop System

which the three crops are grown, and the outer envelope, AHJF, of the bid-rent functions is the rent gradient. Thus, for example, land "at" the marketing center and to a distance OG from it, is devoted to the production of garden crops, and yields rent from OA to HG. As shown in 9-1(b), the model yields concentric rings, each of which is exclusively devoted to a given land use. OF is the limit of cultivation.

Thunen's theory of land use and rent evoked admiration among scholars for generations, but little was done to advance the model until recently when economists, geographers, and others adapted it to an urban setting. In modern versions Thunen's marketing center becomes the central business district (CBD) of a city. His crops became such urban land uses as finance, retailing, manufacturing, and housing. Instead of crops being shipped to the center, labor commutes. The object is still to explain how competition determines the price of space, which is shown to be a declining function of distance from the CBD. However, the tools of modern microeconomics have enriched the model and permitted a wider range of problems to be handled.[2] Thus, Vickrey and Solow have introduced congestion into a land use model.[3] In their work transport cost per unit shipped depends on the total volume of movement rather than being constant as in the Thunen model. Instead of taking the price of goods as given, Muth has developed a model in which prices are determined and goods as well as land markets are cleared.[4] Mills has introduced scale economies into the model, a feature which is essential to an understanding of urban development.[5] Beckmann and Koopmans,[6] Goldstein and Moses,[7] and Mills[8] have attempted to take into account the effect on location and land rent of activities that are interdependent since they use each others outputs as inputs.

While the tools of modern economic analysis have been used to significantly improve certain aspects of land use reasoning, there are other areas where the theory, as against certain empirical understandings, has not been advanced much beyond where Thunen left it. One such area is the effect of time on patterns of land use. To the author's knowledge there are no formal dynamic models that show how time and transport cost interact to determine rents, land uses, and intensities of cultivation at varying distances from a center. This is the subject of this chapter. We have introduced time and its capital theoretic implications into a model of land use in which the output is timber. The effect of time in such a model is of course opposite to that in something like urban housing. Over time a house deteriorates. The quality of the service it yields declines unless there is expenditure for maintenance.[a] At least up to the point where trees reach maturity, time has an opposite effect in forest land. Up to that point the yield from a tree or a stand of trees increases, so that time has a positive rather than a negative marginal productivity. We have chosen to develop our model of dynamic land use in a forestry context because there has been a lively debate on the issue of forestry management for many years. The nature of this debate is explained below.

It is interesting to note that Thunen himself was concerned with some of the dynamic aspects of land use. He considered alternative crop rotation systems, some of which would enrich the soil over time more than others, and some of which would exhaust the soil.[9] Thunen was also interested in the effect of time on the competition for land between forests and annual crops. He attempted to use precisely the same framework as in the remainder of his work, employing specified prices at the town, transport costs, etc., to determine which land would be devoted to commercial wood production for fuel and housing. However, as Samuelson has pointed out, Thunen and most other economists did not understand the capital theoretic aspects of the forestry case.[10]

Thunen assumed a 5 percent interest rate in his isolated state and then observed that there were forests where the annual increment in mass of the trees was 2.5 percent. In these circumstances he concluded that the woodlands would be destroyed and would not be replanted even if their gradual destruction raised the price of timber. He reasoned that each increase in price would simply increase the capital embodied in the timber stock and the owner of the forest

---

[a]Our statement that relatively little has been done to incorporate dynamic reasoning into land use models is not meant to suggest an absence of significant work on the subject. Many economists, planners, and others have been interested in how the quality of the housing stock changes over time and how the stock is filtered to lower income groups. For example, the National Bureau of Economic Research urban simulation model, Ingram, G.F.; Kain, J.F. and Ginn, J.R. with contributions by Brown, H.J. and Dresch, S.P. *The Detroit Prototype of the N.B.E.R. Urban Simulation Model.* New York: 1972 has a sub-model in which decisions are made on maintenance expenditures period by period. However, the complexities of the solution procedure rule out present value calculations and force the authors to adopt a set of ad hoc rules on such things as the net percentage of the stock in each residential area that can be filtered up or down in each period.

would therefore profit from felling the trees and investing at 5 rather than 2.5 percent. Thunen concluded that only a fall in the interest rate to 2.5 percent would halt the destruction of the woodlands. He then added that ". . . if the interest rate does not fall, and such an indispensable commodity as firewood is not to vanish from our earth, the governments will have to take steps to deprive citizens of their rights to dispose as they choose of their woods, forcing them to make do with only half the potential revenue from their forest property.[11] Thunen did understand that in the early years of development of a tree, or an entire forest, its mass might increase at much more than 5 percent per year and therefore that trees cut today might be replanted with young trees. However, he failed to incorporate this understanding into a steady state model.

Thunen's fear that the interest rate could lead to the destruction of forests still haunts foresters, particularly those who manage public forests. The Forestry Service of the U.S. Department of Agriculture, and the corresponding agencies in Canada and other wood-producing countries have adopted a policy known as maximum sustained yield forestry. Essentially the policy comes down to managing the forest so as to maximize the mean annual increment of wood.[12] That is, the forest is permitted to grow until average product with time is a maximum. This amount of timber is then cut each year and replaced with new trees. The influences of the interest rate and even of timber prices and costs of production are ignored in the sustained yield model.

Clearly what many foresters have not understood is that they are not managing forests. They are managing land which can be put to alternative uses, including the planting of new trees. What is needed is a policy based on a model that combines two things: (1) Thunen's conception of rent as it varies with distance and transport costs from a center; (2) Samuelson's capital theory reasoning of the impact of the interest rate and other costs on the steady state solution for any given parcel of forest land without regard to location and transport costs. This chapter attempts to develop such a model. We assume a center in the middle of a forest. This center is a town in which there is a wood processing mill. The price of timber at the mill is given. There are transport costs entailed in shipping timber to the mill and in sending labor out from the town to cut trees and plant new ones. There are other costs of production as well. The timber mill is assumed to operate under perfectly competitive conditions. The model determines the limit of economic cultivation of the forest for such a firm. There is a comparable concept in the forestry literature but it is not clearly defined and does not appear to be determined on the basis of economic considerations. The model shows the impact of transport costs on the length of time that trees are permitted to grow on land located at varying distances from the center. It also shows the impact of these costs on intensity of cultivation. The paper emphasizes the long-run steady state equilibrium rather than the path to equilibrium. The land use decisions a perfectly competitive firm would make are compared with those implied by the policy of maximum sustained yield forestry. We conclude that the latter is a sub-optimum policy.

An Idealized Forest[b]

Initially we ignore transportation costs on output and labor and consider a cyclical model of the forest in which at some time t, labor is used to initiate growth through clearing, planting, etc. At $t + T$, the timber is harvested and then labor is used to initiate a new growth cycle.[c] The available harvest at any date $t + T$ depends on the amount of labor used at t and the length of time, T, growth has ocurred.

Assume that forests grow in accordance with a biological growth law:

$$\dot{M} = f(M(T)) \tag{9-1}$$

where $M(T)$ is the biomass (broad-feet or some other measure) on a given land area at time T, and $\dot{M} \equiv dM/dt$ is the rate of growth of this biomass. Graphically, this growth law is represented in figure 9-2.

Here, $\bar{M}$ is the maximum amount of biomass which the land-area will support. It would be the biomass of a virgin forest. Labor inputs influence outputs because they determine the initial biomass from which growth occurs.[d]

$$M(0) = h(L) \tag{9-2}$$

where L is the amount of labor devoted, for example, to planting. We assume positive but diminishing returns to this type of effort. That is, $h'(L) > 0$ and $h''(L) < 0$.

The combination of biological law (9-1) and technology (9-2) give us our production function. In particular, given L, let $M(T, M_0)$ be the solution to (9-1) through $M_0 = h(L)$. The biomass available for harvest and sale at T, given the labor input, L, is simply

$$X_T = M(T, h(L)). \tag{9-3}$$

---

[b]The model is similar to Waggener's normal forest under full regulation with closed crown cover at each age.[13]

[c]Two additional uses of labor are ignored in this chapter. The first is the labor required to harvest the timber. This could be easily accounted for without changing the analysis by assuming a fixed amount of labor per biomass unit to be harvested. On this point see footnote e.

The second type are inputs used to thin, spray, etc., trees over the course of their development. Such labor increases the intensity of cultivation, and could act as a substitute for planting inputs. Inclusion of the former inputs in the model could affect our results if their impact on growth is large. On this point see footnote j.

[d]Labor is used here to denote all inputs needed to initiate the growth of a forest. i.e., nursery facilities, planting labor, etc.

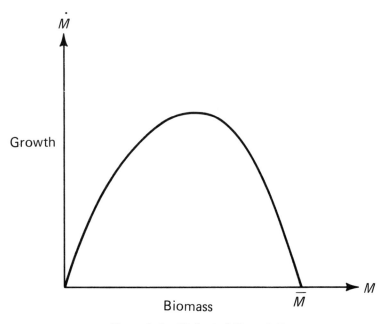

Figure 9-2. Biological Growth Law

In more familiar notation the production function is

$$X_T = F(T,L) \tag{9-3'}$$

where X_T is the output per land area at T.

The Competitive (Optimal) Solution
Without Transport Costs

The forester who is confronted with perfectly competitive markets for output, labor, and land will choose T and L to maximize the present discounted value of profits. Thus, in steady-state competitive equilibrium L and T will be chosen to

$$\underset{T,L,}{\text{Maximize}} \; [pF(T,L)e^{-rT} - wL] \, (1 + e^{-rT} + e^{-2rT} + \ldots) \tag{9-4}$$

or

$$\text{Maximize } V(T,L) \equiv [pF(T,L)e^{-rT} - wL] \, (1 - e^{-rT})^{-1} \qquad (9\text{-}4')$$

where p is the price of lumber and w is the wage rate.[e]

In these competitive markets, the value or competitive purchase price of the land area utilized is

$$V^* = \underset{T,L}{\text{Max }} V(T,L)$$

and the instantaneous rental rate is $R^* = rV^*$. As Samuelson has indicated, an equivalent problem to (9–4) in competitive land markets, is to rent the land for the period of a single cycle.[14] The producer would then

$$\text{Maximize } pF(L,T)e^{-rT} - wL - R \int_0^T e^{-rT} dt = \Pi(R) \qquad (9\text{-}4'')$$

where R is set in competitive markets for land at its highest value, R^*, such that $\Pi(R^*) = 0$. The purchase price of land is $R^*/r = V^*$ as above.

At this point, we note three facts about optimal land use in our model. First, rents and optimal output are simultaneously determined since land is a variable factor of production through the decision variable T. Over the life cycle of one tree the owner of land should take opportunity cost into account even if there is no use for the land other than as a forest. This is true because a tree of age T should be viewed as competing for the land with newly planted trees. The opportunity cost of leaving a tree of age T on the land to grow another year is the present discounted value of profits foregone by not beginning future growth cycles on that date and by waiting until the next year to do so. In our model, the competitive rental, R^*, is the value of this foregone opportunity. The error that Thunen and many foresters have committed is that they have not taken this opportunity cost into account.

A second fact about optimal land use in our model is that if the maximum purchase price a forester should be willing to pay for land, V^*, is less than zero, then the land should not be used to produce timber. It should be left fallow or in a virgin state. This coincides with similar conclusions in traditional land use

---

[e]If b units of harvesting labor are required per unit biomass harvested, then (9–4) would read

$$\text{Max } [(p - wb)F(T, L)e^{-rT} - wL] \, (1 + e^{-rT} + \ldots).$$

The inclusion of harvesting labor would not change any of the qualitative properties of the model.

models. However, as we shall see it is not the conclusion implied in the policy of maximum sustained yield.

A third fact is that if there is an alternative use for the land which would yield a higher competitive purchase price than V^*, then the land should be used for that alternative and not for forests. Such a situation would exist if there were, for example, a one-year crop which yielded a profit on the land each year greater than $R^* (1 - e^{-r})/r = V^* (1 - e^{-r})$, the maximal one-year payment a competitive forester would be willing to pay.[f]

Optimal Land-use with Transportation Costs

As indicated earlier a single point, the mill, exists from which all labor must travel to work and to which all output must be brought for sale. Transport is ubiquitous and labor or output can be moved between any place and the mill at a per unit cost which depends only on the distance between the two locations. As in all land-use models of this type, rings of cultivation are determined within which all output and input decisions are identical.

Let $C_x (d)$ be the cost of shipping a unit of output a distance d to the mill[g] and let $C_L (d)$ be the round-trip cost of transporting labor this distance into the forested area. The competitive forester now chooses $T(d)$ and $L(d)$ to

$$\underset{T,L}{\text{Maximize}}\; V(T,L,d) \equiv [(p - C_x (d))Fe^{-rT}$$

$$- (w + C_L (d))L]\,(1 - e^{-rT})^{-1}. \tag{9-5}$$

In competitive land markets the instantaneous rental rate for land at a distance d from the mill is

$$R(d) = \underset{T,L}{\text{Max}}\; r \cdot V(T,L,d). \tag{9-6}$$

We now turn to the task of describing how rentals, output, labor usage, and

---

[f]Alternatively, if Π' is the maximum profit yielded by a one year crop then the producer of that crop would be willing to pay $V' = \Pi' (1 + e^{-r} + e^{-2r} + \ldots) = \Pi' (1 - e^{-r})^{-1}$. If $V' > V^*$ then the land should be used for the one year crop. $V' > V^*$ holds when $\Pi' (1 - e^{-r})^{-1} > V^*$ or $\Pi' > V^* (1 - e^{-r})$.

[g]This includes the empty trip out and the loaded trip back.

harvesting times vary with the distance from the mill in steady-state competitive equilibrium. The necessary conditions for a solution to (9–5) or (9–6) are

$$[p - C_x(d)] \, (F_T - rF) - R = 0 \tag{9-7a}$$

$$[p - C_x(d)] \, F_L e^{-rT} - (w + C_L(d)) = 0 \tag{9-7b}$$

$$[p - C_x(d)] \, F e^{-rT} - (w + C_L(d))L - R(1 - e^{-rT})r^{-1} = 0 \tag{9-7c}$$

The solution to (9–7) can readily be derived. From (9–3) we note that $F_T = \partial M/\partial T$, and from (9–1) that $\partial M/\partial T = f[F(T,L)]$. Thus $F_T = f(F)$ and equation (9–7a) simply requires that $f(F) - rF = R/(p - C_x)$. Figure 9–3 illustrates how F, and therefore T, can be determined. The first-order condition (9–7a) implies that the profit maximizing output is either X^1 or X^2 in figure 9–3(a). The second-order conditions indicate that X^2 is the appropriate choice.

To demonstrate this result we note that A^*, the matrix of second partial derivatives of the profit function (9–4″), must be negative semi-definite where

$$A^* = (p - C_x) \begin{bmatrix} F_{TT} - rF_T & F_{TL} - rF_L \\ (F_{LT} - rF_L)e^{-rT} & F_{LL} e^{-rT} \end{bmatrix}.$$

By applying comparative dynamics to the growth laws (9–1) and (9–2) it can be

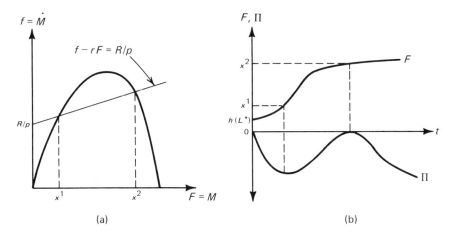

Figure 9-3. Profit Functions and Maximization

shown that $F_L = e^{g(t)} h'(L)$, where $g(T) = \int_0^T f'[F(t,L)]\, dt$. It follows that $F_{TL} = f' F_L = F_{LT}$. Also, $F_{TT} = f' F_T$. Thus A^* can be written as

$$(p - C_x) \begin{bmatrix} (f' - r)f & (f' - r)F_L \\ (f' - r)F_L e^{-rT} & F_{LL} e^{-rT} \end{bmatrix}.$$

Since A^* must be negative semi-definite, $f' - r \leq 0$. Thus, in figure 9–3(a), X^2 is the profit-maximizing output. Figure 9–3(b) illustrates the growth curve $F(t, L^*)$ and the equilibrium single-cylce profit function

$$\Pi(t) = F e^{-rT} - (w/p)L^* - (R/p)(1 - e^{-rT}) r^{-1}$$

for the equilibrium quantity of labor, L^*.

Standard comparative statics analysis can be applied to (9–7) to discover how T, L, and R change as the distance to the mill changes by solving the following system of three equations:

$$\begin{bmatrix} & & \vdots & -1 \\ & A^* & \vdots & 0 \\ \cdots & \cdots & \vdots & \cdots \\ 0 & 0 & \vdots & -(1 - e^{-rT}) r^{-1} \end{bmatrix} \begin{bmatrix} dT \\ dL \\ dR \end{bmatrix} = \begin{bmatrix} C_x'(F_T - rF) \\ C_x' F_L e^{-rT} + C_L' \\ C_x' F e^{-rT} + C_L'(L) \end{bmatrix} d(d). \quad (9\text{–}8)$$

If A^* is assumed to be negative definite, system (9–8) can be solved and it can be shown that

$$dR/dd = -(1 - e^{-rT})^{-1} r [C_x' F e^{-rT} + C_L' L], \qquad (9\text{–}9)$$

$$dT/dd = |A|^{-1} (p - C_x) \{ C_x' e^{-rT} [-F_{LL}(1 - e^{-rT})(f - rF)$$

$$+ (f' - r)F_L (1 - e^{-rT}) r^{-1} F_L + F_{LL} e^{-rT} F]$$

$$+ C_L' [(f' - r)F_L (1 - e^{-rT}) r^{-1} + F_{LL} e^{-rT} L] \}. \qquad (9\text{–}10)$$

$$dL/dd = |A|^{-1} (p - C_x) \{ C_x' e^{-rT} [(f' - r)F_L (1 - e^{-rT}) r^{-1}(f - rF)$$

$$- (f' - r)F_T (1 - e^{-rT}) r^{-1} F_L - (f' - r)F_L F e^{-rT}]$$

$$+ C_L' [-(f' - r)F_T (1 - e^{-rT}) r^{-1} - (f' - r)F_L e^{-rT} L \}. \qquad (9\text{–}11)$$

We now make the eminently reasonable assumption that total transportation costs increase with distance. That is, we assume that C_x' and C_L' are positive.

In addition a positive interest rate, r, is assumed. From these assumptions and equation (9-9) it immediately follows, as one would have guessed, that rent per unit of land is lower the further it is located from the shipping point. That is, $R'(d) = dR/dd < 0$.

Equations (9-10) and (9-11) can be rewritten by recognizing that

$$Fe^{-rT} - (f - rF)(1 - e^{-rT})r^{-1} = Fe^{-rT} - [R/(p - C_x)](1 - e^{-rT})r^{-1}$$

$$= [w + C_L/(p - C_x)]L.$$

One then observes that

$$T' = |A|^{-1}(p - C_x)\{C_x'e^{-rT}[F_{LL}rL(w + C_L/p - C_x)$$

$$+ (F_L)^2(1 - e^{-rT})(f' - r)]$$

$$+ C_L'[F_{LL}Le^{-rT} + (f' - r)F_L(1 - e^{-rT})r^{-1}]\} \qquad (9\text{-}10')$$

and

$$L' = |A|^{-1}(p - C_x)\{C_x'e^{-rT}[(f' - r)F_L(-L)[w + C_L/p - C_x]$$

$$- (f' - r)F_TF_L(1 - e^{-rT})r^{-1}] + C_L'[-(f' - r)(F_T[1 - e^{-rT}]r^{-1}$$

$$- e^{-rT}LF_L(f' - r)]\}. \qquad (9\text{-}11')$$

While it may not be obvious, relations (9-10′) and (9-11′) allow us to conclude that $T' > 0$ and $L' < 0$.[h] In other words, *the optimal management of forests and land requires that the further away land is from the mill, the less labor one should employ in planting, and the longer one should allow the forest to grow before harvesting.*[i,j]

---

[h]One observes that $|A| < 0$ since A^* negative definite implies $|A^*| > 0$. Also $f' - r < 0$, $F_L > 0$, $F_T > 0$, $F_{LL} < 0$, and $(w + C_L)/(p - C_x) > 0$.

[i]The fact that T increases as the net price, $(p - C_x)$, decreases is the "Ricardo effect" of capital theory.

[j]The conclusions so far reached have been based on the assumption that labor inputs only affect output by determining the initial biomass. Suppose, on the other hand, that the forester can also influence rates of growth by applying inputs over time for such activities as thinning, spraying, etc. That is, $\dot{M} = f(M, L)$. Some of the conclusions reached in the chapter may not hold if $\partial f/\partial L$ is large and positive when evaluated at $M = F(T^*, L^*)$, the competitive output level. $R' < 0$ will still hold. However, the expression for T' in (9–10′) will have an additional term $f_L|A|(p - c_x)\{C_x'F_L(1 - e^{-rT}) + C_L'(1 - e^{-rT})r^{-1}\}$ which is negative. The expression for L' in (9–11′) will have the additional term $F_L|A|(p - C_x)\{-C_x'e^{-rT}L$

It is also true that output per land unit at the harvest date, $X_T = F(T,L)$, increases as the distance the land is located from the mill increases, since

$$dF/dd = [d(R/(p - C_x))/dd] \ (f' - r)^{-1} > 0.^{k} \tag{9-12}$$

Finally, it is relatively easy to show that $R'' = dR^2/dd^2 > 0$ if per unit transportation costs do not increase at an increasing rate with distance: that is, if C_x'' and C_L'' are less than or equal to zero. This follows since

$$R'' = (\partial R'/\partial T)T' + (\partial R'/\partial L)L' + \partial R'/\partial d, \partial R'/\partial T > 0, \partial R'/\partial L < 0$$

and $\partial R'/\partial d > 0$.

A representative bid-rent curve, $R(d)$, is graphed in figure 9–4. The number d_c determines the limit of the working circle. Beyond d_c it is unprofitable and non-optimal to engage in commercial forestry.

Land Use Under Sustained Yield Policy

If the policy of maximum sustained yield is interpreted literally, the forester chooses a strategy which yields the highest sustainable output from a normal forest while maintaining a constant vintage structure of trees in the forest.[1] In terms of our model the forester chooses T and L to

$$\underset{L,T}{\text{Max}} \ F(L,T)/T. \tag{9-13}$$

This strategy determines how a particular land unit is to be managed. However, it does not define the size of the working circle, which is to say the amount of land that is to be managed. A search of the forestry literature failed to reveal any specific policy with respect to the size of the working circle for public lands. Therefore we shall examine the implications of two alternative definitions that

---

$[w + C_L/p - C_x] - C_L' \ e^{-rT}L\}$ which will be positive. The expression for F' in (9–12) will have the additional term $-f_L L'(f' - r)^{-1}$ which could be negative if $L' < 0$.

If $f_L < -(f' - r)F_L$, these additional terms will not change the qualitative results reported in the text. Whether labor can have a large enough impact on the rate of growth of a mature forest to cause $f_L > -(f' - r)F_L$ is an empirical issue which cannot be decided in this chapter.

[k] Since L declines with distance, fewer trees are planted. Since T increases, each tree matures longer. The fact that X increases means that the increased maturing more than compensates for the decreased planting. Thus, forests are denser at harvesting date the further one moves from the mill.

[l] This is the maximum mean annual increment discussed by Waggener.[15]

Bid Rent

Figure 9-4. A Representative Bid-Rent Curve

are in keeping with the broad philosophy of sustained yield. As will be shown the first implies a negative annual cash flow.

Equation (9-13) determines the date on which trees should be harvested in order to achieve maximum sustained yield. If contracts are then arranged on a competitive basis with private firms, the maximum amount they would be willing to bid for the privilege of harvesting an acre of land is the revenue they can make from their operation. In our model this is $p - C_x(d)$ per unit biomass harvested from land d units away from the mill.[m] Thus, as long as $p - C_x(d) \geqslant 0$ private firms will be willing to harvest trees from public lands. Under competitive bidding the extensive limit of cultivation will occur at distance d_M from the mill, where $p - C_x(d_M) = 0$. It should be obvious that d_M is greater than the competitively determined extensive limit of cultivation, d_c. A land use policy based on this definition of the working circle generates an annual cash flow of

$$[(p - C_x)F(T,L) - (w + C_L)L]/T. \tag{9-14}$$

This will be negative at d_M and at some other locations within d_M of the mill.

---

[m]If harvesting labor is included in the model, as in footnote e, the revenue per unit harvested at distance d is $p - (w + C_L(d))b - C_x(d)$.

The negative cash flow results from the fact that the private firms ignore the cost of planting new trees.

The second interpretation of the working circle is based on the assumption that the managers of public forests wish to avoid the above losses. They then choose T and L to maximize net sustained cash flow as defined by (9-14). A land use policy consistent with this goal utilizes all land which yields a non-negative cash flow. That is, all land up to a distance d_N from the mill will be used, where d_N is defined by the following equation:

$$\underset{T,L}{\text{Max}}\ [(p - C_x(d_N))F(L, T) - (w + C_L(d_N))L]/T = 0.$$

This approach leads to a less extensive use of land; that is, $d_N < d_M$.

It can also be shown that d_N is greater than d_c, the competitive and optimal extensive limit. To demonstrate this conclusion, we first note that the values of T and L generated by this policy are equivalent to the competitive result if the interest rate, r, equals zero.[n] It can be shown that as r decreases, the competitive value of land increases;[o] that is, $dV^*/dr < 0$.[p] Finally, when the interest rate is zero, competitive rent, R_0, is equal to the maximal value of the net sustained cash flow. Hence d_N, the distance at which $R_0(d_N) = 0$, is larger than d_c (see figure 9-5). Thus, even a policy of maximizing net sustained cash flow leads to a more extensive use of land for timber production than is socially desirable, assuming no externalities.

Summary and Conclusions

This chapter contains a model that combines Thunen's theory of rent and land use, which depends very considerably on transport costs, with capital the-

---

[n]The reader should recall that the competitive choices were made to maximize $pFe^{-rT} - wL - R\int_0^T e^{-rT}dt$. When $r = 0$ this is equivalent to maximizing $pF - wL - RT$, where R satisfies Max $[pF -wL - RT] = 0$. Thus when $r = 0$, L, and T are chosen under competition such that $(pF - wL)/T$ is a maximum.

[o]$dV/dr = d\left(\dfrac{R}{r}\right)/dr = r^{-2}\ [rdR/dr - R]$.

However,

$$dR/dr = -(1 - e^{-rT})^{-1}r[T(p - C_x)Fe^{-rT} + T(R/r)e^{-rT} - R(1 - e^{-rT})r^{-2}] =$$
$$-r(1 - e^{-rT})^{-1}Te^{-rT}\left[(p - C_x)F + \frac{R}{r}\right] + \frac{R}{r}\ .$$

Hence,

$$rdR/dr - R = -r(1 - e^{-rT})^{-1}Te^{-rT}[(p - C_x)F + R/r],$$

which is less than zero.

[p]Despite the fact that $dV/dr < 0$ we cannot conclude that $dR/dr < 0$ since $dR/dr = d(rV)/dr = rdV/dr + R$. The last may be positive even if $dV/dr < 0$. At the extensive limit, however, $V = R = 0$. Thus, at these locations $dV/dr < 0$ and $dR/dr < 0$.

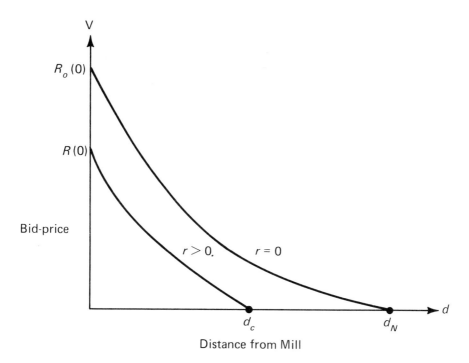

Figure 9–5. The Optimal and Zero Interest Rate Bid Rent Curves for Timber Land

ory. The model was developed for the case of forestry and focused on land use in long-run steady state competitive equilibrium. Among the results derived was the obvious one that the rental value of forestry land declines with distance from the processing mill, which was also treated as the market. In addition, as distance from the mill increases less labor is employed in clearing and planting each acre of land, and trees are permitted to grow for a longer period of time. That is, as distance from the mill increases time is substituted for labor. Finally, the farther an acre of land is from the mill, the greater is output at harvest time because the effect of time more than compensates for the smaller quantity of labor employed.

The chapter also examined some public policy issues involved in the management of public forest lands. In particular, the results of the competitive model were compared with those implied by the policy of sustained yield. We found that the latter entails a more extensive use of land for timber production. In other words, with the competitive model the working circle is smaller and more land is left in virgin forest. Sustained yield can therefore be viewed as a sub-optimum policy so far as the extensive limit of cultivation is concerned. Samuelson reached the conclusion that sustained yield allows trees to grow too long and is, therefore, a sub-optimal policy for any given acre of land, without regard to location.[q]

The conclusion that the policy of sustained yield leads to sub-optimum results is based on the observation which should be familiar to all economists, that in the absence of externalities and in the presence of accurate price expectations, competitive markets will lead decisionmakers to follow policies which are socially optimal. We do not argue that all forestry management should be turned over to the private sector and be subject to market regulation but only that the competitive outcome can be used as a benchmark to judge alternative land use policies.

Certain externality arguments can be made with regard to forests, though it should be noted that these arguments are usually made to justify the existence of forests rather than timber production. We are aware of two such arguments. One is that forested areas benefit the ecological environment through their impact on erosion and flood control, cleaner air, etc. The second is that forests are beautiful and should therefore exist. We have demonstrated that the policy of sustained yield leads to a more extensive use of land for timber production and less virgin forest than the competitive solution. In this respect consideration of externalities therefore reinforces the conclusion that sustained yield is a sub-optimum policy. On the other hand, under the competitive solution trees close to the mill may be harvested at a younger age than under sustained yield. If older trees yield more in the way of flood control or are considered more aesthetically pleasing, the externality argument may go against our conclusion. Whether it does so or not depends on the value of having more virgin forest located at a distance from the mill relative to the value of having older trees close to the mill.

---

[q]Our model leads to the conclusion that the biomass at harvest time is greater under a policy of sustained yield than under competitive conditions. From (9–7a) it follows that

$$(p - C_x)\partial F/\partial r = [(p - C_x)F + \partial R/\partial r](f' - r)^{-1}.$$

Substituting for $\partial R/\partial r$, from footnote o, yields

$$(p - C_x)\partial F/\partial r(f' - r) = [(p - C_x)F + R/r] [1 - rT(1 - e^{-rT})^{-1}e^{-rT}].$$

But

$$1 - rT(1 - e^{-rT})^{-1}e^{-rT} > 0$$

when $rT > 0$ and equals zero when $rT = 0$. Thus, since

$$f' - r < 0, \partial F/\partial r < 0.$$

We cannot conclude that this result is unambiguously due to a longer growing cycle, since it is possible for a fall in the interest rate to lead to a shorter growing cycle, with the greater biomass harvested being due to increased labor. However, if there is little substitutability between labor and time, a condition that seems empirically valid, then our model yields the Samuelson result.

Notes

1. Heinrich Johann Von Thunen, *Von Thunen's Isolated State,* trans. by Wartenberg, Carla M., ed. by Peter Hall (Edinburgh: Pergamon Press, 1966).
2. For a review of the recent literature see G.S. Goldstein and L.N. Moses, "A Survey of Urban Economics," *The Journal of Economic Literature* 11 (June 1973).
3. Robert M. Solow and William S. Vickrey, "Land Use in a Long Narrow City," *Journal of Economic Theory* 3 (December 1971): 430–447.
4. Richard F. Muth, "Economic Change and Rural-Urban Land Conversions," *Econometrica* 29 (January 1961): 1–23.
5. Edwin S. Mills, "An Aggregative Model of Resource Allocation in Metropolitan Area," *American Economic Review* 57 (May, 1967).
6. T.C. Koopmans and M. Beckmann, "Assignment Problems and the Location of Economic Activities," *Econometrica* 25 (1957): 53–76.
7. G.S. Goldstein and L.N. Moses, "Interdependence and the Location of Economic Activities," *Journal of Urban Economics* 2 (1975): 63–84.
8. E.S. Mills, *Studies in the Structure of the Urban Economy* (Baltimore: The Johns Hopkins Press, published for Resources for the Future, 1972).
9. Von Thunen, *Thunen's Isolated State,* Chapter 18.
10. Paul A. Samuelson, "Economics of Forestry in an Evolving Society," paper delivered at a symposium, *The Economics of Sustained Yield Forestry,* College of Forest Resources, University of Washington, November 1974.
11. Von Thunen, *Von Thunen's Isolated State,* p. 119.
12. For a discussion and review of this policy see T.R. Waggener, "Some Economic Implications of Sustained Yield as a Forest Regulation Model," University of Washington, Forestry Paper Contribution No. 6, 1969.
13. Ibid.
14. Samuelson, "Economics of Forestry."
15. Waggener, "Some Economic Implications," p. 9.

10 Social Policy and Uncertain Careers: Beyond Rawls's Paradigm Case

Edmund S. Phelps

> "I'm fed up with symmetry."
> from Buñuel's *Le Fantôme de la Liberté*

This chapter begins as a commentary on the neo-utilitarians' "reaction" against John Rawls.[a] One theme is the difference between the underlying concepts of justice from which Rawls and the neo-utilitarians start. Rawls's theory is addressed to the just division of the fruits of economic cooperation among productive persons, not to the wider problems of justice tilted at by utilitarianism from Bentham to the present. Another theme is the distinction between their views of the good life. Rawls takes the opportunities and chances for self-realization and personal growth to be the desiderata for justice, not the lifetime intake of commodities. The main task here has been to explain, as Rawls and other Rawlsians have tried to do, why the neo-utilitarians' solution to the problem of redistributive social policy does not fit the choice problem that is Rawls's paradigm case: In that case, individuals are born into adulthood with pre-determinedly differing advantages; given the setting of social policy and institutions, their subsequent lives are then laid out deterministically and foreseeably before them. It is therefore hard to see how the neo-utilitarians, with their axioms on behavior toward risk, provide a natural principle for the selection of redistributive measures.

But in the end this chapter succumbs to a far more intriguing question: How would neo-utilitarianism fare against "Rawls" on the neo-utilitarians' own home ground? In *their* paradigm case, all young persons from any generation begin economic life with the same endowment and tastes; in their ultimate success and enjoyment, however, there is a large element of luck. I shall argue that it is a misreading or mis-extrapolation of Rawls to impute to him, as do Samuelson and

---

My understanding of "Rawls" owes much to Columbia colleagues with whom "it" has been a chronic topic of conversation for three years. The present chapter has benefited from additional discussions with David Colander, Thomas Nagel, and Janusz Ordover.

[a]I refer particularly to the recent papers and reviews by Arrow, Harsanyi and Samuelson listed in the references.

By the term *neo-utilitarianism* I mean the use of "expected utility" for social choice as advocated first by William Vickrey in 1945, 1960, and 1961, and later expounded by J.C. Harsanyi and P.A. Samuelson.

some others, the advocacy of redistributive policies that would maximize the minimum realized lifetime utility—the ex post maximin criterion—in this setting of intra-life uncertainty. Yet a Rawlsian cannot go along with the unbridled ex-ante-ism of the neo-utilitarians even in their paradigm case. We need to follow the fortunes of people through their working lives to keep track of their conditional expectations. A 1973 research prospectus of mine glimpses the idea:

> . . . [A]n *unconditional ex ante* notion of social welfare, one which looks from the vantage point of his date of birth solely at the *expected* lifetime utility of each individual, would fail to capture some important aspects of our intuitive feelings about any society's achievement of justice or social welfare. . . . An extreme [approach] would identify social welfare with the worst (lowest) lifetime utility that will be turned into the scorekeeper as the individuals now living (and maybe their descendants) reach death. Such an ex post facto notion of minimum utility would be maximized by a *posterioristic* Rawlsian. An *a prioristic* Rawlsian might maximize the (either subjective or actual) *conditional* expectation of lifetime utility of the persons having the worst such expectation. [first and last italics added.]

The second half of this chapter is an attempt to develop the latter idea in Rawlsian terms, and to define the circumstances in which such an ex ante conditional maximin criterion would be applicable.

Rawlsian Theory in Its Paradigm Case

For simplicity we may usually assume that there are just two sorts of individuals, those born more productive and those born less—top dogs and bottom dogs.

The neo-utilitarians would engage the members of this society in a thought-experiment in which each person (1) accepts the assumption that he had as much chance of being a top dog as anyone else had, and (2) calculates for each redistributive social policy, in view of the relative frequency of top dogs and his attitudes toward risk, the mathematical expectation of the von Neuman-Morgenstern utilities he assigns to each of the two outcomes.

Whatever their full position, the neo-utilitarians then claim that redistribution should not go so far as to reduce everyone's hypothetical "expected utility" so calculated; that would obviously be Pareto inoptimal with regard to these expected utilities. Consider, in particular, that redistributive policy—we may call it the maximin policy with regard to "ex post utilities"—which goes so far as to maximize the realized well-being of actual bottom dogs (their ex post utility level). That policy clearly causes the hypothetical expected utility of any person engaging in the thought-experiment, whether the person is a top or bottom dog, to be smaller than it would be under some more mildly redistributive policy. An "exception" occurs if the person is completely risk-phobic, behaving as though he were fated to be a bottom dog; but that exception is ruled out by the neo-utilitarians' continuity axiom, according to which one will risk crossing the street for a gain on the other side if the chance of accident is sufficiently small.

The Rejection of Neo-Utilitarianism

I shall cite four objections that Rawlsians raise to this neo-utilitarian construction.

1. One objection Rawlsians raise is that the references to "expected utility" suffer from a considerable amount of logical incoherence. If I have an actuarial chance of being a top dog or a bottom dog, then whose utility function and implied risk aversion do I use in calculating "my" expected utility? The notion of averaging top dogs' and bottom dogs' respective risk aversions seems unintelligible; the idea of my entertaining the probability that I will have each person's life prospects cum *my* risk aversion (and other tastes?) seems equally fraught with difficulty. What if I opt *for* special state X on the ground that it is good for you (and I might have turned out to be you) while you oppose X on the ground that it is bad for me (and you might have been me)? Would *these* "ethical preferences" of ours merit any attention? The incapacity to deal persuasively with the diversity of attitudes toward risk has always appeared to be a serious limitation of the neo-utilitarian approach.[b]

The above difficulties over the meaning of "expected utility" notwithstanding, neo-utilitarians are still inclined evidently to pit their approach against Rawls's in the special case where every person's attitude toward risk and implied cardinal utility function is identical to every other person's over the same domain of hypothetical choices. What is said below under points 2, 3, and 4 is compatible with that specialization to identical tastes for risk (though often the assumptions are not couched so as to require that specialization).

2. Another point against neo-utilitarianism is that the willingness or unwillingness of someone (or everyone) to risk his status quo cannot realistically be regarded as independent of his position in the socioeconomic setting.

One of the industrial barons of the '20s remarked that he didn't take risks because he was rich enough not to have to. I suppose he meant relative wealth.

---

[b] A similar difficulty comes up in connection with intergenerational neo-utilitarianism. The beneficiaries of our generation's decision to make positive net investment in favor of the next generation ("we might equally have been in their shoes, so our 'expected utility' is thereby increased") might not have been willing to make such an investment themselves were they us. The next generation may be more risk-averse than we or they may be intergenerational egalitarians.

Accordingly, it is possible that the willingness of a person—hypothetically—to risk greater hardship to bottom dogs on the chance that he will turn out a top dog with still *greater* benefits is attributed in part to the value he places on additional "relative" income rather than "absolute" income. (Recall the Friedman-Savage hypothesis in this connection.)

Now it is one thing for some disinterested party to suggest that half the population sacrifice themselves so that another half could "make something" of themselves. But insofar as the utility gain to the latter group springs from the aversion to having a low *relative* living standard, the appeal to a sporting attitude seems unjustified.

3. The major Rawlsian objection is to the postulate of prenatal choice with symmetrical probabilities. Suppose the bottom dogs each ask for the maximum feasible utility—which will be less than (or equal to) the utility that top dogs are going to get. It would seem like dubious metaphysics to say to them, and a self-serving rationalization for top dogs to say, that each bottom dog had the same chance to be a top dog as each of the top dogs. It is one thing to ask a person to imagine being another person or persons. It is another thing to ask a person to suppose that in fact he might actually have been someone else with equal probability. It's a commonplace that we don't choose our parents. It is equally true that we don't select a lottery determining who our parents will be.

Note first that the particular specification according to which the equal-probabilities-for-all are *estimated* by the observable relative frequencies of top dogs and bottom dogs is totally non-operational (not that every axiom and injunction can be operational). There is no way whatever of testing it, no evidence on its behalf. The assumption seems to be motivated by the desired result. We might just as well employ the postulate that the true probabilities of being an individual of type t, $t = 1, 2, \ldots, T$, are given by $(p_1, p_2, \ldots, p_T)$, not by the relative frequencies, $(f_1, f_2, \ldots, f_T)$ appearing in a *particular sample*. We could invent more than one model in terms of which to estimate those true probabilities, but I can't see clearly which of those models is best or most natural. True, while not really knowing the true probabilities, I can always formulate my subjective probabilities. Perhaps I do this when *I have to make a decision*, in Bayesian fashion. But who I'm going to be, my birth, is not a decision to be made by me. So how can Bayesian prior probability be imputed to me?

f. Yet suppose, arguendo, we were to agree that the true probabilities are none other than the observed relative frequencies, $(f_1, f_2, \ldots, f_T)$. Thus the probability of being a bottom dog is f_b, the proportion in the current generation, and the probability of being a top dog is $1 - f_b$. A crucial question at this point seems to be: What does the willingness of anyone to gamble signify, if anything, for the distribution of utilities over persons that he would accept? Nothing, Rawlsians say.

Imagine that a teacher were to hand out special rewards and offices to those pupils whose last names were highest in the alphabetical order. To a student who complained of the injustice, would it be adequate for the teacher to reply that the pupil had as much chance of a surname beginning A as any other? Might the student not feel that "equiprobability" was irrelevant?

To quote from my earlier, 1971 NSF research proposal:

> . . . recall the problem of the two men and the cake. They agree that it would be unfair if the man who has the advantage of choosing which piece to eat—we assume non-satiation—were also allowed to cut the cake. So the other man cuts the cake, and of course he divides it equally (thus insuring himself half the cake). In the Rawls model, there are incentive effects from redistribution so that (over the interesting range) the cake is bigger the more unequally the first man cuts it. There is assuredly some sense in which it is only fair if the cutter cuts in such a way as to maximize the absolute size of the smaller piece. After all the other man will have the advantage of choosing the larger piece.
>
> Now some neo-utilitarians such as Harsanyi and Vickrey have said to the disadvantaged cake cutter, "Look, you ought to take a larger view, ontologically speaking. When God rolled the dice, you might have been selected to reap the advantage of choosing the larger piece of cake. Had you not known "who you were going to be," your role in the cake business, then surely you would have sought to maximize your *expected* utility by agreeing with the likewise ignorant second man that whoever turns out to be the cake cutter will cut the cake somewhat more unequally [thus shrinking the smaller piece] . . . rather than [to maximize] *ex post* cake-cutter's utility.
>
> To this the cake cutter might well reply, "What dice? What God? I know for a fact that the other fellow has the advantage, the opportunity to take the larger share of the cake. The probability that it is the other way around looks like zero to me."

Let me try again to dispel the alleged connection between acceptance of dispersion in one's own utilities and acceptance of the same dispersion in utilities across different persons. Suppose that I am a risk-lover to the extent that, in preference to the certainty of having the maximin level of utility, I would *if given the choice* opt for the probability mixture of grinding poverty, of quasi-starvation, with probability f_b and the associated improved level of well-being of top dogs with probability $1 - f_b$. By what additional postulates and argumentation is it implied that I would accept as just or satisfactory that a proportion of the people equal to f_b who are bottom dogs, through no choice of gamble of their own, should suffer quasi-starvation for the sake of the associated gain of the remaining proportion $1 - f_b$? It would not seem that the mere fact that I (and every bottom dog) would *risk* the comfort afforded by maximum minimum utility for the probability $1 - f_b$ of having a better-than maximin level of top-dog utility should signal our willingness to impose this level of misery with certainty on the persons who are predetermined to have the bottom-dog position. The chance that bottom dogs would be willing to take to have a top-dog well-being hardly seems to be a justification for making bottom dogs more miserable than they actually need be (*would* be under maximin).

Rawls's Conception and the Neo-utilitarians' Reaction

Rawls's position, of course, is that the relative number of top dogs ought to have nothing to do with the degree to which the welfare of any single bottom dog is traded off, if at all, for that of a top dog. The maximin allocation displays precisely that invariance to relative numbers. Consider two economies in which the maximin level of utility is equal, but in economy A the relative number of top dogs, $1 - f_b^A$, exceeds that in economy B, $1 - f_b^B$. Rawls asks why the bottom dogs in the two economies should be accorded different utilities, when the maximin allocation of utilities would be identical, merely because of the natural accident and irrelevant detail that they are, say, a smaller minority in economy A. To argue otherwise smacks of "numerical superiority makes right."

To aid in deciding what is a just redistributive arrangement, Rawls argues, a person will want to ascend figuratively to the "original position" where "behind the veil of ignorance" he does not know which type of person ($t = 1, 2, \ldots, n$) he is cast to play in the society below. Of course, the idea of the original position, with its dramatization of the notion of impartiality, Rawls has taken from the neo-utilitarians, but he takes little else. In particular, neither the respective probabilities of being of each type nor any information about the relative frequencies of each type at any particular place and moment are divulged to occupants of the Rawlsian original position. In this way it is insured that reflections on the degree to which one type's utility will be traded off for another type's will not be contaminated by information of relative numbers.

Rawls then asserts that most or all individuals, if placed in that original position of actuarial ignorance, would in fact select a *maximin* strategy. They would agree to be bound by a Constitution requiring that the institutions, laws, and social policies in the society they will actually inhabit be dedicated to maximizing the well-being or opportunities of those persons who are least advantaged —who will have "least utility" in utilitarian terms. Some readers remain "non-Rawlsian" because they balk, or hesitate, over this last step. There is no a priori way to *decide*—as distinct from *illuminate*—this issue.

But the neo-utilitarians stubbornly remain non-Rawlsian because they refuse to play his game. They are irrepresible about saying to Rawls what they have been saying for quite some time, as though they had not been heard before, namely: An occupant of the original position ought to consider being a non-bottom type and maximize some corresponding "expected utility." And Rawls will say again that the occupant cannot be expected to know the true probabilities of being of this or that type and that, even if the probabilities were known, one's willingness and everyone else's to exchange one distribution of own-utilities for another riskier one does not justify exchanging the *maximin* distribution of sure-thing utilities over persons for a more *unequal* distribution of sure-thing utilities when people's relative advantages at earning utility in any social state are in fact predetermined and thus not actually the first-stage outcome of some super-lottery purchased by people who were initially equals.

However, the neo-utilitarians rebut, one in the original position must acknowledge *some* positive probability of being of each type $t = 1, 2, \ldots, n$, hence some positive chance of being of non-bottom type under the maximin policy; for otherwise to what end were we to imagine being of each type there in the original position? Why not then "take a chance" that one will not be a bottom type? Why be "so pessimistic" as to opt for the maximin redistributive social policy? So demand Arrow, Harsanyi, and Samuelson.

One answer to that, I should think, is that no particular counterproposal to the maximin strategy has so far been proposed. It is true, however, that one might imagine each person taking a degree of chance according to his "optimism," "sunniness," or whatever. So we must finally let the issue be decided "behaviorally," by whatever risks people do decide to take in choice situations of total ignorance. But until we have more evidence of choice-behavior in such situations it remains plausible, as it seemed to Rawls, that a person, or most persons, would choose the maximin position.

A related quarrel of the neo-utilitarians with the maximin point is based on cases where the utility-feasibility-curve is smooth. In the two-dimensional top-dog/bottom-dog case, one thinks of the point of maximum minimum utility as being fairly "flat." Hence a tiny sacrifice by bottom dogs would reap a much larger gain by the already better-off top dogs in the maximin position. That situation is illustrated by the diagram in figure 10–1 used by Rawls himself. With some assumption about the proportion of the population who are top dogs one can represent the classical utilitarian solution, at W, and the maximin solution, at R. The utilitarians' average utility is measured along the vertical axis along with minimum (bottom-dog) utility. The latter is at a maximum at R and the former achieves a maximum at W.

In a moment I will respond to this quarrel with Rawls in its above, rather unspecific or general form. But let me first deal with a special version of the quarrel that has sometimes been brought up by way of an example. I quote first from Arrow:

> . . . [the maximin theory] . . . implies that any benefit, no matter how small, to the worst-off member of society will outweigh any loss to a better-off individual, provided it does not reduce the second below the level of the first. Thus, there can easily exist medical procedures which serve to keep people barely alive but with little satisfaction and which

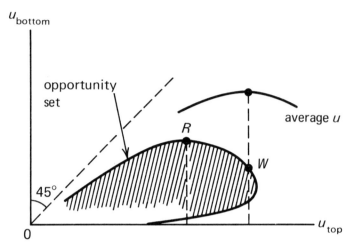

Figure 10-1. Utilitarian and Rawlsian Solutions

are yet so expensive as to reduce the rest of the population to poverty. A maximin principle would apparently imply that such procedures be adopted.

Harsanyi makes the same criticism:

> Even more disturbing is the fact that the difference principle [meaning the maximin principle (au.)] would require us to give *absolute* priority to the interests of the worst-off individual, *no matter what,* even under the most extreme conditions. Even if his interests were affected only in a very minor way, and all other individuals in society had opposite interests of the greatest importance, his interests would always override anybody else's. For example, let us assume that society would consist of a large number of individuals, of whom one would be seriously mentally retarded. Suppose that some extremely expensive treatment would become available which could slightly improve the retarded individual's condition; but the costs would be so high that this treatment could be financed only if some of the most brilliant individuals were deprived of all higher education. The difference principle would require that the retarded individual should all the same receive this very expensive treatment at any event—*no matter how many* people would have to be denied a higher education, and *no matter how strongly* they would desire to obtain one (and no matter how great the satisfaction they would obtain from it).

Actually Harsanyi nearly undermines his case with overstatement. First, a maximin strategy by the state must give a wide amount of latitude to people's ambitions, must allow them nourishing mouthfuls from the invisible hand, if the state is to come up with enough tax revenue to provide maximum support to the bottom groups; unlike the earlier egalitarians, Rawls would harness inequalities and ambition in the name of the least advantaged in that competitive race. Second, if talented scientists and artists were in fact frustrated from acting upon their drives for realization and success, it might very well be them who would be recognized the least favored, most blocked, bottom group; I am sure that Rawls does not mean to fill up the mental wards for the sake of an increase in the motor skills of retardates.

Yet everyone reading Rawls must have wondered at some point or other how he would treat persons whose functioning in and contribution to society are precluded by physical and emotional handicaps. And there is the stickier question of how to treat persons whose impairments place them at the margin of participation in society and its economic activity. Does Rawls envision a state in which the catastrophically disadvantaged are a sink draining off most of available government revenue save for what is deemed necessary to provide incentives for the productive? And if not, how is his position consistent with his endorsement of maximin?

Rawls's oft-cited direct answer rests on the appeal to Kant's principle that people should "treat one another not as means only but as ends in themselves" (p. 179). The answer, couched in the code-words of Kant, has proved too epigrammatic for us economists to understand. But there are enough clues elsewhere in the book for us to be able to figure out Rawls's position.

Rawls's book does not present a general theory of justice, whatever that might mean. It is a theory of social justice, not of justice in all interpersonal transactions. And it is a *special* theory of social justice at that, for it presents only a notion of "economic justice" toward the members of society who can contribute productively to society's "income"—to the vector of satisfactions, achievements, growth of the persons belonging to society.

That this is Rawls's concern and not some wider one embracing unproductive humans, other sentient beings, or indeed even foreigners is made explicit early in the book:

> Let us assume that a society is a more or less self-sufficient association
> of persons who in their relations to one another recognize certain rules
> of conduct as binding and who for the most part act in accordance with
> them. Suppose further that these rules specify a system of cooperation
> designed to advance the good of those taking part in it. Then, although
> a society is a cooperative venture for mutual advantage, it is typically
> marked by a conflict as well as by an identify of interests . . . since per-
> sons are not indifferent as to how the greater benefits produced by their
> collaboration are distributed, for in order to pursue their ends they each
> prefer a larger to a lesser share. A set of principles is required for choos-
> ing among the various social arrangements which determine this division
> of advantages and for underwriting an agreement on proper distributive
> shares. These principles are the principles of social justice: they provide
> a way of assigning rights and duties in the basic institutions of society

and they define the appropriate distribution of the benefits and burdens
of social cooperation (p. 4).

I shall be satisfied if it is possible to formulate a reasonable conception of justice for the basic structure of society conceived for the time
being as a closed system isolated from other societies. The significance
of this special case is obvious and needs no explanation (p. 8).

Justice as fairness is not a complete contract theory. For it is clear
that the contractarian idea can be extended to the choice of more or
less an entire ethical system, that is, to a system including principles for
all the virtues and not only for justice. Now for the most part I shall
consider only principles of justice. . . . Obviously, if justice as fairness
succeeds reasonably well, a next step would be to study the more
general view suggested by the name 'rightness as fairness'. But even this
wider theory fails to embrace all moral relationships, since it would
seem to include only our relations with other persons and to leave out
of account how we are to conduct ourselves toward animals and the
rest of nature (p. 17).

Later in the book, Rawls repeatedly nominates the unskilled worker and his representative expectations as our referent in thinking about the least favored or
bottom group (pp. 78, 96, 98). Never does Rawls identify the least-favored as
consisting of those who are critically impaired from contributing to society, particularly its economy.

So we are to consider a closed society in which a type like the Beatles have
a contribution to social product to make. Less dependably, so does a type like
the Fellows of the Econometric Society. Strong-back types contribute who only
haul their trash. Provided that a manual-labor type can contribute more to total
product when cooperating with the other types of persons in the organized
economy (the market sector, if you like) than that type can produce in isolation
from the organized economy, his utility is one of those utilities which is qualified
for maximin treatment. If there be persons whose faculties are so limited that
their "cooperation" in the organized economy would fail to give rise to a gain
from trade, so that their participation could not make either themselves or
others better off, then those persons are evidently not eligible for "economic"
justice and, in particular, for maximin treatment. These dependents of society
certainly have our moral concern; but their claim is to our sympathy or pity or
some wider sense of right, not to economic justice.

It is an essential feature of this view that no type of person will be expected
to receive less than what that type could produce and consume, that is, achieve,
on its own, without benefit of social cooperation. Indeed, Rawls envisions that
each person will maximize his utility from 9 to 5, subject only to some self-
enforced constraints on law-abidingness and other civic and business ethics.

A difficulty that appears in this respect is that as soon as an individual edges
over the threshold to participation in the social economy, he is at once likely to
be the recipient of substantial support by the state. Because of this unwelcome

discontinuity, it becomes important where the line is drawn between contribu-
tors and non-contributors to society's production. The line becomes hard to
draw if the state's heavy redistribution of the gains of trade in favor of the least
favored has the unavoidable side-effect of actually inducing some of the beneficiaries to withdraw their labor from the organized economy. Rawls regards the
problem of defining the least-favored group or groups—at any degree of redis-
tributiveness, let us say—as a "serious difficulty" (p. 98). But evidently Rawls
does not regard that problem as a fatal weakness of the difference principle, that
is, the maximin criterion.

It would not seem, however, that various types of people would be allowed
to form coalitions against other types. To do so would be to permit the coalition
to appropriate to itself some of the producers' surplus, or gains from trade, in a
way that seems close to their expelling the others from the society; but perhaps
it can sometime be shown that federations within a larger society, if only for
consideration in some hypothetical reasoning, would be of ethical interest.

In this connection one thinks of international justice. If a rich country
should discover a poorer country with which it can profitably trade, is the former
then obligated to *maximin* over each individual utility within the two societies as
if they were now one society? Or is the richer country obliged only to give away
the gains from the trade to the poorer country—which it would do if the poor
country is too small to affect the larger country's relative prices, and the large
country does not think to play monopolist with the terms of trade—as if the rich
country were like a type of person in the closed society? Perhaps a national
coalition is permissible provided it is not exploitive toward others.

Rawls's position seems to be that taken earlier by Koopmans—that the
principles of social choice cannot be established completely independently of the
structure of the choices available. Every principle may be found to have tough
sledding over some terrain or other. Presumably neo-utilitarians stand ready to
amend their criterion in the event it implies enslavement for a few individuals or
a national dividend for cats and dogs. If the neo-utilitarians turn a deaf ear to the
possibility that the last inch toward *their* optimum—say, maximum average
utility or the maximum of some quasi-concave social welfare function of individual utilities—would cause substantial suffering to the least well-off, then how
can they fairly turn the same "paradox" against the Rawlsian extreme under
which at least it can be said that the sufferers are those better off than the gainers?

Toward a Rawlsian Theory for the
Neo-Utilitarians' Case

I have been discussing my understanding of Rawls's theory with reference to
the paradigm case for which it was designed. In that case, given the social structure with its various institutions and governmental redistributions, one sees one's

whole opportunity set laid out before one at the outset of adulthood. At that age, one's fate is predetermined and known. There is no mid-life lottery, either optional or mandated. However, there are some hints in Rawls's *Justice* of how certain kinds of risks or uncertainties might be treated, and we are free to venture our own extrapolations.

The most logical exposition would deal first with the neo-utilitarians' paradigm case, where every young adult's ex ante lifetime prospects is like every other's and only the ex post experiences differ, and thence on to the mixed or general case where both ex ante and ex post well-being (to use the old shorthand) are heterogeneous. However there is another dimension—whether the mid-life hazards are unavoidable, inescapable uncertainties or whether they are voluntarily assumed.

Inescapable Hazards

It might seem at first that it should make no difference for Rawls's theory whether a person's natural disadvantages are known at the beginning of adulthood or whether they occur with a delay. Better to be partially paralyzed later than sooner, a "Rawlsian" might reflect, but no issue of principle is affected. If those handicapped at birth deserve a certain type of aid by the state to assist them in leading productive lives, then those handicapped later in life deserve the same aid—with minor allowance perhaps for the relatively fulfilled youths of the latter.

But neo-utilitarians who conceded that Rawls had a point when dealing with his paradigm case—the configuration of natural disadvantages were not actually insured against in acts of pre-natal choice, so it seems misplaced to inject the rhetoric of tolerance toward risks—might balk at the suggestion that young people must pay the full *maximin* insurance premiums against mid-life calamities when each young person, knowing the risks, would rather take a greater chance that he will be among the lucky ones.

Rawls's *Justice* does not give any clear evidence of how he would come out on this question. The repeated references to the "representative person" among less-favored groups and to the "representative expectations" of various types of people seem intended to evoke the notion of average ex ante lifetime prospects of the members in the group. I know of no passage in the book suggesting that unskilled manual workers, for example, are to define their prospects as those of the unluckiest persons among them. If every type of person in Rawls's scheme can point to one or more victims of some future calamity, though it is not known which member of the type will be a victim, then the purpose of the typing in terms of the "unskilled worker" and so on seems to be lost; every socioeconomic group will have its catastrophic cases, which are much alike.

Let me give one example of an economic model to which it is quite doubtful that Rawls would apply the maximin criterion to ex post lifetime utilities. All people in society live for just one period. They till the soil at the beginning of the period and harvest the crops and consume at the end. There is no carryover of people or capital into the next period. We take the symmetrical case where every person has the same opportunity set and same tastes, hence the same expected (lifetime) utility. Yet it is predictable that bad luck, in the form of floods and drought, will strike some producers, causing an ultimate inequality in ex post before-redistribution incomes across producers. To take an extreme case, corresponding to every allocation of labor in the (identical) "islands" of this society there is a *known* frequency distribution of crop yields across the islands—as if Nature were sampling without replacement. For example, it is known that one-tenth the islands will have half the crops of the other nine-tenths, but it is not known of course which islands will comprise the unlucky tenth.

I find nothing in Rawls's *Justice* to imply that these islanders would, upon original-position reflection, contract to redistribute the aggregate harvest in such a way as to maximize the minimum after-redistribution consumption across islands. These islanders don't need the original position, they are already in it. They all start out as equals, so there is no problem of partiality, and the probabilities of bad luck are actually known (by hypothesis) and can in actual fact be acted upon before the luck of the draw. The probabilities do not have to be postulated retrospectively and imagined to have been acted upon in a hypothetical prior choice.

So it seems to me to be tenably Rawlsian to say that maximin justice has already by accident been realized in this society and it is up to the islanders to decide on the degree of redistribution of ex post harvests in whatever way they (unanimously) prefer; in particular, if they want to maximize expected utility and are not risk phobic (thus, satisfy the continuity axiom), and hence make a compact for less-than-maximin-redistribution to islands with bad crops, it is not unjust toward those who turn out to be unlucky that they do so. Provided that drought would not reduce his well-being below some "social minimum," a person's bad luck would not have prevented him for living the "good life." There is no call to fuss over how the aggregate harvest is divided.

What say the neo-utilitarians? They would advocate that people "insure" against low ex post utility by the payment of premiums—up to the point dictated by their risk-aversion. And they would "prove" that the maximin criterion goes too far. Yet it might be doubted that each islander would *necessarily* have preferences toward frequency distributions of ex post utility across persons that are identical to (and hence derivable simply from) his preferences toward probability distributions of his own utility—even if he knew that all other persons had his preferences toward own-utility distributions. Neo-utilitarianism does not prove the connection between the two sets of preferences, it postulates the connection. I see nothing contradictory about people's being inequality-averse (concave SWFs) while not being risk-averse. So it would not be *irrational,* I believe, if the islanders of the above model *were* to opt for maximin with regard to ex post utilities if that is what they felt like doing.

People's expected utilities are in part a function of the processes, morals, and manners they learn and select among. They may take (utility-enhancing) pride in the cultivation and practice of these traits independently of the terminal consumption of bundles of goods which it gains them or costs them. In this respect, then, the neo-utilitarian theory of the compact which would be made by the islanders—at least the theory in its standard form with egoistic utility functions—is not likely to be descriptive of the social insurance and contingent redistribution compacts that real societies are observed to make. The neo-utilitarian theory is best regarded as an analytical device for rather special situations, such as the model I have just been discussing, in which one would like to be able to say (possibly for some prescriptive purpose), "Even a society of rugged individualists would contract for redistribution of this kind and amount. . . ." It is less effective as a device for deriving propositions like "Rugged individualists who are not risk-phobic would not redistribute by more than that."

Various other modifications of the above model further undermine the neo-utilitarian approach to ex post utilities—where, by that approach, I mean the viewpoint that a person should prefer the "progressive" tax legislation which maximizes his "expected utility."

First, the above model makes the proportion of islands which are going to have a bad harvest a certain fraction which is known universally and deterministically. What if the proportion of islands that will be struck by hurricanes at harvest time is not deterministic but is instead "determinable" only statistically "up to a random white-noise variable with zero mean and other known moments"? If the incidence of hurricanes is above-average, should the islands which are spared send no more food to the unlucky islands than is stipulated by the income-tax legislation which all risk-averting islands agreed upon at the beginning of the period? True, the islanders could draw up redistributive contracts which have contingency clauses to allow for deviations from the mean experience. But such contingent compacts are not a part of neo-utilitarianism.

Second, the problem becomes more Rawlsian once we grant that there is a great variety of catastrophes that can befall us, and the incidence of each tends to rise or fall in ways that were not predicted. So it is grossly unrealistic to say to victims that they could have insured themselves when young, either privately or through public legislation.

Here the neo-utilitarians might reply that the possibility of some unanticipated disasters (or unanticipatable probability of distributions of disaster) does not prevent us from making distinctions according to the degree of insurability. There are certain kinds of risks which, being well-known and presumably constant from year or to, people ought to be left free to insure against by less than the maximin amount; while no island should have to suffer a reduction of its terminal consumption below the maximin level because of a Krakatoa-like explosion or something else never witnessed before. But whatever a neo-utilitarian might feel intuitively about the right way for these islanders to treat Krakatoa-like events whose probabilities are inestimable, I believe it is fair to say that neo-utilitarian theory does not present us with a solution to this problem that is agreed upon by the neo-utilitarians themselves.

Let me now turn to a different model: Overlapping generations have different mid-life fortunes. In view of Rawls's strictures that justice in his sense is owed only to productive, potentially working individuals, let us focus our attention on the coexistence of workers of two ages, disregarding ex-workers now in retirement. For simplicity I maintain at this point our stipulation that all *young* workers have the same ex ante lifetime prospects—in the sense that no young worker is predictably better advantaged than another at the outset of their respective working lives.

Imagine that all thirty-year-olds, though they had the same ex ante prospects as twenty-year olds, have suffered some serious privation owing to a natural disaster, an unprovoked invasion, an economic depression, or whatnot. As a result, let us suppose, the thirty-year-olds are less productive than the twenty-year-olds' expectation of *their* productivity when *they* reach thirty. The question I raise is how the redistributive compacts made by a society of these twenty-year-olds and thirty-year-olds ought to take account of the bad luck of thirty-year-olds.[c]

Now the twenty-year-olds might reply to the thirty-year-old petitioners: "Why didn't you enact (or continue) legislation providing social insurance against misfortunes such as you have experienced? Where are the public entitlements to the state aid that you now claim?" But that position would surely be unjust.[d]

A rejoinder that I have been outlining to this point is that misfortunes come in such varied and novel guises that a generation cannot be expected to anticipate all the contingencies that may befall their members and to enact social insurance programs appropriate to each one of them. Even after the event, we

---

[c]I am not conjuring up a case in which current thirty-year-olds have suffered a loss of first-decade candy, pure and simple. However much a neo-utilitarian might fret over such a problem, it is doubtful that Rawls would worry much over it. The problem posed is that by natural or social accident the thirty-year-olds have suffered a setback in their productivity, their opportunities for achievement and self-realization in relation to the normal projection. After some reasonable correction for their different stages in the life cycle, the thirty-year-olds now find themselves to be disadvantaged relative to twenty-year-olds.

[d]The twenty-year-olds might also be tempted to demand, "What did you thirty-year-olds do for thirty-year-olds when *you* were twenty?". But if each generation of twenty-year-olds refused to do justice to survivors from earlier generations simply because there was no precedent for it, each such generation would find itself in the same boat later. Justice to older generations would never get off the ground. (In some situations the younger generations may have a game-theoretic motive to start the ball rolling, whatever the "requirements" of their conception of justice to the old.)

sometimes do not know "what hit us"—which contingency to ascribe our condition to. There is some element of uninsurability, therefore. Moreover, the existence of public entitlements on the books could hardly be a sufficient condition for meeting the thirty-year-olds' petitions—they could easily have legislated themselves onto easy street at the expense of twenty-year-olds if their legislated entitlements were sure to be paid out—and this even if the thirty-year-olds could demonstrate that they had treated their elders, allowing for different circumstances, in the "same way" they were asking to be treated now.

There is a second rejoinder, once we admit that each fresh generation consists of members with heterogeneous lifetime prospects. I come back to a point I emphasized earlier: What if those persons, particularly new entrants, who are least advantaged within their generation tend to be least risk-averse (or most risk-seeking) precisely because of their unfavorable socioeconomic position? These least advantaged among the young might prefer to take certain chances, but does that give them the right to deny assistance to older persons who, owing to their same disadvantaged situation, took similar gambles and lost? Current thirty-year-olds are actual people, not just hypothetico-probabilistic thirty-year-olds that twenty-year-olds reckon they may possibly become.

What, the reader must be demanding impatiently, is the "Rawlsian" approach to the problem of intergeneration justice that I posed? Of course, I cannot speak for all Rawlsians, let alone Rawls himself, nor for that matter any Rawlsian other than myself. And the solution "for me" I see now only in hazy outline.

One Rawlsian principle that ought, presumably, to remain intact is this: In deciding upon the program of public assistance to be accorded to twenty-year-olds and the (unlucky) thirty-year-olds, the way we trade off between aid to a person from one group and aid to a person from the other group ought not to depend upon the relative numbers of persons belonging to the two groups. A twenty-year-old should not count for more in relation to a thirty-year-old merely because population is booming (or, even, is optimally booming) so there are more of the former types than the latter.

Second, Rawls's maximin principle also retains considerable appeal if what counts in the "min function" is not the duration of time over which one feels "realized" or "successful" but, rather, the opportunity to achieve "self-realization" or "personal success," the chances of reaching it, and the actuality of reaching it. In that case, the maximin principle does not "favor" the old on the ground that they have so little time left just as it does not "favor" the young merely on the ground that they have a longer life-span ahead of them. *Maximin* means maximizing the smaller of the two probabilities of success—those of twenty- and thirty-year-olds, given appropriate provision for future generations. Thus, the probability of success offered twenty-year-olds should be increased by age-free government programs only up to the point that there is also a gain in the probability of success thereby offered to thirty-year-olds, assuming that the thirty-year-olds will have the lesser chance under the maximin social policy. And insofar as middle-aged-favoring policies are feasible which pull the probability of success of the thirty-year-olds toward the success-probability of twenty-year-olds, these programs should be adopted up to the point of equality.[e]

Discretionary Gambles

Consider first some symmetrical cases beloved of neo-utilitarians. Everyone has identical productivities and identical preferences at least with regard to sure-thing commodity bundles. Whatever this society's economic policy, sure-thing prospects are equal over persons and, if attitudes toward risk are also identical, so are persons' expected utilities.

Some or all individuals in this society will want to take certain risks—climb a mountain, speculate on the bourse, plant a riskier crop for a higher average yield, and so on. What is a "just" social policy toward such risk-takings and their outcomes? Should the government share in the gains and losses? Rescue gamblers from all losses? Prohibit some or all risk-taking?

Rawls's position, to repeat my understanding of it, involves his notion of the good life, his emphasis upon the opportunities for self-realization as distinct from the realization of some final bundle of commodities. One's ex post utility in the neo-utilitarians' sense had little or no significance. It is hard to say what minimizing the worst misfortune would mean in a model of any generality; there is no way for the state to guarantee continued life nor continued productivity, thus guarantee any *deterministic* lifetime utility. The prospect of achieving self-realization may require the individuals' acceptance of certain risks that ought not to be removed by the state. If the government were to tax so heavily the rewards from successful explorations and risk-taking as to maximize the floor below which the unsuccessful outcomes would not fall, then there might result such a decline of risk-taking that people would feel their lives to be meaningless, with insufficient challenge and chances, *win or lose.* There is nothing in Rawls's *Justice* to suggest that his conception of the just society boils down to choosing that social policy which maximizes the smallest realized individual income after governmental transfers.

It should be mentioned too that even if Rawls's criterion *were* the ex post maximin utility criterion, that would not imply that Rawls's society would tax away the total winnings from the acceptance of risks, thus killing off the incentives to take risks. People's willingness to take some risks, like their willingness to work or save, are like resources potentially for the benefit of all. If the least fortunate got only their national dividends, their lump-sum demogrants, and

---

[e]Age-specific transfer programs are easily instituted; there is no reason why demogrants should be equalized for persons of all ages. But age-specific expenditure programs to develop skills might often be cumbersome to legislate and administer.

minimum ex post utility were a function of only those poll subsidies, then a society bent on maximizing minimum ex post utility would not want to discourage the taking of all business risks; to do so would cost the society some national income and cost the government some of the revenue with which to pay the national dividend.

But while Rawls's conception of justice countenances certain kinds of risk-taking, and does not maximize ex post utility in the neo-utilitarians' sense of that term, there are some respects in which, I suppose, Rawls would differ from the neo-utilitarians over the matter of ex post eventualities. Some of these differences I have already raised in the previous section: Not all misfortunes are like business risks, the probability distributions being known; hence some misfortunes are more like natural accidents, unanticipatable and uninsurable, than ordinary bad luck. Some misfortunes leave the productivities and remaining lifetime prospects of survivors impaired, so that social policy must confront a particular set of present actualities, not simply prepare for certain future possibilities; my grappling with this problem will be recalled.

There are, in addition, some distinctive attitudes usually shown toward voluntary gambles that should be considered. Let us try to abstract from those kinds of voluntary risks which are in some sense socially productive and which the state wishes to a degree to encourage. There remain a variety of other risks like swimming without lifeguards, traveling great distances for vacations by car or plane, using tobacco or alcohol or other drugs, and so on. An attitude sometimes displayed toward the casualties of such risk-taking is, "You made your bed, now lie in it." Of course, it is not always clear that a strategy or life-style followed by a person is really riskier for him than another strategy, given his particular emotional makeup. To frighten a person from taking certain risks might be riskier for him than to sanction his taking those risks. But let that pass.

It seems fairly clear, however, that that attitude is inappropriate except in regard to behavior toward risk which is in some sense aberrant. Obviously it would be somehow ill-becoming for the parents of a normal child to say to the parents of a defective child that the latter should not have taken the chance when the former took the same chance. It is a little more understandable that those persons who have shied away from taking a certain risk should complain at being taxed for the benefit of those who took the risk and got themselves into trouble as a result: Let those who gambled and won pay the tax, if any must pay. But political arrangements of such a contractarian nature may be too complicated to enact—there are too many contingencies, some unimagined, and too great a variety or risks accepted. Further, everyone has his particular vices; more precisely, there are few persons who could show that their risk-avoidance was greater than another person's across the board. So the fact that some persons can show they have not and will not run the particular risk in question is of doubtful significance for their just obligations toward those who are the casualties of that risk.

Concluding Remarks

I have tried to explain, in the first half of this chapter, why neo-utilitarianism is not relevant to the problem of distributive justice upon which Rawls focused. The neo-utilitarians seem to do their interesting idea a disservice when they try to stretch its application to Rawls's problem.

The harder question, struggled with in the second half of this chapter, is what Rawls's insights have to suggest for the solution to the problem that the neo-utilitarians presumably had in mind—homogeneous prospects plus luck. My suggestion, that something like the maximin criterion with regard to *chances* for self-realization holds good in the neo-utilitarians' setting, is a quite tentative, rather wooly, and not fully-worked idea. One worries that, insofar as some discretionary gambles are available, the institution of that criterion might be abused by excessive risk-taking of certain kinds. But I am not sure that the "costliness" of the maximin criterion—in terms of average well-being maybe—should be decisive against it, just as the "disincentive effects" (dead-weight loss) of maximin taxation is not decisive. Perhaps the best answer, and I do mean "perhaps," to moral hazard is moral restraint.

I stipulated earlier that these latter suggestions of mine are extrapolations from Rawls, not explicit in his work. I suspect the same will be true of most thoughts in welfare theory for a decade or more. Rawls should not be held responsible for them, yet in a sense he is responsible. The mark of a great book is that it is a source-book for new ideas and a provocation for further ideas. I doubt that we shall see, and doubt that we could digest, another like it for quite some time.

References

Arrow, K.J. "Some Ordinalist-Utilitarian Notes on Rawls's Theory of Justice." *The Journal of Philosophy* 70 (1973): 245–263.

Harsanyi, J.C., "Cardinal Utility in Welfare Economics and in the Theory of Risk-Taking." *Journal of Political Economy* 61 (1953): 434–435.

Harsanyi, J.C. "Cardinal Welfare, Individualistic Ethics, and Interpersonal Comparisons of Utility." *Journal of Political Economy* 63 (1955): 309–321.

Harsanyi, J.C. "Can the 'Maximin' Principle Serve as a Basis for Morality?" *American Political Science Review* (1974).

Rawls, J. *A Theory of Justice,* Harvard University Press, Cambridge, Mass., 1971.

Samuelson, P.A. "A.P. Lerner at 60." *Review of Economic Studies* 31 (1964): 169–178.

Samuelson, P.A. "Optimal Compacts for Redistribution," in R.E. Grieson, ed., *Public and Urban Economics: Essays in Honor of William S. Vickrey* (Lexington Books, Lexington, Mass. 1976), pp. 179–190.

Vickrey, W.S. "Measuring Marginal Utility by Reactions to Risk." *Econometrica* 13 (1945): 319–333.

Vickrey, W.S. "Utility, Strategy, and Social Decision Rules." *Quarterly Journal of Economics* 74 (1960): 507–535.

Vickrey, W.S. "Risk, Utility, and Social Policy." *Social Research,* 1961.

11 Optimal Compacts for Redistribution

Paul A. Samuelson

A Theory of Justice by John Rawls (1971) has revived attention to concepts of "fairness" in welfare economics. It has also, by so to speak unnecessary co-incidence, brought back notions of minimaxing. I personally would consider it "unfair" if, under some banner of "fairness," people were forced into doing something none of them wants to do—such as acting in accordance with a mini-max principle. Sketched here are some strong, special cases in which minimaxing would appear to be definitely bad: this would seem to provide a counterexample to it as a *general* principle.

Within the realm of two-person, zero-sum von Neumann games, each of two ideally perfect players will find minimaxing not unattractive. But it was an act of desperation for statisticians of Wald's generation to try to base a system of decision making under uncertainty on minimaxing one's "possible loss." To be-lieve that Nature is an implacable enemy who will attempt to do you in is as good a definition of paranoia as any: Nature, I daresay, is too busy to concern herself so with little old you. Moreover, if the doctrine owes its appeal to your radical skepticism about your ability to form prior probability or plausibility judgments, following that radical skepticism to its logical conclusion will lead to morbid indifference: if no outcome can be ruled out as impossible, then there is no action you can take that will prevent the worst from happening. If, however, you do have some cogent way of separating events into those that can be speci-fied as "impossible" and those "possible," you have already taken the biggest qualitative leap, from which it is a small step to positing quantitative differ-ences in your personal beliefs about the "probabilities" of different events (their "betabilities" in the Ramsey sense.)

Notions of "fairness" can sometimes seem to point toward policies and atti-tudes that twentieth century intellectuals, a fairly well-defined object of anthropologists' studying, generally think of as "conservative" or even "reaction-ary." The minimax principle—whatever its true and intrinsic relation to those symmetry principles that, on sophisticated analysis, "justice" and "fairness" seem to boil down or degenerate to—may provide the opiate or placebo needed by the intellectual who wishes to avoid being reactionary. Thus, minimaxing can lead to egalitarian taxation, an obvious good thing. What is not always realized,

Financial aid from the National Science Foundation is gratefully acknowledged. I have benefited from discussions with Kenneth Arrow, but I fear he still regrets some of my rejec-tions of minimax regret.

179

minimaxing can lead to too much of what seemed like a good thing—even from the viewpoint of a non-conservative concerned with the good.

Regardless of its relationship to Rawlsian concerns, the following analysis has significance in its own right as an excursion into the theory of optimal redistributive taxation and of revealed preferences among social compacts.

Scenario for a Social Compact

Persons $1, 2, \ldots, n$ contemplate forming a compact to determine how their respective non-negative real incomes $(X_1, \ldots, X_n)$ are to be taxed.[a] Each ith person has a concave von Neumann utility function, $u_i[X_i]$, whose expected value he acts to maximize in any stochastic situation. These utility functions need not agree: thus $u_i[X_i]$ may show more or less risk aversion than $u_j[X_i]$, as in the cases $u_i = \log X_i$, $u_j = X_j^{1/2}$; but always $u_i''[X_i] < 0$.

No person knows what his actual pre-tax income will turn out to be. But each person has reason to believe (or, in alternative scenarios, is convinced that he has such reason) that there is a joint probability distribution that will govern the $(X_1, \ldots, X_n)$ outcomes:

$$\text{Prob}\left\{X_1 \leqslant x_1, \ldots, X_n \leqslant x_n \,|\, i\text{'s beliefs}\right\} = P_i(x_1, \ldots, x_n). \quad (11\text{-}1)$$

If there is a true, objective-frequency probability distribution that obtains, and each person's subjective (or personal, or Bayesian) probability agrees with it, then each $P_i(\ )$ and $P_j(\ )$ will be identical, say

$$P_i(x_1, \ldots, x_n) \equiv P(x_1, \ldots, x_n), \, (i = 1, \ldots, n) . \quad (11\text{-}2)$$

But we are free to reject (11-2)'s special case and to stick with the more general case of different subjective probabilities.

An important model is that in which each probability distribution is assumed to be *symmetric,* namely

$$P_i(x_1, x_2, \ldots) \equiv P_i(x_2, x_1, \ldots) \equiv \ldots$$

$$\equiv P_i(x_n, x_{n-1}, \ldots), \, (i = 1, \ldots, n). \quad (11\text{-}3)$$

This means that I think my chances of high or low incomes are no better or

---

[a] Any X_j may be a scalar, such as so many chocolates, or so many market baskets of goods of given composition, or so many dollars spendable at unchanged prices. But it could also be a vector of goods; $X_j = (\text{tea}_j, \text{coffee}_j, \ldots)$, etc.

worse than anyone else's; but it does not mean that the probabilities of low and high incomes are equal to those of middling incomes, as with Laplace's equal-probability axioms.

Egalitarianism Deduced

What will the optimal tax formula be that the ith person would opt for if given his choice? Clearly, consulting his own uncertain (symmetric!) prospects and aversion to risk, he will *solipsistically* vote for completely egalitarian taxa-tion *when incentive distortions can be ignored.*

Concretely, consider the family of tax formulas parameterized by α, the fractional degree to which each person is pushed toward the mean income:

Y_i = after-tax income of person i when all incomes are $(X_1, \ldots, X_n)$

$$= (1 - \alpha)X_i + \alpha\left(\sum_1^n X_j/n\right), 0 \leq \alpha \leq 1. \qquad (11\text{-}4)$$

If $\alpha = 1$, we have completely progressive taxation; if $\alpha = 0$, we have laissez faire and no redistributive taxation.

EGALITARIAN THEOREM. A person with concave utility, wishing to maximize the expected value of his final after-tax income $u_i[Y_i]$, *or in terms of the self-defining notation of Stieltjes multiple integrals,*

$$\bar{u}_i(\alpha) = E\{u_i[Y_i]\}$$
$$= \int_0^\infty \cdots \int_0^\infty u_i\left[(1 - \alpha)x_i + \alpha\left(\sum_1^n x_j/n\right)\right]P(dx_1, \ldots, dx_n) \quad (11\text{-}5)$$

will choose for his optimal α, $\alpha_i^* = 1$. *I.e.,*

$$\underset{\alpha}{\text{Max }} \bar{u}_i(\alpha) = \bar{u}_i(1) = u_i\left[\sum_1^n x_j/n\right].$$

This is proved by verifying

$$\bar{u}_i'(1) = u_i'\left[\sum_1^n x_j/n\right]\int_0^\infty \cdots \int_0^\infty \left[x_i - \left(\sum_1^n x_j/n\right)\right]P(dx_1, \ldots, dx_n)$$

$$= 0 \text{ from symmetry of } P(\ ). \qquad\qquad (11\text{-}6)$$

Even without differentiability, this proof by the principle of Sufficient and Reason applies.

> *UNANIMITY COROLLARY: By unanimous vote, a group of risk averters, each of whom conceives of himself as facing a symmetric prospect of pre-tax income, will opt for completely egalitarian taxation merely out of a* selfish *desire for mutual reinsurance.*

It should be remarked that if each person is a "minimaxer" (or maximizer of his minimum possible outcome), the same egalitarian unanimity follows. But this is a sufficient, not a necessary, condition. And formally it can be regarded as the special polar case of our theorem in which $\gamma \to -\infty$ in $u_i[X_i] = X_i^\gamma/\gamma$, $1 > \gamma \neq 0$. As γ goes to $-\infty$, maximizing (11-5) can be approximated arbitrarily closely by $\text{Max}\{\text{Min}[Y_i \text{ outcomes}]\}$, or so-called minimaxing.

The present theorems are pre-Rawls, going back at least to the analysis in Samuelson (1958, 1966) or Lerner (1944). The next section's advances are developments of what is hinted at in Samuelson (1974a) and earlier suggested as long as thirty years ago by Vickrey (1945).[b]

---

[b]I owe thanks to Kenneth Arrow for reminding me that what I though was original with me in 1964 is actually attributable to William Vickrey, who wrote

> ... If utility is defined as that quantity the mathematical expectation of which is maximized by an individual making choices involving risk, then to maximize the aggregate of such utility over the population is equivalent to choosing that distribution of income which such an individual would select were he asked which of various variants of the economy he would like to become a member of, assuming that once he selects a given economy with a given distribution of income he has an equal chance of landing in the shoes of each member of it ...
>
> Assuming that the marginal utility of money declines with increasing income, maximizing the total utility derived by a population from a given fixed aggregate income implies that this income be distributed equally, due allowance being made for varying needs. On such a basis, the exact shape of the utility function is irrelevant to a determination of the proper distribution.

Vickrey goes on to consider the effects on incentives of redistributive taxation and formulates in the following passage essentially the problem of my next section:

> ... It is generally considered that if individual incomes were made substantially independent of individual effort, production would suffer and there would be less

Deadweight Costs and Limited Redistribution

Suppose we recognize that it may cost something when we take taxes from one person and give transfers to another, that something of real output may be lost in redistributing because of administrative costs, grafts, inefficiencies, and frictions or because of incentive distortions stemming from any feasible taxes. This should temper the amount of egalitarianism that each person will want to have achieved in the social compact (although it may make each want *more* rather than less progression in the tax structure so that at least a little will filter down to a person when he is most destitute!).

Now we will want to replace (11-4) with its assumption that the total of after-tax incomes remains as high as that of pre-tax incomes. The simplest assumption about deadweight loss is that only a fraction, β, of all positive taxes collected ends up being successfully transferred to those who "receive negative taxes."[c]

Let the algebraic tax function that is to be adopted be written as $t(\ )$. If people are to be treated as similar except for differences in their X_j incomes, the tax must be *impersonal* with the special property

$$t_1(x_1, x_2, \ldots, x_{n-1}, x_n) \equiv t(x_1; x_2, \ldots, x_{n-1}, x_n)$$

$$\equiv t(x_1; x_n, \ldots, x_2, x_{n-1}) \equiv \ldots$$

$$t_i(x_1, x_2, \ldots, x_{n-1}, x_n) \equiv t(x_i; x_1, x_2, \ldots)$$

$$\equiv t(x_i; x_2, x_1, \ldots) \equiv \ldots$$

$$\equiv t(x_i; x^i) \text{ for short, } (i = 1, 2, \ldots, n) \tag{11-7}$$

---

to divide among the population. Accordingly, some degree of inequality is needed in order to provide the required incentives and stimuli to efficient cooperation of individuals in the production process. As soon as the need for such inequality is admitted, the shape of the utility curve becomes a factor in determining the optimum income distribution (1945, p. 329).

Then he sets up (pp. 330–331) a variational optimum problem that I would reformulate as follows: Each person's utility depends on his after-tax chocolate consumption and how much he labors; but his pre-tax chocolate output depends probabilistically on his quantity of labor. Any tax formula that depends only on his chocolate output will distort his labor-leisure decision; but subject to this recognized distortion, he selects that tax formula which would maximize his expected utility on the symmetric probability supposition that his productivity luck is the same as anyone else's.

I also owe to Arrow a reference to a similar investigation: J.A. Mirrlees (1971); also a reference to Vickrey (1960).

[c]Since these words were written, I learn that my model is similar to the famous "leaky-bucket experiment" of Arthur M. Okun (*Equality and Efficiency: The Big Tradeoff* [Washington, D.C.: The Brookings Institution, 1975], pp. 91–95).

where $x^i = (x_1, x_2, \ldots, x_{i-1}, x_{i+1}, \ldots, x_n)$ and $t(\ )$ is to be symmetric in the arguments of x^i.

"Positive taxes" are denotable by $\mathrm{Max}[0, t(x_i; x^i)]$ and "transfers received" by the absolute value of negative taxes or by $\mathrm{Max}[0, -t(x_i; x^i)]$. Assuming that only β of all positive taxes end up available as effective transfers, the choice of tax functions available for the social compact is limited by the non-analytic constraint:

$$\sum_{j=1}^{n} \mathrm{Max}[0, -t(x_j; x^j)] - \beta \sum_{j=1}^{n} \mathrm{Max}[0, t(x_j; x^j)] = 0. \qquad (11\text{-}8)$$

This is non-analytic because $\mathrm{Max}[0, z]$ is not an everywhere differentiable function.

> *OPTIMALITY EXISTENCE THEOREM: Each person, given his* $u_i[X_i]$
> *and* $P_i(x_1, \ldots, x_n)$ *functions can now determine in principle the optimum tax function,* $t(x_i; x^i)$, *that he would prefer to have apply to himself (and, of course, under impersonal taxation to each and every other person). The same holds even (a) if each* $u_i[X_i]$ *depends not solely on the* X_i *variable but altruistically or malevolently on all* $(X_1, \ldots, X_n)$ *variables; (b) if each* X_i *is not a scalar of "real income" but rather a vector of diverse goods and services of one date or different dates; (c) if* $\bar{u}_i(\ )$ *of one person's preference is replaced by some Bergson Social Welfare function provided by any ethical observer, the implications of which for optimal taxation we wish to explore.*

Formally, person i must solve a problem in the calculus of variations for *his* solipsistic unknown optimal tax function, which we can denote by $t_i^*(x_k; x^k)$, the affix k being used to emphasize that person i realizes the impersonal tax formula applies to *every* person, $i \gtreqless k = 1, 2, \ldots, n$. Formally, he solves for

$$\underset{t(x_i; x^i)}{\mathrm{Max}} \ \int_0^\infty \cdots \int_0^\infty u_i[x_i - t(x_i; x^i)] \, P(dx_1, \ldots, dx_n) \qquad (11\text{-}9)$$

where $t(x_i; x^i)$ is subject to (11-8). This is not a standard problem because in the Lagrangean-multiplier expression occasioned by the constraint (11-8), terms like $t(x_i; x_1, \ldots)$ and $t(x_1; x_i, \ldots)$ *both* appear. However, in principle the general optimal problem can be solved.

Numerical Example

A simplest case would be a two-person world with only two possible income outcomes characterized by

$$\text{prob}\{ X_1 = 1, X_2 = 3\} = \frac{1}{2} = \text{prob}\{X_1 = 3, X_2 = 1\}. \tag{11-10}$$

Then the sole degree of freedom to be voted on would be how much should be taxed away from the person who happens to get the highest real income for the benefit of the other person: i.e., person i solves (11-9) for his optimal tax function, which reduces to *his* optimal constant value for $t_i^*(3; 1)$. Call it t_i^* for short and derive it from

$$\text{Max}_{t_i} \left\{ \frac{1}{2} u_i[3 - t] + \frac{1}{2} u_i[1 + \beta t] \right\}$$

$$= \frac{1}{2} u_i[3 - t_i^*] + \frac{1}{2} u_i[1 + \beta t_i^*] = \bar{u}_i(t_i^*). \tag{11-11}$$

$$0 = -u_i'[3 - t_i^*] + \beta u_i'[1 + \beta t_i^*]. \tag{11-12}$$

Interestingly, for $\beta < u_i'$ (11-3) u_i' (11-1), (11-12) must be replaced by an inequality and *no* redistribution is worth its deadweight cost. We can deduce from (11-11) and (11-12) an expression for the optimal t_i^*, call it $\tau_i(\beta)$, and for the optimal post-tax income spread, call it $\sigma_i^* = \sigma_i(\beta)$:

$$t_i^* = \tau_i(\beta), \ \tau_i(1) = 1$$

$$\sigma_i^* = \sigma_i(\beta) = 3 - t^* - 1 - \beta t^* = 2 - (1 + \beta)\tau_i(\beta), \ \sigma_i(1) = 0$$

$$\tau_i(\beta) \equiv 0 \ \text{and} \ \sigma_i(\beta) \equiv 2 \ \text{for} \ \beta < u_i' \ (11\text{-}3)/u_i' \ (11\text{-}1).$$

$$\tau_i'(\beta) = \frac{u_i'[1 + \beta t^*] + \beta t^* u_i''[1 + \beta t^*]}{-u_i''[3 - t^*] - \beta^2 u_i''[1 + \beta t^*]}$$

$$\tau_i'(1) > -\frac{1}{2}, \sigma_i'(1) < 0. \tag{11-13}$$

The last expression deduces the intuitive result that when we introduce a little deadweight loss in the system, we increase the optimal after-tax income spread from zero to a positive amount. The expression for $\tau_i'(\beta)$ shows that adding a little loss will increase the degree of tax progression so long as the Pratt-Arrow coefficient of relative risk tolerance, reckoned at the mean income as $-2u_i''[2]/u_i'[2]$, is less than 2: this occurs when people are more risk averse than any person who calculates the certainty equivalent of a lottery ticket as the harmonic mean of its prizes; such a person is definitely more risk averse than a Bernoulli with logarithmic utility, but is not so risk averse as a paranoid minimaxer.

All this general analysis can be confirmed in the special case where the person in question has constant relative risk aversion and has for his utility function $u_i[X_i] = X_i^\gamma/\gamma$, where $\gamma < 1$. Then (11-13) becomes

$$t_i^* = \tau_i(\beta; \gamma_i) = (3 + \beta^\theta)/(1 + \beta\beta^\theta), \; \theta = 1/(\gamma_i - 1) < 0$$

$$\sigma_i \equiv \sigma_i(\beta; \gamma_i) = 2 - (1 + \beta)(3 - \beta^\theta)(1 + \beta\beta^\theta)^{-1}. \qquad (11\text{-}14)$$

$$\tau_i(1; \gamma_i) \equiv 1 \text{ for all } \gamma_i, \; \sigma_i(\beta; -\infty) = 0 \text{ for all } \beta > 0. \qquad (11\text{-}15)$$

For $\beta = 1$ and no deadweight loss, (11-14) and (11-15) confirm our previous section's egalitarian solution no matter what γ_i is. For $\gamma_i = -\infty$, we confirm the minimaxer solution of egalitarianism no matter how small β becomes (and we note that an increase in taxation's *inefficiency* increases the optimal degree of redistributable taxation away from the rich for $\gamma < -1$). For any fixed fractional β, the more risk averse the person is, the larger $1 - \gamma_i$ is, the greater will be the degree of egalitarianism he will vote for. But, unless he is *completely* risk averse (and few such people seem ever to have been observed), he will wish to stop short of complete final income equalization: the last epsilon of mutual re-insurance has too great a deadweight loading cost.

GENERAL THEOREM. If all persons had the same degree of risk aversion and faced the same symmetric probability distribution of fates, they would selfishly agree on a unanimous vote on an optimal compromise between redistributive taxation and the deadweight loss involved there-from. If no person has infinite risk aversion, they will unanimously suffer from an imposed minimaxer's regime of complete (and costly) egalitarian-ism, preferring to be spared that version of non-Pareto-optimal "fairness" or "justice."

If the persons differ in their risk tolerances, and even if they agree on a symmetric probability distribution, it seems unclear whether their sense of "fairness" or "justice" would lead them (a) to be able to identify and calibrate the person who is "hurt most" under any given tax system, $t(x_k; x^k)$, and (b) to agree that the "best" system is to be that $t^{**}(;)$ which leaves the "worst-off person" in the "best feasible position."

Remark: If any person rejects the applicability of a *symmetric* probability distribution, to the degree that the asymmetry is "small," the qualitative conclusions of the present chapter will apply to some degree of approximation. But, of course, if some person knows that *he* will end up affluent, and if he behaves solipsistically and selfishly, then given the chance he would veto any agreement on egalitarian taxation. As Marx and Pareto observed, the last is not a fanciful possibility. To the degree that a person exaggerates his chances for a high (or low) income, he will opt for less egalitarian (or more egalitarian) tax structures: if all exaggerate in the same direction, they may even by unanimous vote agree on a tax structure that would be non-optimal for each were he in command of the true odds.

Negligibility of "Incipient" Deadweight Loss

The example used here to typify "deadweight loss" from redistribution, shrinking of a constant fraction of real incomes transferred with $\beta < 1$ and β a constant, probably exaggerates such costs. Thus, suppose the only important redistributive costs come from distorted "substitution effects" attributable to society's not finding feasible "ideal lump-sum taxes" but instead having to depend on some Ramsey pattern of (so-called "second best" or) optimal-feasible pattern of algebraic excises. And suppose that government has no other function than to provide redistribution (i.e., there is no army, judiciary, or village green concerts—or, if there are any, they are financed out of publicly owned land rents). Finally, continue our assumption that each person conceives of himself as being subject to a symmetric probability distribution as in (11-3).

Can it then be the case that laissez faire is better than *some* degree of egalitarian redistribution? We saw that, with β a small enough fraction, zero redistribution was called for. But once we recognize that β is generated by tax wedges between the prices sellers get and buyers pay (as in a unit or *ad valorem* tax on each bushel of wheat sold), we realize that β is not a constant: we realize that, at the "beginning" of redistribution, β is almost exactly unity, and the initial rate at which deadweight loss is incurred is negligible. This is a basic truth that rarely is explicitly enunciated: yet it follows from the fact that consumer-surplus triangles of deadweight loss, heuristically written as $\frac{1}{2}\Delta p \Delta q$, are of "a second order of smallness" compared to Δp or $q\Delta p$; as $\Delta p \to 0$ or $\alpha \to 0$ in (11-4), $\beta \to 1$—and hence α_i^* *must* be above zero.

The above analysis constitutes the basis for the long reiterated paradoxical theorem of Samuelson (1958, p. 333): a good "frontier" society with "small" public-good responsibilities has for its first responsibility some redistributing of incomes no matter how limited are its feasible tax systems. Actual history, however, which is not a drama playacted in Hegel's seminar room, chose to pursue its own logic.

A Digression of Minimaxing Regret[1]

A discussion that pays some attention to minimaxing should spare a word, a brief word, for the criterion of "minimaxing regret" (or loss in comparison with how one might have fared if a different and more lucky tax decision had been made). In the absence of deadweight distributive cost, $\beta = 1$, the previous numerical case calls for *taxation halfway toward egalitarianism* if maximum regret is to be minimized; i.e., if t_i^* has to be chosen from the real numbers on the interval $[0, 1]$ (and in a moment we shall weaken this requirement and *thereby* change the whole base of calculation of regret!) setting $t_i^* = 1/2$ will minimax regret. If this seems odd (as it does to me at first blush) reflect on the theorem that, if you apply a silly criterion, you must not be surprised at a silly answer (a tautology, since it is by such odd fruits that we learn how odd the tree is).

To see this, note that when you strike it rich, your regret (from not having voted for laissez faire and zero tax rate) is t_i^* itself; when you strike it poor, your regret (from not having voted for completely egalitarian taxation) is $1 - t_i^*$. Therefore, minimax regret requires $\text{Min}\left\{\text{Max}[t_i^*, 1 - t_i^*]\right\}$, which is attained at $1/2$, where $t_i^* = 1 - t_i^* = 1/2$.

Actually, minimaxing regret does not lead to transivity, since it can violate the principle of Independence of Irrelevant Alternatives and leave its practitioner at the mercy of the agenda he confronts. Thus, suppose you had considered it feasible to have taxed *either* outcome by 100 percent. Then your minimaxed regret would be $\text{Min}\left\{\text{Max}[4 - 3 + t_i^*, 4 - 1 - t_i^*]\right\}$, which requires egalitarian taxation, $t_i^* = 1$: that way you never cry over more than two of spilt potential income.

If there is deadweight cost of redistribution, $\beta < 1$, and again *any* degree of taxation is feasible, we achieve $\text{Min}\left\{\text{Max}[3 + \beta - 3 + t_i^*, 1 + 3\beta - 1 - \beta t_i^*]\right\}$ by taxation that falls short of egalitarianism, namely by

$$t_i^* = 2\beta/(1 + \beta) = 1/[1 + \tfrac{1}{2}(1 - \beta)1 < 1 \text{ if } \beta < 1.$$

Actually, the egalitarian solution for the minimaxing of regret, deduced above for our numerical example when $\beta = 1$, holds valid for *any* case in which no two persons can ever have *exactly* the same income. To see this without complicated mathematics, concentrate on after-tax incomes $(Y_1, \ldots, Y_n)$. Compare any possible outcome with the utopia where you get all, $Y_i = \Sigma Y_j$; if ever the tax system could leave you with more than the mean income $\Sigma Y_j/n$, it must leave someone with different income (and that means *you* for a different roll of the die) with an income below the mean and therefore with the high regret greater than $\Sigma Y_j - (\Sigma Y_j/n)$; to keep the high regret at a minimum, you must opt for every after-tax income at the mean! Q.E.D.

However, this simplicity is lost if (a) you really accept the notion of impersonal taxation with $t(X_1; X_2, \dots) \equiv t(X_2; X_1, \dots)$ when X_1 and X_2 happen to be equal. In any outcome with two tied incomes, say $X_1 = 3 = X_2$, $X_3 = 1$, it is not feasible under impersonal taxation to compare for regretting purposes t_2 (3; 3, 1) with $-(3 + 3 + 1 - 3)$. Your wishful thinking can only go so far as dreaming of a feasible $Y_2 = 7/2 = Y_1$ that comes from dividing total incomes evenly among all of you with the same income. Minimaxing regret then leads to solving for $\text{Min}\{\text{Max}\,[7/2 - 3 + t_2(3; 3, 1), 7 - 1 - 2t_2(3; 3, 1)]\}$, which yields the optimum tax $t_i^*(3; 3, 1) = 2\,1/6$. Incredible as it may seem, picking the optimum tax structure that minimaxes regret when two men are rich and one poor leads to an after-tax income where the poor loner gets much more income than the rich, namely: (3; 3, 1) of pre-tax income leads to (5/6, 5/6, 4 1/6) of post-tax income, a case of progression with such vengeance as to lead to reverse inegalitarianism. (However, the effect depends on relative numbers, not on class position in the income scale: if two poor men and only one rich man occur, (1, 1, 3), the same reasoning leads to after-tax incomes of (1/2, 1/2, 6), which comes from taxing the (numerous) poor to subsidize the sparse rich!)

Does all this sound silly? That is because minimaxing regret is a criterion that has only to be understood to be laughed at.[d]

Conclusion

"There but for the grace of God go I." This consideration lies, I believe, at the basis of much of the modern welfare state. Mutual reinsurance is good business. That is why, to improve on Calvin Coolidge, The business of America is (also) government. The present theorems, which avoid all interpersonal comparisons of utility, indicate the sense in which this is true. I would hope that any Rawlsian can reformulate or interpret his syllogisms to agree with the results here deduced.

---

[d]Samuelson (1974b) shows that using it for portfolio decision making requires you, when faced with a choice of safe cash and an only-fair bet (such as the toss of a fair coin that returns you $2 for heads and $0 for tails for each dollar you ante up), to put exactly *half* your wealth into the gamble! Most people would have no such tolerance for profitless and pointless risk. Worse for minimaxing regret is that it makes you put almost half your money in a (slightly) unfavorable bet: thus, if on heads you got only $(2 - ϵ)$ and on tails $0, you'd have to put $(1 - \epsilon)/(2 - 3)$ of your wealth in the unfavorable gamble; for $\epsilon = 1/2$, corresponding to a gamble that gives you nought when a fair coin comes up tails and only 1½ when it comes up heads, you'd still put one-third of your wealth in the gamble and only two-thirds in cash with its safety and higher mean yield. *Remark*: Wald, Savage, and the original discussants of minimaxed regret never recommended it when adequate Bayesian probabilities were present, a reminder that present-day portfolio managers should take to heart.

Notes

1. Savage (1954) discusses minimaxing of regret in statistical decision making. Pye (1974) applies the concept to portfolio decision making (and gives further references); Samuelson (1974b) points out pathologies to which the concept leads.

References

Lerner, A.P. *Economics of Control.* London: Macmillan, 1944, particularly Ch. 3.

Mirlees, J.A. "An Exploration in the Theory of Optimum Income Taxation." *Review of Economic Studies* 38 (1971): 175–208.

Pye, Gordon. "A Note on Diversification." *Journal of Financial and Quantitative Analysis* 9 (January 1974): 131–136.

Rawls, John. *A Theory of Justice.* Cambridge, Massachusetts: Harvard University Press, 1971.

Samuelson, P.A. "Aspects of Public Expenditure Theories." *Review of Economics & Statistics* 40 (1958): 332–338, particularly pp. 332–333; reproduced as Ch. 94, P.A. Samuelson, *Collected Scientific Papers,* II. Cambridge, Massachusetts: MIT Press, 1966.

Samuelson, P.A. "A.P. Lerner at Sixty." *Review of Economic Studies* (1964), pp. 169–178, particularly pp. 173–176; reproduced as Ch. 183, in *CSP* III, (1972).

Samuelson, P.A. "Remembrances of Frisch." *European Economic Review* 5 (1974a): 13–15, particularly around footnote 4.

Samuelson, P.A. "Overdiversification from Minimizing Vain Regret." Paper presented at the Bell Laboratories on Economics of Uncertainty, July 29, 1974(b).

Savage, L.J. *Foundations of Statistics.* New York: John Wiley & Sons, 1954, particularly Ch. 9.

Vickrey, William. "Measuring Marginal Utility by Reactions to Risk." *Econometrica* 13 (1945): 319–333.

Vickrey, William. "Utility Strategy, and Social Decision Rules." *Quarterly Journal of Economics* 74 (1960): 507–535.

12 Collective Consumption and Relative Size of the Government Sector

Carl S. Shoup

I

Wherever population is increasing, the share of the public sector in total output might well be expected to shrink, over time, in view of the collective consumption feature that is attributed to public goods. This feature implies that, ceteris paribus, the cost per capita of a given level of the government service declines as population grows: the price of the product falls. If demand, as expressed through the political mechanism, exhibits a price elasticity numerically less than unity, in the face of this price decline, the share of the product in total output falls. If per capita income is meanwhile increasing, but income elasticity is not large enough to offset a less than unitary price elasticity, that share will still decline. Although the service is here assumed to be distributed free of direct charge, and equally to all, in a non-price-exclusion mode, cost per capita is presumed to influence the political decision as to the amount of the service to be provided, much as the price of a marketed good influences the number of units sold.

It is therefore somewhat puzzling to find that recent studies of trends in or possibilities for the share of the public sector in total output take little or no account of this jointness-over-users that is said to characterize public goods (see Sections III and V below). An attempt is made here to broaden the perspective to allow for the economies of jointness-over-users when population is growing, and to inquire briefly whether those economies outweigh, or are outweighed by, the forces that are deemed to be making for an increase in the public sector share. No firm conclusion emerges, except the need to keep in mind the jointness-over-users attribute as population increases.

Transfer payments, which account for so much of recent growth in total government outlay, are not included in the present discussion, since for them the element of jointness over users does not apply, except for the accompanying externality, that is, the satisfaction that may be felt by others than the recipients.

Section II reviews the concept of collective consumption, suggesting initially a threefold division into simple collective consumption, super-collective consump-

The author is indebted to John G. Head in particular, and to Richard M. Bird, John F. Graham, Cliff Walsh, and to student members of the graduate public finance seminar at Dalhousie University for comments and suggestions on earlier drafts of this chapter. Some of the concepts and analysis in Section II were developed jointly by the author and Robert G. di Calogero in the course of discussions at Columbia University some years ago.

tion, and quasi-collective consumption. There is then noted briefly the possibility of what is here termed decollective consumption, where per capita cost rises as population increases, for a given level of service. Zero and unit price and income elasticities are employed to illustrate the degree to which the level of service (number of units of the good) must rise as population grows, if the public sector share is to expand. Section III summarizes the Baumol thesis of technological lag in the service industries, and explores its implications for the more common governmental services. Section IV considers three other steadily working influences that may affect the size of the public sector share. A concluding section offers some remarks on the combination of jointness-over-users and a technological lag, with respect to certain government services that are direct consumer goods, for which conjectures may be hazarded as to the relevant elasticities of demand.

II

Growth in the number of users of a service—or, for short, growth in population—reduces the average cost per person served, at the given level of the service, if that service is at least to some degree joint over users. Jointness-over-users means that an increase in the number of users of the service does not require an increase in total cost that is in proportion, or more than in proportion, to the increase in number of users. For example, if the number of users doubles, the total cost of rendering the service, at the stipulated level of service, does not double, or more than double.

Level of service refers to quality, length of period over which it is rendered, and other attributes valued by the user. The term "quantity" may be used instead of "level," provided it is not taken to include the number of persons being served. "Level of service," as that phrase is used here, has nothing to do with number of persons served. As that number changes, the level of service is assumed to remain unaltered, unless otherwise specified.

If total cost remains quite unchanged as the number of persons served increases, the service is termed here an "exactly collective consumption good," or "simple collective consumption good." It might also be called a "purely joint good" (joint over users). This is also the meaning intended when "collective consumption good" is used without a modifier, unless otherwise indicated.

If total cost actually declines as the number of persons served increases, as it may in a few unusual instances, the service is a "super-collective consumption good." It is an "exactly super-collective consumption good" if total cost changes in precisely inverse proportion to the increase in population: for example, as the number of users doubles, the total cost of rendering the given level of service falls by one-half.

If, as is common, total cost of the given level of service increases as the number of users increases, but by less than in proportion, the service is here termed a "quasi-collective consumption good," or "partly joint good." For example, if the number of users doubles, total cost may increase by 50 percent.

Accordingly, cost per capita per unit of service (a "level" of service constitutes a fixed number of units of the service) declines by just one-half if population doubles, for a simple collective consumption good, by more than one-half for a super-collective consumption good, and by less than one-half—but at least declines a little—for a quasi-collective consumption good.

These declines in unit cost per capita require some stipulation or conjecture about the price-elasticity of demand for these services, as expressed through the political mechanism, if anything is to be said about whether the share of the service in total economy output will rise, fall, or remain unchanged as population increases. Since the present study is only exploratory, analysis is restricted to two standard cases: perfectly inelastic demand, and unit-elastic demand. Perfectly elastic demand is ignored as being far too unlikely. Intuition can readily suggest what happens when price-elasticity of demand falls between zero and unity, or somewhat exceeds unity.

In an analysis as highly simplified as the present one, and dealing with shares in total output, an assumption about the price-elasticity of demand for one good will commonly fix, or limit the range of, the value that can be assumed for elasticities of demand for other goods. In a two-good economy, for example, an assumption of unit price elasticity of demand for one of the goods necessarily implies unit elasticity of demand for the other. This limitation is one of the reasons why the exploration of effects of varying elasticities is somewhat restricted in the present study.

Perfectly price-inelastic demand is taken in the present context to mean the following. As population increases and per capita cost of the initial level of service falls, the political mechanism for levying taxes and supplying the service acts as if each member of the enlarged group demanded just the same level of the service as had each member of the earlier, smaller group, despite the decrease in cost per capita.

Unit price-elasticity of demand is taken to mean that per capita expenditure on the service remains unchanged when per capita cost of the initial level of service declines with an increase in population. This concept is of course analogous to that of unit elasticity of demand for a separate, marketable good: the amount spent on the good is unchanged when its price alters.

The particular political process or rule by which these elasticity concepts might be implemented are not specified here, e.g., whether the level of service is that demanded by the median voter under some announced general tax formula, or whether a Pareto optimum is reached by, say, a Lindahl pricing policy. The present aim is merely to point out the consequences if the political mechanism acts as if one or the other of these elasticity concepts obtained. In its simplest formulation, this means that everyone is assumed to be alike in tastes and income.

Since population growth is commonly associated with change in per capita income, the income elasticity of demand for the government service must be considered, in estimating whether the share of the service in total product will change over time. This aspect is discussed at the end of this section.

Each of the three types, simple, super-, and quasi-collective consumption goods, will now be exemplified and discussed in terms of share in total product under the different price elasticities, when population grows, with per capita income unchanged.

Among the simple, or exactly, collective consumption goods, national defense is the most important example. Certain public health measures, as distinct from medical care of the individual, fall in this category. So too does weather forecasting, abstracting from the means employed to disseminate the information.

If demand for the simple collective consumption service is perfectly price-inelastic, no more money will be spent on it, in total, than before; yet each user can enjoy the same level of service as did each of the earlier, smaller groups of users. The share of the service in the economy's total output falls precisely in proportion to the increase in population. This outcome is illustrated by a numerical example in table 12-1 (Periods 1 and 2).

If, on the other hand, price elasticity of demand is unity, the share of this kind of service in total product remains unchanged (Periods 1 and 2'). This point deserves some emphasis: even with a demand so price-elastic as to be of unit

Table 12-1
Simple Collective Consumption Goods: Change in Share as Population Increases (Constant Marginal Cost Equals Average Cost, for Level of Service)

	Period 1	Period 2	Period 2'
(1) Population	100	200	200
(2) National income	$1,000	$2,000	$2,000
(3) National income per capita [(2)/(1)]	$10	$10	$10
(4) Level of service, in units	100	100	200
(5) Cost of level of service	$100	$100	$200
(6) Number of person-units of service [(4)/(1)]	10,000	20,000	40,000
(7) Cost per person-unit of service [(5)/(6)]	$.01	$.005	$.005
(8) Amount spent on service, per consumer [(5)/(1)], or [(7)/(4)]	$1	$.50	$1
Total spent on service, as percentage of national income	10%	5%	10%

elasticity, the proportion of the national product represented by this service does not rise, as population increases, with unchanged per capita income. If the level of service is produced at a constant cost (equal to average cost), the level of service demanded doubles (line 5, table 12–1).

The results obtained so far for a simple collective consumption good may be contrasted with those for a private good, that is, one with no jointness at all over users. Let population double, and per capita income remain unchanged. If the per capita level of use of this private good is to remain unaltered, the good will have to maintain its proportion of the national product. That proportion cannot fall by one-half, as it does in the case of the simple collective consumption good. It may be added at this point that if marginal cost of the private good is constant, and equal to average cost, the price-elasticity of demand for the private good is irrelevant in determining the share of the good in total product, as population grows, whereas, as has just been shown, the price-elasticity of demand must be specified for the various types of collective consumption good.

As an extreme, but perhaps illuminating, example involving both types of good, let the economy produce only a simple collective consumption good and a private good with no jointness-over-users. Let each good account initially for one-half the total product. Let population increase, with per capita income unchanged. Under constant cost for the private good and unit price elasticity of demand for the simple collective consumption good, the division of the product remains fifty-fifty. But if the demand for the collective consumption good is perfectly price-inelastic, the public sector share shrinks to one-fourth as population doubles, to one-eighth as it doubles again, and so on.

A super-collective consumption good, almost always a preventive service of some kind (with some significant exceptions), has the peculiar characteristic noted earlier that, as population grows (area remaining constant), total cost of maintaining the initial level of service actually decreases, instead of merely remaining unchanged as with a simple collective consumption good. Per capita cost per unit of service therefore decreases more than in proportion to the growth of population.

An illustration may be drawn from mosquito control.[1] Let the level of the service be measured by the reciprocal of the expected number of mosquito bites per person per day, within a specified area. A mosquito-bite reduction program (the service) is produced by continued spraying of four out of six equal breeding grounds (ponds) to a degree such that no mosquitos at all emerge from these four ponds. Under this regime, there is a certain expected number of mosquito bites per person per day, by mosquitos from the remaining two ponds.

Let the number of persons in this area now double. The mosquitos from the fifth and sixth ponds, being already fully employed, and remaining unchanged in number, will produce only the same number of total bites as before the human population increased. The mosquitos will remain unchanged in number because the number of mosquitos depends simply on the number that complete the larva stage in the ponds; the presence of additional humans does not prolong the lives of the females—the ones that do the biting—or increase their breeding capacity, given an adequate number of humans to start with. Accordingly, the expected number of mosquito bites per person per day will decline, without any increase in spraying input. The level of service automatically increases as population grows.

To lower the service from its new high level to the level at which it was supplied initially, spraying must be reduced to cover only the first and second ponds. The total number of mosquito bites then doubles, as the number of mosquitos doubles. With double the initial human population, the expected number of bites per person per day now rises to what it was initially. If the ponds are equally costly to spray, and abstracting from intra-pond changes in cost as spraying moves toward eliminating all mosquitos from a given pond, the initial service level is maintained at only half the former cost (cost of spraying). The per capita cost of maintaining the initial level of service is reduced, not just to one-half of what it was to begin with, as it is for a simple collective consumption good, but to one-quarter that level.

To illustrate numerically, let the expected number of bites per person per day (EB) be initially 8. When population doubles, with no change as yet in the spraying, the EB falls to 4. The level of service has risen from 1/8 to 1/4. By reducing the spraying, the community pushes the level of service back down to 1/8.

This example of a super-collective consumption good is a special case, an "exactly super-collective" consumption good, in that the total cost of maintaining the initial level of service varies precisely in inverse proportion to the size of the population. More generally, a super-collective consumption good is one that, when population increases, can be maintained at its initial level with some decrease in total cost.[a] The decrease may be less or even more than in inverse proportion to the increase in population, as well as exactly in inverse proportion.

The numerical illustration of table 12–1 is adapted in table 12–2 to the exactly super-collective case, the total cost falling by one-half as population doubles. If demand for the good is perfectly price-inelastic, the level of service continues unchanged, and per capita cost per unit of service declines to one-

---

[a]An example is maintenance of a certain indoor temperature in a cold climate. A given level of heat, say 70° Fahrenheit, can be maintained with less fuel input, the larger the number of persons in a given room, hall, auditorium, etc., as more body heat is given off, (I am indebted to Beatrice Head for this illustration.)

Another example of the same type is suggested by the question, "how many people, as a minimum, are required to be in a 25-man life raft if they wish to maintain the inside temperature at 65 degrees F., while the outside temperature is 30 degrees F. and a wind of 40 knots?" [sic] –one of the questions studied by the Atlantic International Air and Surface Search and Rescue Seminar ("Lantsar '75"). "The . . . lecture raised, but didn't answer, the question of how many occupants would be needed to create a comfortable temperature from body heat."[2]

Table 12–2
Super-Collective Consumption Good: Change in Share as Population
Increases (Constant Marginal Cost Equals Average Cost, for Level
of Service)

	Period 1	Period 2 (inelastic demand)	Period 2' (unit elasticity)
(1) Population	100	200	200
(2) National Income	$1,000	$2,000	$2,000
(3) National Income per capita [(2)/(1)]	$10	$10	$10
(4) Service Level	100	100	400
(5) Total Cost of Service Level	$100	$50	$200
(6) Person-units of Service [(4)/(1)]	10,000	20,000	80,000
(7) Cost per person-unit [(5)/(6)]	.01	.0025	.0025
(8) Amount spent per capita [(5)/(1)]	$1.00	$.25	$1.00
Total spent on service, as percentage of national income	10%	2.5%	10%

fourth its initial value, instead of only to one-half as with the simple collective
consumption good (Periods 1 and 2, table 12–2).

If demand is of unit price elasticity (Period 2'), and cost per unit of level
of service is constant (marginal cost equals average cost), the level of service demanded rises to four times the initial level, instead of to twice that level for the
simple collective consumption good. Total spending increases of course by just
the same amount as with the simple collective consumption good, that is, it
doubles as population doubles, with constant income per capita (line 5 in both
tables).

On the other side of the simple collective consumption good from that of
the super-collective consumption good lie the goods where, as noted above, total
cost of a given level of service increases somewhat as the number of users (population) grows, but not as fast as that number. Such goods are here termed "quasi-
collective consumption goods." For example, let population and national
product both double, and let the total cost of maintaining the initial level of service for this larger number of users increase by, say, 50 percent, so that the per
capita cost of this level of service falls to three-quarters of its initial amount, not
to one-half as under the simple collective consumption good.

This class of goods has been analyzed at length, over a long period of time,
often as "impure public goods" or "imperfect public goods," terms which may
also be used, however, to refer to intra-group discrimination.

The point of view taken in most of those analyses has differed from that of the present essay in two respects. First, the jointness-over-users cost being kept constant in total—e.g., the highway or bridge remains unaltered—the usual question is, by how much do additional users cause the level of service to fall, through congestion or crowding? The question raised in the present analysis is, by how much must total cost be increased to maintain the initial level of service in the face of an increase in number of users?

Second, the congestion case is said to pose the problem, what is the optimum price to charge for use of the facility? This question is modified here, where the service is assumed to be dispensed in a non-price-excludable mode, to read, by how much does the per capita cost of the initial level of service decline, and by how much, consequently, does the demand for that initial level of service increase, if the political process works as if each user were being faced with a uniform price over users and over units of the service? An analogue to the usual price-elasticity analysis is thus employed, but not necessarily with any assumption of optimality.

When the usual congestion analysis is broadened in this manner to include decisions on size of facility—how big should the bridge be? how wide the highway?—the question arises whether the marginal-cost pricing rule will cover total cost, and, if not, how the problem of financing the uncovered part of the cost shall be dealt with.[b] The present analysis does not even approach that problem, since it assumes no direct pricing, dealing as it does with non-price-excludable services.

If the share of the quasi-collective consumption good in total output is to remain unchanged as population doubles, and total output doubles, the total cost of that good must of course double. This result is achieved for the quasi-collective consumption good by having the level of the service, the number of units of the good, rise by less than in proportion to the growth of population, rather than in the same proportion, as with the simple collective consumption good. For example, if total cost of maintaining the initial level of service increases by one-half as population doubles, then, under constant marginal cost (equals average cost) for units of level of service, that level rises by one-third, instead of doubling, as with the simple collective consumption good (total amount spent on the service doubles, since $(3/2)(4/3) = 2$). In terms of table 12–1, level of service rises to 133 1/3 instead of to 200.

---

[b]The distributive issue, by-passed in the present analysis, is dealt with by Professor Vickrey's suggestion of "a suitable choice of increments in the income-tax schedule," such that "the increment of tax in each income class is less than the aggregate increment in consumer's surplus in that class . . . resulting from adopting a marginal-cost-pricing policy in any given class of projects or industries." He points out that this policy requires us to assume, "as seems reasonable, that a redistribution of income within an appropriately defined income stratum can be considered neutral with respect to whatever values are being used as a standard for judgment;" moreover, "if the class of projects to be shifted to a subsidized marginal-cost basis is made sufficiently broad, . . . the number of persons adversely affected by the reorganization might become vanishingly small . . ."[3]

The constant-share assumption implies, of course, unit elasticity of demand for the quasi-collective consumption good, just as it did for the simple collective consumption good and the super-collective consumption good. The total amount spent on the service doubles when population doubles, hence the amount spent per capita remains unchanged under the fall in cost per capita.

It should be noted that unit elasticity of demand has been defined up to this point in terms of unchanged amount spent per capita as population changes. The same results will of course be obtained if the alternative definition of unit elasticity is used: the ratio of proportionate change in quantity to proportionate change in price is unity. Since the computation involves rates of change over a range of values, not instantaneous rates of change, the proportionate decrease in price must be computed by using the new low price as the base, not the initial price. For example, an increase from 1 to 10 in quantity taken, resulting from a decline in price from $1 to $.1, reflect unit elasticity of demand in that the amount spent on the good remains unchanged at $1. The unit elasticity figure is obtained by dividing 9/1 not by .9/1, which would yield 10, but by $[.9/(1 - .9)]$, which yields 1. In the present illustration, cost per capita (price) has decreased by an amount equal to one-third of the new low cost per capita, i.e., it has decreased by one-fourth of the initial cost per capita. The output (level of service) has increased by one-third. Dividing 1/3 by $[1/4(1 - 1/4)]$ yields 1, an elasticity of unity. For the simple collective consumption good example in table 12-1, dividing the proportionate change in level of service, 1/1, by that of cost per capita, $[.005/(.01 - .005)]$, again yields an elasticity of unity.

So far, only constant marginal cost, equal to average cost, has been specified, as to what happens to total cost when, for an unchanged population, the level of service is increased or decreased. Total cost is here assumed always to rise as level of service is increased. With population held constant, total cost may increase less than in proportion to the increase in level of service, or exactly in proportion, or more than in proportion. These instances will be referred to as those of decreasing marginal cost, constant marginal cost, and increasing marginal cost. The term "per capita" may be added, since population is being held constant. This terminology abstracts, for convenience, from any initial lumpiness in cost. In particular, as above, the constant marginal cost will be assumed equal to average cost.

An increase in total cost as level of service is increased, population being constant, is to be carefully distinguished from an increase in total cost of an unchanging level of service of a quasi-collective consumption good as population increases.

This distinction between the two kinds of increase in total cost of course vanishes for the separate, marketable good. With respect to such a good, total cost increases by the same amount whether double the number of persons consume an unchanged average amount per person, or an unchanged number of persons consume a doubled average amount per person. For such a good, a given number of person-units necessarily involves the same total cost, no matter how this number is split between number of persons and average number of units per person. Except for certain special cases, this is not true of any of the types of collective consumption goods.

Another distinction between the kinds of collective consumption goods discussed in the present chapter and separate, marketable goods is that, because of non-excludability, the collective consumption goods are consumed equally by all; the level of service is here assumed to be the same for everyone. In contrast, the number of person-units of a separate, marketable good can, and commonly are, distributed unevenly over persons.

On the other side of the separate, marketable good from the collective consumption goods discussed thus far (quasi-, simple, or super-), symmetry suggests that there lie goods for which the total cost of a given level of service (again, the same level to each user) rises by more than in proportion to the number of users. For example, if the number of persons within a given area doubles, from an already high level, the total cost of providing a given level of fire protection may more than double. This type of good may be called a decollective consumption good. If total cost rises exactly in proportion to the number of persons served, it may be called a neutral collective consumption good.

All of these types of collective consumption good—five altogether—are distinguished from separate, marketable goods in that the change in total cost may—and for the simple or super-collective consumption goods, must—differ according as the total of person-units produced is altered by a given amount by changing the number of persons or by changing the average number of units per person. As already indicated, no such difference exists with respect to the separate marketable good. A further distinction, again already noted, but not essential, although it is assumed in the present analysis, is that units of the collective goods are distributed evenly over persons.

The ways in which total cost may change for a collective good may be expressed symbolically as follows.

Let n = number of users

x = average number of units of service per user (uniform for users, in the present analysis)

$C = an^{\alpha}bx^{\beta}$ = total cost

Then for a good of

simple collective consumption, $\alpha = 0$

super-collective consumption, $\alpha < 0$

exactly super-collective consumption, $\alpha = -1$

quasi-collective consumption $0 < \alpha < 1$

neutral collective consumption $\alpha = 1$

decollective consumption $\alpha > 1$

And with respect to level-of-service marginal cost,

for constant cost $\beta = 1$

for decreasing cost $0 < \beta < 1$

for increasing cost $\beta > 1$

It may turn out that $\alpha = \beta$, in the following cases: quasi-collective consumption good, decreasing cost; decollective cnsumption good, increasing cost; and the two will be equal, for a neutral collective consumption good produced under constant cost. In these three cases, the total cost function will be indistinguishable, in form, from that of a separate, marketable good, since the total cost function of such a good is expressible as follows:

T = total cost of a separate, marketable good

$$k(nx)^\gamma = kn^\gamma x^\gamma, \gamma > 0$$

The distinction drawn here between number of consumers and level of service is similar to that drawn by Professor Vickrey between "intensity" and "mere size," in his discussion of economies of scale in transportation, where he says that "It is important to distinguish clearly between the economies of intensity, which is what concerns us here, and economies of mere size, such as might occur from merger or amalgamation of different entities." The point is that "when the total amount of traffic in a given area or along a given corridor increases, the average cost per unit of service will in most cases tend to decline, or possibly the quality or convenience of the service to the users will improve, or both."[4]

Returning to the first three types (quasi-, simple, and super-collective consumption goods), and exploring further what happens under increasing marginal cost per unit of service, population being held constant, we see of course that a unit-elastic demand still yields an unchanged share of the service in total product when population is allowed to grow. The level of service demanded by the larger population under this elasticity will rise by less than under constant marginal cost. At the point where the unit-elastic demand curve intersects any one of the three new marginal cost curves created by the increase in population, the vertical distance between that point and the point that obtained before the population increased will be smaller than it would be under constant marginal cost. The downward shift of the marginal cost curve caused by the increase in population will be partly negated by its upward slope as the level of service rises.

Figure 12–1 shows a constant (per capita) marginal cost curve, for each of a quasi-collective, a simple collective, and an exactly super-collective consumption good, before and after population doubles, using the numerical examples given in the tables above.

Figure 12–2 shows increasing marginal cost, in a similar fashion. Initially, with population at 100, and level of service at 100 units, per capita marginal cost is 1 cent (from figure 12–1). This cost is assumed to change steadily by 1/2 cent for every 100 units of level of service, that is, by 1/200 cent per unit. If x is the number of such units, per capita marginal cost is, at the 100-unit level, $1/2 + 100/200$. In general, marginal cost per capita is expressible as $1/2 + x/200$, or $(100 + x)/200$.

When population doubles, per capita marginal cost, for a simple collective consumption good, falls by one-half, to $(100 + x)/400$; exactly super-collective consumption good, falls by three-quarters, to $(100 + x)/800$; quasi-collective consumption good of the type stipulated above, falls by one-fourth, to $(300 + 3x)/800$.

Income elasticity of demand for the public good may now be taken into account, to see how it affects the level of service demanded, once the price-elasticity of demand has had its effect on that level.

The tendency toward a decreasing share of the public sector that arises from jointness-over-users, when price-elasticity of demand is less than unity, and population is rising, can be offset, when per capita income rises along with population, by a sufficiently powerful income elasticity of demand (assumed positive). But that elasticity must of course be greater than unity, and considerably greater if price elasticity is much less than unity.

In the table 12–1 example, let price elasticity be only, say, –1/2, so that the level of service demanded rises only from 100 units to 150 units when the cost per unit per capita falls by one-half $(1/2 - [1/2//(1 - 1/2)])$. Let income per capita double, so that, with population 200, national income is $4,000, instead of only $2,000. To maintain its initial 10 percent share in national product ($100 out of $1,000), the amount spent on the public good must rise from the $150 level (which it reaches when population doubles with per capita income unchanged) by $250 when per capita income then doubles. This requires an income elasticity of 5/3, merely to keep the public sector share from falling, over time.

If income elasticity of demand is less than unity, it reinforces a price elasticity of less than unity in depressing the size of the public sector share. Thus, if price elasticity is –1/2 and income elasticity is 1/2, the amount spent on the public good rises from $150, with population doubled but per capita income unchanged, to $225, with per capita income doubled, i.e., $[(225 - 150)/150] / /[4,000 - 2,000)/2,000] = 1/2$. The share in total product falls from 10 percent

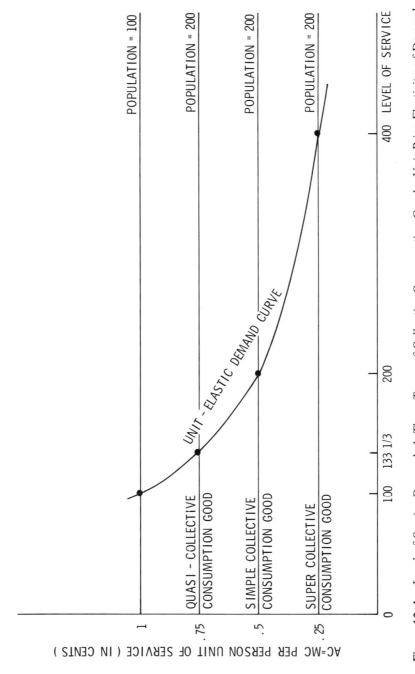

Figure 12–1. Level of Service Demanded, Three Types of Collective-Consumption Goods: Unit Price-Elasticity of Demand, Constant Marginal Cost (= Average Cost)

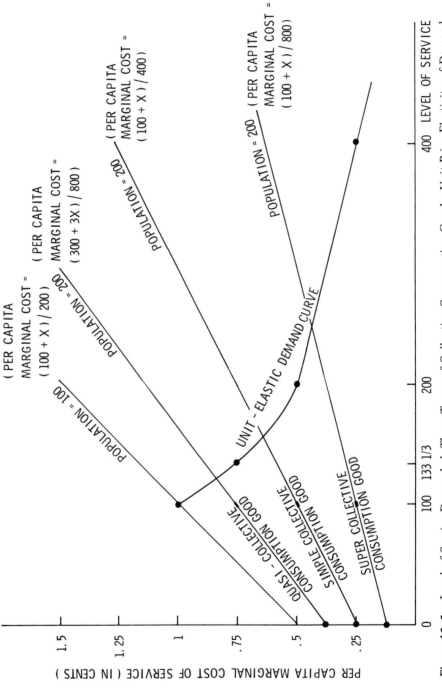

Figure 12–2. Level of Service Demanded, Three Types of Collective-Consumption Goods: Unit Price-Elasticity of Demand, Increasing Marginal Cost per Unit Level of Service

initially to 7 1/2 percent before income per capita doubles (i.e., to 150/2,000), then to 5.625 percent as per capita income doubles (i.e., to 225/4,000).

If both the elasticities are unity, the share of the public sector of course remains unchanged.

III

A technological lag in the service industries has been advanced by William J. Baumol as a reason for expecting the share of the public sector, or at least a considerable part of it, to increase over time.[5] The steps in this argument are as follows.

Continual technological advance in the material goods industries allows wage rates to be increased steadily without raising prices of the products. The service industries, to compete with the material goods industries for labor, must grant similar wage increases. Prices of the services must then rise, because technology does not improve as rapidly as in the production of material goods.

If demand for the service in question is of less than unit price elasticity, the rise in price will be accompanied by an increase in the total amount spent on the service. This tendency toward a larger share in total output may be reinforced, given an increasing per capita income, by an income elasticity of demand for the service that is greater than unity.

Government dispenses chiefly services rather than material goods. Hence the technological lag tends to increase the share of the government in total output, given the elasticities just noted.

The force of this argument that the public sector share may increase seems, however, to be less than might at first be assumed. A large part of the total of services is dispensed by the private sector, much of it in the form of wholesaling, retailing, transportation, and financing. A considerable proportion of these four services is embodied in material goods. A technological lag in these service industries makes it impossible for prices to the final purchaser to remain stable in the face of wage increases large enough to absorb all the technological improvement at the manufacturing level.

Government services, as well as private-sector services, are commonly produced with the aid of material producer's goods, which presumably benefit from technological advance. It is therefore not evident a priori that the cost of services to the users, whether government or private-sector services, must always be at a price disadvantage owing to the uneven technological advance. In the rendering of government services recent developments include, for example, computerized police files, radio-equipped patrol cars, electronic fire-hose nozzles, "Rapid Water" for fire fighting, sophisticated weather forecasting techniques, "smart bombs," and so on.

Moreover, government services are commonly dispensed in a non-excludability mode, and this mode may well be more technically oriented than the marketing mode. Crime prevention appears to be at least no less technologically oriented when rendered through patrol cars and computerized files than when given in an excludable mode through locks, alarms, and private patrol or responding services.

If, on balance, the technological lag adversely affects the prices of services, that effect may be greater in the private sector than in the public, because the type of service where the lag is inherent is often also the kind that can be marketed (exclusion by price). This type of service is one in which the time taken in production, in the final stage, cannot be less than the time taken by the user to consume the service. An example is "live" music. A dimension of such a service is the amount of time occupied in consuming it. In these instances an attempt to speed up rendition of the service simply reduces its amount.

IV

Three other forces at work over time to affect per capita cost of a given level of a government service are considered briefly here. Excluded are those that work only irregularly over time, and that affect transfer payments strongly: for example, the "displacement effect."[6]

The environment may worsen steadily, so that more and more input is needed to achieve a given output. An analogue in the private goods sector would be a downward trend in winter temperatures that would require increasingly large amounts of fuel to achieve a given indoor level of temperature. It is the latter that is the consumer's good (or producer's good, in office or factory), not the amount of coal, gas, or other fuel used up. The price of that service would then have risen, even if the prices of coal, gas, fuel oil, and electricity had remained unchanged.

Similarly for the free public service, the environment, or "atmosphere" in which defense, crime prevention, or education is dispensed may deteriorate over time. With no increase in per unit costs of inputs, and under a given technology and constant population, per capita unit cost of a given level of service rises.

If the atmosphere for government-dispensed services worsens more than that for private-sector goods, the public-sector share will increase, under a price elasticity of demand that is less than unity, or, if that elasticity is greater than unity, under an income elasticity sufficiently greater than unity, in view of the rate at which per capita income is growing.

A second factor that seems to have been at work over time to increase per capita cost of level of government service is a relative increase in unit input costs. The degree of this increase in recent years has evidently been substantial.[c]

---

[c]Morris Beck,[7] studying the experience of thirteen mostly developed countries, has deflated the ratio, current government expenditures to GDP, by two price indexes, one reflecting changes in prices of the inputs covered by government expenditures and applied to

A third factor in some instances is rising density of population or property. Density is to be measured by number of persons per unit area, or, for business districts, by number of patron-hours or value of property per unit area.[d]

In view of finite world space, including oceans, ice caps, mountains, forests, and other absolutely or relatively uninhabitable areas, world density necessarily rises as world population grows. This broad measure of density, however, is useful only in calling attention to possible landfills, leveling, clearing, and other means of creating inhabitable areas. More relevant for the present discussion is change in density in an already inhabited area.

To isolate the per-capita cost effect of increasing density from that of growth of population, which by itself tends to reduce per capita cost, an increase in density may be envisaged as occurring through compression, into a smaller area, of a given number of persons or a given amount of property. For example, if 200 persons are living in single-family houses in each of 100 blocks in Period 1, the Period 2 analysis might deal with 800 persons living in each of 25 blocks of apartments that now fill one-quarter of the original area.

Total cost of a given level of a certain service to this unchanged number of persons might well decrease as density increased: police protection, street maintenance, flood control, drainage, and education, and, after a certain moderate density had been reached, of sewerage, garbage and refuse removal, and recreational and cultural facilities.

The opposite might be true of public health, fire protection, highways, and, up to a certain moderate density, of sewerage and the other items just mentioned.[9]

To be sure, total cost of a given level of any of these services to a fixed number of persons or amount of property seems bound to rise at both extremes: if the persons or property to be served are spaced very widely or are highly compressed.

Some negative externalities that the government may be asked to help combat, air pollution for example, may increase rapidly with density.

---

the numerator of that ratio, the other being the GDP price index, applied to the denominator. Current government expenditure is defined as "Current expenditure for government consumption, transfer payments to households, subsidies to industry, interest on public debt, and miscellaneous current expenditure." From an average for the years 1950 to 1952, to an average for 1968–70, under this dual deflating technique, the public sector share declined in eight of the countries, the greatest decline being in Greece (from 19.1 percent to 12.7 percent, a decline of 34 percent in the percentage), rose slightly in three countries, and rose considerably only in two, the larger being in Sweden (from 23.2 percent to 32.7 percent, an increase of 41 percent in the percentage). For every one of the countries the price index applicable to the numerator rose more rapidly than the GDP price index. Even though in general it would not appear advisable to deflate by two different price indexes in computing a share, the results of doing so in this instance are useful in calling attention to one of the reasons why the public sector share has increased, in current prices.

[d]Much of Wagner's law of increasing public expenditures over time rests, in effect, on the increasing need that is assumed for public services in an industrializing, urbanizing economy.[8]

The net direction of change in total cost of the more common governmental services to a given population or amount of property, as density increases, seems not at all clear a priori. Some increases of total cost that are commonly laid to increase in density may be due simply to increase in numbers served; change in density is sometimes analyzed in terms of constant area.

V

Conjectures as to whether the share of the public sector (aside from transfer payments) will grow or shrink over time should of course consider simultaneously the several forces at work described in Sections II and IV above (as well as others that may be important). Here, only the combined effects of jointness-over-users and a technological lead or lag for government services will be so considered, partly because of their special significance, and partly because the public finance literature has paid considerable attention to both features, but almost completely in isolation from one another.[e]

There are two combinations of jointness over users and technological lag, together with the appropriate elasticities of demand, that lead to an increase in the share of the public sector in total output.

One of these combinations links a high price elasticity of demand with a high degree of jointness-over-users, and relative technological progress, or at least not much technological lag. As time passes, and population grows, cost per unit per capita declines; the technological lag, if any, is not large enough to offset the influence of population increase. The price-elastic demand, not offset by a low income elasticity of demand as per capita income increases, causes a larger total amount and larger share to be spent on the good (by taxation, through the political process).

The other combination consists of a low price elasticity of demand, a low degree of jointness-over-users, a technological lag, and, again, an income elasticity of demand not too low. If the technological lag is large enough, relative to the degree of jointness-over-users, cost per unit per capita rises, and the low

---

[e]The jointness-over-users attribute of public-sector services (which extends to some private-sector services as well) is not noted in Baumol's article.[10] Dean A. Worcester, Jr., discussing Baumol's thesis, does refer to marginal cost pricing, apparently in terms of marginal cost over users, as possibly implying zero price, but only in the context of a change in the area distribution of population, not an increase of population over time. Baumol's only reference to population in his article implies that this factor is accompanied by an increase in density and a consequent increase in negative externalities that will rise roughly as the square of the number of inhabitants, as when "total domestic sootfall will be equal to soot per home times number of homes . . ."[11] Certain more recent studies of local government expenditures have similarly made no reference to possible reduction in per capita cost arising from at least partial jointness over users, given some growth in population.[12]

price elasticity of demand causes a larger total amount and a larger share to be spent on the good.

The first of these combinations will be referred to below as Category I, the second as Category II. Corresponding categories, with reverse consituents, can be formulated for goods that become a smaller part of the total product over time.

Government expenditure data for the United States suggest that neither Category I nor Category II goods account for a substantial part of government outlays, and that the same is true of their opposites. In·the fiscal year 1972–73 the "direct general expenditure" of the governments in the United States (federal, state, and local) came to $344 billion. If "public welfare," $27 billion, is subtracted, the remainder is accounted for by: national defense and international relations, 25.1 percent of this remainder; education, 23.9 percent; highways, 6.0 percent; health and hospitals, 5.9 percent; postal service, 3.0 percent; veterans' services, 2.3 percent; police protection, also 2.3 percent; sanitation, 1.7 percent; local fire protection, 0.9 percent. There remains 23.7 percent not allocated among activities: interest on general debt, 7.9 percent, and "other functions," 15.8 percent.[13]

Most of the federal outlay, apart from transfer payments (not covered in the the present analysis) is for the military. Price and income elasticities of demand for services of the military are difficult even to conjecture in the roughest way.

At the state level, the bulk of non-transfer expenditure goes for higher education, highways, health and hospitals (mostly hospitals) and "natural resources." Appreciable proportions of each of these services are consumer's goods, for which, therefore, elasticities of demand may be somewhat more readily conjectured than if they were producer's goods.

At the local level, non-transfer expenditure is chiefly for local schools. Substantial amounts are spent on highways and streets, health and hospitals, and police protection. Somewhat smaller amounts go to sewerage, housing and urban renewal (part of this consists of transfer payments), fire protection, parks, recreation and cultural facilities, and sanitation other than sewerage. Again, only a portion, but an appreciable one, of each of these services is a consumer's good.

Aside from certain aspects of elementary education, and secondary education also, to be treated separately below, most of these state and local services seem to be only quasi-collective consumption goods, i.e., without full jointness-over-users.

Technological lag, relative to all the rest of the economy, may well be zero or negative for highways, health (if not hospitals), police protection and fire protection.

As to price elasticities of demand (through the political process), the private sector supplies moderately good substitutes, up to a point, for increments of police service, sanitation other than sewerage, health and hospitals, and recreational and cultural facilities, but not for highways, streets, sewerage (save in rural areas), fire protection, and, for the groups of persons affected, housing and urban renewal. Price elasticities for the publicly supplied good may therefore be fairly high for the first group, fairly low for the second.

Income elasticities of demand are probably at least not too far enough below unity to negate the net effect of the other forces when that effect is share-increasing.

In general, then, few if any of the consumer goods supplied free of charge in the United States by the various levels of government possess all the characteristics of the Category I combination or of Category II, or of the reverse types. In this conjectural survey, therefore, apart from elementary and secondary education, no clear tendency emerges for either growth or shrinkage in the share of consumer's goods distributed free of charge by government, over time, with respect to population growth and technological lag.

Expenditure on education ranks with defense plus international relations outlay as a proportion of direct general expenditure by all levels of United States governments combined. The remarks below apply chiefly to elementary and secondary education.

Education reflects three kinds of demand, since it is a bundle of three different services: a consumer's good, prized for its own sake by the person receiving it; a producer's good, creating human capital; and, from the viewpoint of all others than the person being educated, an externality that is both a consumer's good and a producer's good, this externality consisting of an improved milieu arising from the ability of others to read, write, and compute.

As a producer's good, a form of human capital, which tends to lower the cost of creating consumer's goods in the future, education poses a particularly difficult problem in conjectures of elasticities of demand, a problem that will not be pursued here.

As a consumer's good, valued by the direct recipient for its own sake, education is of course demanded only by those not already educated, or not educated to the level they desire. In an almost totally illiterate society, this demand might be virtually zero or very strong, depending on whether the illiterate would recognize the disadvantages of illiteracy.

In any event, education viewed solely from the point of view of the pupil does have good substitutes, indeed almost perfect substitutes, in the private-sector market. On this score, the price elasticity of demand for public education should be fairly high. Education as commonly dispensed exhibits only a moderate degree of jointness-over-users, and this jointness does not extend beyond small groups. Some technological lag probably exists. Income elasticity may not be far from unity. Again, in summary, the requirements for Category I or Category II are not fully met (nor for their opposites).

The externalities created by primary and secondary education (public or private) cannot themselves be purchased, by any single beneficiary of the externalities, on the market. Being externalities, they can be supplied only in a non-price-excludable mode. Moreover, there are no private-market close substitutes.

Price elasticity of demand (through the political process) should therefore be fairly low. Income elasticity of demand for the externalities may be fairly high. There is complete jointness-over-users (simple collective consumption, not super-collective consumption). Some technological lag probably exists. Once more, education, now as a creator of externalities for the community, does not fit easily into either Category I or Category II or their opposites.

To summarize, for the direct-consumer and the externalities aspects of education: education is not precisely a Category I good as a direct consumer's service to the pupil, because it is not highly joint over users, nor as a bundle of externalities, because its price elasticity of demand is probably low; and education is not precisely a Category II good either, because, as a service to the pupil, its price elasticity of demand is probably high, and, as a bundle of externalities, it is highly joint over users. Similar reasoning would show that education does not fall easily into categories of goods the share of which in total product will decline over time (abstracting from its role as a capital good).

Notes

1. For circumstances under which crime prevention might be a super-collective consumption good, see Carl S. Shoup, "Non-Zero Marginal Cost per Consumer, with Non-Excludability," in Warren L. Smith and John M. Culbertson (eds.), *Public Finance and Stabilization Policy, Essays in Honor of Richard A. Musgrave* (Amsterdam: North-Holland, 1974), pp. 37–52, espec. pp. 41–42.

2. *New York Times,* April 27, 1975.

3. William S. Vickrey, *Microstatics* (New York: Harcourt, Brace & World, 1964), pp. 259–60.

4. William Vickrey, "Current Issues in Transportation," in Neil W. Chamberlain (ed.), *Contemporary Economic Issues,* revised edition (Homewood, Ill.: Irwin, 1973), pp. 219–20.

5. William J. Baumol, "Macroeconomics of Unbalanced Growth: The Anatomy of Urban Crisis," *American Economic Review* 57 (June 1967): 415–26; and, in the same journal, September 1968, Vol. 58, Carolyn Shaw Bell, pp. 877–84; L.K. Lynch and E.L. Redman, pp. 884–86; Dean A. Worcester, Jr., pp. 886–93; J.W. Birch and C.A. Cramer, pp. 893–96; and William J. Baumol, pp. 896–97, all under the caption, "Macroeconomics of Unbalanced Growth: Comment;" and, again in the same journal, September 1969, Vol. 59, Joan Robinson, "Macroeconomics of Unbalanced Growth: A Belated Comment," and William J. Baumol, "Comment on the Comment," p. 632.

6. Alan T. Peacock and Jack Wiseman, *The Growth of Public Expenditures in the United Kingdom* (Princeton, N.J.: Princeton University Press, National Bureau of Economic Research, 1961).

7. Morris Beck, "The Expanding Public Sector: Some Contrary Evidence" (preliminary draft), and "Letters to the Editor," *New York Times,* Feb. 21, 1975, and correspondence with the present author.

8. See Herbert Timm, "Das Gesetz der wachsenden Staatsausgaben," *Finanzarchiv* 21, 2 (Sepbember 1961): 201–47.

9. For conjectures on this score, see Carl S. Shoup, *Public Finance* (Chicago: Aldine, 1969), Ch. V, especially p. 143.

10. See note 5 above.

11. Baumol, "Macroeconomics of Unbalanced Growth," p. 424.

12. D.F. Bradford, R.A. Malt, and W.E. Oates, "The Rising Cost of Local Public Services: Some Evidence and Reflections," *National Tax Journal* 22, 2 (June 1969): 185–202, an "investigation inspired by Baumol's contention . . ." (p. 190); and Roger S. Smith, "Financing Cities in Developing Countries," *International Monetary Fund Staff Papers* 21, 2 (July 1974): 329–88.

13. United States Department of Commerce, Bureau of the Census, *Governmental Finances in 1972–73*, Series GF73-No. 5 (Washington, D.C.: U.S. Government Printing Office, 1974).

13

Optimal Fishing with a Natural Predator
Robert M. Solow

Ideas and events have combined to generate increased concern about the adequacy of the world's natural-resource base for continued economic development. In turn, this concern has awakened and reawakened interest in the economic theory of renewable and non-renewable resources. There has always been, if I may make a joke, an undercurrent of interest in the economics of fisheries, but the subject has attracted wider attention recently, and will no doubt attract still more as the problems of managing a 200-mile coastal limit are seriously considered.

In the first section of this chapter I outline briefly one of the standard problems of the economics of fisheries: the optimal exploitation of a single species obeying a logistic growth law. In the remainder of the chapter, I consider a generalization: a situation in which the original species is also being "exploited" by a natural predator, presumably of lesser economic value. The original fishery can then be "farmed" in a sense, by capturing the predator, I have no idea if this situation plays any important role in real fisheries; but I hope to show that in any case it has some general interest, for the light that it throws on the principles of the economics of complex ecological systems.

I

Imagine a localized fishery, occupied by a single species. In the absence of fishing, the fish population would grow according to the logistic law:

$$\dot{x} = x(a - bx) \tag{13-1}$$

where $x(t)$ represents the aggregate population size or biomass. The constants a and b can be interpreted: a is the maximum growth rate of the population, achievable only when the population is very small relative to the carrying capacity of the environment R; while $\bar{x} = a/b$ is the largest sustainable population size—any larger population will decrease in size. It is easy to see that x converges to a/b from any positive initial size.[a]

---

[a]Any growth function with these qualitative properties would do. The logistic has time-hallowed familiarity on its side, and it leads to easy computations. It is a much more important defect that this model lumps all ages together.

If a local fishing industry catches fish at the rate $g(t)$ [i.e., takes $g(t)dt$ fish in the sort time interval between t and $t + dt$] then (13-1) can be replaced by

$$\dot{x} = x(a - bx) - g(t) \qquad\qquad (13\text{-}2)$$

on the assumption that fishing does not interfere with the normal reproductive process.

Suppose that inputs into fishing can be summed up in units of generalized "fishing effort." The application of E units of fishing effort when the size of the fish population is $x(t)$ will result in a catch

$$g(t) = mEx(t). \qquad\qquad (13\text{-}3)$$

Here m is a "catchability" coefficient; it gives the fraction of the fish population that will be caught per unit of fishing effort. Obviously (13-3) can be at best a local approximation, because it can hardly be literally true that $E = 1/m$ units of fishing effort will catch every last haddock in the sea in time dt.

There are several things the literature can do with this model. The one I want to summarize asks for the socially optimal pattern of fishing effort over time. Even here there are several alternatives, of which the simplest is a partial-equilibrium approach. If one takes it for granted that there are other fisheries catching the same species, or that other species are very close substitutes, then the demand curve will be very elastic and the social value of the catch can be taken to be its market value at the going price, pg, rather than the area under the demand curve. Similarly, if fishing effort has a variety of uses elsewhere in the economy—often not the case in isolated fishing communities—then the social costs can be taken as wE, where w is the market price—or some adjusted price—of a unit of effort. Then the problem is to choose a discount rate and maximize

$$\int_0^\infty e^{-rt} \left[pg(t) - wE(t) \right] dt$$

subject to (13-2), (13-3), and, for technical reasons, an upper bound on E.[b]

This problem has been studied and solved by Clark [1973], Neher [1974], Spence [1973], and others. See also Mohring [n.d.].

The outcome is interesting and easily characterized. There is an optimal stationary state with fish stock x^*, effort E^*, and catch g^*, all constant. The best strategy is to get to that stationary state as quickly as possible: if the initial stock is less than x^*, refrain from fishing until it grows to x^*; if the initial stock exceeds x^*, apply the maximal fishing effort until it is reduced to x^*; afterwards

---

[b]The unit cost of catching a fish is w/mx when the fish stock is x. Since one can not expect ever to observe a stock greater than the carrying capacity a/b, unit cost can never be less than wb/ma. We must assume that $p > wb/ma$ or it will never pay to exploit the fishery at all.

keep to the optimal stationary state forever. The optimal stock x^* is the unique positive root of the quadratic equation

$$(2/\bar{x})x^2 - \left(1 - \frac{r}{a} + \frac{w}{pmk}\right)x - \frac{wr}{pam} = 0. \tag{13-4}$$

Once x^* is calculated, set $\dot{x} = 0$ in (13-2) to find $g^* = x^*(a - bx^*)$. Then from (13-3) $E^* = g^*/mx^* = (a - bx^*)/m$.

I do not wish to repeat all of the interesting economics that others have built onto this simple analysis.[c] The literature is fun to read. Let me just point out that (a) the stationary solution does not coincide with "maximum sustainable yield" $(= \bar{x}/2)$ unless the rate of time discount is zero *and* the ratio of unit fishing cost to price is negligible; and (b) the stationary optimum will not be achieved by an atomistically competitive fishing fleet unless the appropriate rate of time discount happens to be infinite. Competition will lead to overfishing because there is a classical "common-property" externality. The stock of fish is common property, and its depletion is not a private cost to anyone. For given x, fishing exhibits constant returns to scale in E. Individual fishermen will enter until price equals unit private cost, i.e., $p = w/mx$. Even if price is fixed, the mechanism for achieving zero-rent equilibrium is the entry of fishermen until the stock of fish is reduced and unit cost driven up to meet p. This is the solution one gets by dividing both sides of (13-4) by r and letting r go to infinity. The reason is that when the discount rate is very large, the social value of the fish is negligible, because the world effectively ends tomorrow, and individual fishermen are right to ignore it.

II

Now suppose there are two species of fish sharing the same territory, one as predator and the other as prey. Let x be the population or biomass of prey and y the stock of the predator species. Then Volterra's equations for the interaction are:

$$\dot{x} = x(a - bx - cy)$$

$$\dot{y} = y(-f + c'x). \tag{13-5}$$

For discussion, see Maynard Smith [1974, pp. 19-35]. In the absence of the

---

[c]One supposes that E^* is less than the preassigned upper limit to E. We need that boundedness because otherwise it would be optimal to get to x^* from above "instantaneously." Boundedness of E is just an extreme form of increasing marginal cost.

predator, $y = 0$ and (13–5) reduces to (13–1). Otherwise the term $-cxy$ gives the capture of prey by predators per unit time; the assumption is that the catch is proportional to the number of predators for fixed prey population and proportional to the number of prey for fixed predator population. The second equation of (13–5) is not symmetric or even antisymmetric with the first; it presumes that the availability of prey is the only environmental limit on the growth of the predator population. Ecological theory has alternatives to this model, but it seems a sensible starting point for the economics. (By the way, (13–5) generates damped cycles converging to a stationary equilibrium.)

Suppose that both species can be fished and let $g(t)$ and $h(t)$ be the rates parent–characterization of the best fishing strategy. (This characterization also holds in the single-species situation, but there the most-rapid-approach property is much more descriptive.) In the usual way for such problems, one can define and, in principle, compute a time-varying shadow-price for a unit of biomass in the stock of fish. Let $\lambda(t)$ be the shadow-price for prey and $\mu(t)$ the shadow-price for predator at time t. Then $e^{-rt}\lambda(\bar{t})$ measures the largest achievable increment to the present-value integral (13–8) if one unit of prey were exogenously added to $x(\bar{t})$ at time $\bar{t}$ along an optimal path. Similarly, $e^{-rt}\mu(\bar{t})$ answers the same question for an exogenous addition to $y(\bar{t})$ at time $\bar{t}$. They are standard dual variables. Now the present value of the marginal benefit from applying an extra unit of fishing effort E at time t is $e^{-rt}[w + \lambda(t)mx(t)]$. Here w is the out-of-pocket private cost of a unit of fishing effort; $mx(t)$ is the reduction in stock from the marginal unit of fishing effort and its shadow value of $\lambda(t)mx(t)$ is not a cost to the individual fisherman though it is a cost to the whole fishery.

The best path has the property:

$$\text{if } pmx(t) < w + \lambda(t)mx(t), E = 0$$

$$\text{if } pmx(t) > w + \lambda(t)mx(t), E = E_{max}$$

$$\text{if } pmx(t) = w + \lambda(t)mx(t), 0 \leqslant E \leqslant E_{max}. \qquad (13\text{–}8a)$$

By exactly similar reasoning,

$$\text{if } qny(t) < w + \mu(t)ny(t), F = 0$$

$$\text{if } qny(t) > w + \mu(t)my(t), F = F_{max}$$

$$\text{if } qny(t) = w + \mu(t)ny(t), 0 \leqslant F \leqslant F_{max}. \qquad (13\text{–}8b)$$

Notice that $\mu(t)$ might easily be negative; the presence of an extra unit of predator will certainly diminish the value of the prey fishery and probably the value of the whole fishery, unless the predator species is itself very valuable. So even if the predator is a valueless trash fish, i.e., $q = 0$, it will be socially valuable to fish for it so long as $w + \mu(t)ny(t) \leqslant 0$. In any case, a fishery should shut down if the marginal benefit from a unit of fishing effort exceeds the full shadow cost, and should fish at maximal intensity if the marginal benefit exceeds the full shadow cost.

One other property of the best path is very important: marginal benefit and marginal social cost can be equal in both fisheries simultaneously during an interval of time only when the combined fishery is in its optimal stationary state. Once that state is achieved, the best strategy is to stay there. In other words, along an optimal path either (a) one or both fisheries must be shut down, or (b) one or both fisheries must be at its maximal permissible effort, or (c) both fisheries must be at their optimal stationary state. This conclusion justifies concentrating further analysis on the stationary optimum.

III

The optimal stationary values for the populations of predator (y^*) and prey (x^*) are given as the roots of the equations

$$(pc - qc')x = rw/ny + (wc/m - rq - fq)$$

$$(pc - qc')y = rw/mx - 2pbx + (bw/m - wc'/n - rp + ap),$$

provided, of course, that x^* and y^* are non-negative. In discussing these equations, I shall take it for granted that p is much bigger than q, so that the coefficient $pc - qc'$ is positive. If the predator is the valuable species, the industry would hardly want to compete with it for its food supply; there may be intermediate cases, but I have not thought about them. It is a little more transparent to rewrite these equations as

$$y = A/(x - B) \tag{13-9a}$$

$$v = C/x - Dx + G \tag{13-9b}$$

where

$$A = rw/n(pc - qc') > 0$$

$$B = (wc/m - rq - fq)/(pc - qc')$$

$$C = rw/m(pc - qc') > 0$$

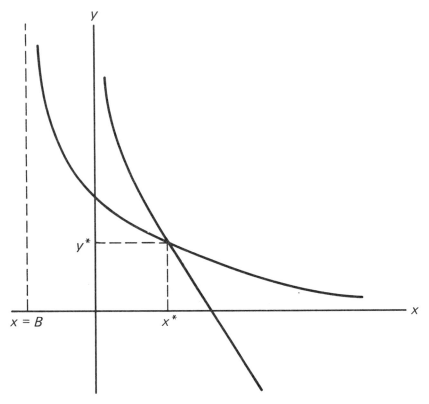

Figure 13-1. Optimal Stationary State, $B < 0$

$D = 2pb/(pc - qc') > 0$

$G = (bw/m - wc'/n - rp + ap)/(pc - qc').$ (13-10)

For computational purposes, y can be eliminated between (13-9a) and (13-9b) to leave a cubic equation in x. For qualitative inspection, however, it seems better to plot (13-9a) and (13-9b) separately. Since x and y are intrinsically non-negative, we need only look at the branches that intersect the first quadrant. Three configurations are possible, as shown in figures 13-1, 13-2, and 13-3.

The graph of (13-9b) has the y-axis as a vertical asymptote; for large x it is asymptotic to a straight line of slope $-D$ (see figure 13-1). The graph of (13-9a) has a vertical asymptote at $x = B$ and falls toward the x axis as x gets large. In figure 13-1 B is negative and the two curves intersect just once at the optimal stationary state (x^*, y^*).

In figure 13-2, B is sufficiently large that the two curves do not meet. There is no optimal stationary state; presumably the best path has one or both

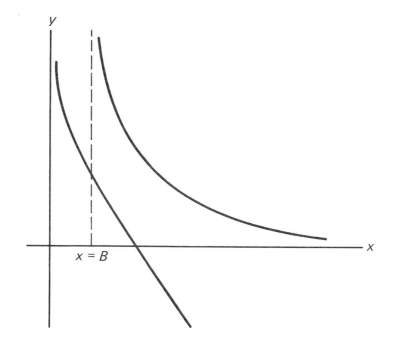

Figure 13-2. No Optimal Stationary State, B Sufficiently Large

fisheries operating with zero or maximal effort all the time. (That may be the case even if the curves do intersect.)

In figure 13-3, the curves intersect twice, and the question arises as to which of the solutions represents the optimal steady state. The following line of reasoning suggests convincingly that the lower-right-hand intersection is the one that counts. Inspection of (13-10) shows that the parameter n enters the definitions of the constants A and G. If n were higher, A would be smaller and G bigger. That is to say, the graph of (13-9a) would be shifted downward and that of (13-9b) upward. In the configuration of figure 13-3, the NW intersection would move further to the NW, the SE intersection further to the SE. Now an increase in n is simply an increase in the productivity of effort applied to the capture of the predator. That must presumably lead to a steady state with a smaller population of predator and a larger population of prey, i.e., must shift the point (x^*, y^*) to the SE. So the SE intersection is the relevant one.

A similar intuitive argument follows from imaging a rise in f. The parameter f enters only the constant B, and a higher value of f reduces B, translating the graph of (13-9a) to the left. In the two-intersection case, a higher value for f moves the NW intersection further to the NW and the SE intersection further to the SE. Now from (13-5) or (13-6), a higher f means a greater natural mortality of the predator species for any given size of the prey population. Again, it seems

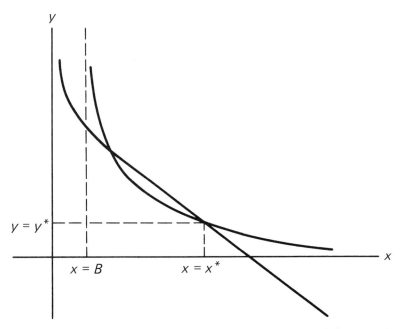

Figure 13-3. Possible Optimal Stationary States and Intuitive Solution, $B > 0$

implausible that such a shift in the ecology would lead to an increase in the predator population and a decrease in the valuable prey population in the optimal
stationary state. But then again it is the SE solution that must be the relevant
one. Obviously these arguments need to be made rigorous. (There is also a possible case with three solutions in the first quadrant; this intuitive reasoning suggests that only the middle one is economically relevant.)

Once x^* and y^* are determined, we have from (13–6) with $\dot{x} = \dot{y} = 0$ that
$g^* = x^*(a - bx^* - cy^*)$ and $h^* = y^*(-f + c'x^*)$. Then (13–7) gives $E^* = (a - bx^*$
$- cy^*)/m$ and $F^* = (-f + c'x^*)/n$. These formulas provide some inequalities on
the stationary populations of the two species. If the industry reaches a stationary optimum with g^* and h^* (and therefore E^*, F^*, and y^*) positive, it follows
that

$$a/b > x^* > f/c'$$

$$y^* < (a - bx^*)/c. \qquad\qquad (13\text{-}11)$$

The first of these inequalities says that x^* can not exceed the carrying capacity
of the environment in the absence of both predation and fishing and can not fall
short of the population of prey needed to sustain a positive population of preda-

tor.[d] The second inequality says that y can not be so large as to hold the prey population constant, because then there would be no room for fishing. These bounds are too weak to be really useful.

One's first hope in analyzing simplified models like these is to find strong, simple qualitative results in comparative statics or comparative steady states, if only because they are likely to transcend the details of the model. Thus in the one-species case, it is easy to show by implicit differentiation of (13-4) that a higher interest rate leads to a smaller stationary population, a larger input of effort, and a rate of catch that could go either way. Similarly, a higher value of w/pm leads to a larger population, a smaller input of effort, and again an ambiguous effect on the rate of catch. I have not found any comparably pithy statements for the predator-prey model. I suppose I can take some comfort from the thought that the very fact is interesting; it suggests that in dealing with complex ecological systems—even the two-species system is after all not terribly complex—the formulation of good policy will have to depend more on precise empirical knowledge of the behavior parameters and less on rules of thumb derived from strong special cases. But that is just a thought, not a tried and true conclusion.

As an illustration, consider how variations in r and in w/p affect the stationary populations of the two species. For this purpose, we can simplify (13-9) and (13-10) by taking the special case $q = 0$, when the predator species has no market value. It is easy to see that a higher r corresponds to a higher value for A and C, no change in B and D, and a reduction in G. When $q = 0, B = 0$, so we must investigate the consequences for x^* and y^* in terms of figure 13-3, where there are two first-quadrant intersections, of which one (the SE one) is relevant. The graph of (13-9a) is shifted upward proportionally to its ordinate in the original situation. If that were all, we could say unambiguously that x^* falls and y^* rises. But the graph of (13-9b) also shifts; it is translated downward parallel to itself because of the reduction in G, and it is shifted upward proportionally to its original ordinate because of the rise in C. As far as I can tell, the economically relevant solution can move in any direction depending on the catchability coefficients m and n, about which anything could in principle be true. It seems to me, just from playing with the graph, that it is "easier" for y^* to rise than to fall, and that makes economic sense: when $q = 0$, catching the predator is almost a pure investment, so a higher interest rate might be expected to inhibit fishing for the predator, and allow its population to increase. But that is not an airtight theorem, because any reduction in the stock of prey also operates on y, and in the opposite direction. It's an excellent example of the conflict between complex ecology

---

[d]This merely reflects the assumption that $h^* > 0$. For some values of the parameters, it may be optimal to drive the predator species to extinction by direct capture or by limiting its food supply.

and simple economics. An increase in r might also move the fishery from the situation of the third to that of the second figure.

If we turn to the case of an increase in w/p, the same ambiguity is present. When $q = 0$, a rise in w/p entails a rise in A, B and C, no change in D, and a change in G that has the sign of $g/m - c'/n$, and so could go either way. Again, both curves can shift upward in the diagram, and one can not be certain about the direction in which x^* and y^* change. (Perhaps I should note explicitly that the graph of (13-9a) shifts upward in both examples, so that it is impossible for both x^* and y^* to fall with an increase in r or w/p, but that is hardly an earth-shaking (ocean-shaking?) result.)

IV

In the single-species fishery, the common-property character of the marine resource generates an externality that makes exploitation of the fishery by atomistic competitors non-optimal, and maybe even inefficient (in the sense that effort is larger *and* output smaller than in some other feasible situation). As the literature has pointed out, this defect would disappear if rights to the fishery were auctioned off or turned over to a sole owner, which could be a cooperative. This would internalize the cost of depleting the fish stock. (Competition in the product market could still be preserved if there were other fishing grounds for the same species, or many close substitutes.) Given security of tenure, the sole owner would presumably maximize the present value of future rents, and optimality would be achieved, provided the discount rate were socially "right."

The same reasoning is true in the two-species case, but in spades. There is an added complication. In the automatic case, nobody is motivated to fish for the predator; there may be an out-of-pocket loss if the market value of the predator is small, certainly if it is zero, and in any case the situation is a classic instance of the "free rider." Thus if the defect is to be removed by the device of exclusive rights, it is necessary that the local monopolist understand the interspecies relation. In the simple one-predator–one-prey model, that is enough, subject always to the proviso that private and social discount rates coincide. The holder of exclusive rights to the fishing ground would be motivated to deal properly with the predator species. But the main advantage of the simple two-species model is to alert us to the full scope of the problem. For sole ownership to work, the range of exclusive rights must cover the full range of (important) ecological interrelationships. For example, suppose the prey species does not travel, but the range of the predator covers several fishing grounds, and it feeds on several species. Then if these relations are quantitatively important, the exclusive-access solution has to confer rights to all the affected fisheries in the same agency. Otherwise the free-rider problem persists, and more subtle externalities arise: the size of each prey population affects the size of other prey populations indirectly through effects on the predator.

Decentralized control of the fishery can be achieved in another way, through the imposition of a tax (or the payment of a bounty) on the capture of various species. The raw materials for such a policy have already been introduced in (13–8a) and (13–8b) in the form of the shadow-prices λ and μ. It is plain from the characterization of an optimal path in (13–8ab) that the appropriate policy is to levy a tax equal to λ for each member of the prey species captured, and a tax equal to μ for each predator captured. If the appropriate tax is negative, as will usually be the case with μ if q is small, the tax becomes a bounty (or sub-sidy). There is an indeterminacy when equality holds in (13–8a) and (13–8b) that will probably be taken care of by the demand for fish; otherwise a touch of quantitative control might be needed.

The solution of the optimization problem generates differential equations for λ and μ. I will write down only the stationary values of the shadow prices corresponding to an optimal stationary state in which neither fishery is operating at either zero or maximal effort:

$$\lambda^* = \frac{rpmE^* + c'y^* qnF^*}{r(r + bx^*) + cc'x^* y^*}$$

(13–12a)

$$\mu^* = \frac{(r + bx^*)qnF^* - cx^* pmE^*}{r(r + bx^*) + cc'x^* y^*}.$$

(13–12b)

In these equations one can substitute $mE^* = a - bx^* - cy^*$ and $nF^* = -f + c'x^*$. Notice that λ^* is always positive when the fishery actually operates, but μ^* may well be negative if q is small, and certainly if $q = 0$.

The normal situation in an optimal stationary state is that the government taxes the capture of prey and offers a bounty on the capture of predator. It is natural to wonder whether the aggregate tax on the fishery is positive or negative. (There is not enough constant returns to scale in this model to offer any hope that the aggregate tax or bounty will usually vanish.) It is easy enough to calcu-late, using (13–12ab), that when $q = 0$

$$\frac{\lambda^* g^* + \mu^* h^*}{pg^*} = \frac{1}{H} \frac{rg^*}{x^*} - ch^*$$

where H is the (positive) denominator that appears in (13–12a) and (13–12b). It follows, then that the aggregate tax $\lambda^* g^* + \mu^* h^*$ is positive or negative according as

$$rg^* \lessgtr cx^* h^*$$

$$y^* \lessgtr \frac{r(a - bx^*)}{c(r - f + c'x^*)}. \tag{13-13}$$

We can see from (13-11) that, when plotted as a curve, (13-13) decreases from $x = f/c'$, $y = (ac' - bf)/cc'$ [which is the natural equilibrium of (13-5) when there is no fishing] to $x = a/b$, $y = 0$. If this curve is plotted on one of the previous diagrams, one can read off the sign of the aggregate tax-bounty according as (13-9a) and (13-9b) intersect below or above the graph of (13-13).

V

The only other point I want to make is that the predator-prey set-up is only one of several possible two-species interactions. Ecologists distinguish a "competitive" situation and a "commensal" situation. The interaction is competitive when each species responds negatively to the presence of the other, presumably because they compete for limited resources. In that case, the second equation of (13-5) or (13-6) would look just like the first, with α, β, γ replacing a, b, c. In a commensal interaction, each species responds positively to the presence of the other, perhaps because each uses a by-product of the other, or because they have a common enemy. In that case, the term $-cy$ in the first equation of (13-5) or (13-6) would be replaced by $+cy$, with a similar rewriting of the second equation. The optimal fishing problem can be analyzed in those contexts as in the predator-prey context. The results will be different, but the principles and the general implications the same.

References

Clark, Colin W. "Profit Maximization and the Extinction of Animal Species." *Journal of Political Economy* 81 (1973): 950–60.

Mohring, Herbert. "The Costs of Inefficient Fishery Regulation." Unpublished, n.d.

Neher, Philip. "Notes on the Volterra-Quadratic Fishery." *Journal of Economic Theory* 8, 1 (May 1974): 39–49.

Smith, J. Maynard. *Models in Ecology.* Cambridge University Press, 1974.

Spence, Michael. "Blue Whales and Applied Capital Theory." Unpublished, 1973.

14 Estate Taxes, Growth, and Redistribution

Joseph E. Stiglitz

Introduction

One of Vickrey's major contributions was his thorough analysis of estate and inheritance taxes, and his attempt to devise a scheme which would reduce some of the distortions associated with the present system of inheritance taxes. The object of this short essay is to extend Vickrey's discussion of estate taxes, and to show, in particular, that under certain circumstances, the estate tax may not achieve the objective to which it is presumably directed, equalizing the distribution of income.

Capital Accumulation and Inequality

The reason for this is that the estate tax may reduce savings, the reduction in savings and capital accumulation will, in the long run, lead to a lower capital labor ratio, and the lower capital labor ratio will, if the elasticity of substitution between capital and labor is less than unity, lead to an increase in the share of capital. Since capital income is more unequally distributed than is labor, the increase in the proportion of income accruing to capital may increase the total inequality of income.

This result hinges on three key assumptions (besides the assumption that the elasticity of substitution be less than unity).

Estate Taxes and Savings

The first assumption in the above argument is that the estate tax leads to a reduction in savings. There are two aspects to this. First, the estate tax can be thought of as a transfer from the individuals who would have inherited the wealth, to the population as a whole. The latter is effected, for instance by the reduction in income tax which the revenues raised through the estate tax allows. The question is, what is the effect of this transfer?

The increased income to the population as a whole will have associated with it the conventional marginal propensity to consume out of income. The effect of the transfer depends on the magnitude of marginal propensity to consume out of income relative to the marginal propensity of individuals to consume out of inheritances. If the latter is treated like any other wealth (rather than like any other income), as seems likely, then since the marginal propensity to consume out of wealth is much lower than that out of income, the estate tax has a significant effect on the aggregate consumption rate.

The second aspect is concerned with incentive effects. If bequests are treated like consumption the $n + 1^{st}$ period of the individuals life (where the individual lives n periods), then there is an income effect and a substitution effect associated with the tax. The income effect leads the individual to consume less during his lifetime; the substitution effect to consume more. On a priori grounds it is not possible to say which effect is stronger. But even if the individual is induced to consume less to increase his gross bequest (so that his net bequest is reduced by less than the magnitude of the tax) it does not seem likely that this effect will overcome the transfer effect described above.

The Concept of Balanced
Growth Incidence

The second assumption in the argument that the estate tax may lead to greater inequality because of reduced savings is that the government does not or cannot take countervailing actions.

Presumably, the government, through monetary policy could offset any effect on the pattern of capital accumulation.

The question raised here is of import for more than just the analysis of the estate tax. A wide variety of taxes effect savings, and the question is in a general equilibrium context, how are we to evaluate such taxes. The questions raised are analogous to how are we to evaluate the incidence of a tax, in the context of the standard macroeconomic model, for the tax will have a deflationary effect on the economy, so that the equilibrium level of national income will be reduced. There is now widespread agreement that the most meaningful comparisons are to policies which leave the level of output constant; e.g., we *substitute* one tax for another tax.

Here, it seems to me appropriate to introduce some notion of *balanced growth path incidence,* where we compare policy changes which leave the aggregate capital labor ratio unchanged. Such policy comparisons might include offsetting the savings effect of the inheritance tax by an interest subsidy on savings (essentially substituting life-cycle savings for inheritance savings), or, offsetting the reduced private savings by increased government savings, or, as mentioned above, offsetting the reduced savings through monetary policy.

The Distribution of Wealth

The third basic assumption in our argument that the estate tax might increase the inequality of income was that capital is more unequally distributed than labor. Although this is undoubtedly true at the present time, the question may legitimately be raised of whether this would be the case if we had larger inheritance taxes. The answer depends on the particular theory of the determination of the income and wealth distribution. We now show that, indeed, the inheritance tax may have an effect on the equilibrium distribution of wealth, but *even if the estate tax has no effect on the aggregate capital labor ratio it may increase the inequality of wealth ownership.*

The argument is presented in a model which is a modification of that presented by Stiglitz (1969). We assume (a) individuals leave as a bequest to their children an amount which is a linear function of their lifetime income

$$B = sY - a$$

where B is the bequest, s is the marginal propoensity to save out of lifetime income $a \geqslant 0$ is the intercept of the consumption function (consumption at zero income) Lifetime income for the ith family is equal to their wage income plus interest income, i.e.,

$$Y_i = w_i L_i + rC_i$$

where C_i is the amount of (inherited) capital of the family, w_i is the wage received, r the rate of interest, and L_i is the number of wage earners in the family. (b) Individuals differ in productivity, but the productivity of children is identical to the productivity of their parents (the assumption of perfect correlation of abilities). (c) All families reproduce at the same rate. In continuous time, we let n be the rate of increase in the size of the family. (d) Parents divide their wealth equally among their children.

If we let y_i be income per capita in the family, and c_i be wealth per capita, and represent the dynamics of capital accumulation of the family in continuous time, we obtain

$$\dot{c}_i = sw_i - a + (sr - n)c_i$$

or, in equilibrium

$$c_i = \frac{sw_i - a}{n - sr}.$$

Thus, the coefficient at variation is wealth is given by

$$\gamma_c = E(c_i - \bar{c}_i)^2 / \bar{c}_i^2 = s^2 \sigma_w^2 / (s\bar{w} - a)^2$$

where σ_w^2 is the variance of w and $\bar{w}$ is the mean of w. To obtain this result, we observe that in equilibrium, if P_i is the proportion of the population in the ith group,

$$k = \bar{c} = E\, p_i c_i = \frac{s\bar{w} - a}{n - sr}.$$

We now impose an inheritance tax, distributing the proceeds as income transfers, if τ is the tax rate, the wealth accumulation equation becomes

$$\dot{c}_i = [sw_i - a + src_i - + s\tau nk]\,(1 - \tau) - nc_i$$

and

$$\dot{k} = [s\bar{w} - a + s(r + n\tau)k]\,(1 - \tau) - nk.$$

Thus in long-run equilibrium

$$c_i = \frac{(sw - a + sn\tau k)(1 - \tau)}{n - sr(1 - \tau)}$$

$$k_i = \frac{(sw - a)(1 - \tau)}{n(1 - s\tau(1 - \tau)) - sr(1 - \tau)}.$$

It is clear that if s were constant, an increase in τ (for small τ) would reduce k and the coefficient of variation of c_i,

$$\gamma_c \equiv \frac{s^2 \sigma_w^2}{(s\bar{w} - a)^2}\left[\frac{n(1 - s\tau(1 - \tau)) - sr(1 - \tau)}{n - sr(1 - \tau)}\right]^2$$

$$= \frac{s^2 \sigma_w^2}{(s\bar{w} - a)^2}\left[1 - \frac{s\tau n}{\dfrac{n}{1 - \tau} - sr}\right].$$

The effect on the coefficient of variation on income depends on the magnitude of the elasticity of substitution. In steady state

$$y = \frac{n(w + n\tau k) - a(1 - \tau)}{n - sr(1 - \tau)}$$

$$\gamma_y = \frac{n^2(\sigma_w^2/\bar{w}^2)\alpha^2}{(n - sr(1 - \tau))^2}$$

where $\alpha = \bar{w}/\bar{y}$ is the share of labor in national income if individual's productivities are related to each other in a Harrod-Neutral way, i.e., w_i/w_j is independent of k, then $\sigma_w^2/\bar{w}^2$ is a constant, and the coefficient of variation then depends simply on α and $r(1 - \tau)$. It is then possible that the increase in τ includes an increase in γ_y.

Assume, on the other hand, that s changes so that k remains constant. Then,

$$\gamma_y = \frac{n^2(\sigma_w^2/\bar{w}^2)\alpha^2}{(s\bar{w} - a + sn\tau k)^2(1 - \tau)^2}.$$

Thus

$$- \text{sign}\left(\frac{\partial\gamma_y}{\partial\tau}\right)_{\tau = 0} = \text{sign}\,\frac{\partial(1 - \tau)(s\bar{w} - a + sn\tau k)}{\partial\tau}\bigg|_{\tau = 0}$$

$$= \alpha srk - (1 - \alpha)k(n - sr - sn)$$

$$= [sr - (1 - \alpha)(1 - s)]\,k$$

which may be of either sign. For reasonable values of the parameters

$$\left(\frac{\partial\gamma_y}{\partial\tau}\right)_{\bar{k}} > 0.$$

If the marginal savings rate adjusts to keep the capital labor ratio constant, the inequality of income (as measured by the coefficient of variation) increases.

The Distribution of Consumption

It is not clear, however, that the inequality of the variable which we are ultimately interested in is the distribution of income or wealth; in some sense, the relevant variable is consumption. Under certain circumstances, it seems clear that the *estate tax may actually lead to an increase in the inequality of consumption.*

This is the case, for instance, if the conventional adage of "from rags to riches to rags in three generations" were correct; for the effect of inheritances in that case is to spread the consumption of the productive antecedent over three generations; disallowing inheritances would have forced the antecedent to consume the entire amount himself.

Within a generation, there is little incentive for an individual to transfer wealth to an individual, even a relative, who is better off than he is. Most gifts are thus unambiguously equality increasing, in the sense discussed by Atkinson and Rothschild-Stiglitz. It is clear that within a given generation, taxing such voluntary redistributions might well increase the degree of inequality, and certainly forbidding them would.

Similarly, it would seem that one of the motivations of parents in leaving bequests to their children is that parents who are both able (have a high wage) may, if they believe in the process of regression towards the mean, expect their children (on average) to be less able than they are. Thus, if their children's welfare enters their utility function, they will make a transfer payment to their child. On average, it is clear that this is inequality reducing, but under certain circumstances we can make an even stronger statement. Assume that there were only two ability groups, the more able, and the less able. Regression towards the mean, in that case, simply means that there is a finite probability of a parent of one type having a child of the other. Assume also that the rate of interest is small (more precisely, zero). Then a parent of the more able type who inherits less than a critical amount C^* will leave to his children (assuming for simplicity that he does not know their ability at the time of bequest) an amount in excess of the amount that he has inherited, i.e., he consumes less than his own wage income. A parent of the more able type who inherits more than C^* will consume out of his inheritance, but in steady state, no one will even inherit more than C^*. Thus all individuals of the more able type consume an amount less than or equal to their wage incomes, i.e., the income that they would have consumed if inheritances are not allowed. The same argument establishes that all individuals of the lower ability group consume an amount equal to or more than their consumption if inheritances were not allowed. Thus putting a prohibitive tax on inheritances would be unambiguously inequality increasing. Exactly how general the conditions are in which this result obtains, remains an open question. But, as we noted earlier, even if a policy of limiting inheritances did not unambiguously increase inequality, in the strong sense defined above, under weaker conditions it is likely to increase the average degree of inequality.

Distortions of the Estate Tax on the Form of Transfer

Earlier we briefly discussed the incentive effects of the estate tax on the total amount of bequests left. But there is a further effect of the tax, on the form in which bequests take. This distortion arises because of the inability to monitor all transfers. In particular, by giving his child human capital, he transfers wealth to his child without paying inheritance or gift taxes. Since much of the acquisition of human capital does not occur within the market sector, it would be virtually impossible to tax such transfers. To the extent that this offsets effects associated with imperfect capital markets for human capital, the distortion may be desirable; it may however have lead to excessive expenditures on human capital relative to physical capital. The ability of parents to transfer wealth to their children in the form of human capital also limits the ability to equalize incomes through an inheritance tax. Finally, differences in wage incomes may be more invidious (in terms of individuals views of themselves, their status, etc.) than differences in capital income.

Concluding Comments

In this essay we have focused on several aspects of the economics of estate taxes that have received perhaps too little attention in recent discussions. These taxes may not lead to the reduction in inequality which their proponents desire; but rather may increase the degree of inequality. The importance of these considerations depends not only on the values of certain economic parameters, which we have identified in our earlier discussion, but also on the importance ascribed to these economic considerations relative to the non-economic considerations. Accumulations of wealth may, it is argued, lead to accumulations of political power, and effect the nature of our political processes. Opponents of estate taxes are concerned with the ethical grounds for restricting this particular class of choices of individuals. They ask, why should parents who do not wish to leave wealth to their children, but prefer to consume it themselves, restrict the ability of parents who do wish to leave wealth to their children? Although these ethical and political questions may in the final analysis be more important in determining policies towards inheritances, it is at least worth noting the important economic effects of such policies.

References

Rothschild, M. and J.E. Stiglitz. "Some Further Results on the Measurement of Inequality." *Journal of Economic Theory,* April 1973.

Stiglitz, J.E. "Distribution of Income and Wealth Among Individuals." *Econometrica,* 1969.

Vickrey, W. *Agenda for Progressive Taxation,* 1947.

Part II
Urban Economics

15

Welfare Implications of Various Pricing Schemes in Monopolistic Competition Due to Location

Ronald E. Grieson

A literature concerned with the questions of monopolistic competition's existence and possible inefficiencies has recently arisen. Barzel (1970), Demsetz (1968, 1971, 1972), Schmalensee (1972), Telser (1969, 1971), and Vickrey (1964) have participated in this literature.

Schmalensee sees the production inefficiencies which result from a firm facing a downward sloping demand curve as the major issue. Demsetz takes the position that firms with U-shaped cost functions could only face non-infinitely elastic demand if they produce significantly different products in which case he sees the inefficiency that results ($P = AC > MC$) as a cost of worthwhile diversity. However, Demsetz acknowledges that inefficiencies do result and are undesirable only in the case of indivisibilities. It might be noted that indivisibilities usually present us with natural monopoly, as do persistent economies of scale.

Monopolistic competition can result from differences in location and the subsequent transportation costs. Increasing the quantity sold will require attracting customers from further away who will require lower prices as compensation for increased transportation to the firm or store. We will show that the existence of monopolistic competition's production inefficiencies (when significant) can be mitigated (inefficiency reduced) by the provision of free delivery within a given (set) area only.

By analogy, the location-transportation case will be extended to advertising and sales costs which will also be provided free ("c.i.f." not "f.o.b."), leading to greater efficiency in production and transportation (distribution or advertising). Similarly, the model applies to all firms experiencing increasing returns due to the above factors.

Without free delivery, locational differences would lead to an individual paying the average cost of physical production of the good plus the marginal cost of transportation from the firm. Conversely, free delivery will lead to the consumer paying a price equal to the marginal cost of the good plus the marginal cost of delivery (to the furthest customer), the service area being such that this is equal to the minimum average cost of production plus transportation. The average cost of production will be lower than for the f.o.b. case, though not a minimum. Minimizing the average cost of production alone would be undesirable, since it would not minimize the average total cost of the good to the purchaser,

I would like to thank William S. Vickrey, Donald Dewey, Lester Telser, Robert Mundell, and especially Ralph Beals for their comments.

235

that is the average cost of production and transportation combined, as production cost minimization would involve excessive transportation costs. It will be shown that, under certain assumptions, free delivery is the lowest cost-most "efficient" solution possible in the absence of government subsidies which permit the price of production to be set equal to marginal cost. The chapter provides a solution to location created monopolistic competition discussed in the Telser (1969, 1971)–Demsetz (1968a, 1971) debate.

Monopolistic Competition Caused by Location or Transportation Costs

Our case is that of spatially separated firms producing an identical product.[a] Different delivery distances and thus transportation costs are involved in obtaining goods from different firms and cause consumers to consider the delivered products of firms to differ significantly in transportation cost. This is the Demsetz case in which there must be some costs other than production to cause consumers to consider significant differentiation to exist. Retail (drug, etc.) stores would be a good example. If the nth consumer is willing to pay $\bar{P}_n$ for the good delivered to his door, he is only willing to pay $\bar{P}_n - t_{in}$, where t_{in} is the transportation cost from the ith producer, if he pays for delivery. Without price discrimination with regard to customers' location, the firms' f.o.b. price (P_i) will be a uniform $P_i = \bar{P}_n - t_n$, where t_n is the freight cost to the most distant consumer.

We shall assume that customers are uniformly distributed over a featureless plain and that they have identical demand curves. The individual demand curves are assumed completely inelastic at a quantity qth for all $P \leqslant P$ and a quantity zero for all $P > P$. Any distribution that is invariant with respect to the price of the good will lead to the same conclusion, though the featureless plain is easiest to conceive of. The extent to which the elasticities of demand and/or location with respect to the price of the good could be different from zero is a function of the derivatives of the average costs of production and transportation.

Free Delivery

If each firm provided no charge ("c.i.f.") delivery to all of its customers, a superior, lower average cost, allocation of resources would be achieved than with f.o.b. pricing. With free delivery, consumers become indifferent to which firm supplies the good and the demand for the output of each firm becomes perfectly

---

[a]We shall assume that the demand for the goods is large enough to achieve competition in the absence of spatial separation and transportation costs.

elastic over the range of output in which the free delivery zones overlap sufficiently to guarantee competition. The price of the good would be equal to the
marginal and minimum average total cost of production plus transportation.

   The cost of transportation of the good is an addition to marginal cost. In
equilibrium (*with free delivery*), at q_1,

$$P_1 = \frac{C(q_1)}{q_1} + \frac{t(q_1)}{q_1} = C'(q_1) + t'(q_1), \tag{15-1}$$

where P_1 is the price of the good including delivery, $C(q)$ and $t(q)$ are the total
costs of production and transportation at equilibrium q respectively and $C'(q)$
and $t'(q)$ are their marginal values. The marginal cost of transportation is the
transportation cost of the furthest customer or the additional cost of adding him
to an existing route.

   With *customer paid delivery*, demand would slope downward, with

$$P_0 = \frac{C(q_0)}{q_0} > C'(q_0),$$

the average cost of production at equilibrium quantity, q_0. The total price (cost)
of the good plus transportation to any given customer, P, would be;

$$P = P_0 + t'(q) = \frac{C(q_0)}{q_0} + t'(q) > C'(q_0) + t'(q), \tag{15-2}$$

where $t'(q)$ is the cost of transportation to customer i. The larger the firm's output, q, the greater the distance from the firm that the marginal customer is located. Hence, transportation cost is a function of the quantity sold, q.

   With customer paid delivery, the maximum price a firm can charge customers will decline with distance and be equal to a constant minus the cost of
transportation to the customer(s);

$$P = \bar{P} - t'(q). \tag{15-3}$$

The constant $\bar{P}$ will be the maximum the closest customer would pay (we will assume all customers have the same rectangular demand curve). $\bar{P}$ would be equal
to P_1 if the pay delivery firm is competing with free delivery firms.

   Since average cost and demand are tangent at equilibrium and the slope of the demand curve is the negative of that of the marginal cost of transportation, equilibrium occurs at

$$t''(q_0) = \frac{C(q_0)}{q_0^2} - \frac{C'(q_0)}{q_0}, \text{ where } P_0 = \frac{C(q_0)}{q_0}, \qquad (15\text{-}4)$$

or similarly, by the use of $MC = MR$,

$$C'(q_0) = \frac{C(q_0)}{q_0} - q_0 t''(q_0),$$

from (15-2) and (15-3).

In order for free delivery to increase efficiency and output of the firm, the average total cost of transportation and production must be lower than in the case of customer paid delivery (classical monopolistic competition) at its equilibrium, q_0. Average costs to consumers are

$$\left(\frac{C(q_0)}{q_0} + \frac{t(q_0)}{q_0} \right) \text{or } [C'(q_0) + t'(q_0)]$$

given customer paid delivery or free delivery respectively.

Free transportation minimizes average total consumer cost if

$$C'(q_0) + t'(q_0) < \frac{C(q_0)}{q_0} + \frac{t(q_0)}{q_0}, \qquad (15\text{-}5)$$

the sum of the marginal costs of production and transportation are less than the sum of the average costs, which may be rewritten as

$$t'(q_0) - \frac{t(q_0)}{q_0} < \frac{C(q_0)}{q_0} - C'(q_0). \qquad (15\text{-}6)$$

Our contention is correct if marginal transportation costs exceed average by less than the amount by which average production costs exceed marginal in the customer paid transit equilibrium.

If the marginal cost of transportation is declining for a firm adding additional customers to its free delivery route at q_0, $t''(q_0) \leqslant 0$, due to initial economies of scale inherent in a central delivery system (a J- or U-shaped cost curve which may or may not be available in paid delivery),

$$t'(q_0) \leqslant \frac{t(q_0)}{q_0}$$

and the left-hand side of (15-6) will be negative and (15-6) will hold true. If $t'(q)$ is rising at q_0, $t''(q_0) \geqslant 0$, as is more likely, we must further investigate the necessary and sufficient conditions for (15-6) to hold!

Substitution of the equilibrium tangency condition (15-4) into (15-6) and rearranging terms yields

$$t'(q_0) - \frac{t(q_0)}{q_0} < q_0 t''(q_0). \qquad (15-7)$$

Now let us postulate the general rising marginal transportation[b] cost function $t'(q) = bq^n$. Thus $q_0 t''(q_0) = nbq_0{}^n$ and

$$\frac{t(q_0)}{q_0} = \int_0^{q_0} \frac{bq^n \, dq}{q_0} = \frac{1}{n} bq_0{}^n.$$

Substituting the above in (15-7) yields

$$bq_0{}^n - \frac{1}{n} bq_0{}^n < nbq_0{}^n$$

$$1 - \frac{1}{n} < n,$$

which is true for all $n \geqslant 0$.

Producer-paid transportation minimizes the average total cost of production plus transportation (equal to the marginal cost of transportation). Making the usual assumption that the marginal cost of transportation is rising, it reduces, but does not minimize the average cost of production. Hence a non-free delivery firm could not compete unless it is willing to sustain negative profits, since the average cost of production incurred by the free delivery firm is below that which

---

[b]This was the first production cost function postulated. Other more and less general ones tried also yielded the same result.

would permit zero profits to be earned by the paid delivery firm. Consumers located within the free delivery zone of several firms would buy from any of them at the same price. Those within the range of only one would also pay the same price. Any higher price would create positive profits and induce the entry of additional firms until free delivery zones overlap for the consumer in question. It has been shown that a paid delivery firm will have higher production costs (with consumers having equal transportation costs) than a free delivery firm and thus would earn negative profits. The losses would be even greater if the paid delivery firm was not at the same location as the free delivery firm.[c]

Free delivery is the best (lowest average total cost of production and transportation) solution that can be achieved without government subsidies permitting price to be equal to marginal cost of production alone, $C'(q)$, for all consumers. The price discrimination involved in this solution does involve some inefficiency for all but the furthest customers. This solution *does not minimize average production costs. Minimizing just operation or production costs would be less efficient*, by which we mean it would involve excess transportation costs to customers beyond the point q_i, the furthest point to which free delivery is provided. Average total (production plus transportation) costs are above both their marginal and minimal values in the customer paid transportation case. Free delivery may raise or lower the total cost of the good to those located closest to the firm, changing it from P_0 in equation (15-2) to P_1 in equation (15-1).

Free transit may raise or lower local land values, depending on whether it is available elsewhere and its effect on the price of the good to nearby consumers. If free transit raises the good's price to those located adjacent to the firm and there exists perfect competition in structural (and land) markets, free transit will reduce equilibrium structure and land rents near the firm and raise them further away. Hence, the shift to "free" transport may not cause any loss to consumers located near the firm even if they wind up paying more, but instead change equilibrium structure and land rents to be uniform throughout the relevent area (lower near the firm and higher further away). Those residing near the firm would reduce their consumption of the good and those living further away would increase it. The average cost of production (and production plus transportation) would decrease as quantity demanded and per capita consumption increase. If all consumers have the same utility functions and incomes and the density of structures was uniform, no movement of consumers would occur. If structural density did vary, as it would, then the higher structural rents would have brought about greater structural density near the firm. Free transport would equalize

---

[c]If the density of consumers is uniform, as in a featureless plain, the free or paid delivery firms would locate at equidistant points. Otherwise they will locate where the density of consumption is greatest. In either case, free delivery will dominate as our specification of the consumer density-delivery cost function was completely general.

structural price and density and be accompanied by movement away from the firm.[d]

The good under analysis is not the only one in the consumer utility function and therefore may or may not be the only one having transport costs or being subject to monopolistic competition for any reason. Hence, consumers may locate uniformly over the area or tend to concentrate around firm(s), with variable structural density. Either would have no effect on the qualitative impact of the analysis but only result in different patterns of structure (land) prices (and perhaps construction costs depending on whether or not variable density occurs). However, utility will be the same at any location for consumers with the same utility functions. Again, even differing utility functions and locational attributes will have no effect on our analysis.

The Effect on Price to Nearby Consumers

The switch to free transit will raise the price (cost) of the good to consumers located adjacent to, at zero distance from, the firm if

$$\frac{C(q_0)}{q_0} < C'(q_1) + t'(q_1) = \frac{C(q_1) + t(q_1)}{q_1}, \tag{15-8}$$

average production cost of the good under monopolistic competition is less than the marginal, equal to minimum average, cost of the good and freight with producer paid freight.

Rearranging terms in (15-8) yields

$$\frac{C(q_0)}{q_0} - \frac{C(q_1)}{q_1} < \frac{t(q_1)}{q_1}. \tag{15-9}$$

If the average cost of "free transportation" exceeds the reduction in average production cost that it will bring about, it will raise prices to adjacent consumers.

Substituting (15–4) in (15–8) and rearranging terms yields

$$q_0 t''(q_0) - t'(q_1) < C'(q_1) - C'(q_0). \tag{15-10}$$

We know $C'(q_1) - C'(q_0) > 0$, the marginal cost of production with free trans-

---

[d]For a fuller discussion of structural densities, land values and capitalization, see Grieson (1972 and 1974).

port is more than with customer paid transport because of the larger output in
the former case.

Hence, if the left-hand side of (15-10) is negative, the inequalities (15-8),
(15-9), and (15-10) hold, and free transit raises transport costs to nearby customers. If $t''(q_0) < 0$, the left-hand side of (15-10) will be negative and the inequality will hold. If $t''(q_0) > 0$, the effect is indeterminate.

It might be argued that free transportation could reduce society's welfare,
in spite of the reduction in average total cost $(C + t)$, if the elasticity of demand
for the good on the part of nearby consumers was very much larger than that of
more distant ones. However, given some rather obvious and reasonable simplifying assumptions about demand, it could easily but tediously be shown that free
transit would not occur under that case since it would reduce aggregate demand
for the firms' output thus raising its average costs of production.

The last two questions with which we need deal are the optimal number of
firms and how our pricing system is arrived at. The market demand for the good,
Q, would be determined from P_1 and the market demand curve. Since the optimal firm output is q_1, the optimal number of firms is Q/q_1.

Competition would prevent an independent firm from entering the market
and offering to sell at a lower price on an f.o.b. basis. Thus, the competitive
equilibrium is possible without regulation or other restrictions on competition.
If an f.o.b. firm entered the market, it would face the downward sloping demand
curve, D, in our analysis, determined by delivery costs. The f.o.b. firm would
have the same average cost of production schedule, $C(q)/q$, as a free delivery
firm. Hence, the equilibrium price and quantity for the firm would be

$$P_0 = \frac{C(q_0)}{q_0}$$

and q_0 at the point of tangency. The free delivery firm minimizes the average
cost of transportation plus production and any other output would not. Monopolistic competition would give a solution to the left of free delivery while minimizing the cost of production alone would yield a solution to the right of the
free delivery solution and both would be at higher total cost.

The cost of the good to a consumer would be

$$P_0 + t'(q_0) = \frac{C(q_0)}{q_0} + t'(q_0)$$

from an f.o.b. firm which is more than the cost

$$P_1 = C'(q_1) + t'(q_1) = \frac{C(q_1) + t(q_1)}{q_1}$$

from a free delivery firm.
Our proof that

$$\frac{C(q_0)}{q_0} + t'(q_0) \geqslant C'(q_1) + t'(q_1) = \frac{C(q_1) + t(q_1)}{q_1}$$

is as follows. Since

$$t''(q_0) > 0, \frac{C(q_0)}{q_0} + t'(q_0) > \frac{C(q_0) + t(q_0)}{q_0},$$

we need only show

$$\frac{C(q_0) + t(q_0)}{q_0}$$

has a negative slope at q_0, for then

$$\frac{C(q_0) + t(q_0)}{q_0} \geqslant \frac{C(q_1) + t(q_1)}{q_1}, q_1 > q_0.$$

The slope of average cost at q_0 is

$$\frac{C'(q_0) + t'(q_0)}{q_0} - \frac{C(q_0) + t(q_0)}{q_0^2}.$$

We have already shown in equation (15–6),

$$C'(q_0) + t'(q_0) < \frac{C(q_0) + t(q_0)}{q_0}$$

and therefore the slope of

$$\frac{C(q_0) + t(q_0)}{q_0}$$

is negative and our contention that the cost of the good is less in the free delivery equilibrium than in the monopolistic competition equilibrium is true for
both the cost of the q_0 customer and the average cost to all q_0 customers. It is
obviously true for all $q \gtrless q_0$, for as q becomes progressively smaller than q_0,
$C(q)/q$ increases more than and has a larger absolute slope than $D, = t''(q)$. Similarly, as q rises above q_0, $C(q)/q$ decreases more slowly and has a smaller slope
than $-t'(q)$ and D, as in the well-known condition for a tangency at q_0. Thus at
any output, q, the f.o.b. firm will have to charge a price below average cost,

$$P < \frac{C(q)}{q},$$

in order to compete with the free delivery firm(s) involving both a welfare and
profit loss.

These results *allow* the price of the good to effect consumers' location decisions, since the initial demand curve, D, was based on the location of consumers
when only an f.o.b. firm existed.

Our analysis of demand and output with free delivery permits the free delivery firms to have overlapping areas bring about competition among them.[e]

Conclusions and Extensions

This result can be extended to include all firms in which the marginal cost
of production lies below the average and can be extended to include the cost of
advertising and sales to reach those informationally and knowledgeably distant
from a producer. Companies having marginal less than average costs would provide free transportation, sales services and advertising within the minimum average total cost range or distance indicated by q_1. Those firms experiencing constant or decreasing returns to scale would not provide free delivery, advertising,
distribution, etc.

These firms would add the cost of any of these services to the price charged
at the warehouse. Auto parts wholesalers, etc., would fit into this category,
while a monopolistic competitor like the Encyclopedia Britannica or Xerox
would charge the same price whether a consumer just called in and ordered a few

---

[e]For our proofs to always hold, we must rule out the possibility that all customers will
order from the most distant of the free delivery firms whose radii overlap the customers' location. The customers need not always order from the closest free delivery firm for our conclusions to hold.

We can however, easily postulate reasons why individuals would order from the nearest
free delivery firm in spite of the fact that all firms charge the same total price. It may be
that the closest firm will probably deliver the good slightly more quickly. By slightly, we
mean only an epsilon more quickly.

units or was subject to expensive and extensive sales and advertising pressure. Large detergent ads may increase the efficiency of and lead to minimum average cost of production plus information combined, as detergent production may be subject to economies of scale in production.

References

Archibald, G.C. "Chamberlin vs. Chicago." *Review of Economic Studies* 29 (October 1961).

Archibald, G.C. "Monopolistic Competition and Returns to Scale." *Economic Journal* 77 (June 1967).

Barzel, Y. "Excess Capacity in Monopolistic Competition." *Journal of Political Economy* 78 (September/October 1970).

Demsetz, H. "Do Competition and Monopolistic Competition Differ?" *Journal of Political Economy* 76 (January/February 1968a).

Demsetz, H. "Why Regulate Utilities." *Journal of Law and Economy.* (April 1968b).

Demsetz, H. "On the Regulation of Industry: A Reply." *Journal of Political Economy* (March/April 1971).

Demsetz, H. "The Inconsistencies in Monopolistic Competition: A Reply." *Journal of Political Economy* 80 (May/June 1972).

Dewey, D. "Imperfect Competition No Bar to Efficient Production." *Journal of Political Economy* (February 1966).

Dorfman, R. and Steiner, P.O. "Optimal Advertising and Optimal Quality." *American Economic Review* 44 (December 1954).

Grieson, R.E. "The Economics of Property Taxes and Land Values: The Elasticity of Supply of Structures." *Journal of Urban Economics* (October 1974).

Lancaster, Kelvin "Socially Optimal Product Differentiation." *American Economic Review* 65 (September 1975).

Schmalensee, R. "A Note on Monopolistic Competition and Excess Capacity." *Journal of Political Economy* 80 (May/June 1972).

Stigler, G.J. *Five Lectures on Economic Problems* (New York: Macmillan, 1950).

Stigler, G.J. "A Theory of Oligopoly." *Journal of Political Economy* (February 1964).

Telser, L. "On the Regulation of Industry: A Note." *Journal of Political Economy* (November/December 1969).

Telser, L. "On the Regulation of Industry: Rejoinder." *Journal of Political Economy* (March/April 1971).

Vickrey, W.S. *Microstatics* (New York: Harcourt, Brace & World, Inc. 1964).

16

Crime Prevention and the Police Service Production Function

Werner Z. Hirsch
Sidney Sonenblum
Jeffrey I. Chapman

Introduction

Police agencies frequently claim that they could improve citizen's welfare if they had additional funds. These claims can be substantiated only if generally accepted output measures of police agencies can be systematically related to resources required to provide the outputs. There are important difficulties in measuring agency output particularly if the objective is to prevent something from happening, e.g., crime. Empirical analyses have proceeded along two lines: attempts to explain the behavior of police agencies and attempts to explain the behavior of criminals.

Empirical attempts to explain governmental agency behavior with expenditure determinant studies [6] and then moved on to cost function studies [8, 9] in which various agency and service characteristics are seen as affecting costs of production. Although cost studies are theoretically more rigorous than expenditure studies they do not directly face the issue of appropriately defining output agencies which seek to prevent something from happening. Consequently, in recent years attempts have been made to reexamine agency cost functions [4, 15] and through cost-benefit analyses to define agency outputs [1, 13]. The other line of development has focused on the sources of crime rather than on the police agency. Thus, there have been crime determinant studies which identify various community and criminal characteristics as influencing crime [5, 11, 12, 13] and there have been theoretically based crime function studies which identify crime producing behavior of criminals in economically rational terms [3, 14].

In the model described below police agency activity and criminal behavior are related in the following way:

The potential criminal's behavior is partly influenced by his/her perception of the police agency's capacity for catching criminals. This factor is incorporated in a crime function. The relative extent to which a police agency prevents crimes can be estimated from the crime function. But crime prevention is only one dimension of output. Once a crime has been committed society generally seeks

This research was supported by grant #GS 3309 of the National Science Foundation, to whom we express our appreciation. We also benefited from advice on econometric problems given by Michael Intriligator, John McCall, and Don Atwater and from institutional information on the police by James Fisk, all of the University of California, Los Angeles. We of course assume responsibility for any mistakes.

247

punishment of the criminal and the police department initiates this process by making arrests. The punitive component of police output is estimated with the use of arrest data. The two components—preventive and punitive—are then combined to define an index of real output of the police agency. This is incorporated in agency output equations. The agency's behavior is then analyzed in terms of the effects of resource utilization on the output it generates. This is incorporated in the police agency production function

Thus a link between behavior and police agency is established if agency output can be defined as including the agency's effect on preventing crime [4]. However, prevented crimes are not recorded; they can only be inferred. The measurement of prevented crimes, therefore, becomes somewhat arbitrary and raises some econometric difficulties. In spite of these difficulties the model provides with a high reliability theoretically explainable results—the amount of crime produced in cities through its crime function and the output produced by police agencies through its production function.

The Crime Function

A conventional economic behavior model for criminals has been adopted. The model postulates that crime is a potential source of income which the individual compares with potential legal income before making a decision as whether or not to commit a crime. The amount of crime in a city results from six factors affecting the criminal's perception of the relationship between his legal and illegal wage. We would expect that the number of crimes committed in a community would be higher the greater the population, the higher the per capita real wealth, the larger the percentage of nonwhites, the lower the median education, and the lower the average household size in the community.

It is expected that the larger the *population* of a community, the more people in absolute numbers would engage in criminal activity, perhaps even at an increasing rate; *per capita real wealth* reflects a potential for illegal gains and acts to encourage crime because the "wage" gained from robbing a wealthy person is greater than that obtained from robbing a poor person; increasing education raises legal income more than illegal income; nonwhites are more discriminated against in the legal than in the illegal labor markets, thereby lowering their legal wage relative to their illegal wage; the larger the household, the greater the probability that someone will be at home at any one moment of time and that her presence will deter the commission of a crime.

Before committing a crime the rational criminal will consider the probability of being caught and punished. This probability is to a large extent influenced by the operations of the police agency. A change in the number of crimes committed in a community will reflect the criminal's perception of the likelihood that she will be caught and therefore her realized illegal wage. Thus the greater

Table 16-1

Property Crime Function: Eighty-two California Cities in 1960*

$$LCP = a + b_1 LD + b_2 LVAL + b_3 LPUSH + b_4 LPOP + b_5 LE + b_6 LNPL$$

	Crime Elasticity Coefficient	Standard Error	t	Mean
LCP = log (number of property crimes)	—	—	—	6.29
a	1.25	1.9	.66	—
LD = log (percent nonwhite)	.012	.04	.32	−3.81
$LVAL$ = log (locally assessed property value)	.13	.16	.87	.46
$LPUSH$ = (population per occupied household)	−1.12	.40	−2.79	1.14
$LPOP$ = log (population)	1.01	.07	15.2	10.8
LE = log (median years of schooling)	−2.0	.73	−2.74	2.49
$LNPL$ = log (change in crime between present and previous year)	.08	.02	3.41	4.03

R^2 = 0.8576
n = 82
SSR = 10.7584
SER = 0.3787
F = 79.6

*Recorded crime data are not wholly adequate. Most important is that many felony crimes are not even reported. But also the police department, by the way in which it engages in its activities, can encourage or discourage the reporting of crimes. Since reported crimes are often a factor in determining the police budget, biased reporting may be a common occurrence.

Annual Los Angeles data are available for all variables except percentage nonwhite and median years of education, for which data are available for only 1960 and 1970; with these as benchmarks, the number of nonwhite and median years of education were linearly estimated for 1956–1970.

the rate at which crimes have been increasing in the community, the preceding five factors being kept the same, the smaller the perceived probability of being caught and the greater the probability that additional crimes will be committed.

An ordinary least-squares regression equation has been estimated, relating property crimes to the above six independent variables for eighty-two California cities (excluding the city of Los Angeles) using 1960 Census data. All variables are measured in logarithms so that their coefficients can be interpreted as crime elasticities.

The fitted crime function in table 16-1 shows an R^2 of 0.86. Four of the six independent variables are statistically significant with their coefficients showing that a population increase will bring about the same proportionate crime increase while an increase in home protection (measured by population per occupied household) will lead to approximately the same proportionate decline in crime. At the same time an increase in income (measured by median years of schooling) will lead to a decline in crime which is proportionately twice the rate of the income increase while an increase in the criminals perception of the police agency's capacity to catch criminals (as measured by annual change in crime) will induce a crime increase which is proportionately only one-tenth of the perceived agency effectiveness. The per capita wealth variable (as approximated by assessed property value per capita) is found to be positively correlated to the number of property crimes but is not statistically significant.[a] The discrimination variable (percentage nonwhite) has the expected sign but is not statistically significant, perhaps because number of years of schooling explains the number of crimes committed better than does race. This would suggest that crimes can be better explained by economic than discrimination variables.

Police Output

Preventing Crimes

How many crimes are prevented by the police agency? Even if there were no police agency to catch criminals there would be a limit set to the number of crimes committed because at some point the legal wage would become greater than the illegal wage for the individual criminal. The difference between this hypothetical total potential number of crimes and the actual number of crimes committed would then be the number of crimes prevented.

However, the total potential number of crimes in a city is not recorded nor is it possible to estimate such a number indirectly through statistical techniques. What can be estimated is the amount of crime in a city which is predicted by the crime function. It is reasonable to expect that a ranking of predicted crimes among cities would be similar to a ranking of the hypothetical total potential crime among cities. The reason for this is that the crime function and particularly the coefficient of the annual change in crime variable reflects the effects of an intercity "average" police agency on preventing crime.

However, it is not an average but a real police agency which exists in a city and it is this real agency which influences the actual number of crimes committed. Therefore, the difference between a city's predicted crime (as estimated from the crime function) and its actual crime (as reported) is a measure of rela-

---

[a] Absence of a statistically significant correlation may have two basic causes. First, there is a high negative correlation between the logarithm of per capita property value and the logarithm of the population per household (r = .51). This colinearity might bias the coefficient of the property value variable and make it insignificant. Second, while wealthy people because of large assets may be victimized by property crimes more than poor people, they may also commit fewer crimes. Thus, the coefficient would be biased downward.

tive crime prevention; for this implicitly reflects the difference between the number of crimes which would be prevented by the "average" police agency and the number of crimes actually prevented by the city police agency. Also, relative crime prevention can be measured as a crime prevention rate, i.e., the ratio of predicted to actual crime.[b]

We have assumed that the structure of the crime function is applicable to Los Angeles, even though Los Angeles is much larger than the sample cities. Inserting Los Angeles data into the crime function, the annual number of expected Los Angeles property crimes for the period 1956 to 1970 were estimated and from these estimates the number of relative prevented property crimes and the relative prevented property crime rate could be calculated.[c]

The Punishment of Crime

Arrests can be considered as contributing to police output because society prefers that once a crime has been committed the criminal be punished. The police agency initiates this punitive process by employing resources in finding and apprehending criminals.

The number of arrests that can be made are not only limited but also influenced by the number of crimes committed. Thus an increase in arrests need not reflect an increase in police output (even though it requires increased resources) but may be due to other factors. For this reason the difference between arrests and crimes may be more appropriate than number of arrests as a representation of the output resulting from the punitive activities of the police agency. This difference might be called "unsuccessful crimes" and police output grows as this number increases (since arrests less crimes is always negative, an increase in this number, disregarding sign, implies an output decline). Unsuccessful crimes can be considered the punitive component of police output, analogous to prevented crimes as the prevention component.

---

[b]Our measure of relative crimes prevented—the difference between predicted and actual crimes—is equivalent to the negative of the error term as calculated in the crime function. In the crime equation the residuals are randomly distributed among cities, satisfying the Gauss-Markov assumptions. When the error term for a given city is calculated, it is assumed to be non-random and therefore can be used as a measure of prevented crime for that city.

[c]W. Patrick Beaton [2] in an interesting paper shows that insofar as police expenditure functions are concerned care must be taken that the regression equation is not fitted to too broad a population size range, since it may produce heteroscedastic residuals as found in New Jersey.

We tested for heteroscedasticity in our sample using the recommended Goldfeld-Quant test (1965). We found no heteroscedasticity in the residuals of our sample. We believe the difference in our results from those of Beaton is mainly because the cities in our sample are relatively homogeneous—with similar population mixes, population increases, growth rates, police traditions, etc.

However, unsuccessful crimes are rarely viewed as a key indicator of police performance. More commonly the arrest rate—arrests divided by crime—is viewed as a summary measure to evaluate the performance of the police agency in terms of how it responds to crimes committed. It is analogous to the crime prevention rate which summarizes performance in terms of preventing criminal activities.

Is the arrest rate satisfactory as the punitive component of police output, inasmuch as a police department can readily generate arrests in response to political pressure? If the crime rate rises, the police may make dubious arrests just to placate critics. The clearance rate—the ratio of crimes considered solved by the police department to crimes reported—does not avoid such difficulties. It too is subject to police discretion as to what constitutes a solved crime and could include even more distortions than the arrest rate [10]. In this sense, the arrest rate is at least as good a punitive component of output as the clearance rate.[d]

Combining the Components of Output

The prevention and punitive components of crime need to be combined in order to estimate police output. However we have already suggested two measures of prevention—relative prevented crimes and relative prevented crime rate—and two punitive measures—unsuccessful crimes and the arrest rate. It makes a difference as to which components are combined to obtain police output since prevented crimes change at a different pace than the prevented crime rate, and the arrest rate changes at a different pace than unsuccessful crimes.

There are several reasons for preferring the combination of relative prevented crime rate and arrest rate over the combination of unsuccessful crimes and relative prevented crime.

First, work with the Los Angeles Police Department suggests that their goals are established and their resource allocation decisions are made in terms of rates.[e]

---

[d]Most misdemeanors and some felonies are counted as a crime only when someone is arrested, e.g., drunk driving. If the arrest rate to be used as an output component includes such crimes, its numerator and denominator are simultaneously determined and upward-biased. To minimize this bias we limit the arrest rate (and unsuccessful crimes) to arrests and crimes for Part I felonies.

Part I felonies include murder, rape, assault, theft, larceny, robbery, and vehicle theft. Only the first four of these refer to the property crimes which are used in the measurement of the prevention component of police output.

The police agency acknowledges that while its activities can prevent some robberies, burglaries, larceny, and vehicle theft, which are the property crimes, it has little influence over murder, rape, and assault, which are the remaining felonies.

[e]For example, the police department, as well as the city council, newspapers, community groups, etc., closely monitor the arrest rate and the rate of crime in the community in

A second reason is the desirability of having the prevention and punitive components of output independent of one another. The combination of rates tends to mitigate interdependence.[f]

A third reason relates to how the community is likely to compare the punitive and prevention components. If weights are assigned to prevented and unsuccessful crimes the interpretation would be that the community values each prevented crime as being equal to (or twice as high as, etc.) each unsuccessful crime; if weights are assigned to the rates the interpretation would be that the community values crime prevention activities as being equal to (or twice as high as, etc.) the punitive activities of the police department. The latter interpretation seems more appropriate for output measurements, since attaching weights to the individual units of crimes not prevented and arrests not made produces output results solely affected by changes in community size.

Finally, while Part I felonies are the data base for estimating the punitive component, only property felonies are the prevention base. Combination of rates produces a smaller bias resulting from differential coverage between property crimes and all Part I felonies.

Although police output seems more appropriately estimated by combination of the crime prevention and the arrest rates for the indicated reasons, its use as the dependent variable in a police production function may bias the production function coefficient. This occurs because there is a relationship between the error term of the production function and actual crimes which is eliminated when prevented crime is used as an output component but does not cancel out when the prevented crime ratio is used. Empirical test of the bias shows that it grows as the arrest component becomes smaller in the output measure. Our calculations indicate that this bias ranges from -0.004 percent to $+2.16$ percent of the input coefficients. Usually, the coefficients are biased upward, indicating that the production inputs are calculated to have a slightly greater effect on output than is warranted.[g]

Even if we decide that the prevention and punitive components of police output should be measured as ratios we are still confronted with the issue of the importance which society attaches to each of these components. Is an ounce of prevention worth a pound of punishment or are there other standards?

Both police officers and the community recognize that police duties include

order to evaluate performance. Standards are set to reduce the rate of crime or increase the rate of arrest rather than to reduce the amount of crime or increase the number of arrests. This observation is supported by our production function analyses which show that net regression coefficients are more often statistically significant and their signs more often as hypothesized when the combination of prevention and arrest rates is used to measure output.

[f]The simple coefficient of correlation between the arrest rate and the crime prevention rate is $+0.165$ while that between prevented crimes and unsuccessful crimes is $+0.912$.

[g]The methodology and calculation of the biases are available upon request from the authors.

more than punitive and preventive activities. The most important are traffic control and providing miscellaneous services to families and the community such as
quieting family quarrels, patrolling parades, and finding lost children. Together
these account for about 40 percent of the patrolman's time [11].

However, it is inappropriate to seek to weigh components by the way in
which resources are used. Proper weights would relate to benefits and there is no
a priori way to know the relative weight that society or even the police give to the
prevention versus the punitive component of output. Therefore we have calculated alternative outputs for the years 1956-1970 as based on a 100 percent,
one-half, one-third, and two-thirds weighting combination for each component.[h]

Alternative estimates of police output in Los Angeles city since 1956 are
shown in table 16-2. Between 1956 to 1970, reported property crimes and felony crimes have almost tripled, predicted property crimes increased by almost
one-third and felony arrests doubled. Relative prevented crimes (the excess of
actual over predicted property crimes) increased by a factor of four during this
period, while unsuccessful crimes (the difference between felony arrests and
crimes) tripled. The relative prevented crime rate (ratio of predicted to actual
property crime) was cut in half over the interval while the felony arrest rate remained relatively constant. There seems to have been a major reduction in the
prevention component of police output while there has been a smaller reduction
in the punitive component. As compared with other cities the Los Angeles police
agency prevents fewer crimes and this gap has been increasing over the past fifteen years.

Police Production Functions

Not only is the police service highly labor intensive but different occupational classes of labor—motorcycle officers, field officers, nonfield officers, and civilian employees—are technologically related to the different classes of capital: motorcycles are the tools of motorcycle officers; automobiles are essentially the
tools of field and nonfield officers; and computers, communications equipment,
laboratory equipment, and office equipment are used mostly by civilians and
nonfield officers. Since changes in the mix of employees and kinds of capital are
highly correlated we define as real resource inputs the joint labor and capital input by occupational class, and measure this input by the number of employees

---

[h]In broad terms the overall police output is relatively insensitive to the alternative
weights assigned to the prevention and punitive components. In all cases output of the Los
Angeles police agency declined between 1956 and 1970, although generally at a faster pace
the greater the weight given to the prevention component; and generally at a slower pace
when measured by the combination of crime prevention and arrest rates as compared to the
combination of prevented and unsuccessful crimes.

Table 16-2
Los Angeles Police Output Measures 1956-1970

Year	Reported Property Crimes (X1,000) C	Predicted Property Crimes (X1,000) CP	Felony Arrests (X1,000) CA	Felony Crimes (X1,000) CT	Prevented Property Crimes (X1,000) $CP-C$	Prevented Crime Ratio CP/C	Unsuccessful (X1,000) $CA-CT$	Arrest Rate CA/CT
1956	82	46	22	88	-36	.557	-66	.251
1957	95	45	25	102	-49	.478	-77	.244
1958	104	46	27	112	-58	.442	-85	.241
1959	97	23	26	105	-75	.231	-79	.247
1960	115	51	32	124	-64	.441	-91	.258
1961	111	24	36	120	-88	.212	-85	.296
1962	117	49	36	126	-68	.415	-91	.282
1963	124	51	34	133	-73	.409	-99	.255
1964	137	55	34	147	-82	.400	-133	.233
1965	153	57	37	164	-96	.374	-127	.225
1966	163	56	33	175	-107	.341	-141	.191
1967	174	57	37	189	-116	.331	-151	.199
1968	194	61	44	209	-132	.318	-166	.208
1969	199	56	46	217	-143	.282	-171	.213
1970	209	58	46	226	-151	.279	-180	.203

Year	$\left(\dfrac{CP}{C}\right)^{1/3}\left(\dfrac{CA}{CT}\right)^{2/3}$	$\left(\dfrac{CP}{C}\right)^{1/2}\left(\dfrac{CA}{CT}\right)^{1/2}$	$\left(\dfrac{CP}{C}\right)^{2/3}\left(\dfrac{CA}{CT}\right)^{1/3}$	$\dfrac{1}{3}(CP-C)+\dfrac{2}{3}(CA-CT)$	$\dfrac{1}{2}(CP-C)+\dfrac{1}{2}(CA-CT)$	$\dfrac{2}{3}(CP-C)+\dfrac{1}{3}(CA-CT)$
1956	.327	.374	.428	-56	-51	-46
1957	.304	.341	.383	-68	-63	-58
1958	.295	.327	.362	-76	-71	-67
1959	.242	.239	.237	-78	-77	-76
1960	.308	.337	.369	-83	-78	-74
1961	.265	.250	.237	-86	-86	-87
1962	.321	.342	.366	-83	-79	-76
1963	.298	.323	.350	-91	-86	-82
1964	.279	.306	.335	-103	-97	-92
1965	.266	.290	.316	-117	-112	-106
1966	.231	.255	.282	-130	-124	-119
1967	.235	.256	.280	-140	-134	-128
1968	.239	.257	.276	-155	-149	-143
1969	.233	.245	.257	-162	-160	-152
1970	.225	.238	.251	-171	-166	-161

in each class.[i] Capital inputs are therefore assumed to enter into the production process through the combined productivity of the labor and capital package as represented by the input coefficients.

We anticipate these coefficients to have positive signs. We also expect field officer coefficients to be large relative to those for nonfield officers, motorcycle officers, and civilian employees because field officers are the primary agents for making arrests, and their visibility tends to prevent crime. Since a large part of the time of motorcycle teams (each consisting of one man, one cycle) is associated with traffic duties, which do not enter our output measure, we anticipate their effect on output to be smaller than that of other officers. However, since their visibility—and therefore crime deterrence—is high, their influence on output should be greater, the larger the prevention component in the output measure. Finally, it is expected that civilian employees, i.e., laboratory technicians, other investigatory (but not sworn) personnel, clerks, and stenographers, are expected to have smaller coefficients than sworn police officers.

There are two variables which are not labor/capital inputs. The first represents police knowledge about the potential criminal population in their jurisdiction. As this knowledge increases, it becomes easier to make arrests and prevent crimes. Recidivism is high, and released prisoner is likely not only to commit further crimes but also to know others who may again commit crimes. An approximation for police information is the number of newly released criminals in the community which is expected to be positively related to output. However, as the prevented crime component becomes more important, this variable is expected to become less important, perhaps even becoming negatively related to output, because the more exconvicts in the community, the harder it is to prevent crime.

Finally, a proxy variable in introduced into the police production function to account for possible structural crime changes in 1956–1970. It extends from 1965, the year of the Watts riots; its value is one for 1965 to 1970 and zero for earlier years. If there were structural changes in the crime function, the absolute value of the dummy variable's coefficient should become larger as the prevention component of output increases.

---

[i]Within each class of input, the mix of labor and capital varies. Motorcycles have retained a one-to-one relation to motorcycle officers. The ratio of cars to field officers has been gradually increasing over the period, while the ratio of cars to nonfield officers has remained about the same. Information on other classes of equipment is not available, although the amount of equipment has probably been increasing relative to the number of civilian employees and nonfield officers. For field officers, with an increasing car to labor ratio, the estimated coefficient will be larger than it would be if the ratio were constant. This bias may have some influence on the estimated coefficients of the other variables.

Also we attempted to explicitly introduce as a capital variable police cars per capita and police cars per sworn officer. Aside from that production function which gave a 100 percent weight to the arrest rate, there was no equation in which the variables were significant or had the anticipated (positive) sign. When a time variable was introduced to measure technological progress, it was not significantly different from zero, although its sign did indicate that there might be some small technological increases over time.

Production functions for each output category have been estimated for the period 1956–1970, with output and input variables measured in logarithms. Table 16–3 shows the estimated production functions which are based on combining the crime prevention and arrest rates to measure police output. Each R^2 is sufficiently high that the hypothesis that all estimated coefficients are equal to zero in any equation can be rejected at the 95 percent significance level. Furthermore, use of the Cochrane-Orcutt method gives Durbin-Watson statistics that are acceptable.

As hypothesized, an increase in per capita field officers is positively associated with an increase in police output, the effect of motorcycle teams on output increases as the proportion of prevention in the output measure increases, there is a positive relationship between police output and civilian employees, and a negative relationship between police output and the number of exconvicts living in the community.

However, the relationship between police output and nonfield officers is negative in four of the five equations though not significant,[j] and the hypothesis that the size of the input coefficients would be highest for field officers and then decline as we move to nonfield officers, motorcycle teams and civilian employees was not confirmed. Although we find that the importance of the input coefficients in terms of their impacts on output increases as the proportion of the prevention component of output increases, the explanatory power of the production function declines.

Finally, the dummy variable is consistently negative and always highly significant. It therefore appears that after 1965 it became harder for police to produce output.

Table 16–4 shows the estimated production functions when police output is measured by combining prevented and unsuccessful crimes. It was suggested earlier that such equations might be preferred to those in table 16–3, since they would eliminate the bias resulting from the relationship between the error term of the production function and crimes committed. However, while these equations result in a higher R^2, which is partly spurious, there are no significant factor input variables other than motorcycle teams.

Summary

The empirical analysis has sought to test the hypothesis that increasing police resources significally affect police output which is defined as including both prevention and punitive activities of the police agency. The results support this

----

[j]The negative relation may occur because much of the time of nonfield officers is spent on duties not directly related to the production of police output as defined, e.g., taking calls, dealing with citizen complaints, guarding jails, engaging in community relations, etc. A second possible reason may be employees successfully bargain for work rules that assure a "redundant" number of nonfield officer positions.

Table 16-3
Police Service Production Functions, City of Los Angeles, 1956–1970:
Police Output Equal Crime Prevention Rates and Arrest Rates

$$O_j = q_j \left(\prod_{i=1}^{3} \left(X_i^{b_{ij}} \right) \right) P^{c_j} D^{d_j} e_j$$

for all $i = 1,2,3$
output $j = 1,2,3,4,5$

Number of observations = 14
(Under Cochrane-Orcutt technique)

Police Output (O_j)	Constant (a_j)	$X_i^{b_{ij}}$ Log Per Capita[a]				p^{c_j} Ex-Convicts	D^{d_j} Dummy	R^2	Durbin-Watson (C-O Tech)	SSR
		Motorcycle Teams	Field Officers	Nonfield Officers	Civilian Employees					
$\log \dfrac{C_A}{C_T}$	17.20** (2.63)	.01 (.059)	.718* (1.66)	1.02** (2.29)	.74** (2.16)	.078 (1.05)	—	.9013	1.85	.0205
$\log \left(\dfrac{C_A}{C_T} \right)^{2/3} \left(\dfrac{C_P}{C} \right)^{1/3}$	12.81** (2.93)	1.21*** (3.89)	.55 (1.35)	−1.31 (−2.98)	1.80** (2.66)	−.62** (−2.69)	−.61*** (−4.20)	.8827	2.34	.0243
$\log \left(\dfrac{C_A}{C_T} \right)^{1/2} \left(\dfrac{C_P}{C} \right)^{1/2}$	22.03*** (3.51)	2.02** (4.49)	1.24** (2.09)	−2.12 (−3.34)	2.60** (2.70)	−1.03*** (−3.08)	−.84*** (−3.99)	.8321	2.67	.0508
$\log \left(\dfrac{C_A}{C_T} \right)^{1/3} \left(\dfrac{C_P}{C} \right)^{1/3}$	31.15*** (3.45)	2.82*** (4.35)	1.93** (2.26)	−2.89 (−3.17)	3.34** (2.42)	−1.41** (−2.95)	−1.07*** (−3.51)	.7729	2.72	.1055
$\log \dfrac{C_P}{C}$	48.33*** (3.21)	4.32*** (4.00)	3.24** (2.27)	−4.32 (−2.85)	4.72** (2.05)	−2.14** (−2.67)	−1.48** (−2.92)	.6957	2.66	.2939

***Significant at 99% level 1-tail t-test $t > 2.998$.
**Significant at 95% level 1-tail t-test $t > 1.895$.
*Significant at 90% level 1-tail t-test $t > 1.415$ t values in parenthesis.

Note:
[a] Ordinary least-squares estimation resulted in Durbin-Watson statistics that are quite low, and therefore a serial correlation coefficient was estimated (and in all cases significantly different from zero) and used to transform the variables.

Factor inputs were specified in per capita terms in order to eliminate the effect of population change. When the production function was estimated with non per capita inputs and population as right-hand variables, the hypothesis that the population elasticity was different from one was rejected for four of the five cases and therefore the right-hand variables can be measured in per capita terms.

Table 16-4
Alternative Police Production Functions: Police Output Equal Prevented Crimes and Unsuccessful Arrests[a]

(Number of observations = 15)

Police Output[c]	Constant	Motorcycle Teams	Field Officers	Nonfield Officers	Civilian Employees	Ex-Convicts	Dummy	R^{2}[b]	Durbin-Watson (OLSQ Tech)	SSR
				Log Per Capita						
$(CA - CT)$	12.256*** (18.32)	.026 (.54)	.076 (-1.02)	.038 (.82)	.26 (-4.05)	.072*** (4.50)	—	.95	1.85	.0014
$2/3 (CA - CT) + (CP - C)$	13.39*** (27.66)	.11*** (3.13)	-.03 (.66)	-.11 (2.45)	-.02 (.33)	-.013 (.57)	-.05*** (3.74)	.98	1.60	.0004
$1/2 (CA - CT) + (CP - C)$	13.49*** (30.30)	.115*** (3.62)	-.017 (.40)	-.12 (2.97)	-.011 (.17)	-.02 (.98)	-.06*** (4.19)	.98	1.69	.0004
$1/3 (CA - CT) + (CP - C)$	13.60*** (30.44)	.12*** (3.91)	-.004 (-.09)	-.14 (3.32)	.001 (.016)	-.028 (-1.35)	-.059*** (4.38)	.98	1.89	.0004
$(CP - C)$	13.80*** (26.31)	.14*** (3.75)	.022 (.44)	-.17 (3.38)	.02 (.32)	-.04* (1.75)	-.06*** (4.00)	.98	2.31	.0005

***Significant at 99% level   1-tail t-test $t > 2.896$.
**Significant at 95% level   1-tail t-test $t > 1.860$.
*Significant at 90% level   1-tail t-test $t > 1.397$.

Notes:

[a] Ordinary least-squares, rather than Cochrane-Orcutt, has been used in estimating these equations, since the results show little serial correlation between the error terms of the production functions.

[b] The high R^2 is misleading because of the large constant added to transform output into positive numbers.

[c] One million was added to all dependent variables in order to transform the data into positive numbers.

view. Under the circumstances analyzed, increasing the real resources made available to the police agency will increase both the prevention and the punitive components of output, particularly if these resources are put into field officers, motorcycle teams, and civilian support. A 1 percent increase in police employees and their associated equipment, except for nonfield officers, would on the average increase output by substantially more than 1 percent—often by 2 to 4 percent. Thus there appears to be some indication of increasing returns to the police agency as a whole.

The production functions describe what police actually do and therefore reflect what police consider to be important. The equations with the highest R^2 are those that give a heavy weight to the punitive component of output; the production function explains the least when the prevention component of output is emphasized. This suggests that when allocating their resources the police may consider arrests to be more important than preventing crimes. However, since the input coefficients have an increasing impact on output as the prevention proportion of output increases the police agency would get more return from an increment in inputs if it allocated resources to preventing crimes rather than making arrests.

Whether it is worthwhile for the Los Angeles community to increase the output of its police agency by providing more resources to the agency has not been answered in this study. Such an answer depends, among other things, on how much society values police output and the price it must pay to acquire the appropriate resource inputs.

References

1. Anderson, Robert W. "Toward A Cost Benefit Analysis of Police Activity." *Public Finance* 1 (1974).
2. Beaton, Patrick W. "The Determinants of Police Protection Expenditures." *National Tax Journal* 27 (June 1974).
3. Becker, Gary. "Crime and Punishment: An Economic Approach." *Journal of Public Economies* (March-April 1968): 169–217.
4. Carr-Hill, R.A. and M.H. Stern. "An Econometric Model of the Supply and Control of Recorded Offences in England and Wales." *Journal of Public Economies* 2 (1973).
5. Chapman, Jeffrey I. *A Model of Crime and Police Output*. Ph.D. dissertation, University of California, Berkeley, 1971.
6. Colm, Gerhard et al. "Public Expenditures and Economic Structure." *Social Research* 3 (February 1936): 57–77.
7. Goldfeld, Stephen M. and Richard E. Quandt. "Some Tests for Homoscedasticity." *American Statistical Association Journal* 60 (June 1965): 540–43.
8. Hirsch, Werner Z. "Expenditure Implications of Metropolitan Growth and Consolidation." *The Review of Economics and Statistics* 41 (August 1959): 323–41.

9. Hirsch, Werner Z. "Cost Functions of an Urban Government Service: Refuse Collection." *The Review of Economics and Statistics* 47 (February 1965): 87–92.

10. Maltz, Michael D. "Evaluation of Crime Control Programs." Washington, D.C.

11. Misner, Gordon E. and Richard B. Hoffman. "The Urban Police Mission." *Issues in Criminology* 3 (Summer 1967).

12. Morris, Douglas and Luther Tweeten. "The Cost of Controlling Crime." *The Annals of Regional Science of the Western Regional Science Association* 5 (June 1971): 33–49.

13. Shoup, Donald C. and Stephen L. Mehay. *Program Budgeting for Urban Police Services.* Praeger, 1972.

14. Sjoquist, David Lawrence. "Property Crime and Economic Behavior: Some Empirical Results." *American Economic Review* (June 1973): 439–446.

15. Walzer, Norman. "Economics of Scale and Municipal Police Services: The Illinois Experience." *Review of Economics and Statistics* (November 1972).

Appendix 16A

It has been pointed out that using the relative prevented crime rate (CP/C) rather than relative prevented crimes $(CP-C)$ creates a bias when used in the police agency production function. This can be demonstrated as follows:

We begin with a cross-sectional crime equation which, when Los Angeles values for the right-hand variables are introduced, predicts Los Angeles crime, i.e.,

$$\hat{CP} = \hat{a}_1 + \hat{b}_i \bar{D}_i + \hat{c}_1 \Delta \bar{C} + \hat{E}$$

where

$\hat{CP}$	= predicted property crime for Los Angeles
$\hat{a}_1, \hat{b}_i, \hat{c}_1$	= estimated coefficient values from cross section equation
$\hat{E}$	= error term for Los Angeles
$\bar{D}, \Delta \bar{C}$	= Los Angeles values for D (demographic and wage variables) and ΔC (change in crime).

We use $\hat{CP}$ in the production function analysis as part of output. If there is a bias because we have used $\hat{CP}$, then it will be strongest when the prevention component is given the total weight and the punitive component is zero.

1. Production Function for Relative Prevented Crimes

$$\hat{CP}_t - C_{LA_t} = a_2 + b_2 I_t + v_t$$
$$\hat{CP}_t = C_{LA_t} - \hat{E}$$
$$(C_{LA} - \hat{E} - C_{LA})_t = a_2 + b_2 I_t + v_t$$
$$-\hat{E} = a_2 + b_2 I_t + v_t$$

where

I	= production function inputs

263

v_t = production function error term

a_2, b_2 = production function coefficient,

which gives rise to unbiased results for b_2.

2.   Production Function for Relative Prevented Crime Rates

$$\left(\frac{\hat{CP}}{C_{LA}}\right)_t = a_3 + b_3 I_t + v_t$$

$$\left(1 - \frac{\hat{E}}{C_{LA}}\right)_t = a_3 + b_3 I_t + v_t$$

$$\left(-\frac{E}{C_{LA}}\right)_t = a'_3 + b_3 I_t + v_t$$

which gives rise to biased results for b_3 because of the presence of C_{LA}.

3.   In order to calculate the bias we use the following procedure:

$$v_t = p v_{t-1} + u_t$$

where

P = serial correlation coefficient

u_t = error term.

So, we can say, using the Cochrane-Orcutt technique

$$\left(-\frac{E}{C_{LA}}\right)_t = a'_3 + b_3 I_t + p v_{t-1} + u_t$$

and

$$-E_t = a'_3 C_{LA_t} + b_3 C_{LA_t} + n_t$$

with

$$n_t = C_{LA_t} (p v_{t-1} + u_t)$$

Using covariance relationship, we know

$$b_3 - \frac{S_{(CI, n_t)}}{S_{(CI, CI)}} = \tilde{b}$$

with

$\tilde{b}$ = unbiased estimate

$S_{CI, n}$ = covariance between CI and n

The values for $S_{(CI, n)}$ and $S_{(CI, CI)}$ are:

	$S_{(CI, n_t)}$	$S_{(CI, CI)}$
with I – motorcycle teams	– .235	9.6
I = field officers	+ .106	1.51
I = nonfield officers	+ .025	4
I = prisoners	+ .794	9.10
I = civilians	≈ 0	1.14

Thus, the results of the relative crime rate production function are biased by the following:

	Estimated $\hat{b}_3$	Bias	True $\tilde{b}$
motorcycle teams	4.32	– .02	4.34
field officers	3.24	+ .07	3.17
nonfield officers	– 4.32	≈ 0	– 4.32
prisoners	– 2.14	+ .09	– 2.05
civilians	4.72	≈ 0	4.72

17 Race, Ethnicity, and Residential Location

John F. Kain

Introduction

The residence patterns of black and ethnic populations in the Cleveland SMSA in 1970 permit tests of several hypotheses about the determinants of racial and ethnic segregation. Cleveland is particularly well suited to an investigation of these questions, since the extent of racial segregation is very great and since it has an unusually large and prominent ethnic population.

The analysis begins with a discussion of both current and past racial segregation in Cleveland. Section II describes the extent to which the residence patterns of black and ethnic populations can be predicted from a knowledge of their incomes and household composition. Comparision of black and ethnic group segregation is pertinent because the segregation of the latter is frequently presented as evidence of the normality of the segregation of black households. Section III then considers other explanations of racial segregation.

I. Extent of Racial Segregation

In 1970, all but 1.3 percent of Cleveland's blacks and 19.6 percent of its white population lived within Cuyahoga County, the central county of the Cleveland SMSA. The intensity of segregation within Cuyahoga County is evident from figure 17–1, which is a computer map depicting the proportion of persons in each census tract that were black in 1970. Fully 92 percent of black residents of the Cleveland SMSA lived within the central city and east of the Cuyahoga River.

The principal black satellite community west of the river, clearly visible in figure 17–1, is known as the Linndale-Bellaire section. This small black Cleveland neighborhood, which housed 508 black families in 1970, had permanent black

Numerous individuals made valuable contributions to the preparation of this chapter. William Apgar, Jr., and J. Royce Ginn devised and programmed the scaling algorithms used in the analysis. William Apgar, with the assistance of Patricia Beckett, performed the computer analysis and computations required for this paper. Apgar, John Jackson, Robert Schafer, Jeffrey Zax, and Gary R. Fauth all read drafts of the chapter and their valuable substantive and editorial suggestions greatly improved the chapter. Finally, Madeleine Lane typed the several drafts and the final manuscript, drew the maps, and assisted in the preparation of the manuscript in too many other ways to list.

Figure 17-1. Percentage of Population Black: Cleveland, 1970

residents as early as 1880. It was settled by blacks who worked at the nearby Nickel Plate Railroad yards, and in particular by porters and other black train crews who boarded and left the trains at Linndale. The remaining central city tracts located west of the river whose populations are more than 5 percent black reflect the racial composition of public housing projects located in them.

The small industrial town of Berea, in Southwest Cuyahoga County, also contains a small concentration of black households. The Berea enclave, clearly visible in figure 17-1, originated in the 1920s, when the Dunham Company, manufacturers of plows, harrows, cultivators, and other farm implements, recruited blacks from the South to work in its foundries in Berea. It housed 147 black households in 1970.

In addition to the Linndale-Bellaire and Berea enclaves, the Cleveland SMSA has two other outlying black residential areas, with established black populations. The first of these, Oakwood-Walton Hills, clearly visible in figure 17-1 to the southeast of the Cleveland ghetto, housed 238 black households in 1970. This settlement originated during the 1920s when a number of black families settled in what at that time was Bedford township, attracted by lenient zoning laws which permitted development on smaller than usual lots and the sale of these lots to low income households on a land contract basis.

The final outlying black neighborhood, Chagrin Falls Park, is located in Geauga County and thus does not appear in figure 17-1. The 207 black households who resided in Chagrin Falls Park in 1970 are the descendents of a much larger number of blacks who settled in the area starting in the 1920s. The proposed factory, which attracted them to the area, never materialized, but a small black enclave remained.

II. Socioeconomic Determinants of Segregation

Numerous explanations have been offered for the virtually total segregation of blacks in United States metropolitan areas. One of the most common is the contention that blacks are concentrated within particular neighborhoods because they are poor, spend too little on housing, and differ systematically from the majority white population in other characteristics that influence residential choices. This socioeconomic hypothesis is easily evaluated empirically, and several studies have examined it.[1]

Karl Taeuber completed an analysis of this kind which illustrates that little of Cleveland's existing pattern of racial segregation can be explained by income differences.[2] Taeuber multiplied the areawide proportion of black households in each income class times the number of households in each income class in each Cleveland census tract, summed over the tracts' income distribution, and divided by the total number of households in the tract. This simple procedure produced an estimate of an "expected" proportion of black residents by census tract. The segregation index between expected black tract population and actual white population for tracts in the Cleveland metropolitan area was 5.3 in 1960 as contrasted to a segregation index of 90 between the actual black and white populations of each tract.[3]

A frequent criticism of analyses such as Taeuber's is that white and black households differ in ways other than income. Fortunately, data from the *1970 Census of Population* can be used to make more recent and more precise estimates of the kind reported by Taeuber for Cleveland in 1960. The estimates of predicted black population by census tract and similar estimates for various ethnic groups presented in this chapter employ two types of data from the 1970 census, the county group 5 and 15 percent public use samples and tract statistics.

Shown in figure 17-2 is the predicted or expected black proportion of each census tract calculated on the assumption that color has no effect on residence location. More specifically, the estimates shown in figure 17-2 are the predicted black percentage of each tract's total population, based on the assumption that black households have the same probability of living in each census tract as actual tract residents with the same socio-demographic-economic characteristics. To obtain the estimates shown in figure 17-2, we classified each black and white person as belonging to one of 384 types of households defined in terms of those characteristics which previous research has shown to have the most significant effect on the housing and residential choices of both black and white households. There is a considerable body of evidence that demonstrates that, except for the restrictions imposed on them by housing market discrimination, black households choose the same types of housing as otherwise identical white households.[4] The 384 types of households used in the analysis are defined in terms of family type, family size, age of head, and household income.[a]

The procedure used involved the use of the public use sample and the Fourth Count (census tract) tapes to obtain estimates of equation 17-1 for the entire SMSA,

$$\alpha_{jk} = \frac{P_{jk}}{P_j} \qquad\qquad (17\text{-}1)$$

where P_{jk} is the number of persons belonging to each of j household categories and k racial and nationality groups in the entire SMSA. The predicted racial or ethnic group populations of each tract, i, p_{ij}^e is then given by equation 17-2, where P_{ij} is the actual population in each tract i of household type j. The predic-

---

[a]The categories are: (1) family type (husband and wife, other families, and primary individuals), (2) age of head (less than 30 years of age, 30–44 years, 45–64 years, and more than 65 years for husband-wife families; and less than 65 years or more than 65 years for other families and primary individuals); (3) family size (1, 2, 3, 4, 5 and 6 or more); and (4) income class (less than $2,000, $2,000–2,999, $3,000–4,999, $5,000–6,999, $7,000–9,999, $10,000–14,999, $15,000–24,999, and more than $25,000).

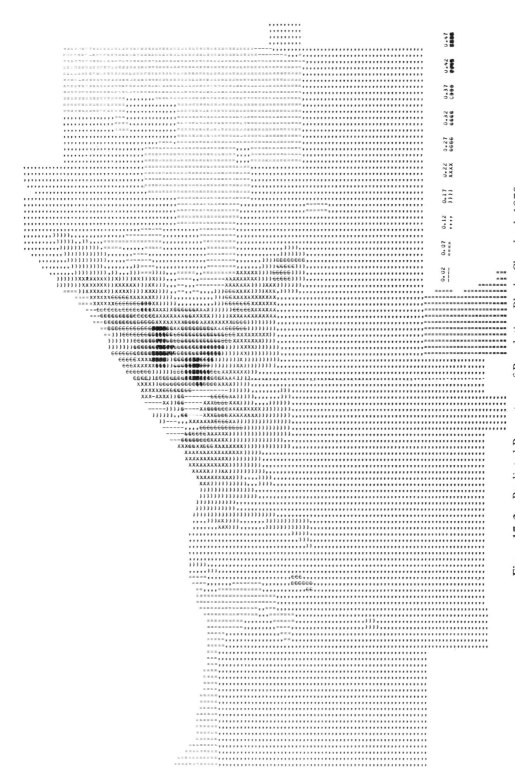

Figure 17-2. Predicted Percentage of Population Black: Cleveland, 1970

ted proportion of each tract's population that belongs to ethnic group k is given
by equation 17-3.

$$P^e_{i_{jk}} = \alpha_{jk} P_{ij} \qquad\qquad\qquad (17\text{-}2)$$

$$\frac{P^{ek}_i}{P_i} = \frac{1}{P_i} \sum_{j=1}^{384} p^e_{i_{jk}} \qquad\qquad\qquad (17\text{-}3)$$

The procedure is quite straightforward except that not all elements of the household type matrix are included in the census tract tables and the sample estimates
obtained from the two sources differ somewhat. Therefore, a scaling routine developed by William C. Apgar, Jr., and J. Royce Ginn, was used to estimate the
full matrix and to make the two sets of sample data consistent. These procedures
are described in Appendix 17A.

The effects of housing market discrimination and racial exclusion are clearly evident in figure 17-2. When the racial composition of each tract is predicted
in the way described blacks are still somewhat overrepresented in the city of
Cleveland and especially in its more central portions, but the tracts that were
more than 10 percent black in 1970 are predicted to have only 43 percent as
many black residents as they actually had in 1970. It should be noted that the
predicted distribution of the black population, shown in figure 17-2, is almost
certainly more concentrated geographically than it would be if racial discrimination had never existed. This is because the actual concentration of poor households in the central city and in predominantly black tracts was far greater in
1970 than it would have been in the absence of racial discrimination.

Ethnicity and Residential Segregation

The concentrations of various ethnic groups evident in United States cities
and in cities throughout the world is often used to explain or justify racial segregation and the almost totally white complexion of many suburban communities
and central city neighborhoods. These areas are, it is often claimed, tightly-knit
ethnic enclaves consisting of persons with a similar cultural heritage and common
religious beliefs. They do not exclude blacks, but the competition of individuals
with strong preferences to live in these ethnic areas discourages other groups,
such as blacks, from moving there.

The importance of ethnicity in determining residence patterns in Cleveland
can be examined by using the methods described previously to estimate the predicted black population of Cleveland census tracts. Figure 17-3 illustrates the

actual proportion of persons in each tract who are foreign-born or of foreign or mixed parentage, and figure 17–4 shows the predicted proportions.

While there are obvious ethnic concentrations, the computer maps clearly indicate that neither the ethnic population as a whole or persons of Polish stock exhibit the intense segregation characteristic of black households in the Cleveland SMSA. The visual impressions obtained from an examination of the computer maps are further supported by the statistics shown in table 17–1, which describe the actual and predicted percentages of foreign stock and black population in twenty-three geographic subdivisions of the Cleveland SMSA. The twenty-three areas included in table 17–1 include all incorporated communities of more

Table 17–1

Actual and Predicted Percentage of Foreign Stock and Black Population for Selected Geographic Areas

| | | | | Percentage Foreign Stock | |
| | Percentage Black | | | Predicted | |
Area	Actual	Predicted	Actual	Model I	Model II
Brook Park	.3%	13.3%	20.8%	19.0%	21.7%
District I	10.9	16.7	35.4	27.1	29.4
District II	78.4	31.2	8.5	21.6	7.6
District III	54.2	20.8	20.1	24.7	15.8
District IV	1.4	20.2	27.8	24.0	29.2
District V	.2	15.8	37.5	27.0	31.6
District VI	2.7	14.3	31.1	25.9	29.3
Cleveland Hgts.	2.5	11.4	36.7	28.8	31.6
East Cleveland	58.6	19.3	15.9	24.4	15.6
Euclid	.4	18.1	33.1	27.2	30.9
Garfield Hgts.	4.3	13.7	35.9	26.7	29.6
Lakewood	a	13.0	28.3	27.9	31.8
Maple Hgts.	2.0	13.6	33.3	25.8	29.2
North Olmstead	a	12.6	24.0	22.6	25.8
Parma	a	12.7	36.1	25.7	29.3
Parma Hgts.	a	12.1	32.6	26.2	29.6
Shaker Hgts.	14.4	8.5	28.3	30.4	29.1
South Euclid	.1	11.2	45.8	30.0	33.4
Balance of Cuyahoga	2.6	14.9	39.9	35.4	38.9
Mentor	.5	13.7	14.4	22.8	26.1
Geauga County	1.2	13.8	20.4	21.7	24.7
Balance of Lake County	1.6	14.0	21.7	23.1	26.2
Medina County	.8	14.7	12.8	22.9	26.5
Mean	10.3	15.0	27.8	25.7	27.1
Standard Deviation	21.3	4.4	9.5	3.4	6.5
Mean Error	—	15.7	—	6.4	4.5

a = less than 0.1 percent.

Figure 17-3. Percentage of Population Foreign Stock: Cleveland, 1970

Figure 17–4. Predicted Percentage of Population of Foreign Stock: Cleveland, 1970

than 25,000 population in the Cleveland SMSA, the remaining portions of the four counties that comprise the SMSA, and six districts within the city of Cleveland. The six central city districts and the incorporated communities of more than 25,000 located in Cuyahoga County are shown in figure 17-5.

Careful examination of table 17-1 reveals important differences between the residence patterns of blacks and of persons of foreign stock in the Cleveland SMSA. First, as the actual proportions of blacks and foreign stock in the twenty-three areas illustrate, blacks are far more geographically segregated than the ethnic population as a whole. In 1970 87 percent of the black population of Cleveland SMSA lived within the central city and 84 percent lived within District II and III, whose populations were 78 percent and 54 percent black. Districts IV, V, and VI, west of the Cuyahoga River, housed 13 percent of the SMSAs white population but only 0.2 percent of its black population. District I which was 10.9 percent black in 1970, housed 5 percent of the SMSA black population. In addition, the black population living outside the central city in 1970 was heavily concentrated in two communities: East Cleveland, which was 59 percent black in 1970, and Shaker Heights, which was 14 percent black in 1970. Both communities are located adjacent to the central city ghetto.

The predicted black proportions for the twenty-three areas shown in table 17-1 are much more uniform than the actual proportions. The highest predicted proportion, 31 percent, was obtained for District II, while the lowest predicted proportion, 8.5 percent, was obtained for Shaker Heights. The differences in predicted percentages among the twenty-three areas, of course, reflect differences in the socioeconomic-demographic composition of the twenty-three areas.

The final summary statistic included in table 17-1, the mean error, provides one measure of how well the probability model described previously predicts the racial and ethnic composition of the twenty-three areas. Both the mean difference and a comparison of the actual and predicted proportion black in these areas indicate that information on the socioeconomic-demographic characteristics of households residing in each area do not permit very satisfactory predictions of the black population in each area. The average prediction error, 15.7 percent, is nearly as large as the overall proportion of blacks living in the Cleveland SMSA and is 50 percent larger than the mean percentage black for the twenty-three areas.

The statistics in table 17-1 also reveal that foreign born persons and persons of foreign or mixed parentage are much more uniformly distributed among these twenty-three geographic areas. The lowest fraction, 8.5 percent, is found in Cleveland District II, where housing market discrimination against blacks produces a crowding out of all but a very small number of whites. Since all but a few persons of foreign stock are white, they are crowded out as well. The remaining areas that have unusually low concentrations of foreign stock are low density counties on the fringes of the SMSA, where much of the population continues to be engaged in farming and related activities. Moreover, as a comparison

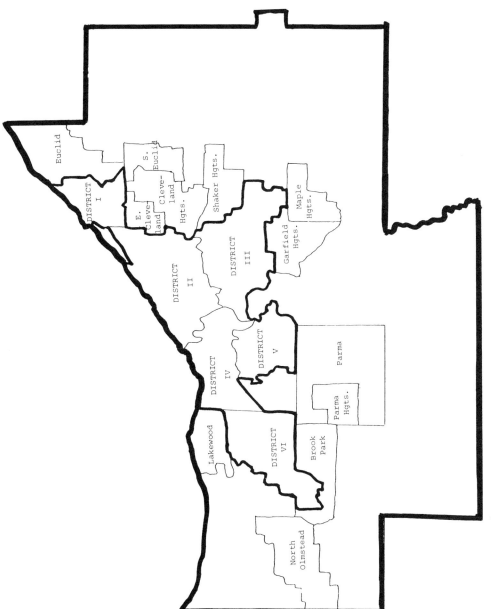

Figure 17–5. Central City Districts and Cuyahoga County Communities of More Than 25,000 Population in 1970

of the actual and predicted proportions of foreign stock indicates, the same procedures that do so poorly in predicting the black proportion of the twenty-three areas shown in table 17-1, do a highly credible job of predicting the percentage of foreign stock in each area.

Two predictions of the proportion foreign stock are included in table 17-1. The first predicts the proportion of the population who are foreign stock in precisely the same way that the black proportion was obtained. The second estimate, labeled Model II, takes account of the fact that white ethnics are crowded out of the ghetto by black households. It takes as given the black population of each area and uses only whites to compute the αjk's and p_{ijk}^e's in equations (17-1)-(17-3). The actual census tract population, P_i, in equation (17-3) includes both blacks and whites, however. The mean prediction error obtained using Model II is only 4.5 percent, which is less than one-fifth as large as the overall foreign stock percentage for the SMSA and about a fourth as large as the mean of the twenty-three areas. Moreover, even if the intense segregation of blacks is ignored the mean prediction error for the twenty-three areas shown in table 17-1 is only 6.4 percent.

Table 17-2, which compares the frequency distribution of the actual number of Cleveland tracts with various proportions of Negroes and persons of foreign stock in 1970 with the distribution of tracts by the predicted proportion of these same groups, provides more evidence on the effects of housing market discrimination and on the dissimilarity of the patterns of racial and ethnic segregation. Table 17-2 includes all SMSA census tracts, while the computer map shows only those Cuyahoga county tracts.

Table 17-2

Frequency Distribution of Cleveland SMSA Census Tracts by Actual and Predicted Percentage Black and Foreign Stock

| | Black | | Total Foreign Stock | | |
| | | | Actual | Predicted | |
Percentage of Tract	Actual	Predicted	Actual	Model I	Model II
90–100	46	–	–	–	–
80–89	15	–	1	–	–
70–79	3	–	1	–	–
60–69	6	–	2	–	–
50–59	7	1	7	–	–
40–49	7	13	46	1	2
35–39	3	6	49	3	23
30–34	4	21	54	40	160
25–29	6	29	58	187	134
20–24	5	46	61	178	38
15–19	6	109	57	30	11
10–14	5	193	33	1	8
5–9	14	22	24	–	15
0–4	313	–	44	–	49

As the frequency distributions in table 17-2 illustrate, 46 census tracts in the Cleveland SMSA were 90 percent or more black and 77 tracts were 50 percent or more black in 1970. In contrast, only one of the 448 census tracts in the Cleveland SMSA had a predicted 1970 percentage of black residents as high as 50 percent. Similarly, while 313 census tracts had fewer than 5 percent black persons in 1970, no census tracts had a predicted percentage of blacks below 5 percent.

As the statistics on persons of foreign stock in table 17-2 illustrate, the combined population of foreign stock does not exhibit the intense segregation that characterizes the black population. Even though persons of foreign stock are a larger share of Cleveland's population than blacks are, 25.5 percent, as compared to 16.1 percent, only 11 tracts were more than 50 percent foreign stock in 1970 as contrasted to 77 tracts that were more than 50 percent black in the same year. It should be recognized that these data on foreign stock include only foreign born persons and persons of mixed or foreign parentage. Many third generation individuals may have strong ethnic attachments and may concentrate in ethnic neighborhoods; if these unenumerated ethnics were included, the ethnic proportions of some tracts might be much larger.

The predicted proportions of foreign stock obtained from Model I cluster much more tightly around the areawide proportion than is true of the actual proportions. This greater clustering reflects the effect of variables omitted from the projection model that produce more segregation than would be predicted from the household characteristics included in Model I. Model II accounts for one of these factors, discriminatory practices in Cleveland's housing market and the resultant crowding out of persons of foreign stock from ghetto tracts. When persons of foreign stock are distributed among tracts in the same proportions as all white households of the same characteristics, the actual and predicted distributions of tracts by percent foreign stock are much more similar. In particular, Model II does a reasonably good job of identifying those tracts with small proportions of foreign stock. The reason is obvious, the tracts have very few whites of any kind. Neither Model I nor Model II can reproduce those tracts with disproportionately large foreign stock populations.

Shown in table 17-3 are summary statistics describing the actual and predicted population distributions for nine individual racial and nationality groups, which are heavily represented in the Cleveland SMSA, including the summary statistics for blacks and total ethnics shown in table 17-1. In addition, the first column of table 17-3 gives the SMSA wide proportion of each group and the final two columns give the mean percentage error of prediction of the population of each group. For individual ethnic groups the areawide proportions vary from a high of 3 percent for Italians and Poles to a low of 1.4 percent for Russians. The small size of these nationality groups adds another complication to the prediction problem. The Public Use (1 percent) samples for a number of these groups number fewer than 400 persons, who are allocated among 384 household types. The resulting sampling error would be expected to be quite large. The pro-

Table 17-3
Actual Means and Standard Deviations and Model I and Model II Prediction Errors for Selected Racial and Ethnic Groups: Twenty-three Subareas of the Cleveland SMSA

		Actual (23 areas)		Mean Error		Mean Percentage Error	
	SMSA Proportion	Mean	Standard Deviation	Model I	Model II	Model I	Model II
Total Foreign born	25.5	27.8%	9.5%	6.4%	4.5%	29%	19%
German	2.6	2.8	1.0	.8	.6	39	26
Polish	3.0	3.2	2.4	1.6	1.6	70	70
Czech	2.6	2.8	1.7	1.2	1.1	80	66
Austrian	1.5	1.7	.7	.4	.4	34	23
Hungarian	2.0	2.1	.8	.5	.5	59	35
Yugoslavian	2.0	2.0	2.0	1.2	1.4	113	115
Italian	3.0	3.4	2.1	1.5	1.3	123	118
Russian	1.4	1.8	2.0	1.2	1.2	63	54
Other	7.4	8.0	2.9	2.1	1.6	35	21
Black	15.1	10.3	21.3	15.7	—	11,028	—

cedures used in the analysis insure that the predicted total number of persons belonging to each nationality group agree with the estimated number obtained from the census tract tables, but the sampling errors around the α_{jk}'s shown in equation (17-1) are quite large. Given this consideration, the predictive accuracy of both Model I and Model II are surprisingly high.

In several cases the prediction error is less than a fourth of the mean proportion of the twenty-three areas used in the analysis. If this criterion is used to evaluate predictive accuracy, the probability models are most successful in predicting the residential distributions of the German, Austrian, and Hungarian populations. They are least successful in predicting the residential distributions of the Russian, Yugoslavian, and Polish populations. At the same time, it can be claimed that this criterion of success is inappropriate. Comparison of the mean proportions for the twenty-three areas with their standard deviations makes it clear that the groups with the poorest predictions, according to this criterion, are also the groups with the largest standard deviations relative to the means of the twenty-three areas used in the analysis. This latter statistic can be interpreted as a measure of how segregated or clustered these nationality groups are. This measure indicates that Russians and Yugoslavians living in the Cleveland SMSA are far less uniformly distributed among the twenty-three areas used in the analysis than are Germans, Austrians, or other ethnic populations as a whole.

Even so, in very case the socioeconomic-demographic prediction model is far more successful in predicting the population distribution of these small nationality groups among the twenty-three areas used in the analysis than it is in predicting the distribution of the larger black population. This important finding is vividly illustrated by the final statistic in table 17-3, which is the mean percentage error. This statistic, which, to repeat, is the mean absolute value of the percentage error of prediction of the persons belonging to each racial or ethnic group, ranges from a low of 19 percent for all ethnics using Model II to a high of 123 percent for Italians using Model I. It is 11,028 percent for blacks.

The preceding analyses demonstrate that family income, family-size and composition, and age of the household head explain only a small part of the spatial distribution of the black residences in the Cleveland SMSA. In particular, they provide no explanation for the almost total exclusion of blacks from 80 percent of the region and their intense segregation in Cleveland's ghetto. In contrast, these same household characteristics explain a good deal of the spatial distribution of persons of foreign stock taken as a whole and that of individual ethnic groups. Previous studies of ethnic segregation in Cleveland and in other American cities provide additional evidence that the current and historical segregation of black Americans is close to unique, and cannot be dismissed as analogous to the history of various ethnic groups. These studies are unanimous in their conclusions that the current intensity of black residential segregation is greater than that documented for any other identifiable racial or ethnic group in

American history and that in contrast the experience of ethnic groups, who experienced rapid dispersal from their original ethnic concentrations, black Americans have become more rather than less segregated with time.

Stanley Lieberson's classic, *Ethnic Patterns in American Cities* provides the most detailed historical analysis of the extent, causes, and trends of ethnic segregation in American cities.[5] Lieberson calculated segregation indexes and analyzed the extent and character of racial and ethnic segregation in ten American cities in 1910, 1920, 1930, and 1950 for the major ethnic and racial groups living in these cities. The segregation indexes for 1910 and 1920 were based on ward data, while the indexes for 1930 and 1950 were based on tract data. As a result the indexes for the earlier two periods cannot be directly compared to those for the more recent periods. Even so, trends can be analyzed between 1910 and 1920 and between 1930 and 1950. Lieberson discovered that the mean residential segregation indexes of immigrant groups from native whites declined between 1910 and 1920 and between 1930 and 1950 in each of the ten cities under consideration, and that the ethnic second generations in 1930 were less segregated from whites of native parentage than were the first generations.

The first of these conclusions is evident from table 17–4 which presents mean indexes of residential segregation for blacks and ethnic groups in each of the four years and the ten cities studied by Lieberson. The division between old and new ethnic groups refers to the period when each nationality group first migrated to the United States in large numbers. Old ethnic groups include immigrants from England and Wales, Scotland, Ireland, Norway, Sweden, Denmark, France, Switzerland, and Germany. New ethnic groups include immigrants from Poland, Czechoslovakia, Austria, Hungary, Yugoslavia, Russia, Lithuania, Rumania, Greece, and Italy. The distinction between old and new ethnic groups is important because both theory and empirical evidence suggest that the segregation of immigrant groups will decline over time. Individual ethnic groups are at first highly segregated, but they tend to disperse as they learn the language and become assimilated in other ways. The dispersal of the children of immigrants, as is noted above, is even more pronounced.

The Cleveland experience shown in table 17–4 is fairly typical of that of the remaining nine cities. New ethnic groups are more segregated from native whites than old ethnic groups and blacks are more segregated from native born whites than either old or new ethnic groups. Moreover, the difference is much larger for more recent than for earlier years, reflecting a decline in the segregation of the several ethnic groups and an increase in the segregation of blacks.

III. Other Determinants of Racial Segregation

In addition to the socioeconomic and demographic determinants of residential segregation analyzed in the previous section and the possible relevance of the experience of various ethnic groups, there are a number of other factors that

Table 17–4

Mean Indexes of Residential Segregation of Blacks and Ethnic Groups, 1910–1950

| City and Groups | | Foreign Born White and Black vs. Native White | | | |
| | | Wards | | Tracts[a] | |
		1910	1920	1930	1950
Boston	Old	20.6	23.2	26.2	25.4
	New	53.3	45.8	54.6	49.6
	Negro	64.1	65.3	77.9	80.1
Buffalo	Old	28.4	27.9	30.0	28.4
	New	60.3	55.2	55.7	48.1
	Negro	62.6	71.5	80.5	82.5
Chicago	Old	32.6	29.8	27.7	27.8
	New	52.6	41.1	47.1	41.4
	Negro	66.8	75.7	85.2	79.7
Cincinnati	Old	22.4	21.5	28.4	28.7
	New	54.6	46.0	51.6	49.2
	Negro	47.3	57.2	72.8	80.6
Cleveland	Old	24.2	22.6	28.8	27.0
	New	52.2	43.1	51.8	45.7
	Negro	60.6	70.1	85.0	86.6
Columbus	Old	25.6	26.9	28.4	24.3
	New	52.7	50.6	57.2	46.3
	Negro	31.6	43.8	62.8	70.3
Philadelphia	Old	21.6	21.1	29.3	28.4
	New	57.8	47.7	52.9	48.0
	Negro	46.0	47.9	63.4	74.0
Pittsburgh	Old	23.5	20.9	25.1	24.1
	New	51.0	47.7	52.7	46.6
	Negro	44.1	43.3	61.4	68.5
St. Louis	Old	21.3	21.8	26.1	27.6
	New	57.2	46.5	61.9	43.4
	Negro	54.3	62.1	82.1	85.4
Syracuse	Old	28.4	23.6	33.2	27.2
	New	55.6	50.9	59.2	48.9
	Negro	64.0	55.2	86.7	85.8

Source: Stanley Lieberson, *Ethnic Patterns in American Cities* (Glencoe: Free Press, 1963), pp. 66–67, and 122.

[a]Community areas used for Chicago.

may explain all or part of the residence pattern of Cleveland's black households. In this section we consider the potential role of three such factors: workplace location, black preferences for segregation, and discriminatory practices.

The Effect of Workplace Location

Economic theories of residential location emphasize the role of workplace location as a determinant of the residential location choices of urban households. Specifically, urban households are depicted as choosing their residential locations on the basis of a locational calculus in which they trade-off savings in housing or location costs against increases in transport costs as they commute further from their place of work. In addition to this general theoretical observation, a number of studies have shown that the specific workplaces of employed household members have a major effect on the household's residential location.[6] This suggests the possibility that the observed differences in the residence locations of otherwise comparable black and white households may reflect differences in the location of their workplace.

A superficial examination of published data on the geographic distributions of black and white employment appears to support this view. In 1970 61 percent of black but only 47 percent of white workers held central city jobs, a finding that might lead some persons to conclude that differences in workplace location account for the underrepresentation of black households in suburban residence areas. A more sober evaluation indicates, however, that differences in the workplace locations of black and white workers can at best explain only a small fraction of the difference in actual and predicted black residence patterns and that the smaller proportion of blacks working in suburban workplaces is more a consequence of the observed pattern of residential segregation than its cause.

Geographic limitations on the residential choices of non-whites insures that blacks can reach many jobs only by making time consuming and expensive journeys-to-work.[7] If blacks seek, obtain, and accept jobs distant from the ghetto, their real wages (money wages minus the money and time outlays for commuting) will be less than those of comparable white workers. Often they will not even learn of available jobs far from the ghetto or will not bother to apply because of the cost and difficulty of reaching them. Faced with these difficulties, they may accept low paying jobs near the ghetto or no job at all, choosing leisure and welfare as rational alternatives to low pay and poor working conditions.

Several years ago, I completed a statistical analysis of the effects of housing market discrimination in Detroit and Chicago on the location of black employment and on black employment levels.[8] These analyses determined that the proportion of black households employed at each of ninety-nine workplace zones in Detroit and Chicago decreased with the workplace's distance from both the major and secondary black ghettos in both areas. The same study indicated that the

level of black employment was also strongly influenced by the racial composition of the resident population of the surrounding neighborhood.

While the detailed place of work and place of residence data that would be
required to replicate this analysis for Cleveland are unavilable, census data on
black and white employment levels in various portions of the Cleveland SMSA
indicate a similar situation exists there. Cleveland's black workers are underrepre-
sented in suburban workplaces. For example, in 1970 black workers held an estimated 7.5 percent of all jobs in Cleveland's suburban ring as contrasted to 18
percent of all central city jobs.[9] Part of this difference may be attributable to
differences in the characteristics of central city and suburban jobs, but the larger
part is no doubt explained by the accessibility considerations discussed previously. In 1960 when the black population of Cleveland was even more centralized
than in 1970 and when central city employment was greater, black workers held
only 3.6 percent of jobs in Cleveland's suburbs as contrasted to 15.8 percent of
jobs in the central city.[10]

The effect of racial discrimination on blacks is illustrated further by the extent of reverse commuting by black and white households. Typically workers
commute down the houseing price gradient to obtain better and lower cost
housing at less central locations. Few workers will willingly commute from suburban workplaces to inferior and more expensive housing located in the central
city and most of the exceptions to this general rule are accounted for by workers belonging to multiple wage earner families or those who do not wish to have
not yet changed their residence locations.

As table 17–5 indicates, 46.7 percent of Cleveland's white workers and 61.1
percent of Cleveland's black workers were employed in the central city in 1970.
Of the 319,000 white workers employed at central city workplaces in 1970, 61

Table 17–5
Percentage of White and Black Workers by Place of Work and Place of
Residence: Cleveland City and Suburban Ring in 1960 and 1970

	1960		1970	
	White	*Black*	*White*	*Black*
Total SMSA Employment	100.0	100.0	100.0	100.0
Working in Central City	65.6	84.1	46.7	61.1
Living in City	36.4	83.1	18.1	52.4
Living in Ring	29.2	1.0	28.6	8.7
Working in Ring	29.5	7.4	44.6	21.6
Living in City	3.2	5.4	6.0	16.6
Living in Ring	26.3	2.0	38.6	5.0
Other	4.9	8.5	8.7	17.3

Source: U.S. Bureau of the Census, Census of Population: 1970, *Subject Reports,* Final
Report PC (2)–6D, Journey to Work (Washington, D.C.: U.S. Government Printing Office,
1973).

percent commuted to suburban communities to obtain better or cheaper housing. For the reasons discussed previously, only 14 percent of the 70,000 black
households employed in the central city in 1970 commuted to suburban residences.

Even larger differences are obtained for white and black workers employed
at suburban workplaces. As table 17-5 indicates, only 21.6 percent of Cleveland's
black workers as contrasted with 44.6 percent of its white workers were employed at suburban workplaces. This difference reflects the restrictions on the
residential choices of black households in the Cleveland metropolitan area. Moreover, as the estimates in table 17-6 indicate, 87 percent of whites employed at
suburban workplaces in 1970 resided in suburban areas, while only 23 percent of
blacks employed at suburban workplaces lived in the suburbs.

Black Preferences and Discriminatory Practices

To conclude that "voluntary" self-segregation is responsible for much of
the current pattern of black residential segregation, it is necessary to assume that
blacks have much stronger ties to their community than other groups. Although
there is evidence of a growing cultural pride and sense of community among
blacks, it is impossible to assign much weight to this increased awareness as an
explanation of these durable segregation patterns. While we recognize the difficulties of interpretation, recent surveys of black attitudes provide little support
for the self-segregation hypothesis. In 1969, 74 percent of a random sample of
U.S. blacks interviewed by the Harris Poll indicated a preference for living in in-

Table 17-6
**Percentage of Central City Workers Residing in the Central City and
Suburban Ring and Percentage of Suburban Workers Residing in the
Central City and Ring by Race: Cleveland SMSA in 1960 and 1970**

	1960			1970	
	White	Black		White	Black
Working in Central City					
Living in City	55.4	98.8		38.7	85.7
Living in Ring	44.6	1.2		61.3	14.3
Total	100.0	100.0		100.0	100.0
Working in Ring					
Living in City	11.1	72.3		13.4	76.9
Living in Ring	88.9	26.7		86.6	23.1
Total	100.0	100.0		100.0	100.0

Source: U.S. Bureau of the Census, Census of Population: 1970, *Subject Reports,* Final
Report PC (2)–6D, Journey to Work (Washington, D.C.: U.S. Government Printing Office,
1973).

tegrated neighborhoods. This fraction is somewhat larger than the 68 percent expressing this opinion in 1966 and still larger than the 64 percent with this opinion in 1963. Similarly, only 16 percent of blacks interviewed in 1969 and 17 percent in 1966 expressed a preference for all black neighborhoods.[11]

It is also true, however, as Pettigrew points out, that the trend among blacks toward a greater willingness to live in mixed areas reflects a strong preference for better housing and does not imply there is a widespread desire among blacks to live in "mostly" or overwhelmingly white areas.[12] A 1969 survey conducted by Gary Marx asked black respondents, "If both neighborhoods were equally well kept up, would you rather live in a neighborhood that was mostly Negro or mostly white?" Asked to choose between these two alternatives, only 4 percent of black respondents in non-southern metropolitan areas favored "mostly white" neighborhoods, while 55 percent registered a preference for "mostly Negro." Even though the alternative was not included, 38 percent of black respondents volunteered they preferred "mixed" neighborhoods or that it made no difference.[13]

In spite of the lack of any systematic evidence which supports the self-segregation hypothesis, it is difficult to dispose of. The problem is that it is virtually impossible to determine finally the role of self-segregation as long as strong traces of white community antagonism toward black efforts to leave the ghetto remain. The physical dangers of moving out of the ghetto probably are less today than in the past, but many subtle and indirect forms of intimidation and discouragement still exist. Moreover, violence against blacks moving into white neighborhoods remains an ever present possibility, as witnessed by incidents reported recently in Boston and New York.

Evidence of the methods used to enforce housing market segregation is more difficult to obtain today than in the past. Open occupancy laws, which forbid discrimination in the sale and rental of housing on the basis of race, and a decline in clear-cut community approval for such practices, have caused opponents of open housing to resort to more subtle and secretive methods. Until very recently, however, the most effective devices used to enforce segregation could hardly be called subtle. Deed restrictions (racial covenants), the appraisal practices of the FHA and of private lending institutions, the actions of local officials, and the practices of real estate agents were among the most important of them.[14] Because residential patterns have a great deal of inertia, the effect of these now discredited devices will long be felt. Even if there were no future resistance to black efforts to leave the ghetto, the cumulative effects of decades of intense discrimination will have long lasting impacts.

Summary and Conclusions

This chapter considers the highly important question of the roles of racial and ethnic preferences and prejudices on the residence locations selected by urban households. The analysis is lengthy and relatively complex. The conclusions are not.

The central question concerns the roles of measurable socioeconomic characteristics, self-segregation, and racial discrimination in producing the intense segregation of black households in U.S. urban areas. While this question by its very nature cannot be answered with absolute certainty, the findings of this research strongly point to racial prejudice, deep rooted discriminatory practices, real and imagined fears by blacks, and subtle forms of collusive behavior as the principal causes of racial segregation.

The empirical analyses deal with the residence patterns of Cleveland black and ethnic populations. An unusually elaborate analysis of the effects of family income, family size, family type, and age of head reveals these measurable characteristics of black households explain only a small part of their geographic distribution and provide no explanation for their almost total exclusion from some areas. To provide a benchmark, the same methods are used to predict the residence patterns of the foreign born population and of several nationality groups. The same model that was virtually unable to explain the geographic distribution of the black population within the Cleveland SMSA was remarkably successful in explaining the geographic distribution of various ethnic groups. Some segregation of these nationality groups exists beyond what can be explained by socioeconomic and demographic variables, but it is a fraction of that exhibited by blacks.

Notes

1. Karl E. Taeuber and Alma F. Taeuber, *Negroes in Cities: Residential Segregation and Neighborhood Change* (Chicago: Aldine Publishing Co., 1965). A.H. Pascal, "The Economics of Housing Segregation," Memorandum, RM-5510-RC (Santa Monica: The RAND Corp., November 1967); John R. Meyer, John F. Kain and Martin Wohl, *The Urban Transportation Problem* (Cambridge, Mass.: Harvard University Press, 1965), Chap. 7; and Davis McEntire, *Residence and Race* (Berkeley: University of California Press, 1960).

2. Karl E. Taeuber, "The Effect of Income Redistribution on Racial Residential Segregation," *Urban Affairs Quarterly* 4 (Sept. 1968): 5–15.

3. Karl and Alma Taeuber calculated segregation indexes for Cleveland and most other large central cities in 1940, 1950, and in 1960. These indexes, which assume values between zero and 100, measure the extent to which observed racial patterns of residence by block differ from a pattern of proportional representation. A value of zero indicates a completely even distribution of blacks, i.e., the proportion in the entire central city. A value of 100 indicates the opposite situation of a completely segregated distribution, i.e., each block contains only whites or blacks, but not both. The higher the value of the index, the higher the degree of residential segregation.

   Values for the 207 central cities analyzed by the Taeubers in 1960 ranged from 60 to 98 with only a few cities having values in the lower range of observations—only 5 cities had values below 70. Cleveland is no exception to these generalizations: the city of Cleveland had block segregation indexes of 92 in 1940, 91.5 in 1950, and 91.3 in 1960 and 87 in 1967.

As indicated in the text, Taeuber and Taeuber calculated census tract segregation indexes for Cuyahoga County. This index is 86.6 for 1950 and 89.7 for 1960. Taeuber and Taeuber, *Negroes in Cities.*

Taeuber also compared the Census tract distribution of expected high income blacks (those earning over $10,000 in 1960) with the actual distribution of high income blacks. The segregation index comparing *expected* high income blacks with *actual* high income blacks in 1960 is 89. Similarly, when segregation indexes are computed comparing the expected residence patterns of low income households (those with incomes below $3,000 in 1960) with the actual low income black residence patterns an index of 77 is obtained. Karl E. Taeuber, "The Effect of Income Redistribution."

4. John F. Kain and John M. Quigley, *Housing Markets and Racial Discrimination: A Microeconomic Analysis,* (New York: National Bureau of Economic Research, 1975); and Mahlon Straszheim, *An Econometric Analysis of the Urban Housing Market* (New York: National Bureau of Economic Research, 1975).

5. Stanley Liberson, *Ethnic Patterns in American Cities* (Glencoe: The Free Press, 1963).

6. Mahlon R. Straszheim, *An Econometric Analysis of the Urban Housing Market,* (New York: National Bureau of Economic Research, 1975); John F. Kain, "A Contribution to the Urban Transportation Debate: An Econometric Model of Urban Residential Location and Travel Behavior, *The Review of Economics and Statistics* 46 (February 1964); John F. Kain, *Essays in Urban Spatial Structure* (Cambridge: Ballinger Publishing Co., 1975), Chaps. 1–3, Gregory K. Ingram, John F. Kain, and J. Royce Ginn, *The Detroit Prototype of the NBER Urban Simulation Model* (New York: National Bureau of Economic Research, 1972); John M. Quigley, "The Influence of Workplaces and Housing Stocks upon Residential Choice," Paper presented at the Toronto meeting of the Econometric Society, Dec. 30, 1972 (processed).

7. John Kain, "Housing Segregation, Negro Employment and Metropolitan Decentralization," *Quarterly Journal of Economics* 82, 2 (May 1968): 175–97, Joseph D. Mooney, "Housing Segregation, Negro Employment and Metropolitan Decentralization: An Alternative Perspective," *The Quarterly Journal of Economics,* May 1969, pp. 298–311; and National Committee Against Discrimination in Housing, *Jobs and Housing: A Study of Employment and Housing Opportunities for Racial Minorities in Suburban Areas of the New York Metropolitan Region,* (New York: National Committee Against Discrimination in Housing, Inc., March 1970).

8. Kain, ibid.

9. U.S. Bureau of the Census, Census of Population: 1970, *Subject Reports* Final Report PC (2)-6D, Journey to Work, (Washington, D.C.: U.S. Government Printing Office, 1973).

10. U.S. Bureau of the Census, Census of Population: 1970, *Subject Reports* Final Report PC (2)-6D, Journey to Work, (Washington, D.C.: U.S. Government Printing Office, 1973).

11. William Brink and Louis Harris, *The Negro Revolution in America* (New York: Simon and Schuster, 1964).

12. Thomas F. Pettigrew, "Attitudes on Race and Housing: A Social-Psychological View," in Amos H. Howley and Vincent P. Rock, (eds.), *Segregation in Residential Areas,* (Washington, D.C., National Academy of Sciences, 1973), p. 44.

13. Ibid., p. 45.

14. For a discussion of these questions see: David McEntire, *Residence and Race* (Berkeley, University of California Press, 1960); John F. Kain and John M. Quigley, *Housing Markets and Racial Discrimination: A Microeconomic Analysis* (New York, National Bureau of Economic Research, 1975), Chap. 3, U.S. Commission on Civil Rights, *Hearing,* St. Louis, Missouri, Jan. 14–17, 1970.

Appendix 17A

The 1970 County Group Public Use Samples consist of two one-in-one-hundred samples of the U.S. population identified by place of residence in 408 county groups having populations of more than 250,000 population. The two county group samples correspond to the two extended questionnaires used by the Census in 1970, the so-called 5 percent and 15 percent samples. The α_{jk}'s in equation 17–1 are calculated from the 5 percent sample for the two county groups comprising the Cleveland SMSA. (Questions about national origin appeared only on the 5 percent questionnaire.) The sample used to estimate the α_{jk}'s provides information on approximately 12,000 individuals and 3,000 households located in the Cleveland SMSA.

To calculate provisional α_{jk}'s each sample person was identified in terms of their race or ethnic origins and by membership in each of 384 household types. The resulting matrix had 4,608 elements, 384 household types times 12 racial and ethnic groups. Then to improve the efficiency of the estimates of the α_{jk}'s, the provisional estimates were scaled to agree with the complete count published estimates of the distribution of Cleveland's ethnic population.

To predict the racial or ethnic population of each census tract, the areawide values of α for each ethnic (racial) group are multiplied by P_{ij}, the number of households of each type residing in each tract. Unfortunately, no exact counts of the number of households in each of the 384 household types are available by tract. Specifically, elements of the P_{ij} matrix are missing by tract. Fortunately, good estimates of these missing elements can be obtained from available data. As Leo Goodman has observed, any three-dimensional array can be exactly described in terms of a set of one-, two-, and three-dimensional interactions.[1] Adequate estimates of each of these interaction terms can be obtained from tract and SMSA-wide data and these estimates are sufficient to derive good estimates of the unknown three dimensional array for each tract. The scaling procedures used to complete the census tract matrices are described briefly below.

For each census tract, the Fourth Count Summary tape for households presents a cross-tabulation of household income by number of persons in the household, and of household income by family type. These tables are two-dimensional marginal summaries (or two-dimensional interactions) of the unknown three-dimensional table of household income, by household size, by family type. The missing interactions at the SMSA level are estimated from the combined 5 and 15 percent Public Use Samples (a one-in-fifty sample). The procedure thus assumes that the interaction between family type and household size, and the three dimensional interaction is constant across all tracts in the SMSA.

The procedure used to combine this information into a single estimate of the complete 384-cell matrix for each tract is known as "iterative scaling." A full discussion of the method is presented by Bishop.[2] The iterative scaling procedure used in this analysis preserves exactly the known two-dimensional margins available for each tract and provides estimates of the unknown three-dimensional array which reflect to the fullest extent possible the estimated third level interactions obtained from the Public Use sample data.

The procedure was performed separately for the total households and for white households. In all, over 900 separate tract matrices were obtained in this way. The procedure will lead to biased estimates of the 384-cell tract arrays if the omitted interactions, say, the relationship between household type and household size, vary systematically by census tract within the SMSA. It is highly improbable that the small estimation errors inherent in this procedure would affect the analyses presented in this paper in any way.

After the estimates of P_{jk} and P_{ij} were obtained using the procedures described previously, estimates of the numbers and proportions of each racial and ethnic group were obtained from equations 17-2 and 17-3.

One final problem appeared during the analysis of the actual ethnic population counts obtained from the summary tapes. In certain instances, these data differed from similar information published in the Census Tract series for Cleveland. We assumed these differences reflected differences in error editing, and that the published figures were the most accurate estimates.

Notes

1.   Leo A. Goodman, "The Multivariate Analysis of Qualitative Data: Interactions Among Multiple Classifications," *Journal of the American Statistical Association* 65, 329 (March 1970): 226–256.
2.   Y M M. Bishop, "Full Contingency Tables, Logits, and Split Contingency Tables," *Biometrics* 25 (1969): 383–400.

18

The Distributive Effects of Local Taxes: Some Extensions

Peter Mieszkowski

Introduction

The recent literature on local taxation has reexamined the conventional wisdom on the distributive effects of local property taxes. Contrary to the conventional wisdom that the property tax is a regressive excise tax, it has been argued by Henry Aaron,[1] Peter Mieszkowski,[2] and Procter Thompson[3] that it is important to distinguish between the global (nationwide) effects of the property tax and local excise tax effects. As capital can be assumed to be perfectly mobile between communities (cities) a community that unilaterally raises its tax will have to pay more for the services of capital. However, if all communities raise their property tax simultaneously, then the effect of property tax system is to depress the after-tax rate of return on capital in the nation by the average rate of property tax in the economy. Hence the property tax system is effectively a tax on capital income.

This is quite a general argument and is based on a number of strong assumptions. Among them: that capital markets are perfectly competitive; that the property tax is a general tax as it applies to all capital; and that the *overall* supply of capital in the economy is fixed. The work of R.A. Musgrave,[4] Dick Netzer,[5] and Martin Feldstein[6] has questioned these assumptions and some of this work develops the necessary qualifications to the central argument that a property tax system is a tax on capital.

Nevertheless, in this chapter I propose to remain within the confines of most of the simplifying assumptions made in earlier work and to remedy one limitation of this work; namely, the lack of attention paid to the benefit aspects of local government expenditures.

Another objective of this chapter is to compare the distributive effect of property taxes with wage taxes. The analysis of the differential tax incidence of various tax systems imposed by local governments has not been developed to any significant extent.

Some Models Where Only Residential Capital Is Subject to Tax

I shall begin by repeating a result first presented by Bruce Hamilton[7] for a world where property taxes are imposed solely on residential capital. Suppose that all metropolitan areas in the United States are sufficiently similar so that we can ignore differences in tax rates and benefit levels between areas and regions. We shall proceed as if the whole country was one giant SMSA and within this SMSA capital and households are very highly, if not perfectly, mobile. For the moment we shall also ignore questions of urban structure and difference in density of development within the SMSA. Following Hamilton we shall assume that there are a very large number of independent communities each with its own fiscal powers that provide diverse bundles of public services. Also, we shall assume that each community is perfectly homogeneous, or nearly so in terms of house types. Within each community, zoning or development controls insure that the housing will be maintained at some designated level of quality or assessment. As there exists a large number of house types and a larger number of communities with varying public service levels, the household's decision regarding the consumption of housing is independent of the decision of how much public services to consume. As there are a very large number of communities to chose from, a household first decides on a housetype and from the subset of communities consisting of that housetype finds the community that best suits its public service requirements.

In this world of perfect stratification, enforced with zoning or deed restrictions, the property tax becomes in effect a user price. If people want more public goods they have to pay for it in the form of higher property taxes. It is as if each developer of each community simply charged each household a given annual fee for the use of the public facility.

The key assumptions that underly this result are the assumptions of perfect stratification, perfect mobility between communities and the wide range of choice over varying levels of public services. In effect, any tax system can be transformed in a set of user charges under essentially the same sort of assumptions made above. Under a wage, or an income tax imposed on the household, communities would become stratified according to wage level rather than according to house type. The zoning or residence requirement would be written in terms of minimum wage levels rather than in terms of minimum floor space or lot size requirements.

Similarly, if the source of revenue was an expenditure tax on cigarettes then heavy smokers would reside in communities composed solely of heavy smokers, moderate smokers with other moderate smokers, and so forth. Although this last possibility is rather far fetched, it is clear that, constitutionality considerations aside, a property tax system on residential property and a wage tax are essentially interchangeable in this world of perfect stratification. Communities would not look, or be, quite the same under a wage tax as under a property tax. Under the wage tax, communities would be more hetrogeneous with respect to housetype and more homogeneous with respect to wage level. And if one system was to replace the other, there would be a period of transition where households would resuffle themselves among communities and community development would be modified in response to the tax change.

The first assumption that I shall weaken is the assumption of perfect stratification or perfect homogenity of different communities. Bruce Hamilton[8] has
also analyzed this case and has concluded that if communities remain homogeneous in the sense that each household residing in a community wishes to consume
the same amount of the collectively provided good when faced with a use charge
for that service, then property tax differences will be fully capitalized in land
values. Thus, if we have some perfectly stratified high income communities (H
housing) and some low income communities (L housing) and some mixed communities, H and L housing, then H residents can calculate the tax disadvantages
of living in mixed communities and will lower their bids for land in these communities while L income households will recognize the tax advantages of residing
in mixed communities relative to residing in perfectly stratified L housetype (income) communities.

So, the value of $H(L)$ housing will be depressed (selling at a premium) in
the mixed community. In fact, for the special case of identical demands for the
public good and taking the lots to be of the same size, the *total* value of land in
the mixed community will be independent of the composition of the town between H and L housing.

This neat proposition has to be qualified, of course, when the demand for
public services varies across income groups. Large houses in low-income, high-tax
communities that provide little in the way of public services will sell for very
little, first because of the high tax assessments and also because of the very low
public service levels. On the other hand, small houses in wealthier communities
may not fully reflect the tax saving associated with a higher level of public services in such a community. Low income residence will not value dollar for dollar
the higher benefit levels they are consuming relative to what they would voluntarily "buy" in stratified low income communities.

The basic result that seems to come out of this analysis is that in a system
of decentralized local governments where there exists considerable choice between residential locations, residents "pay" for the public service that they consume. Higher levels of benefits will be more expensive either in terms of taxes
paid or in terms of higher property values. Similarly, lower benefits and/or higher
taxes will be offset by lower capital costs.

It is useful in developing this proposition to note what would occur in a
world where all housing is rental housing. In communities which are perfectly
stratified the renters will pay for the extra public services just as they pay for
additional floor space or for built-in appliances.

In mixed communities where high income and low income apartments coexist side-by-side, the tax rate difference on specific pieces of property in these
mixed communities and the same type of apartments in perfectly stratified communities will be capitalized in the value of the land on which the apartments are
built. In other words, for the same level of public services renters who occupy the
same units will pay the same rents.

However, what I would like to stress is that this type of result is not particular to the property tax. If local wage or income taxes were employed instead, the value of expensive housing in mixed communities would be depressed relative to its value in more homogeneous communities. This is due to the fact that in mixed communities the wage tax will have to be higher than in stratified high income communities.[a] Due to high correlation between wages (income) and the consumption of housing services, the types of fiscal zoning we currently observe would very likely persist or continue under a system of local wage taxes. The reason why a decentralized local tax system approximate a set of user charges is that consumers have, by assumption, a considerable number of residential choices throughout the metropolitan region and are more or less indifferent as to where they reside within the region.

It is useful to contrast a decentralized situation with a highly centralized situation where there is only one fiscal jurisdiction. Since we are abstracting from differences between metropolitan areas a centralized fiscal structure essentially implies a national or federal government. Consider a property tax system levied on residential housing which provides a uniform system of public services throughout the nation. For a unitary system of government this will increase the cost of housing and consumers will decrease their purchases of these services relative to other commodities.[b] This raises the possibility first suggested by H.G. Brown[9] that a property tax on residential housing may turn out to be a tax on capital in general. This result is possible as capital will shift out of housing into manufacturing and other industries and as housing is capital intensive relative to other industries, this reallocation of capital will decrease the rate of return to capital throughout the economy. Following the lead of A.C. Harberger[10] I analyzed elsewhere[11] the possible general equilibrium adjustment of a tax on housing and concluded that under some special circumstances the cost of housing will rise by the amount of the tax revenues and the rate of return to capital will fall by the amount of the tax. The explanation of this result lies in the fact that the cost of the commodities other than housing will fall in value relative to wages so that consumers lose as purchasers of housing but gain as purchasers of all other commodities. Consequently, the Brown-Harberger result that a capital tax in one sector (housing) is essentially a tax on capital in general may be the main effect of a property tax on residential capital. However, as it is not my intent to emphasize this type of adjustment I shall assume that flows of capital from housing to industry is quite small or that the overall return to capital is little affected by a tax on housing capital.

So, a tax on residential real estate imposed at a centralized level of govern-

---

[a]This is not to suggest that wage tax and property tax are perfectly equivalent, as wage tax would impinge on the work-leisure decision while the property tax will directly affect the relative cost of housing. However, the differences that arise from adjustments at the margin are secondary in importance relative to general similarities between a local property tax system and a system of local wage taxes.

[b]This adjustment would also occur in a system of local government where zoning or development controls are insufficiently strict to prevent adjustments to the tax.

ment will increase the cost of housing by the amount of tax. Thus, we have the conventional result that the tax burden of the residential property tax should be allocated to the consumers of housing services. In contrast, a tax on wage income imposed at a centralized level of government will, under the assumption of competitive labor markets, fall on persons in proportion to their wage income.

The result that households pay the property tax in proportion to their consumption of housing in a centralized situation may appear to be similar to the result of the decentralized situation where households are said to "pay" for the benefits of the public services they consume. However, both the distribution of tax burdens and welfare (utility) are likely to be very different between the two extreme fiscal systems.

In a centralized world everyone will tend to get the same level of public services, and pay the same rate of tax. In such a world high income groups will subsidize the collective consumption of low income groups and probably consume suboptimal levels of public services. For example, when the "quality" of public education is low, high income groups will tend to send their children to private schools. They are not "compensated" for this private expense through lower land values as by assumption; there exists no alternative fiscal jurisdictions for them to "buy" their desired level of public goods.

On the other hand, in a decentralized fiscal structure high income groups will tend to stratify themselves into homogeneous communities, and this stratification will decrease their subsidies for the collective consumption of low income groups. Also, high income groups will be able to approximate their desired or preferred level of collective consumption.

When mixed communities exist and low income groups share in the higher benefit levels and/or low taxes, they either pay for these advantages in the form of higher rents or higher housing prices. Land prices or housing value will be anchored to the reproduction costs of perfectly stratified communities. The values of different housing in "mixed" communities will be determined relative to these prices. The principal difference between a centralized and decentralized fiscal structure is that there is less redistribution under a decentralized situation. Unfortunately, one can say little beyond this very general statement unless one has rather detailed information on the time-profile of development of various metropolitan areas. As a way of illustrating the empirical complexities of the problem consider a metropolitan area which initially consists of a central city which has a unified fiscal government; distinguish between two groups, H and L, that live side-by-side in this city. Suppose that the land area in the central city is filled in and ignore the possibility of demolition and increases in density levels there. Consequently, the next stage of development occurs in brand new suburbs which are fiscally independent of the central city. Suppose there are a sufficient number of these new communities so that the price of these new houses is competitively determined. Assume that initially H-type housing is the only housing built in the suburbs and that these suburbs are built in a reasonably short period of time, say three of four years, and that they constitute only a small fraction of the H-type housing in the metropolitan area. As a result of the creation of the new suburbs both the L and H households in the central city are somewhat worse off than they would have been had the suburbs been annexed by the central city or had the new housing been built within the confines of the central city. The reason for this is that the tax base per unit of H housing is higher than the average tax base of central city housing.

This means that taxes on central city will have to rise slightly relative to a situation where annexation occurred and this would lead to increases in rents. However, on current or income account the residents in the central city are initially little affected by the formation of the new suburbs. However, on capital account the owners of H housing will probably have suffered a rather large capital loss. The new suburbs now represent a much more attractive fiscal jurisdiction to purchasers of H-type housing and as a consequence these buyers in the metropolitan area will purchase in the central city only if the fiscal disadvantages are compensated by lower housing prices. On the other hand, the new residents of the area who have bought the suburban housing are no better off on wealth account as a result of the formation of the new suburbs. On the assumption that there is free entry in the formation of suburbs, the prices of housing there will be the same as they would have been had the central city extended its boundaries. But they are much better off on current account as they are paying lower taxes and enjoying a more appropriate level and composition of public goods than they would have consumed in an extended central city.

As the development process continues more and more residents of the central city or their heirs realize their capital losses. The new H residents of the metropolitan area remain on an equal footing as the fiscal disadvantages of residing in the central city are capitalized. For simplicity, we assume for a moment the low income population does not grow. While these groups are no worse off than they were before the formation of the new suburbs, low income groups become increasingly worse off than they would have been in an extended central city or under a metropolitan form of government. A somewhat more general form of this proposition is that as long as low income groups continue to reside in the central city in housing which is provided at competitively determined rates of return on capital the amount of fiscal redistribution that will accrue to them depends on the number of H households residing in the central city. Even if all members of the L group are renters, their rents will be lower when the amount of fiscal redistribution is increased. If fiscal reorganization were to occur and a metropolitan form of government was adopted, low income groups would benefit as the taxes paid on their housing for the same level of public services are likely to fall and so their rents will fall. However a lion's share of the benefits, that are made at the expense of the suburban residents of annexation, will accrue to the *owners* of high income housing located in the central city. The increase in the tax base and the possible standardization of benefit levels will put better quality housing in the central city and the suburbs on a more equal footing. In the somewhat unlikely situation that development of L-type housing will occur in stratified suburbs, the owners of L housing in the central city will experience a capital gain as the new suburbs are formed. For the same service levels, and consequently rent levels, taxes on L houses in the central city will be lowered due to the existence of H houses there and so the value of L housing in the central city will be higher. Consequently, after a metropolitan reorganization the value of L housing in the central city may well fall and the benefits of a larger tax bases will accrue to higher income central city residents and to low income suburban residents. The interesting general issue which arises is whether tax relief to a high tax jurisdiction from a higher level government or through fiscal centralization accrues to the owners of the housing capital or to the user of this capital (the renters). We are suggesting that depending on the situation, a large part of the tax relief may accrue to the owners of capital. However, it is not unrealistic to assume that due to exclusionary zoning and the fiscal difficulty of setting up low income suburbs the bulk of L-type housing will be supplied in the Central City. To the extent that taxes level the effect of the supply price of housing, low income residents will benefit directly as renters as well as owners if the suburbs are annexed by the central city.

In closing this section we wish to remind the reader that the capitalization of tax differentials and benefit differences take place relative to a norm or an average. In the models where stratified communities coexist with mixed or hetrogeneous communities, the price structure is anchored to the reproduction costs of perfectly stratified communities.

When we begin with a diverse set of communities with varying benefit levels and varying tax rates and then move to a uniform system of taxation on residential property that will finance the previous benefit levels, the prices of houses will change depending on whether their respective tax rates go up or down. So in this example of tax capitalization value moves up or down with reference to an average rate of tax. When property taxes are imposed on housing capital, the incidence of the average tax or the norm falls on the consumers of housing services.

Local Taxes on Industrial and Commercial Capital[c]

To this point the analysis has been partial in a number of respects. First we have assumed that local taxes are imposed only on residential (household) capital and that the benefits of the local expenditures accrue only to households. Second, the wage rate and the return to capital has been taken to be predetermined,

[c]By industrial capital we mean, in this section, all capital that is not used as residential real estate.

or exogeneous. We have in effect assumed that the supply of capital to the household sector is perfectly elastic at a predetermined rate of return. While it is the joint demand for capital by the household and the industrial sectors that determines the return to capital, the explicit introduction of an industrial sector closes the model and makes before tax factor prices endogeneous. On the adoption of marginal product factor pricing, it is the technology and the ratio of labor to capital in the industrial sector that determines the wage rate.

One of the principal questions which we address in this section is whether the introduction of local taxes on industrial property changes the supply price of capital to the household sector. The principal conclusion of the previous section was that if the cost of capital to the household sector is given and if communities are fully or partially stratified, according to benefits levels provided, then households will pay for the benefits of local public services. So if the supply price of capital is 10 percent a 1 percent local property tax will represent a particular bundle of public services and will increase the cost of capital in that community to 11 percent. A 2 percent property tax will represent, other things being equal, a higher benefit level and will raise the cost of capital in that community to 12 percent and so on. To the extent communities are not perfectly stratified, fiscal advantages and disadvantages will be capitalized. The important conclusion is that a local property tax system restricted to residential capital and a system of local wage taxes will approximate a system of user charges.

As the first step in analyzing the effects of local taxes on the industrial sector we shall search for conditions under which industrial property taxes will be perfect benefit taxes (user charges). Consider a dual fiscal structure where separate industrial tax levies are used to finance public services that benefit only industrial capital. To be more specific suppose that police services and fire protection are capital saving in the sense that cost of capital is directly decreased. The police prevent the vandalism of the capital stock (but not the theft of finished commodities). Fire protection decreases the amount of capital destroyed and decreases insurance rates.

As for households, there will be an incentive for firms to stratify themselves according to their capital intensity. For under an industrial property tax, capital intensive firms will pay a lower rate of tax, for the same level of services if located in industrial parks with other capital intensive firms. Similarly, for a system of wage tax, wage-intensive firms will wish to exclude capital intensive firms. Should mixed (mixed with respect to capital intensity) industrial parks form, land prices will adjust to account for various fiscal advantages and disadvantages relative to stratified industrial zones.[d] It appears that in a fragmented fiscal system industrial firms will pay for the benefits of public services. If they want

---

[d] In mixed communities a switch from profit taxation to wage taxation is not a matter of indifference. Firms have bought land on the basis of certain expectations regarding the tax systems and a change-over from a property base to a wage base will result in capital gains for some firms and capital losses for others.

more fire protection they will locate in industrial parks with elaborate protection facilities and will pay a higher rate of tax for these services. Hence to the extent that industrial capital is taxed on a benefit basis, it appears that the supply price of capital to the residential (household) sector is unaffected by taxes on industrial capital.

Also, it appears that a change-over from property taxation to wage taxation will not change this conclusion. Firms located in high tax, high service industrial parks will have to pay higher wage taxes or higher wages if the legal liability is imposed on workers. Factor proportions will be affected, but this effect it might be argued is a secondary one. Local taxes, imposed on capital or on labor, will, if they finance services beneficial to industry, approximate a system of user charges.

I now wish to argue that this line of reasoning is misleading at best and that the distributive effects of using property taxes to finance local services for industry are very different from the distributive effects of using wage taxation to finance the same benefits. At the risk of running together two separate issues let us first drop the assumption that the benefits of public expenditures accrue in the form of decreases in the cost, or use, of capital. Many public services unquestionably can be represented as a form of "technical progress" or a shift in the production function. Improvements in transportation facilities decreases the delivered price of commodities. The police protect not only capital but labor and finished commodities as well. Hence if the public services beneficial to industry can be represented as a form of Hicks neutral technical change then the benefits of these services will accrue to labor and capital in proportion to their shares in industrial output, and the only true benefit tax will be a commodity tax, or a value added tax on industrial output.

Consequently, if we begin with a uniform level of public services throughout the industrial sector financed by a commodity tax and then substitute either a wage tax or a property tax for the commodity tax, the distribution of income will be significantly affected. Under competitive factor and commodity markets, a uniform wage tax will fall on labor, while the burden of a uniform industrial property tax will fall on capital. Although we abstract from the use of labor in the household sector, and restrict ourselves to the consideration of residential real estate, a change in the tax system will affect the supply of capital to the residential or household sector.[e]

One point which needs to be emphasized is that this result in no way depends on the assumption that capital and labor share in the benefits of public expenditures in proportion to their shares in industrial output. The difference in income distribution between a property tax on industrial capital and a tax on industrial labor *arises from different methods of financing and not effects of the*

---

[e]The supply of labor will also be affected as workers will shift from household work to work in the market sector.

expenditures that can be taken to be as given and unchanged from tax system to tax system.

Two points come out of this analysis. First, for a local fiscal system that provides benefits to industry the nature of the tax system used to finance these benefits does affect the distribution of income between labor and capital. Second, it will be only under very special circumstances that a set of property tax on industrial capital will be a perfect benefit tax in the sense that, at the margin, the return to industrial capital is increased by an amount equal to the cost of the industrial property tax.

In general, the benefits of public expenditures for industrial purposes will be imperfectly related to the property tax on industrial capital. And this will be true even if the taxes imposed on the industrial sector are *not* used to finance household public goods such as education and recreation. The imperfect relationship between benefits and taxes will affect the supply of capital to the residential sector.

In order to highlight this effect we shall make the rather extreme assumption that there is no relationship between the tax rate on industrial capital under the property tax and the benefits from public expenditures that accrue to industrial capital in the form of a higher rate of return. This assumption does not imply that industry does not receive the benefits of police and fire protection, local transportation facilities, local water supplies, and so on. What it does mean is that the level of benefits accruing to capital is *independent* of the taxes collected on industrial property and/or that most of benefits of the services that affect the industrial sector accrue to consumers and labor.

We begin with a system of communities which for simplicity we shall assume are identical and which initially do not impose taxes on industrial capital. All communities provide an identical level of public services and pay for them out of residential property taxes which average out to be 3 percent. So, in the initial equilibrium, the total cost of capital to residential sector including the property tax is 13 percent, while the cost of capital to the industrial sector is 10 percent.

Suppose that a 3 percent tax is imposed on all industrial capital and that the proceeds are used to finance educational, cultural, and recreational facilities for household sector or are used to increase transfer payments to the poorer members of the household sector. The after-tax rate of return on industrial capital will fall from 10 percent to 7 percent as a result of the tax. As equilibrium in capital markets will not be established unless capital earns the same after-tax rate of return in the industrial and the residential sectors, the cost of capital will fall from 10 percent to 7 percent in the residential sector. So, in effect, what was initially a tax on households consuming the services of residential real estate has been transformed, through the addition of a tax on industrial capital, into per-unit tax on all of the capital in the economy.

We can contrast this conclusion with a situation where local public goods are financed, initially, by wage taxes and an industrial wage tax is imposed. For such a system the rate of return on capital would be 10 percent and household would, in the form of lower wage payments, bear the burden of the wage tax. Alternatively, we could imagine the imposition of an industrial wage tax to provide property tax relief to the household sector. In this case households will lose in their role of workers, and gain as consumers of the services of residential real estate.

Although these points are made in the context of uniform taxation across communities, they also apply to a fragmented fiscal situation where tax rates vary across communities.

When we add an industrial property tax system to a set of property taxes on residential capital in a decentralized fiscal structure, the effects will vary greatly across communities. The distribution of industrial capital varies across jurisdiction as does the level of taxes they impose. If communities simply impose the same rate of tax on industrial capital as they do on residential capital some very rich communities will collect nothing in the way of additional taxes while other rich communities enjoying the presence of offices and shopping centers will reap large windfalls. Industry and residents are bound to reallocate as the result of the tax changes. Some industrial land will become very expensive in response to the low taxes and high benefit level, while other industrial land will lose value, relatively, as a result of the imposition of the industrial property tax.

Although I have no easy way of characterizing these changes, I would like to stress once again that the imposition of industrial taxes will depress the rate of return on industrial capital and will also lower the cost of residential capital by the average rate of industrial property tax. The changes in land values, reallocations of industry, and declines in wages, if labor is immobile, will also occur, but one of the dominant (primary) effects will be a fall in the return to capital.

Thus, I repeat the basic conclusion of earlier work that it is important to distinguish between global or macro effect of changes in tax with local or partial changes that will affect the relative position of particular communities. We have moved away from previous emphasis on excise tax effects that reflect tax differentials between communities in the form of price difference and have emphasized the capitalization effects that reflect tax difference and benefit differences in terms of differences in sites or land values. Ideally, one should allow for both types of effects and in the next section we shall sketch such an attempt.

A Simple Model of Central-City
Suburban Location

There are a number of weaknesses in the analysis above. First, little if any reference is made to the structure of urban areas. The location decision of households and industry is based on the assumption that all sites in the metropolitan area are identical and are perfect substitutes for one another.

One of the main weaknesses of the simple capitalization hypothesis is that it overlooks the possibility of varying the density or intensity of land development. To say that tax rate differences are capitalized in the value of land is really precise only when the two sites are identically developed. Earlier work has shown that if land in the proximity of the central business district (CBD) has certain unique characteristics and the demand for residential or commercial floor space is not perfectly elastic at this site, then the imposition of a tax on property on this site will *increase* the cost of floor space at this site and will lower the value of land there, as the intensity of development will be decreased. The most general work of this type is due to Grieson[12] and it suggests that a substantial part (about 70 percent) of a property tax on the CBD capital will be passed onto consumers and 30 percent absorbed by owners of land.

In this section I attempt to extend the analysis to two sites, the central city and the suburbs; and two commodities, residential housing and manufacturing industry. The key question is the degree of substitutability between central city and suburban sites for both residential and business activity. There are a number of reasons for believing that these two broad, general locations are not perfect substitutes.[f] One of the main reasons why the two locations are imperfect substitutes for each other is that households vary in their life style, preference for suburban living, attitudes towards commuting, and so on.

The model that we use is set out in more detail in Appendix 18A. Here we shall give a verbal sketch of the model and shall present the results of a few numerical simulations.

We assume that there are two sites, the central city and the suburbs. These two locations represent independent fiscal jurisdictions. We shall assume that the central city has extraordinary expenses such as welfare payments or higher wages to militant labor, that are of little benefit to the average taxpayer. The analysis will concentrate on comparing the effect of a property tax imposed on the central city with a wage tax imposed by the central city on an origin basis.

There are two production activities at each of the two sites, housing and manufacturing. So in effect there are four commodities: central city housing H_1, suburban housing H_2, central city manufacturing X, and suburban manufacturing Y.

Central city and suburban housing are not perfect substitutes for each other in demand. As suggested above some persons may prefer to live in the central city (or the suburbs). However, equivalent housing at the two locations are expected to be close, if not perfect, substitutes. Similarly the two manufactured

---

[f]There are a number of activities, cultural and recreational, which are unique to any metropolitan area and these are typically located in the central city. The central city may also have unique transportation facilities such as a port or rail terminals. These may also be substantial economies of scale in certain activities that may preserve a production advantage for the central city in the face of an eroding fiscal base. Public transportation and established neighborhood associations are other central city advantages. Also there is the point that depreciating industrial capital may be replaced bit by bit so that central city abandonment may be very expensive for an enterprise.

goods X and Y are not perfect substitutes though their substitutability in demand may be very high.

In addition to substituting between housing sites persons will change their work-sites if relative wage rate changes and/or if relative housing price changes. If wages rise in the suburbs a person will be more likely to offer his labor services to a suburban firm even though he continues to reside in the central city. Also, if central city housing increases in price relative to suburban housing, people are not only likely to move to the suburbs, but other things being equal, to work there also.

We assume that the *overall* labor supply is given but that the supply of labor to the central city is a function of the difference in the wage rate, in the two locations and of the difference in housing prices between the central city and the suburbs. A more general version would make labor supply a function of the two wage rates and the two housing prices.

In order to simplify the model we assume that labor is not used in the production of housing services, and that land is not used in the production of manufactured goods. This last assumption is strongly contrary to reality, and bypasses the existence of expensive central business district land. However, it is an assumption of considerable convenience and is really an extreme form of the assumption that housing is relatively more land intensive than is industry and commerce. Another important assumption is that the *overall* stock of capital is given, and is perfectly mobile between various activities and locations so that the after-tax return to capital is equalized throughout the economy. We also assume that the supply of land in the central city is fixed; however, the supply of land in the suburbs is positively related to the land rental earned on urban (residential) activity.

Although we have taken a number of shortcuts and have made a number of strong assumptions the model is sufficiently complicated that we do not attempt explicit qualitative analysis of the factors that effect the differential incidence between a central city property tax and a wage tax on labor employed in the central city.

Instead, we present two sets of numerical results for the changes in five factor prices, the change in after-tax return to capital, dp_k, the changes in the wage rate in the central city and suburbs, dw_1, dw_2, respectively, and the changes in per-unit land rents in the central city and the suburbs, dr_1 and dr_2, respectively.

The two sets of results differ in terms of the assumptions regarding the response in the demand for housing at different sites, the elasticity of substitution between the two manufactured commodities X and Y, and the elasticity of labor supply with respect to changes in relative wages in the central city and the suburbs, and with respect to relative housing prices at the two locations. The first set of results are derived on the basis of the general assumption that all the elasticities are high. All the assumed parameter values are set out in Appendix 18A. Some representative parameter values are a value of -5.0 for the own price elasticity of central city housing, a labor supply elasticity of $+5.0$ to central city manufacturing with respect to the difference in wages between the central city and the suburbs, and a supply elasticity of suburban land of + 5.0 with respect to the return to land at this location.

In *both* sets of results the elasticity of substitution between labor and capital in manufacturing and between land and capital in housing are taken to be equal to – 1.0; i.e., the production functions in both types of activity are taken to be Cobb-Douglas.

In the second set of results the elasticity of demand is taken to be 1/5 of the values assumed for the first set of parameters. The own price elasticity of demand for housing is taken to be – 1.0, and so on.

In interpreting the results in table 18–1 one should bear in mind that the price of the manufacture, X, is taken as the numeraire. As this commodity is subject to tax, under the property tax and the wage tax, the after-tax returns to factors will typically fall in terms of this commodity. Even if this occurs, it is quite possible that the price of Y will fall sufficiently so that a particular factor may experience an increase in real income.

The units of measurement for the factors are so chosen that the original prices or returns to various factors are all equal to 1. Consequently, a 1 percent property tax is equivalent to a 10 percent tax on profit income (assuming a 10 percent rate of return) and T_{xk} is equal to 0.10. So a result $dp_k = -0.70T_{lk}$ means that a 10 percent tax on capital will decrease after-tax capital earnings measured in terms of the value of X by 7 percent, and if $dr_1 = -1.74T_{lk}$ the same tax will decrease land rents in the central city by 17.4 percent.

The important measure for incidence are the relative magnitudes of the factor price changes. When the change in factor prices are identical relative factor prices have not changed and the burden of the tax for these factors will be in proportion to their original share in national income.

Table 18–1
Numerical Estimates of Changes in Urban (CC) and Suburban Factor Prices Due to Taxes on Capital and Labor

	High Elasticities		Low Elasticities	
	Tax on Capital In CC*	Tax on Labor In CC	Capital Tax	Labor Tax
Profit dp_k =	$- .70T_{1k}$**	$-.53T_{xL}$***	$-.65T_{1k}$	$-.29T_{xL}$
Land Rents (CC) dr_1 =	$-1.74T_{1k}$	$-.21T_{xL}$	$-.20T_{1k}$	$-.18T_{xL}$
Land Rents (Suburbs) dr_2 =	$.25T_{1k}$	$-.07T_{xL}$	$.07T_{1k}$	$-.03T_{xL}$
Wages (CC) dw_1 =	$-.13T_{1k}$	$-.70T_{xL}$	$-.15T_{1k}$	$-.87T_{xL}$
Wages (Suburbs) dw_2 =	$-.12T_{1k}$	$-.69T_{xL}$	$3.2T_{1k}$	$.28T_{xk}$

*Central city.
**T_{1k} is the per-unit tax on capital imposed on housing capital and industry located in the central city.
***T_{xL} is a per-unit tax on labor in the central city.

Although the results presented in table 18-1 are specific to the parameter values on which they are based, and are partial and incomplete, I wish to draw one basic conclusion from these results; namely, that the distributive effects of a partial property tax system are very different from the distributive effects of partial wage tax.

These results bear out the proposition that a partial property tax imposed on one of the two sites, the central city will impose a much larger burden on capital than on equal yield tax on labor employed at the same location. Also, while a tax on capital in the central city may lead to a substantial fall in the return to land, capital—while it will bear a smaller relative burden—will typically bear a substantial part of the absolute burden of the tax. At the same time it is very clear from these results, and others that we have calculated, that it is very difficult to pin down precisely the relative tax burdens on various factors of production.

When labor and consumers of housing are highly mobile between communities, land in the high tax areas will bear a large share of the burden of a property tax. When households are less mobile, the decline to land rents will be relatively small and the return to suburban workers will be enhanced. When we made the supply of land less elastic in the suburbs, we found, other things being equal, that for a tax on central city capital the increase in suburban land returns will be dramatic, the decline in wages and land values in the central city will be somewhat less, and that the burden of capital will increase.

While these results accord well with common sense, they are, because of limitations of quantitative information, quite general. Nevertheless the results do effectively illustrate the main point of this chapter, as well as other work; namely, that it is misleading to analyze the effects of a property tax from a partial perceptive, where taxes on industrial and commercial sectors are ignored. Secondly, a partial property tax though it may impose large burdens on land owners and will certainly raise the prices of the commodities subject to tax, will also tend to depress the return to capital relative to labor. On the other hand, a partial wage tax will depress wages relative to profit income.

Finally, while a general accounting of the benefits of public expenditures complicates the analysis, the introduction of the benefit side does not in any way upset the general conclusions reached on the differential incidence of a wage tax and a profits tax, once the taxation of the industrial and commercial sectors are accounted for.

Notes

1. Henry J. Aaron, "A New View of Property Tax Incidence", *American Economic Review, Papers and Proceedings*, 64 (May 1974); 212-221.
2. Peter Mieszkowski, "The Property Tax: An Excise Tax or a Profits Tax?" *Journal of Public Economics* 1, (April 1972): 73-95.
3. Procter Thompson, "The Property Tax and the Rate of Interest," *The*

   American Property Tax (Claremont, California: The Lincoln School of Public Finance, 1965).

4. Richard A. Musgrave, "Is a Property Tax on Housing Regressive?" *American Economic Review, Papers and Proceedings* 64 (May 1974): 222–229.

5. Dick Netzer, "The Incidence of the Property Tax Revisited," *National Tax
   Journal* 26 (December 1973): 515–535.

6. Martin Felstein, "Tax Incidence with Growth and Variable Factor Supply,"
   Quarterly Journal of Economics 88 (Nov. 1974): 551–573, and "Incidence
   of a Capital Income Tax in a Growing Economy With Variable Savings
   Rates," *Harvard* Institute of Economic Research, Discussion Paper Number
   300, June 1973.

7. Bruce Hamilton, "Zoning and Property Taxation in a System of Local Government," Urban Institute Working Paper 1207–14, October 1972.

8. Bruce Hamilton, "Capitalization of Intro-Jurisdictional Differences in Local
   Tax Price, mimeo, June 1974.

9. H.G. Brown, *The Economics of Taxation* New York, Holt: 1924.

10. H.C. Harberger, "The Incidence of the Corporate Income Tax," *Journal of
    Political Economy* 70 (June 1962): 215–240.

11. Peter Mieszkowski, "Tax Incidence Theory: The Effects of Taxes on the
    Distribution of Income," *Journal of Economic Literature* 7 (Dec. 1969):
    1103–1124.

12. Ronald E. Grieson, "The Economics of Property Taxes and Land Value:
    The Elasticity of Supply of Structures," *Journal of Urban Economics* 1
    (October 1974): 367–381.

Appendix 18A

A Model of Central City–Suburban Activities

There are four commodities produced in the metropolitan area $H_1, H_2, X,$ $Y,$ where H_1 is housing consumed in the central city, H_2 is housing consumed and produced in the suburbs, X is a manufactured good produced in the central city, and Y is a manufactured good produced in the suburbs. The four production functions are:

$$H_1 = f_1 (K_1^H, S_1) \tag{18A-1}$$

$$H_2 = \quad (K_2^H, S_2) \tag{18A-2}$$

$$X = X (K_x, L_x) \tag{18A-3}$$

$$Y = Y (K_y, L_y) \tag{18A-4}$$

where $K_1^H, K_2^H, X, Y,$ are the inputs of capital in each of the four industries, S_1 and S_2 are the amounts of land used in the production of housing in the central city and suburbs respectively, and L_x and L_y are the inputs of labor in central city and suburban manufacturing, respectively. By assumption, labor is not used in the production of housing and land is not used in the production of the two manufactured goods.

The factor supply relations are as follows:

$$K_1^H + K_2^H + K_x + K_y = \bar{K} \tag{18A-5}$$

$$L_x + L_y = \bar{L} \tag{18A-6}$$

$$S_1 = \bar{S} \tag{18A-7}$$

$$S_2 = f(r_2) \tag{18A-8}$$

Equation 18A-5 says the overall stock of capital is fixed; equations 18A-6 and 18A-7, define the fixed supply of land in the central city and the overall supply of labor, $\bar{L}$; equation 18A-8 defines the supply of land in the suburbs as a function of the land rental r_2.

$$L_x = f(w_1, w_2, P_1^H, P_2^H).$$ (18A-9)

Equation 18A-9 is a supply function of labor to central city manufacturing and relates labor supply to after-tax wage rates in the central city and the suburbs, w_1 and w_2 respectively and the price (cost) of housing in the central city and suburbs, P_1^H and P_2^H respectively.

In specifying the demand side of the model we have ignored income effects and have made demand a function of the four commodity prices. P_x, P_y, P_1^H and P_2^H. There are three independent demand functions, and in carrying out the numerical work reported in the text of the chapter, we dropped the demand relation for the manufactured good produced in the central city.

By assuming the production functions, equations 18A-1 through 18A-4, to be homogeneous of the first degree we can specify factor demand functions, or factor proportions, as a function of the relative factor prices in each of the four industries.

$$\frac{K_1^H}{S_1} = g_1\left(\frac{P_{K1}^H}{r_1}\right)$$ (18A-10)

Factor proportions in central city housing

$$\frac{K_2^H}{S_2} = g_2\left(\frac{P_{K2}^H}{r_2}\right)$$ (18A-11)

Factor proportions in suburban housing

$$\frac{K_x}{L_x} = g_3\left(\frac{P_{Kx}}{w_{x1}}\right)$$ (18A-12)

Factor proportions in central city manufacturing

$$\frac{K_y}{L_y} = g_4\left(\frac{P_{Ky}}{w_2}\right)$$ (18A-13)

Factor proportions in suburban manufacturing

These thirteen equations, plus the three demand relation and four equations which relate commodity prices to factor prices and taxes, plus the arbitrary choice of a numeraire define a determinant system. Taxes are introduced as per-unit taxes. The two taxes considered are a tax of capital on central city housing and manufacturing, T_{1K}, and a wage tax on central city labor, T_{xL}. The after-tax return to capital is P_K. The relationship between after-tax and before-tax factor prices (cost) differs by the amount of tax. For example, the cost of capital for central city housing P_{K1}^H is equal to $P_K + T_{1K}$, and the total cost of labor in central city manufacturing $w_1^x = w_1 + T_{xL}$.

In comparing the differential incidence of a property tax on capital located in the central city with a tax on central city labor, we assume that no taxes exist at the outset; introduce a capital tax and solve for the *change* in the five after-tax factor prices dP_K, dw_1, dw_2, dr_1, and dr_2 as a function of the per-unit capital tax and then repeat the same type of calculation for a per-unit tax on labor, T_{xL}.

In carrying out the numerical experiments reported in the text we assume the share of capital in housing in both the central city is equal to 0.8, while the share of land is 0.2. We assume the same initial factor intensities in both manufacturing industries and assume the share of labor and capital to be 0.70 and 0.30, respectively. We assume that initially housing capital is equally divided between the suburbs and the central city and it represents 50 percent of the total capital stock. We assume that initially there is twice as much labor and capital in the central city as there is in the suburbs.

Two sets of parameter values are assumed. We shall refer to the two sets as High Elasticity and Low Elasticity. These values are:

	High	*Low*
Own price elasticity of central city housing	−5	−1
Cross price elasticity of central city housing with respect to price of suburban housing	4	.8
Cross price elasticity of central cith housing with respect to manufacturer's price produced in the suburbs	.5	.1

Exactly the same elasticities are assumed in the demand function for suburban housing.

Own price elasticity for commodity Y	−1	−.5
Cross price elasticity for commodity Y with respect to price of central city housing	.5	.25
Cross price elasticity for commodity Y with respect to price of suburban housing	.5	.25
Elasticity of labor supply to central city with respect to differences in wages between central city and suburbs	5	1

	High	*Low*
Elasticity of labor supply to central city with respect to difference in housing prices between central city and suburbs	–1	–.20
Elasticity of substitution between labor and capital in manufacturing in both industries	–1	–1
Elasticity of substitution between land and capital in housing at both locations	–1	–1

19
Planning and Market Processes in Urban Models

Edwin S. Mills

Urban land use models, like other economic models, fall into two fairly clear categories, positive and normative. Most normative models in economics use the following paradigm: a market resource allocation is derived from a model; a welfare criterion, such as Pareto-optimality, is introduced; the market allocation is shown to be suboptimum; measures that governments could take to achieve optimum resource allocation are suggested. It is now widely recognized that this paradigm is something of a travesty in that it takes no account of the incentives that government agencies have to behave in particular ways and of their ability to administer particular kinds of programs. Yet it is firmly rooted in an interesting and attractive view of society; that in a free enterprise and democratic society, private institutions (especially households and firms) further their parochial interests, whereas governments further broader social interests.

Normative concepts are much more primitive in urban models than elsewhere in economics. Typical models in the city planning tradition, such as those surveyed in Brown (1972), have as their solution a spatial representation of private resource allocation in an urban area. Certain public service "needs," e.g., in transportation, are then judgmentally inferred from the solution despite the facts that the public service does not appear in the model and that the model contains no welfare criterion.

Alternatively, some models, including several presented in the *Swedish Journal of Economics* (1972) are explicitly optimization models in which a central planning agency is assumed to control all resources in the urban area and to use them so as to maximize a social welfare criterion. This is unsatisfactory in that, in virtually all western economies, some urban resources are controlled privately and some by governments. Presumably, relatively few western economists believe it would be desirable for governments to plan all major urban activities, although that seems to be the ideal envisaged by many city planners.

Optimization models represent an improvement on the traditional city planning model in that it is sometimes possible to establish whether competitive markets can sustain an optimum solution of the model, usually by using theorems about duality. The best model of this kind is that by Mirrlees in the *Swedish Journal of Economics* (1972).

Support for the research reported in this chapter was provided by a grant from the Ford Foundation to Princeton University.

313

All these approaches miss the essential normative issue, the interaction between public and private sectors. The usual view in a mixed economy is that some goods and services should be produced privately and some publicly in urban areas. It would be desirable if urban models could shed light on this controversial issue. Perhaps even more important and controversial is the issue of government regulation of private activities. Local governments impose a complex web of regulation on almost all private activities in modern cities, and mathematical models should be able to shed light on the desirability of regulation and the efficacy of alternative regulatory programs.

The purpose of this chapter is to present and analyze a model that begins to come to grips with the issue of interaction between public and private sectors in an urban land use model. It introduces assumptions that indicate why it is desirable for government to undertake certain activities. It then specifies the effect of government activity on private resource allocation, and the effect of private activity on the use of the public service. It is an optimization model and permits calculation of an optimum allocation of both public and private resources. Finally, it is demonstrated that competitive markets can sustain an optimum allocation of resources if the public sector provides its service in optimum fashion.

The public service studied in detail in this model is the provision and pricing of transportation facilities. Transportation is an important local public service, whose study is certainly justified. More important from the point of view of this chapter it has strong interactions with the private sector. All private activities require the movement of goods and people. Locations of these activities, means of production, and origins and destinations of trips are affected by the provision and pricing of transportation facilities. Conversely, locations of private activities strongly affect the demands placed on the transportation system. Finally, transportation, like most local public services, has a strong spatial component. It matters a great deal exactly how much transportation is provided at each of many locations in an urban area. Thus, a model that is to be useful for planning purposes must be capable of providing a detailed spatial representation of the urban economy.

The foregoing remarks strongly suggest the formulation of urban land use models in a linear or nonlinear programming framework. It is really the only computational technique that permits numerical analysis on a large enough scale to be useful for detailed spatial planning. Equally important, it is an optimization technique with a natural and well-worked out relationship with welfare economics. Finally, duality then tells us something about the ability of competitive markets to sustain optimum resource allocation. The model presented in the next section is the third generation in a series of programming models of urban land use.[a] The model is presented in the next section. Some numerical analysis

---

[a]References to earlier models are Mills (1972–1974a, and 1974b).

is presented in the third section. The chapter concludes with suggestions for extensions and modifications in the fourth section.

The Model

The primal problem is the construction of an entire optimum urban area. The center of the urban area is fixed by a predetermined point at which goods can be exported from (and, in an easy generalization of the model, imported into) the urban area. The model constructs the urban area on a homogeneous plain stretching in all directions from the central export point. The model determines the amount and production technique of each of an arbitrary number of goods and services to be produced at each location in the urban area. Each good or service can be exported, consumed by residents or used as an input in the production of any other good or service. However it is used, each product must be shipped from where it is produced to where it is used. Among the goods produced are houses where workers live: Each worker must travel from his residence to his place of work. Thus the computer also builds a transportation system designed optimally to carry the traffic placed upon it by optimum locations of production and consumption activities.

To fit into the programming framework, space is represented by a square grid centered on the central export point. Assumptions introduced below imply that all squares a given distance from the center have identical patterns of production, consumption and transportation. This means that squares need to be identified only by their distance from the center. In fact, it is conceptually easy to identify each square separately, but it greatly increases the computational burden. Separate designation would be imporant if, for example, there were geographical irregularities or a partially pre-built city to contend with. Land is treated as homogeneous within each square and transportation entirely within a square is ignored. These assumptions can be made as accurate as desired by making the squares sufficiently small. In fact, square-mile squares are used in the calculations reported below.

The transportation system consists of a single north-south and east-west road through the center of each square. All transportation from a given square is to other squares either closer to or further from the city center. There are no shipments between squares the same distance from the center. Movements thus need to be classified by only two directions, toward and away from the center. There are several routes to get from one square to another, and assumptions made below imply that traffic is shared equally among all efficient routes. Squares are designated by the number of miles of travel necessary to get from the center of the square to the center of the urban area. There is one square at the center and there are $4u$ squares that are u miles from the center.

The following is a complete glossary of notations used:

Endogenous variables

$x_{rs}(u)$ = output of good r using production technique s per square u
miles from city center

$x_r^e(u)$ = export of good r per square at distance u

$t_r^i(u)$ = units of r shipped across square boundary in direction i per
square at u ($i = 1$ is toward city center, $i = 2$ is away from city
center)

$t_{rk}(u)$ = unit miles of r shipped at congestion level k per square at u

$L_k(u)$ = land used for transportation at congestion level k per square
at u

$\delta_k(u)$ = $\begin{cases} 1 \text{ if congestion } k \text{ isused in squares at } u \\ 0 \text{ otherwise} \end{cases}$

Exogenous variables and parameters

x_r^e = total export of r

a_{qrs} = input of q per unit output of r using production technique s

$b_{\bar{r}+1,k}$ = land input per unit of transportation at congestion level k

$b_{\bar{r}+2}$ = capital-land ratio in transportation facility

g_r = congestion effect of r in transportation facility

e_r^u = unit cost of exporting r from square at u

c_{rk} = time and operating cost per unit of shipping r at congestion
level k

R_A = rental rate per square mile of land if land used for non-urban,
e.g., agricultural, purposes

R = rental rate per unit of capital

The urban area produces $\bar{r}$ goods. Housing is the only good that is not exported. It is conceptually easy to introduce an arbitrarily large number of housing types, classified by income, demographic status or tastes of households. In the computations reported below, only two types of housing are considered: that for low and high income residents. This is the minimum number that will permit study of residential location by income level, and the number was kept to two to economize on computing costs. Each house type can be produced by a variety of techniques. ($\bar{r} - 1$) refers to low income housing and $\bar{r}$ to high income housing.

All goods other than housing are exported in exogenously determined amounts. A more complete model would make exports endogenous, but that would require major extensions of the model. Goods can be exported not only from the center but also from suburban export nodes, one in each square at $u = \hat{u}$. The optimum value of $\hat{u}$ can be found by repeated solution of the model for various values of $\hat{u}$. Intuitively, the export point at $u = 0$ is thought of as a railhead or port, whereas those at $u = \hat{u}$ are trucking terminals. Thus, choice of export node determines shipment mode and therefore export cost. This consideration will be introduced below. At least x_r^e units of r must be exported from the various export nodes:

$$x_r^e(0) + 4\hat{u}x_r^e(\hat{u}) \geqslant x_r^e \qquad r = 1, \ldots, \bar{r} - 2 \qquad (19\text{-}1)$$

In each square, sources and uses of each good must add up:

$$4t_r^1(1) + \textstyle\sum_s x_{rs}(0) - t_r^2(0) - \textstyle\sum_s \sum_q a_{rqs} x_{qs}(0) - x_r^e(0) = 0 \qquad (19\text{-}2.0)$$

$$8t_r^1(2) + t_r^2(0) + 4 \textstyle\sum_s x_{rs}(1) - 4t_r^1(1) - 4t_r^2(1) - 4 \textstyle\sum_s \sum_q a_{rqs} x_{qs}(1) = 0$$
$$r = 1, \ldots, \bar{r} \qquad (19\text{-}2.1)$$

$$4(u + 1)t_r^1(u + 1) + 4(u - 1)t_r^2(u - 1) + 4u \textstyle\sum_s x_{rs}(u) - 4ut_r^1(u) - 4ut_r^2(u)$$

$$- 4u \textstyle\sum_s \sum_q a_{rqs} x_{qs}(u) - 4ux_r^e(u) = 0 \qquad u = 2, \ldots, \bar{u} - 1 \qquad (19\text{-}2.u)$$

$$4(\bar{u} - 1)t_r^2(\bar{u} - 1) + 4\bar{u} \textstyle\sum_s x_{rs}(\bar{u}) - 4\bar{u}t_r^1(\bar{u}) - 4\bar{u} \textstyle\sum_s \sum_q a_{rqs} x_{qs}(\bar{u}) = 0$$

$$r = 1, \ldots, \bar{r} \qquad (19\text{-}2\bar{u})$$

These identities ensure that shipments into each square plus production in the square equal shipments to other squares plus use as input or final consumption in the square plus exports, if any, from the square. The identities for $u = 0$ and $u = \bar{u}$ (the furthest square in the city) must be written separately, as (19-2.0) and (19-2.$\bar{u}$) because there can be no outward shipments to or inward shipments from the former and no inward shipments to or outward shipments from the latter. Likewise, the identity for $u = 1$ must be written separately, as (19-2.1), because there is one square at $u = 0$, not $4u$. For other squares, the identity is as written in (19-2u). In each case, there must be one identity for each r.

Most of the complexity in the model is in the specification of the transportation system. The model msut design a system in each square and calculate the use to be made of it. A given facility may be used more intensively by congesting it. Thus, a given amount of traffic can be handled by a small facility and a high congestion level or by a large facility and a low congestion level. The roadway is built with land and capital. A unit-mile shipment of each commodity requires a given amount of roadway at each congestion level, but less roadway is required at higher congestion levels.

Production and use of commodities give rise to units shipped across square boundaries in equations (19-2). These must be converted into unit-miles to calculate demands on the transportation system. From the assumption that activity is uniformly distributed within squares it follows that the average unit shipped across a boundary travels half a mile each in the square from which it comes and the square to which it goes. A unit that goes in and out of a square crosses two boundaries and travels the full mile across the square. Square zero is an exception since nothing travels more than half way through it. Again remembering the restrictions on shipments to and from squares O and $\bar{u}$, units shipped across boundaries, $t_r^i(u)$, are converted into unit-miles shipped, $t_{rk}(u)$, by the following inequalities:

$$\sum_k t_{rk}(0) \geqslant \frac{1}{4} \left[4t_r^1(1) + t_r^2(0) \right] \qquad r = 1, \ldots, \bar{r} \qquad (19\text{-}3.0)$$

$$4 \sum_k t_{rk}(1) \geqslant \frac{1}{2} \left[8t_r^1(2) + t_r^2(0) + 4t_r^1(1) + 4t_r^2(1) \right]$$

$$r = 1, \ldots, \bar{r} \qquad (19\text{-}3.1)$$

$$4u \sum_k t_{rk}(u) \geqslant \frac{1}{2} \left[4(u+1)t_r^1(u+1) + 4(u-1)t_r^2(u-1) \right.$$

$$\left. + 4ut_r^1(u) + 4ut_r^2(u) \right] \qquad r = 1, \ldots, \bar{r} \quad u = 2, \ldots, \bar{u}-1 \quad (19\text{-}3.u)$$

$$4\bar{u} \sum_k t_{rk}(\bar{u}) \geqslant \frac{1}{2} 4(\bar{u}-1)t_r^2(\bar{u}-1) + 4\bar{u}t_r^1(\bar{u}) \qquad r = 1, \ldots, \bar{r} \quad (19\text{-}3.\bar{u})$$

In the glossary, $\bar{r}+1$ refers to land $b_{r+1,k}$ represents the input of land required per standard unit of transportation (an arbitrary measure) at congestion level k. g_r converts unit-miles of r shipped into standard units of transportation. If congestion level k is used at u, enough land must be used for transportation at that congestion level to handle the demands placed upon the facility. This condition is satisfied by the following inequalities:

$$b_{\bar{r}+1,k} \sum_r g_r t_{rk}(u) \leqslant L_k(u) \qquad u = 0, 1, \ldots, \bar{u} \qquad k = 1, \ldots, \bar{k} \quad (19\text{-}4.u)$$

All traffic goes over the same road system and therefore, at a given u, all traffic is subject to the same congestion level. Of course, roads are not uniformly congested throughout the day or week, and some travel is at off-peak times. In principle, the amount of travel at peak and off-peak times should be endogenous, determined by costs of movement at various times. That would require a very complex model. In this model, all traffic in a given square is subject to the same congestion level, but off-peak travel is allowed for informally by making some c_{rk}'s rise more rapidly with k than others. By and large, commuting is at peak travel hours, whereas goods tend to be shipped off-peak. Thus, in the numerical analysis in the next section, the c_{rk}'s that pertain to commuting are made sensitive to k whereas those that pertain to goods movement are made insensitive. This is satisfactory to the extent that time of travel is insensitive to congestion.

Exactly one congestion level must be chosen at each u. This is ensured by the following equalities and inequalities:

$$L_k(u) \leqslant \delta_k(u) \qquad k = 1, \ldots, \bar{k} \qquad u = 0, 1, \ldots, \bar{u} \qquad (19\text{-}5.u)$$

and

$$\sum_k \delta_k(u) = 1 \qquad u = 0, 1, \ldots, \bar{u} \qquad (19\text{-}6.u)$$

$$\delta_k(u) = 0, 1 \qquad u = 0, 1, \ldots, \bar{u} \qquad k = 1, \ldots, \bar{k} \qquad (19\text{-}7.u)$$

Equations (19-7.u) restrict the δ's to integer values and place the problem in the category of non-linear programming. If $\delta_k = 0$, (19-5) says no land can be used for transportation at that congestion level, in which case (19-4) says there can be no travel at that congestion level. If $\delta_k = 1$, (19-5) merely says that no more than one square mile of land can be used for transportation at that congestion level. Equation (19-5) then becomes redundant in view of (19-8) below. Equation (19-6) ensures that exactly one congestion level is used in each square. Of course, the congestion level used can vary from square to square.

The final inequalities ensure that land used for all purposes not exceed that available in any square:

$$\sum_r \sum_s a_{\bar{r}+1,rs} x_{rs}(u) + \sum_k L_k(u) \leqslant 1 \qquad u = 0, 1, \ldots, \bar{u} \qquad (19\text{-}8.u)$$

Equations and inequalities (19-1)–(19-8) are the complete set of constraints on the urban system. The constraints as written permit an arbitrarily large variety of production techniques to be considered, equal to the number of values s can take. Interest in this chapter is focused on the intensity of urban land use and the a_{qrs} are chosen with this in mind. In principle, any input can be a substitute for land, but capital is by far the most important substitute for land in urban activities. The most common way to economize on land in urban areas is to build tall structures on it, housing correspondingly large amounts of other inputs. In addition, substitution of capital and other inputs for land provides the most prominent interaction with the transportation system. Increasing the ratios of capital and other inputs to land increases the traffic a given pattern of land use imposes on the transportation system. Then, optimum design of a transportation system requires knowledge not only of the uses to which land will be put but also of the ratios of capital and other inputs to land.

To focus on this issue, it is assumed that only the capital-land ratio varies with s in production. Specifically, s is assumed to represent building height, so that a large value of s means a small value of $a_{\bar{r}+1,rs}$ and a large value of $a_{\bar{r}+2,rs}$, where $\bar{r}+1$ is land and $\bar{r}+2$ is capital, the second nonproduced input. In the calculations presented below, no other a_{qrs}'s are permitted to vary with s. This implies, for example, that labor-input output coefficients are independent of building heights. Although not quite true, this is probably a good approximation.

The preceding assumption has the implication that the urban area's labor force and output of all produced goods are determined by the export requirements via the input-output matrix. Only transportation costs and land and capital requirements vary with the endogenous variables in the model. Therefore, the appropriate optimization procedure in the primal problem is to minimize the sum of land, capital, transportation and exports costs needed to produce the required export goods. It is assumed that as much land as needed can be rented at the rental rate R_A by expanding $\bar{u}$, the geographical dimension of the urban area. Thus, R_A is the opportunity cost of land to urban areas. Likewise, it is assumed that unlimited amounts of capital can be acquired at a rental rate R per unit. $a_{\bar{r}-1,rs}$ and $a_{\bar{r},rs}$ are low and high income labor input requirements per unit of output of r. But $a_{r,\bar{r}-1,s}$ and $a_{r\bar{r}s}$ represent consumption of good r per low- and high-income household. In this respect, but not in others, this model is like a closed Leontief model.

The criterion function can now be written:

$$\min 2 = R\left[\sum_u \sum_{\bar{r}} \sum_s 4u a_{\bar{r}+2,rs} x_{rs}(u) + \sum_{\bar{r}} \sum_s a_{\bar{r}+2,rs} x_{rs}(0) + b_{\bar{r}+2} \sum_k \sum_u 4u L_k(u)\right.$$

$$+ b_{\bar{r}+2} \sum_k L_k(0)\right] + R_A\left[\sum_u \sum_{\bar{r}} \sum_s 4u a_{\bar{r}+1,rs} x_{rs}(u) + \sum_{\bar{r}} \sum_s a_{\bar{r}+1,rs} x_{rs}(0)\right.$$

$$+ \sum_k \sum_u 4u L_k(u) + \sum_k L_k(0)\right] + \left[\sum_u \sum_r \sum_k 4u c_{rk} t_{rk}(u) + \sum_r \sum_k c_{rk} t_{rk}(0)\right.$$

$$+ \sum_r e_r^0 x_r^e(0) + 4\hat{u} \sum_r e_r^{\hat{u}} x_r^e(\hat{u})\right]. \tag{19-9}$$

The first square bracket in (19-9) is total capital used in the urban area. The first two sets of terms are capital used in goods production, and the last two are capital used in the transportation system. The second square bracket represents land use and the terms are similar to corresponding terms in the first square bracket. The final square bracket represents transportation and export costs. The first two sets of terms multiply the c_{tk}'s, representing time and operating costs of shipping people and goods at various congestion levels, by unit miles travelled.

The last two terms multiply unit export costs by amounts exported for the commodities exported at the two export nodes.

The above is a mixed-integer programming problem, now a well studied mathematical and computational problem (Hadley 1964), although no substantial example seems to have appeared in the economics literature. Literally, the primal problem is a central planning problem in which a single decisionmaker builds the transportation system, decides the amount and production technique of each good to be produced in each square, and chooses the origin and destination of each shipment, and hence the congestion level in each square. In linear programming, duality theory tells us that competitive markets can sustain an optimum allocation of resources without government interference (Dorfman 1958). No usable theorems are available regarding duality for this kind of non-linear programming problem. There is a presumption, but no proof, that competitive markets cannot sustain an optimum resource allocation in this model. This certainly accords with economists' and planners' intuition since few of these specialists would claim that private firms could build and operate an efficient urban road system.

The only non-linearity in the model is the integers used to represent road congestion levels. Thus, the key observation is that, if the public sector builds an optimum road system and charges optimum congestion fees, which would depend on the c's, the model becomes a standard linear programming system. Then, well-known duality theorems tell us that competitive markets can construct and operate an optimum set of production facilities, including homes, and that the optimum congestion fees will induce the private sector to make optimum use of the transportation system. Provided the transportation system is appropriately built and priced, there is no justification for any controls on land use in this model. Many theoretical and applied studies have investigated the resource misallocation from underpricing of congested urban roadways in a partial equilibrium framework. But changes in urban travel patterns usually entail changes in land use and the important issues can be studied only in a model that represents the interaction between transportation pricing and land use. I believe this is the first model to do this satisfactorily.

In principle, the public sector must know the solution of the entire model to be able to calculate the optimum road system to build and the optimum tolls to charge. Congestion on a given road length depends on land use throughout the urban area. Although no proof is available, there seems to be no reason in principle why the public sector cannot approach an efficient transportation system incrementally. It appears that, if the government acquires land for transportation at its competitive market price, and widens roads whenever revenues from doing so will pay the cost of doing so, then an optimum road system will result. Of course, revenues must be calculated at appropriate tolls. This unproven result is contrary to that obtained with other models, such as that in Solow (1972), where it is shown that land acquisition at competitive prices leads to a sub-optimum transportation system. But such results appear to follow from implausible assumptions about inputation of travel costs. Of course, all such results, in this model and elsewhere, ignore the problems that arise in connection with land acquisitions when bordering sites are already developed.

In a sense, there is nothing surprising in the conclusion that governments must take responsibility for constructing and operating an urban road network. Nevertheless, it should be valuable to have a model in which it is made clear why the government should do so. It should be more surprising, at least to some, that the transportation system is the only responsibility the government must assume in this model. There is no need for government controls on building heights, land uses or population densities in this model. It is an important conclusion of this chapter that optimum construction and pricing of the transportation system are sufficient government measures to enable private markets to allocate land uses optimally. Of course, by no means all the characteristics of urban land use alleged to justify government interference are included in this model. But congestion is often used as a justification for elaborate land use controls, and the model makes it clear that many such claims are groundless. Indeed, many planners and others believe that the very fact that the profitability of using a plot for one purpose depends on the uses of neighboring plots deprives markets of their ability to allocate land efficiently. That claim is clearly false.

A Numerical Example

In this section, a moderately realistic illustrative calculation is presented. The purpose is not only to give the reader a sense of how the model works, but also to gain insight into the magnitude of realistic calculations with the model.

The example entails construction of an urban area of about one million people, using data approximately representative of U.S. urban areas of that size at about 1970. The main determinants of computational burden are the details with which the urban area is represented rather than its size. Relatively little detail is included in the calculations reported here.

Urban activities are divided among five sectors, so $\bar{r} = 5$. Sector number one produces services typical of those produced in central parts of U.S. urban areas. They are mainly office activities and large amounts are exported from the urban area. Sector two mainly serves the local population, and is typified by local retail firms. Sector three produces largely for export and is typified by manufacturing firms. Sector four is low income housing and sector five is high income housing. The above statements are merely tendencies; in fact each sector produces at least some output used by each other sector.

All the parameters used in the illustrative calculations are presented in table 19-1. U.S. data imply a labor force of about 300,000 in an urban area with a million people. People are here measured in thousands, so the urban labor

Table 19-1
Parameter Values

a_{qrs}	1	2	3	4	5
1	.00	.03	.06	.07	.14
q 2	.07	.00	.06	.27	.54
3	.03	.02	.00	.03	.06
4	.34	.40	.37	.08	.16
5	.50	.47	.37	.03	.06

$\bar{u} = 11$
$\bar{s} = 20$
$\bar{k} = 3$
$\bar{r} = 5$
$\hat{u} = 7$
$b_{\bar{r}+2} = 0.4$

$x_1^e = 30$
$x_2^e = 20$
$x_3^e = 60$

$R_A = 250$
$R = 1,000$

LAND

s	a_{61s}	a_{62s}	a_{63s}	a_{64s}	a_{65s}
2	.30	.42	.36	.34	.68
5	.24	.36	.31	.29	.54
8	.18	.31	.27	.25	.50
11	.14	.27	.24	.22	.44
14	.10	.23	.22	.20	.40
17	.06	.20	.21	.19	.38
20	.04	.17	.20	.19	.38

k	c_{1k}	c_{2k}	c_{3k}	c_{4k}	c_{5k}	c_{6k}
1	60	30	15	30	45	.07
2	75	45	25	50	75	.05
3	100	65	40	80	110	.03

CAPITAL

s	a_{71s}	a_{72s}	a_{73s}	a_{74s}	a_{75s}
2	.94	.76	1.38	.80	1.60
5	.96	.78	1.40	.82	1.64
8	.98	.80	1.42	.84	1.68
11	1.00	.82	1.45	.86	1.72
14	1.02	.84	1.48	.88	1.76
17	1.04	.86	1.52	.90	1.80
20	1.06	.88	1.57	.93	1.86

r	e_r^0	$\hat{e}_r^{\bar{u}}$	g_r
1	0	200	1.25
2	0	100	0.75
3	0	50	1.20
4	—	—	1.00
5	—	—	1.00

force is 300. Units for outputs of sectors one–three are arbitrary, so units were chosen so that total output is also 300. The complete input-output matrix is in the upper left-hand corner of table 19–1. Sectors four and five are low and high income housing. Income groups are divided at the median for this calculation, so there are 150 low income workers and 150 high income workers. U.S. data imply that the average income of the richest half of the population is roughly twice that of the poorest half, and it is assumed here that high income households consume twice as much of each of the five goods as low income households. These consumption quantities are the last two columns of the matrix. The last two rows are employment coefficients in the five sectors, the elements in both the last two rows and columns being direct employment in households.

The right top of table 19–1 presents the dimensions of the model. $\bar{u}$ is 11, implying an urban area of about 250 square miles. $\bar{s}$ is 20. This is about the height of the tallest building in most U.S. urban areas of about a million people. In fact, the land and capital input-output coefficients in the middle of the table were chosen to produce maximum building heights of about 20 stories, but $\bar{s}$ does not constrain building heights. $\bar{s}$ was made great enough so that the tallest building was less than $\bar{s}$ stories. To ease computing, only values of s that are multiples of three were used in the calculations. Thus, buildings of 1–3 stories are represented by $s = 2$ in these calculations, and so on.

$\bar{k}$ is the number of possible congestion levels. The cost of the computing depends mainly on the number of integer-valued variables, which depends strongly on $\bar{k}$. Thus, although congestion is actually a continuous variable, $\bar{k} = 3$ was used here. $k = 1$ is uncongested travel, and $k = 3$ is heavily congested travel. After some experimentation, the suburban export node was put at $\hat{u} = 7$.

The value of R_A of 250 at the middle top of table 19–1 is the annual rental in thousands of dollars per square mile of land valued at \$4,000 per acre and using a discount rate of 10 percent. \$4000 per acre was estimated to be a typical land value near the edge of a U.S. urban area in 1970. $R = 1,000$ is the annual rental in thousands of dollars per \$10 million worth of capital. Other units in table 19–1 were chosen to make these parameters consistent with the fact that the share of property (capital and land) in value added is about 0.25 in the United States.

The land and capital input-output coefficients are shown in the middle of the table for the five sectors. The land coefficients should fall with building height. It takes less land to produce a unit of output in a high building than in a low building. Capital coefficients should rise with building height, for three reasons. Foundations and structures must contain more capital per unit of enclosed area the taller the building to support the weight and stresses of tall buildings; there are costs of raising materials to great heights in construction of tall buildings; and the usable floor space per unit of enclosed area falls as buildings become taller because more interior space must be devoted to vertical movement of occupants.

The pattern of the coefficients differs among the sectors. Good number one is office type activities for which it is relatively easy to substitute capital for land. Thus, capital coefficients rise little, and land coefficients fall considerably, with building height. Sector three produces manufactured goods, which is difficult in tall buildings, so capital coefficients rise rapidly, and land coefficients fall little, with building height. The pattern for sector two is between those of sectors one and three. In housing, sectors four and five, substitution of capital for land is easy for low buildings but becomes difficult for tall buildings.

In U.S. urban areas, housing occupies about half the land area, transportation about 25 percent and goods production the remaining quarter. The land input-output coefficients were chosen to reproduce this pattern.

The c_{rk}'s, representing transportation costs, are shown at the bottom of the table. Auto costs were about 0.10 per vehicle mile in 1970 and varied little with speed or congestion. Time costs were assumed to be half the wage rate and are inversely proportional, per mile, with speed. Thus, vehicle operating costs are independent of the driver's income and of travel speed, whereas time costs are proportionate to income and inversely proportionate to speed. Little is known about unit-mile costs of shipping goods. Sector one produces services, whose delivery requires movement of people, and transportation costs are therefore high except that much delivery is probably off-peak. Coefficients for sector two and sector three were chosen so that transportation costs were modest fractions of production costs.

$b_{\bar{r}+1,k}$ and $b_{\bar{r}+2}$ represent land and capital coefficients for transportation facilities. They are less the greater the congestion level. They also reflect the fact that land costs are about half of road costs in U.S. urban areas. Finally, the land coefficients are chosen so that about a quarter of the land area is devoted to transportation.

The g_r's represent road space requirements per unit-mile of transportation in the five sectors. Their values are quite arbitrary, but reflect the fact that most urban road space is devoted to movement of people rather than of goods.

The e_r^u's respresent cost of exporting the three goods from the two export nodes. For each good, only the relative value of e_r^0 and $e_r^{\hat{u}}$ matters, since total exports of each good from the two nodes are exogenous. Thus, the e's only affect which node is used. Thus, all three e_r^0's were set equal to zero. Good one was made most expensive to export from the suburban node and good three least expensive.

The dimensions in table 19-1 imply that there are 788 variables, excluding slacks, in the problem. Of these, 36 are integer valued. But exactly one of each triplet of integer-valued variables must equal one, implying 3^{12} possible combinations of zeros and ones. There are 219 constraints in the example, ignoring non-negativity conditions on the variables.

These numbers are small for modern linear programming calculations, and of moderate size for mixed integer-programming calculations. The calculations were done on Princeton's IBM 360/91 computer, using a modification of IBM's M for 360 linear programming package. It is a branch-and-bound iterative procedure. It starts with guesses as to the values of the integer-valued variables and solves the linear programming problem. It then modifies the values of the integer-valued variables, at first ignoring the integer constraints, searching for new values that, upon resolving the linear programming problem, reduce the value of the criterion function. The example presented here required $400k$ of the $1100k$ of usable capacity in the core of the computer, and took just over six minutes, at a total cost of $70, to solve the 70 linear programming iterations needed to find an optimum feasible integer solution.

The solution is presented in table 19-2. The city built by the computer has many of the characteristics of real cities. Square zero is devoted to production of good one in seventeen-story buildings, and to transportation at congestion level three. Square one is devoted to production of good one in smaller buildings, to some low income housing, in five-story buildings, and to transportation. Square two contains both low and high income housing as well as sector one. It is interesting to observe that there is a ring of low income housing surrounding the city center, as in most U.S. cities. All subsequent squares contain at least some of each sector except that square seven, the suburban export node, contains none of sector three. Building heights mostly fall with distance from the center until they rise at or near the suburban export node. About two-thirds of good one exports go from the city center, whereas all the exports of goods two and three go from the suburban node.

The congestion pattern is somewhat unpersuasive. Congestion level falls from three to one from square zero to one, rises to two and then three in squares six and seven, and stays at three to the edge of the urban area.

The final column is the shadow rental value of land from the solution of the dual problem. Land rent is high at the center, falls off rapidly at first, then slowly. It rises near the suburban export node, then falls. It is zero in square eleven since not all the land in that square is used. This is at least roughly the pattern observed in real cities.

Extensions

The model could easily be modified to include many additional phenomena of importance in cities.

Perhhaps the most obvious modification would be to introduce alternative transportation modes. If the second mode had its separate right-of-way, as a subway, this would be simple. All that is needed is a second set of input-output coefficients for its construction, a second set of time and operating cost coefficients, and a set of constraints to ensure that all travel went by one mode or the other. If the second mode used the same right-of-way, as a bus system, some-

Table 19-2
Solution for Illustrative City

Distance	Good 1 Output	s	Good 2 Output	s	Good 3 Output	s	Good 4 Output	s	Good 5 Output	s	Congestion Level	Land Rent
0	14.35	17	0.00	—	0.00	—	0.00	—	0.00	—	3	6.35
	1.26	14										
1	0.23	8	0.00	—	0.00	—	1.87	5	0.00	—	1	2.50
2	0.22	8	0.00	—	0.00	—	0.32	2	1.38	5	1	1.29
3	0.16	2	0.79	2	0.13	2	0.56	2	0.63	5	1	0.72
4	0.16	2	0.93	2	0.08	2	0.60	2	0.60	5	1	0.44
5	0.16	2	0.93	2	0.08	2	0.60	2	0.60	5	1	0.53
6	0.16	2	0.77	2	0.25	2	0.60	2	0.59	2	2	0.82
7	0.53	8	0.77	5	0.00	—	0.65	2	0.69	5	2	1.16
8	0.17	2	0.51	2	0.52	2	0.59	2	0.56	5	3	0.70
9	0.17	2	0.52	2	0.53	2	0.60	2	0.57	5	3	0.54
10	0.16	2	0.48	2	0.49	2	0.56	2	0.54	2	3	0.26
11	0.09	2	0.26	2	0.26	2	0.30	2	0.29	2	3	0.00

$x_1^e(0) = 19.75$ $x_1^e(7) = 0.37$

$x_2^e(0) = 0.00$ $x_2^e(7) = 0.71$

$x_3^e(0) = 0.00$ $x_3^e(7) = 2.14$

what more complex modifications would be required. At least if accurate data were available, these modifications would make it possible to investigate the benefits and costs of various modal mixes and to study the effects of various modes on the structure of the city.

It would also be possible, though somewhat more complex, to modify the model to study the effects of inappropriate congestion tolls. As has been well studied, absence of congestion tolls implies excessive use of congested streets and consequent loss of welfare. The present model permits such calculations to be made in a general equilibrium framework in which land uses are affected by pricing policy.

The model can easily be used to study effects of government policies such as land use controls and real estate taxation. It would be somewhat more complex, but possible, to include effects of polluting discharges from urban activities and various government actions to control them.

It would be easy to modify the model to study the growth of an existing city. This would entail omission of certain constraints and addition of some others representing transportation to and from existing land uses.

Perhaps the greatest defect in the model is that it does not include scale economies in production of goods one and three. The simplest way to include scale economies is to introduce additional integer valued variables and constraints that ensure that production takes place only above some minimum scale. That is conceptually easy but computationally expensive because it increases the number of integer-valued variables. More important, if there are scale economies, it may not be optimum to require equal production in all squares a given distance from the center. Thus, introduction of scale economies suggests the desirability of separate identification of each square. That would provide a much richer model, but it would make computations very expensive and would quickly strain the capacity of even large computers.

The second important defect of the model is the absence of an articulated demand side. Demands for goods should depend on prices as well as incomes. Perhaps most important, the population of the urban area should depend on wages, prices, congestion, etc., in the urban area. These changes would require major modifications in the model and a quite different criterion function. The simplicity of the present criterion function is made possible by the fact that the population of the urban area does not depend on alternatives considered by the model.

References

Brown, H. James et al. *Empirical Models of Urban Land Use: Suggestions on Research Objectives and Organization.* Columbia University Press for National Bureau of Economic Research, 1972.

Dorfman, Robert, et al. *Linear Programming and Economic Analysis.* New York: McGraw-Hill, 1958.

Hadley, George. *Nonlinear and Dynamic Programming.* Reading: Addison-Wesley, 1964.

Mills, Edwin. "Markets and Efficient Resource Allocation in Urban Areas." *Swedish Journal of Economics* 74, 1 (March 1972): 100–113.

Mills, Edwin. "Sensitivity Analysis of Congestion and Structure in an Efficient Urban Area." In Jerome Rothenberg and Ian Heggie (eds.), *Transport and Urban Environment.* New York: John Wiley, 1974a, pp. 192–208.

Mills, Edwin. "Mathematical Models for Urban Planning. In Alan Brown et al (eds.), *Urban and Social Economics in Market and Planned Economies.* New York: Praeger, 1974b, pp. 113–129.

Solow, Robert and William Vickrey. "Land Use in a Long Narrow City." *Journal of Economic Theory* 3, 4 (December 1972).

Swedish Journal of Economics 74, 1 (March 1972).

20

Externalities Incurred by Movement into a Polluted Area

Ezra J. Mishan

The question to be answered is whether, under conditions to be specified, the movement of people or firms into a polluted area, and/or the output of the polluting industry, should be controlled through taxes or subsidies to as to meet the Pareto criterion. The models to be used in this chapter belong to partial equilibrium analysis, in which in addition to make the particular assumption that optimality conditions are met in all economic activities save those under examination. In order to reduce the analysis to its simplest terms we suppose that marginal resource costs in the competitive industry in question are constant, that all welfare or "income" effects are zero, that relevant information about the particular pollution is known to all concerned, and that there is no way of dealing with the pollution other than by controlling the movement of people or firms, or by taxes and subsidies.

The specific conditions to be considered arise from pair-wise combinations of two sets of alternatives. The first set consists of (a) situations in which the pollution is invariant to the amount of immigration into the polluted area, and (b) situations in which it varies directly with that immigration. The second set consists of (c) situations in which there are advantages to immigrants into the polluted area (other than wage-differentials) and (d) situations in which there are no such advantages.

Model I comprises (a) and (c), Model II, (a) and (d), Model III, (b) and (d), Model IV (b) and (c). In all of the models we assume the existence of a smoky area, the result of the establishment there of a competitive industry producing x but generating smoke. At some fixed distance from the smoky area is a nonsmoky or clean area, where people also live and work.

We begin with two persons A and B, who work and reside in the clean area and contemplate a movement to the smoky area. Person A perceives a gain (above all costs of movement) of $16 a week from moving permanently into the smoky area, whereas person B perceives a gain of only $8 a week. Since in both cases the damage to be endured in living in the smoky area is reckoned as equal to $12 a week, person A will decide to move and person B to stay. A weekly lump sum tax or subsidy of $12, or indeed of any amount, will not alter their decisions since it is to be paid or received unconditionally. It affects each person's welfare but not his behavior. (Specifically because of the assumption of

I would like to thank Ronald Grieson for useful comments on a first draft of this chapter.

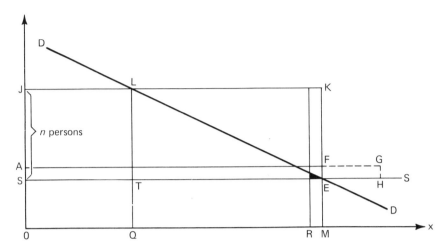

Figure 20-1.

zero welfare or "income" effects.) But a large enough *conditional* subsidy or tax does affect behavior. If, for example, there is a tax on such immigration into the smoky area that works out at more than $4 a week, say $5 a week, it will deter A's migration there. For A's not benefit from moving will now include -12 (smoke damage to be incurred) +16 (advantage from moving) -5 (tax to be paid), an algebraic total of -1. Nevertheless there is a positive net *social* benefit of 4 from his moving into the smoky area, for the tax of 5 paid by A is received by taxpayers; that is to say, to A's private net benefit of -1, we must now add +5 for the rest of society, giving a social aggregate of +4. This net social benefit of 4 is, of course, equal to the algebraic sum of the real loss and real benefit of A's movement—respectively -12 and +16.

If we now make the assumption that the smoke damage to be suffered by person A once he enters the smoky area is directly related to x, the output of the competitive smoky industry, the $12 of damage incurred by A's moving into the area can be represented by the strip[a] SAEF in figure 20-1, laid on top of the constant unit resource cost SE for output OM. The broken line extensions EFGH serves to remind us that person A has an excess gain of $4—the damage of $12 (SAEF) being exceeded by his gain of $16 (SAGH). Thus when A moves into the area the social marginal cost of the industry moves from SE to AF.

In general, a number of people, say n altogether, will gain by taking up residence in the smoky area, and, on the same reasoning, society as a whole is better off on a cost-benefit criterion from their movement. Given an unchanged output

---

[a]This is drawn as a rectangle on the assumption of constant damage per unit of output. There is no change of conclusion if instead we assume rising marginal damage. (It simplifies further to assume that factors used in producing OM of x are exactly compensated by receiving the market price of their factors.)

OM each person adds a strip of damage, equal say[b] to \$12, but reckons that his gain from the movement exceeds \$12. Thus the total damage endured by the n migrants is represented by the rectangle SJKE, the total social cost of OM of x now being OJKM. In the absence of any bargaining between the new immigrants, the industry, and the consumers of x, and in the absence of any government intervention, the industry continues to produce an output of OM.

In order to show that further improvement is possible, consider the shape of DD, the demand curve for x. A reduction of but one unit of x, from OM to OR, would entail a small loss of consumer surplus (equal to the small shaded triangle to the left of point E), but it removes a unit of smoke damage from all n persons with a total damage cost of EK $\times$ MR. This reduction of a unit of x therefore confers a clear gain on society. Each subsequent reduction of output would yield a (diminishing) net benefit of this sort until output were reduced to OQ, after which point any further reduction of output would involve a loss of consumer surplus greater than the saving in smoke damage. Thus the movement from output OM to the optimal output OQ implies a net social gain of LEK—equal to the removal of smoke damage LTEK minus the loss of consumer surplus LTE.[c]

We conclude as follows: those who wish to move into the smoky area of their own free will, so incurring damages without assurance or anticipation of any subsequent reduction of the damage, should be allowed to move unhindered on a cost-benefit criterion.[d] Secondly, in consequence of his migration, the output of the smoky industry may be curbed, if necessary by a tax[e] to OQ optimal

---

[b]The width of the strips can differ inasmuch as the damage endured by each person will differ in general. But this "refinement" makes no difference to the conclusions.

[c]For completeness we should have to include the damage incurred by those additional persons who would choose to move into the smoky area only *after* the output of x (and therefore the associated smoke damage also) had been reduced from the initial amount OM. Thus if n persons choose to move, on the assumption of output OM, more than n persons will move in as output is reduced, and the resultant optimum output OQ' (not shown in figure 20-1) will be smaller than OQ in figure 20-1.

[d]Schultze and D'Arge (1974) demonstrate that when firms in the polluted industry are compensated for damages, *and potential entrants to the industry are aware of these compensatory payments,* the resulting industry output, and number of firms in the long run, will be too large. They therefore conclude (incorrectly) that a "liability rule" leads to a misallocation of resources in the long run.

In our initial two-person example, person B should not enter the smoky area and, indeed, will not enter the area if he is not compensated (or even if he is, later, compensated, provided he does not anticipate compensation for the damage he suffers). Clearly then it is not the "liability rule" per se, but the awareness in advance that compensation will be paid to him if he moves into the area that causes the misallocatior This payment, which is conditional upon his acting in a way different from that which he would otherwise choose when in possession of all the relevant data, can as indicated be regarded as a subsidy—one having no allocative rationale.

[e]If costless bargaining were possible then those who would move in would be able to overcompensate consumers for their loss, assuming factors employed in industry x can move elsewhere at zero cost.

output, so as to increase net social gains further. If the numbers who wish to move into the smoky area are large enough optimal output of x may well be zero.[f]

These conclusions can be extended to firms (including laundries) as well as people, that choose to move into the smoky area—again, without anticipation of any reduction in smoke damage over the future. No tax on their movement should be used to deter their migration into the smoky area. Moreover, as a result of the damage so incurred, the output of the smoky industry has to be reduced to optimal size in order to secure further social gains. This general result extends also to downstream bathers or downstream factories. Their choice of that part of the stream for their activities, notwithstanding its pollution, invites subsequent net social benefits via a reduction in the outputs of the upstream factories.[g]

II

We now assume instead there is no one who perceives any advantage in moving into the smoky area, at least no net advantage above damages to be suffered there. The only way for the competitive x industry to recruit workers—who are either to live in the area or to work there each day—is to offer them wages above the market rate. In order to maintain the assumption that immigration into the area (when that immigration is of workers into the x industry) does not of itself increase the smoke, we are now obliged to make the restrictive assumption that the smoke produced by the industry is invariant to the output of x. The smoke generated is not quite invariant or it could be classified as an "overhead" external diseconomy or "separable externality." Since some output, if only a single unit of output, has to be produced for a factory to be working, this minimal output is needed for smoke to be generated. Above this minimal output, however, there need be no further increase in smoke, which is our assumption in the text.

Since the marginal product (ignoring pollution) per worker is assumed con-

---

[f]This conclusion contradicts Coase's view of the matter as expressed in his famous 1960 article. There he regards the excise tax on the output of the smoky factory as absurd just because the free movement of persons into the smoky area could eventually close down the factory.

Addressing himself principally to Coase's criticisms, Baumol in an elegant paper (1972) vindicates the Pigou thesis. His reply to Thompson and Batchelor's Comment (1974) concerning the problems that arise when the smoky factory is a monopoly could have been made more forcible by a reminder that Pigou never proposed that an excise tax be set equal to the marginal pollution damage. The Pigovian proposal is more general, since irrespective of market organizations the excise taxes or subsidies are to be chosen such as to equate price to social marginal cost in all sectors.

[g]Compare these results with those reached by Mohring and Boyd toward the end of their *Economica* article (1971).

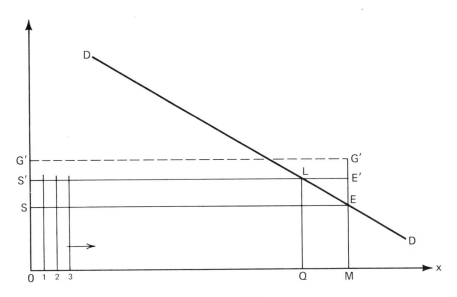

Figure 20-2.

stant, we can choose units of x equal to the worker's marginal product. This choice of a unit x allows us the convenience of measuring both the wage rate and the marginal labor cost for any output by the same vertical distance in figure 20-2.

Thus, in order to induce one worker to move to the smoky area, the minimum premium above the market wage rate OS is SS'. If we assume that all workers are equally averse to smoke, the marginal labor cost of output x to the industry rises from SE to S'E'.[h] At this higher wage, industry chooses to produce OQ of x which is the optimal output since at Q the social marginal cost is equal to the demand price (equal to marginal value of x).

In this case, in which no worker moves into the smoky area without compensation, no intervention is called for either to curb the workers' movement into the area (as in the preceding example) or (as distinct from the preceding example) to reduce the competitive industry's equilibrium output. The latter result differs from that of the preceding example because, in contrast to the situation there depicted, the damage inflicted on others by industry x is now being borne

---

[h]If, more generally, we assume that additional workers can be attracted into the x industry only by offering increasingly higher wages, the correct marginal labor cost S'E" (not shown in figure 20-2) will slope upward, implying that intra-marginal workers make rents. If the competitive industry is assumed to pay the same efficiency wage to all workers the upward-sloping supply curve S'E" will be an average cost to the industry. But since it is also a marginal social cost to society the resulting equilibrium output is optimal.

Since our results are unaffected by varying this assumption, we shall continue to work with the simpler one of uniform worker-aversion to the smoky area, and to infer a constant marginal social cost curve S'E' (equal to the industry's perceived average labor cost) as in figure 20-2.

by that industry in the form of compensatory payments to labor. Its supply
curve or curve of average resource cost is, however, equal to the social marginal
cost, and in equating the former with price, it equates the latter with price also.

This result is unaltered, in the more general case in which, in the long run,
the industry minimizes resource costs by efficient combination of many factors,
and the factor-owners in varying degrees are averse to placing their factors in the
smoky area.

Those who would not wish to interfere with the working of the market
would be justified wherever the situation is that depicted by this rather restrictive model—at least if zero costs of movement are assumed. This latter proviso is
critical. For if the costs of movement are positive, which they obviously are in
the real world, then the attainment of the optimal output can depend on whether workers happen to be living outside the area to start with or whether, instead,
they were living within the area before the smoke began to be troublesome. Suppose the situation were the latter, then if the costs of movement of each worker
exceeded the cost of the damage he has come to endure by staying in the area he
will choose to remain there even though he is not paid any wage premium. The industry, that is, does not have to pay him more than the going wage in the "clean"
industry in order to retain the services of the workers employed there. To illustrate
with figure 20-2, the cost of movement per worker is measured by the vertical distance SG' which cost exceeds the saving in damage SS' from moving out of the
area. The industry continues therefore to pay OS per worker. Its average resource
cost is then no greater than OS, and the competitive equilibrium output OM exceeds the optimal OQ. Provided that transactions costs associated with the imposition of an optimal excise tax, equal to EE', is less[i] than the triangle E'EL,
there is a residual net benefit in imposing an excise tax to reduce output to the
optimal OQ.

This same crucial amendment applies if workers are initially attracted by
the wage premium to move their homes into the smoky area. Once the smoky
industry ceases to expand and, therefore, to require additional workers, it can
maintain the existing work force by paying no more than the going wage rate
OS (or for that matter, if institutionally feasible, by paying up to (G'S'−SS') less
than the going wage rate) whenever the costs for each worker of moving out of
the area exceed the costs of the smoke damage he has to endure.

III

A less restrictive model is one in which the smoke damage is not invariant
to the output of x and, therefore, not invariant to the employment of labor in
the smoky area.

[i]Less also than the costs of bargaining between interested parties; otherwise voluntary
agreement between consumers and workers would be the more economic method of attaining optimal output OQ.

Again, nothing is lost in qualitative conclusions by assuming a linear relation between smoke damage and output of x, along with a uniform response of
workers to the smoke damage they sustain by working in the smoky area. The
vertical distance OS in figure 20-3 (as in figure 20-2) measures the constant
wage rate in the absence of smoke damage, and also the constant marginal and
average labor cost of x. Thus the first worker employed in x, produces one
"unit" of x which generates one "unit" of smoke requiring compensation above
the wage OS of, say, $1. This is represented by the first small shaded rectangle
above the SE line. The second worker produces another unit of x and so generates another unit of smoke. He therefore suffers from two smoke units and requires, we suppose, $2 in compensation, a sum that is represented by the second
shaded rectangle (above the SE line) that is twice as high as the initial rectangle.
Similarly the third worker would require a $3 premium to compensate for three
units of smoke, a sum represented by the third shaded rectangle (over the third
unit of output) above the SE line. Continuing in this way, the wage OS plus
shaded rectangle over the M'th unit of output is just equal to the demand price.

However, when the second worker receives $2 for the two units of smoke
he suffers, so must the first worker as he also suffers from two units of smoke.
For an output of two units of x, and therefore two units of smoke, the premium
for *each* worker becomes $2. The average wage and (on our construction) the
average labor cost for the industry therefore goes up by $2. Again, when the
third worker receives $3, each of the other two workers also suffers the three
units of smoke, and each must also receive $3. Thus the average wage, and aver-
age labor cost, to each firm in the x industry continues to rise as output and em-

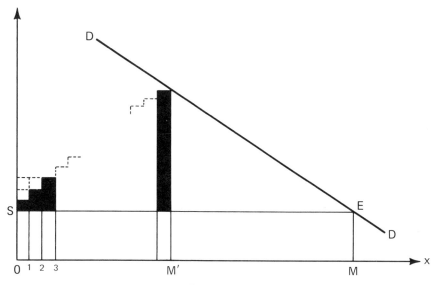

Figure 20-3.

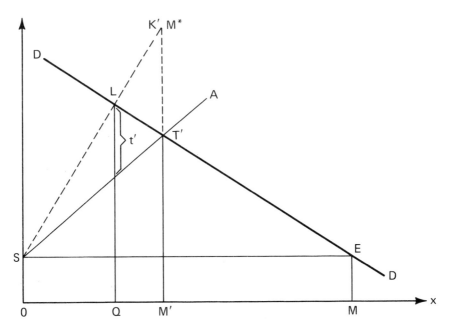

Figure 20–3a.

ployment is increased until at M′ output it is equal to the demand price, at
which point a competitive equilibrium exists. (If the less smoke-sensitive workers
entered the x industry first, they would be making rents once the more sensitive
workers entered the industry and required greater sums as compensation for a
given smoke damage.)

But this resulting average labor cost curve to the x industry is *not* equal to
the marginal social cost. For the employment, say, of the second worker increases the total smoke damage from $1 to $4 (two workers each suffering $2 of
smoke damage) i.e., by $3, which is the increment of total damage incurred by
the employment of the second worker. Similarly, the employment of the third
worker increases the total smoke damage from $4 to $9 (three workers each suffering $3 of smoke damage), or by $5, this being the increment of damage incurred by the employment of the third worker, and so on. This marginal damage
curve, which has to be added to SE to give the marginal social cost curve, SM* in
figure 20–3a, is above the average social cost curve, SA in figure 20–3a. This SA
curve is, of course, the industry supply curve.

Competitive industry therefore has an equilibrium output[j] equal to OM′,

---

[j]If, as in the preceding example, we consider the case in which workers already live in
the smoky area, and the costs of moving out exceeds for each worker the damage suffered,
the industry supply curve will not rise but will remain constant at SE. In that case the equilibrium will be OM of x, which is still larger than optimal output OQ.

whereas the optimal output is OQ at which the marginal social cost is equal to the demand price.

If imposing an excise tax t' involves smaller transactions costs than the net benefit LK'T' from reducing output from OM' to OQ then it is economical to establish the optimal output OQ in this way.[k]

On reflection it will be apparent that this analysis is but another example of external diseconomies that are internal to the industry—more familiar examples, perhaps, being commercial fishing and road congestion, in which cases the industry expands along its average cost curve, ignoring the damage inflicted on all intra-marginal units by the marginal unit.

Finally, the inclusion of smoke damage suffered over the long period by factors other than labor acts to reduce the optimal output further, but the formal analysis follows the same lines.

We may conclude that in the more plausible case, that in which pollution varies with output and, therefore (in this model) with the recruitment of immigrant labor into the smoky area, the competitive market solution is too large and can be corrected by an optimal excise tax.

IV

The final model we consider is similar to the preceding one except that workers no longer have to be attracted by wage premia into the smoky area, but for one reason or another, perceive some net advantage in working there or living there. As we might suspect, the desire to work or live in the smoky area acts to offset the total damage each additional worker inflicts on intra-marginal workers, so that the optimal output will, to that extent, be larger than it is where the worker perceives no advantage in moving into the smoky area.

Figure 20–4 has the same construction as figure 20–3. Ignoring smoke for the moment, the advantage the first worker perceives in moving to the area is measured by S'S, so that the minimum wage that would induce him to live or work there is OS'. Successive workers perceive smaller advantage as a result of which the minimum curve S'E' slopes upward, is equal to the market wage at OV and, thereafter, continues to rise as subsequent workers perceive increasing disadvantage.

S'A measured vertically from S'E', is the curve of average smoke damage

---

[k]By introducing a budget constraint covering the two areas, Seskin (1973) contrives an optimal output in the smoky area by an excise tax there and an excise subsidy on the good in the clean area.

In a two-good economy there can, of course, be any number of combinations of excise taxes and subsidies on the polluting and "clean" good respectively that will yield optimal outputs. But in partial analysis, in which the smoky industry x is a minute fraction of the total economy, an excise tax on x is only practical tax solution.

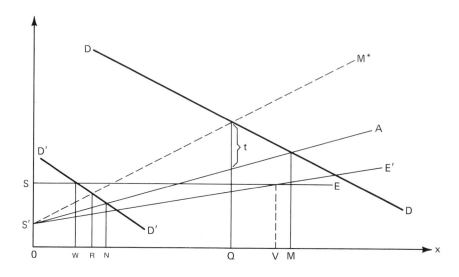

Figure 20-4.

with respect to output and to number of workers. Measured from the x axis it is the average wage curve and average labor cost curve (or supply curve) to the industry once workers have to be compensated for the smoke damage they suffer. The industry equilibrium is therefore at output OM, whereas the optimal output OQ is derived from the intersection of the $S'M^*$ curve, which is marginal to an $S'A$ curve that is measured vertically from $S'E'$. An optimal tax t is called for to bring the x industry into equilibrium at output OQ.[1]

References

Baumol, W.T. "On Taxation and the Control of Externolities." *American Economic Review*, June 1972.

Coase, R.H. "The Problem of Social Cost." *Journal of Law & Economic*, Oct. 1960.

Mohring H. and J.H. Boyd. "Analysing Externalities: Direct Interaction vs. Asset Utilization Framework." *Economica*, Nov. 1971.

Pigon, A.C. *The Economics of Welfare*. London: MacMillan, 1946.

---

[1]If the demand for x were small enough, say D'D' and (a) it was institutionally possible to pay some workers less than the market wage OS, the industry equilibrium would be ON. If, indeed, (b) it was not institutionally possible to pay any worker less than the going wage rate OS, the industry equilibrium would be smaller, at OW.

The optimal output however is OR, so that in the (a) case an excise tax is required, and in the (b) case an excise subsidy is required, in order to move the industry equilibrium to the optimal output, OR.

Schultze W. and R. D'Arge. "The Coase Proposition, Information and Long Run Equilibrium." *American Economic Review*, Sep. 1974.

Seskin, E. "Residential Choice and Air Pollution." *American Economic Review,* Dec. 1973.

Thompson E.   and R. Batchelor. "On Taxation and Control of Externolities: Comments." *American Economic Review*, June 1974.

21

Spatial Equilibrium in a CBD-Oriented City

Herbert Mohring

The original motivation for undertaking the analysis reported in this chapter was the implausibility of conclusions reached in studies by Pendleton[1] and myself.[2] This research used data on the relationship between property values and proximity to the central business districts (CBDs) of Washington, D.C., and Seattle, Washington, respectively, to infer the values households place on the time they spend traveling. The model underlying both studies involved the following assumptions: A city is located on an undifferentiated plain. Except for housing, all of the economic, social, and cultural activities of its residents take place in its CBD. The elasticities of demand for both land (which is useless except as housing sites) and trips to the CBD are zero. Each household places the same value on the travel time of its members. Travel time from a house to the CBD is proportional to the crowline distance between the two and is unaffected by the rate at which travel occurs.

These assumptions lead directly to a linear rent gradient, i.e., one that can be written as:

$$R(t) = VT(t^* - t) + T[C(t^*) - C(t)] \tag{21-1}$$

where $R(t)$ is the annual rental on a housing site t minutes away from the CBD, V is the value of a minute's travel time, T is twice the annual number of round trips a household makes to the CBD, t^* is travel time to the city limits—the outer edge of the residential zone surrounding the CBD— and $C(t)$ is the money cost of a trip to the CBD.

In a community of this nature, it would be possible to determine the value residents place on travel time even though this commodity is not traded in any market. To do this, one need merely determine the relationship that exists between t on the one hand and the rental value of a dwelling minus the rental

I am deeply indebted to Edward Foster, Marvin Kraus, Thomas Pinfold, Marcel K. Richter, Robert Solow, and Helen Tauchen for helpful suggestions and to the National Science Foundation for financial support. The discussion of Sections I and II was, to a large degree, stimulated by William Alonso.[3] The original version of this chapter was prepared for a 1968 conference of the Committee on Taxation, Resources, and Economic Development which Wiiliam Vickrey organized. During the interval since this version was written, a number of excellent studies (notable examples are those of Richard Muth[4] and Robert Solow[5]) dealing with CBD-oriented cities have appeared in the literature. I have not attempted to take the results of these studies into account in revising this chapter.

value of the structure it contains on the other. The value of travel time could then be inferred from

$$V = -(R' + C'T)/T.$$

Both Pendleton and I found that land values did, indeed, decline with travel time to the CBD. However, the absolute value of R' was less than $C'T$ in both studies. Thus, taking our results at face value leads to the implausible conclusion that the representative household in our study areas would prefer more commuting time to less and is deterred from locating so as to satisfy this preference only by the increase in the money cost of travel that would result.

As a basis for analyzing real world land markets, the model underlying this conclusion is clearly not without its elements of unreality. The model developed in Section I eliminates some of these unrealistic assumptions. Specifically, it deals with the spatial equilibrium of a household in a city in which tastes and incomes differ, in which nonzero elasticities of demand for housing services and travel prevail, and in which land is valued not in its own right but rather as an input to the production of housing services. Section II describes land market equilibrium in a city comprised of households with identical tastes and incomes and provides a specific illustration—that generated by a Cobb-Douglas-type utility function—of these equilibrium relationships. Throughout the chapter, the assumption is retained that the CBD is the only focus of economic activity. However, the analysis can be extended in a straightforward fashion to deal with areas having any number of activity centers.

I. Household Equilibrium in Space

Consider a city much like that described above: It is located on an undifferentiated plain. Except for housing, all economic, social and cultural activities take place in its central business district. In spending its fixed income, I, a representative household residing in the city gains satisfaction from consuming (1) a composite good, X, which, for convenience, is measured in units of dollars per year and which is available at the same price in all parts of the city; (2) trips downtown (and, of curse, back home), T; and (3) the services of land, L.[a] In addition, residents incur *dis*satisfaction from the time, $tT = \tau$, they spend traveling downtown. Trips, then, are objects of desire not in their own rights but rather for what takes place at their ends. They are intermediate rather than final

---

[a]As will be shown later in the chapter, the conclusions reached are not appreciably altered when L is replaced by housing services, H, a homogeneous commodity manufactured from land and X by an industry in long-run competitive equilibrium.

goods.[b] The dollar cost of a trip from home to the CBD, $C(t)$, and the annual rent on an acre of land, $R(t)$, is a function only of the time, t, required for a trip between the dwelling and the CBD. For convenience, t is assumed to be the same for a given dwelling at all times of day and under all weather conditions, and $C(t)$ is assumed to be the same for all individuals living at distance t. Neither peak hour congestion problems nor differences between the costs of operating Cadillacs and Volkswagens are around to complicate equilibrium in the city. Given these assumptions, the problem of an individual household can be written as:

$$\max Z = U(X, T, t, \tau) + \lambda [I - X - C(t)T - R(t)L]. \qquad (21\text{-}2)$$

Differentiating this expression with respect to X, L, T, and t yields, as first order conditions for utility maximization,

$$U_X = \lambda \qquad (21\text{-}3)$$

$$U_t = \lambda R(t) \qquad (21\text{-}4)$$

$$U_T + U_\tau t = \lambda C(t) \qquad (21\text{-}5)$$

$$U_\tau T = \lambda (C'T + R'L). \qquad (21\text{-}6)$$

The signs of U_τ and U_X are respectively negative and positive. Their dimensions are utils per dollar and utils per travel hour. The ratio, $-U_\tau/U_X$, can therefore be interpreted as the rate at which the household would be willing to give up the general purpose commodity in return for a reduction in travel time—the (marginal) value of travel time, for short. Denoting this ratio by V, dividing equation (21-5) by equation (21-3) yields

$$U_T/U_X = C(t) + Vt \qquad (21\text{-}7)$$

This relationship can be interpreted as saying that a utility maximizing household equates the ratio of the marginal utility of what occurs at the end of a trip to the marginal utility of dollars with the sum of the money ($C(t)$) and time (Vt) costs of a trip. This sum will henceforth be termed $P(t)$, the "full price"[c] of a trip.

With this interpretation of the ratio of equation (21-5) to equation (21-3),

---

[b]Robert Strotz' first and third parables provide both precedent and justification for regarding travel time and an intermediate good, trips, as arguments in a consumer's utility function.[6]

[c]A term which I have borrowed from Hayden Boyd.

equations (21-3), (21-4), and (21-5) together with the household's budget constraint suffice to determine, e.g., $X = X(R(t), P(t), C(t), I)$—annual consumption of X if the consumer chooses to live t hours from the CBD as a function of $R(t)$, $P(t)$, $C(t)$ and I—and similar demand functions for T and L. Dividing equation (21-6) by equation (21-3) and rearranging terms yields

$$(C' + V)T + R'L = 0 \qquad\qquad\qquad (21\text{-}8)$$

as the condition for the household to be in spatial equilibrium. This condition can be interpreted as saying that the household will locate at that time distance from the CBD at which the saving (R' is presumably negative) in land rent that would result if it moved one minute farther away would exactly offset the resulting increase in the time and money costs of its trips.

In the city currently under examination, equation (21-8) provides essentially the same basis for drawing inferences about a household's travel time value as does equation (21-1) in a city of zero elasticities of demand for trips and land. A household's land and trip consumption rates and the slopes of the land rent and travel cost functions at its residence are all measurable directly albeit with perhaps considerable error. At least in principle, therefore, the value of a household attaches to its travel time could be inferred from the same sorts of information as Pendleton and I employed.[d] The fact that real world land and trip demand elasticities are not zero does not create additional measurement difficulties of any consequence.

At first blush, it might appear that application of equation (21-8) to observations on a household's location would lead to biased estimates of its travel time value if land is valued not in its own right but rather as an input to the commodity, housing services. It can quite easily be shown that such is not the case, however, *if* the housing industry is in long-run competitive equilibrium. In such an equilibrium, the market rental, $r(t)H$, of a house containing H units of housing services would equal the market value of the inputs required to construct it. That is,

$$r(t)H = R(t)L(H,\ t) + X(H,\ t)$$

where $L(H,\ t)$ and $X(H,\ t)$ are respectively the land and X used in providing H units of housing services t hours from the CBD. The rate at which the rental

---

[d]"In principle" must, unfortunately, be emphasized. In an attempt to apply a multi-center generalization of the model outlined in this section to Minneapolis data on sales of single family residences, Allan Maslove[7] found significant *positive* relationships to exist between site values and distance from a house to both the Minneapolis CBD and the University of Minnesota, the city's two largest trip generators.

value of H units would change with t can be written:

$$r'H = R'L + RL_t + X_t = R'L + L_t(R + X_t/L_t)$$

$$= R'L + L_t(R + dX/dL) \qquad\qquad (21\text{-}9)$$

where dX/dL is the rate of technical substitution between X and land in the production of housing services. For cost minimizing producers of these services, $-dX/dL = R$. If the first order conditions for cost minimization hold, then, the sum of the second two terms on the right of (21-9) is zero. Hence, $r'H = R'L$. Regardless of the way in which land services enter utility functions, equation (21-8) will hold for a utility maximizing consumer *if,* to repeat, the housing industry is in long-run competitive equilibrium.

Equation (21-8) can be regarded as a first order differential equation in R. Solution of this equation would yield a family of functions of the form

$$R = R(t, k). \qquad\qquad (21\text{-}10)$$

Given a specific value of the constant of integration, k, equation (21-10) would define a relationship among land rents at alternative time distances from the CBD such that equation (21-8) would be satisfied at all admissable values of t. Given k and, in the background, the household's income and adjustment of its L, T, and X consumption rates so as to maintain tangency with the relevant indifference surface, equation (21-10) shows those alternative rents at which the consumer would be indifferent among locations.[e] That is to say, equation (21-9) is a transformation of the household's indifference map, an indirect indifference curve.

It seems plausible to suppose that the value a household attaches to its travel time is positively related to its income. This being the case, if other things (trip and land consumption, in particular) were independent of income, higher income families could be expected to preempt housing sites near the CBD leaving the suburbs to those with lower incomes. Precisely the reverse pattern prevails in most urban areas, of course. A variety of factors—e.g., putatively better schools, proximity to open space, distance from ghetto dwellers—that are negatively correlated with distance from the CBD suggest themselves as explanations for this phenomenon. Still, it seems worthwhile to explore the conditions under which distance and income would be positively related in a CBD oriented city in which these other explanatory factors are of no concern.[f]

---

[e]Although the two developments differ, equation (21-10) seems to be the equivalent of what William Alonso refers to as a "bid price curve."[8]

[f]Becker[9] discusses this problem but under considerably more restrictive conditions than those assumed here.

In equation (21-8), the values of travel time, V, and of trip and land consumption, T and L, can be regarded as functions of time to the CBD, t, and family income, I. Differentiating equation (21-8) with respect to I and t with t being regarded as a function of I yields

$$V_I T + (V + C')T_I + RL_I = -\partial W/\partial t \cdot dt/dI \qquad (21-11)$$

where W denotes the left-hand side of equation (21-8). Second order conditions for utility maximization dictate a positive value for $\partial W/\partial t$.[g] Hence, if dt/dI is to be positive—if an increase in income is to result in an outward movement—the left-hand side of equation (21-11) must be negative. Using equation (21-8) to eliminate R' from this portion of (21-11), multiplying through by I/VT, and rearranging terms yields

$$E_{LI} > E_{TI} + E_{VI} V/(C' + V)$$

as the condition for dt/dI to be positive. In this expression, E_{LI} and E_{TI} are respectively the income elasticities of demand for land and trips and E_{VI} is the income elasticity of the value of travel time. This inequality can therefore be interpreted as saying that a household will move outward when its income increases if its income elasticity of demand for land exceeds its income elasticity of demand for trips by more than $V/(C' + V)$ times the income elasticity of its value of travel time. In turn, $V/(C' + V)$ can be interpreted as the ratio of the value of travel time to the change in the full price of a trip resulting from an outward movement.

II. Equilibrium of the Land Market with Identical Incomes and Tastes

Suppose, now, that residents of the city have identical tastes and incomes. The rent gradient established in the real estate market would then have to be such that each household is indifferent to the value of t associated with its residence. That is, one of the family of equations defined by (21-10) would be the

---

[g]Equation (21-8) can be rewritten as $R' = -(C' + V)T/L$. The left-hand side of this expression is the slope of the prevailing land rent gradient. Hence, the right-hand side is the slope of the household's indirect indifference curve in $R - t$ space. Since utility increases with a movement toward the origin in this space, this indifference curve must be *below R* except at their point of tangency. This implies that R'' must be greater than the derivative of $-(C' + V)T/L$ with respect to t in the neighborhood of equilibrium. Substituting this condition into $\partial W/\partial t$ yields a relationship that can be written

$$\partial W/\partial t > L_t \, [(C' + Y) \, T/L + R'] = 0.$$

prevailing rent gradient. Two conditions would serve to determine precisely which member of this family would be established: First, at a distance of t^*—the travel time from the CBD to the city limits—the rent on an acre of land, say R^*, would equal its opportunity cost in farming or whatever other activity takes place just beyond the city limits. Second, those values of t^* and k, the constant of integration in equation (21-10), would be established for which the supply of land equals the demand for its services.

Regarding the latter condition, if no land is allocated to roads, parks, or other nonresidential uses, the amount of land at a travel time of t or less from the CBD is $\Pi[D(t)]^2$ where $D(t)$ is the distance that can be covered in t hours by traveling along a radial route starting from the CBD. The change in the supply of land with a change in t is therefore $2\Pi DD'$ at a travel time distance of t. The consumption of land services by a household living at a distance of t is given by its land services demand function, $L = L(P(t), R(t), C(t), I)$. Since, by assumption households have identical demand functions, the total consumption of land services at a distance of t is $n(t)L$ where $n(t)$ is the number of households living at distance t. Since land services consumed at t must equal land services supplied at that distance,

$$n(t)L = 2\Pi DD'$$

$$n(t) = 2\Pi DD'/L$$

Adding up the number of households at each time distance between the CBD and the city limits yields the number of households in the city, N. That is,

$$N = \int_0^{t^*} n(t)dt = \int_0^{t^*} (2\Pi DD'/L)dt. \tag{21-12}$$

To recapitulate, equation (21-12) together with

$$R^* = R(t^*, k) \tag{21-13}$$

determine k and t^*. Once these values are known, aggregate land values in the city can be determined from

$$LV = \int_0^{t^*} 2\Pi DD' R(t, k)dt$$

and similarly for aggregate travel expenditures or any other aggregate magnitude of interest.

To take a specific example, suppose that the utility function of each household is:[h]

$$U \equiv \alpha_X \ln X + \alpha_L \ln L + \alpha_T \ln T - \alpha_\tau \ln tT \qquad (21\text{-}15)$$

where $\alpha_X + \alpha_T + \alpha_L - \alpha_\tau = 1$. It can fairly easily be shown that maximizing this utility function subject to the budget constraint, $I = X + CT + RL$, leads to demand functions of the form

$$X = \alpha_X I \qquad (21\text{-}16a)$$

$$L = \alpha_L I/R \qquad (21\text{-}16b)$$

$$T = (\alpha_T - \alpha_\tau)I/C . \qquad (21\text{-}16c)$$

The value of travel time can be written

$$V = \alpha_\tau X/\alpha_X tT = \alpha_\tau I/tT . \qquad (21\text{-}16d)$$

Substituting equation (21-16) into equation (21-8) yields

$$\alpha_T - \alpha_\tau)C'/C + \alpha_\tau/t + \alpha_L R'/R = 0. \qquad (21\text{-}17)$$

This spatial equilibrium relation integrates directly to

$$(\alpha_T - \alpha_\tau)\ln C + \alpha_\tau \ln t + \alpha_L \ln R = k . \qquad (21\text{-}18)$$

Making use of the fact that rent at the city limits, t^* hours from the CBD,

---

[h]This Cobb-Douglas-type utility function is considerably more restrictive than I would like. Before reluctantly settling on it as the basis for an illustration, I experimented with variants of a CES production function:

$$U = (\alpha_X X^\gamma + \alpha_L L^\gamma + \alpha_T T^\gamma (1 - \beta t^\gamma))^{1/\gamma}$$

$$U = (\alpha_X X^\gamma + \alpha_L L^\gamma + \alpha_T T^\gamma (1 - \beta t)^\gamma)^{1/\gamma}$$

where $1 \geqslant \gamma \geqslant -\infty$. Both the time and the money cost of a trip is zero for a household living adjacent to the CBD. T^γ and hence U are therefore infinite for each such household if γ is positive. Given a positive γ, the population of the city would congregate with infinite density at zero distance from the CBD. With γ negative, the first CES variant leads to rent gradients which, for reasons I have been unable to fathom, behave perversely in the vicinity of the origin. While the second variant leads to a value of travel time which is independent of income ($V = \beta C/(1 - \beta t)$), it does generate a perfectly sensible looking rent gradient when γ is negative. However, I have as yet been unable to perform the integration dictated by equation (21-12) except for very special cases.

must equal the opportunity cost of land in farming, R^*, to evaluate the constant of integration in equation (21-18) yields

$$R = R^* \, (t^*/t)^{\alpha_T/\alpha_L} \, [C(t^*)/C(t)]^{(\alpha_T-\alpha_\tau)/\alpha_L} \qquad (21\text{-}19)$$

as the prevailing rent gradient. Using equation (21-12) to determine t^* requires exact functional forms for $C(t)$ and $D(t)$. Suppose they are $C(t) = Ct^a$ and $D(t) = Dt^b$. This specification changes the rent gradient to

$$R = R^* \, (t^*/t)^B \qquad (21\text{-}19')$$

where

$$B = [\alpha_\tau + a(\alpha_T - \alpha_\tau)] \, /\alpha_L.$$

Equation (21-12) then yields:

$$t^* = [NI\alpha_L (2b - B)/(2\Pi D^2 bR^*)]^{\, 1/2b} \qquad (21\text{-}20)$$

A few implications of equations (21-19') and (21-20) are worth noting. First, as B approaches $2b$ from below, t^* approaches zero. That is, the city contracts as the weight attached to trips in the utility function increases relative to that attached to land. Beyond some critical value—$\alpha_T \geqslant 2\,\alpha_L$ if $a = b = 1$—the city's residents congregate with infinite density at zero distance from the CBD.

Second, if $M = Dt^b$ miles are traveled in t hours, the time required to travel D miles is $t = (M/D)^{1/b}$. Substituting this relationship for t and its counterpart for t^* in (21-19') leads to an expression for rent per acre that is a function only of geographic, not of time distance from the CBD. Raising both sides of equation (21-20) to the power, b, and then multiplying through by D leads to the conclusion that the geographic distance between the CBD and the city limits is independent of the coefficients C and D in the travel cost-time and distance-time relationships respectively. This being the case, a transportation improvement which alters either of these parameters has no effect on the structure of the city. In particular, it leaves land rents unchanged.

Third, substituting $(M^*/D)^{1/b}$ for t^* in equation (21-20) reveals that

$$(M^*/D)^{1/b} = k \, (N/D^2)^{1/2b}$$

where k refers to the remaining parameters on the right-hand side of (21-20). Hence, geographic distance to the city limits is proportional to the square root of the city's population. This being the case, population density—$N/\Pi M^{*2}$—is independent of city size.

Despite these elements of unreality in the system, it seems worthwhile to see what more or less realistic numerical values of the parameters in equation (21-19) and (21-20) would imply about the structure of the city. The values settled upon after some experimentation are:

N: 333,333 families (i.e., a city of roughly 1,000,000)

I (income): $10,000 per year

$C t^a$ (Cost of t hour trip): $1.50 $t^{0.8}$

$D t^b$ (miles covered in t hours): 25 $t^{1.25}$

α_L (share of income spent on land): 0.10

$\alpha_T - \alpha_\tau$ (share of income spent on trips): 0.125

α_τ (coefficient of income in value of travel time): 0.10

R^* (rent at city limits): $500 per acre.

The reasons for selecting most of these parameter values are hopefully either self-evident or apparent from the economic magnitudes to which they give rise. Some of these magnitudes are shown in table 21-1 for geographic distances equal to 10, 25, 50, 75, and 100 percent of that between the CBD and the city limits. As for the remainder, U.S. Bureau of Public Roads data suggest that including depreciation, maintenance and insurance as well as direct operating costs but excluding the opportunity cost of invested capital, the average cost of operating an automobile is about 15 cents per mile. This is an approximate weighted (by population) average of the values shown in line (4) of table 21-1.

Beesley[10] found that the choice mode for travel to work by a sample of British civil servants implied that they valued their travel time at about one-third

Table 21-1
Spatial Structure of "Cobb-Douglas City"

	Dwelling Distance from CBD				
Miles:	*0.81*	*2.04*	*4.07*	*6.11*	*8.14*
Fraction of D*:	*0.1*	*0.25*	*0.5*	*0.75*	*1*
(1) Rent/Acre	$19,905	$4,595	$1,516	$792	$500
(2) Acres/Family	0.05	0.22	0.66	1.26	2.00
(3) Money Cost/Trip	16.7¢	30.1¢	47.0¢	60.9¢	73.2¢
(4) Money Cost/Mile	20.6¢	14.8¢	11.5¢	10.0¢	9.0¢
(5) Trips/Day	20.4	11.4	7.3	5.6	4.7
(6) Miles/Year	6,073	8,446	10,840	12,543	13,912
(7) Minutes/Trip	3.9	8.1	14.1	19.4	24.5
(8) Travel Hours/Day	1.32	1.53	1.71	1.82	1.91
(9) Travel Time Value/Hour	$2.08	$1.79	$1.60	$1.50	$1.44

of their wage rates. A number of other investigators have come to a similar conclusion. Dividing $10,000 a year by 40 hours per week times 50 weeks per year yields $5 an hour—roughly three times the average of the values given in the last line of table 21-1.

Budget studies suggest that the average American household spends about 25 and 12 percent of its income respectively on housing and transportation. In turn, Muth[11] cites data suggesting that raw land accounts for about 8–15 percent of the total cost of urban housing or about 2–4 percent of total family income. Values of α_L in this range produced very densely populated cities. Using larger value therefore seemed essential. Census data indicate that 1960 "urbanized area" densities in United States metropolitan areas with a population of one million or more ranged between four (Houston) and twelve (New York) people per acre. With this frame of reference, the value of 7.5 yielded by the parameters underlying table 21-1 seems about right for a city of exactly one million which has no space devoted to commercial or industrial establishments, roads, or parks —uses which all enter into the denominator of the Census density data.

Notes

1. William C. Pendleton, *The Value of Highway Accessibility*, doctoral dissertation, University of Chicago, 1963.
2. Herbert Mohring, "Land Values and the Measurement of Highway Benefits," *Journal of Political Economy* 69 (June 1961): 236–249.
3. William Alonso, *Location and Land Use* (Cambridge, Massachusetts: Harvard University Press, 1964).
4. Richard Muth, *Cities and Housing* (Chicago: University of Chicago Press, 1969).
5. Robert Solow, "On Equilibrium Models of Urban Location," in Michael Parkin, ed., *Essays in Modern Economics*, (London: Longman, 1973), pp. 2–16.
6. Robert Strotz, "Urban Transportation Parables," in Julius Margolis (ed.), *The Public Economy of Urban Communities* (Washington: C.O.U.P.E. 1965).
7. Allan Maslove, *Travel Rent Gradients and the Value of Travel Time in a Multi-Nodal City*, doctoral dissertation, University of Minnesota, 1972.
8. Alonso, *Location and Land Use*, Chapter 4.
9. Gary S. Becker, "A Theory of the Allocation of Time," *Economic Journal* 75 (September 1965): 493–517.
10. Michael Beesley, "The Value of Time Spent in Travelling: Some New Evidence," *Economica*, N.S. 32 (May 1965): 174–185.
11. Richard Muth, "Economic Change and Rural-Urban Land Conversions," *Econometrica* 29 (January 1961): 1–23.

22

Central City Taxation for Redistributive Expenditure

Richard F. Muth

Since the publication of Peter Mieszkowski's paper (1972), it has become more widely realized that the economic effects of a real property tax depend upon the size of the taxing jurisdiction. When a single municipality increases its property tax relative to rates prevailing in the rest of the economy, less non-land capital is invested in it in the long run, the rental value of real property rises, and thus the relative prices of real property intensive commodities rise. Especially affected are the rental values of housing, since it is the most real property intensive of all major categories of consumption. The effects of a rise in the property tax throughout the economy as a whole are quite different, however. Though owners of non-land capital might seek to escape the tax, their only outlets for doing so are foreign investment or investment in forms of capital not subject to the tax, principally consumer durables. Since the economy's capital stock is quite insensitive to changes in the returns to saving, the principal effect of an economy-wide real property tax is to reduce the net returns to saving.

An interesting intermediate case of considerable interest for policy purposes is when property tax rates are raised in a fraction of the economy which is substantially greater than zero and substantially smaller than unity. Such a case is provided by central cities in the United States following World War II. During and following the war there occurred a substantial inmigration into central cities of lower income persons, many of them members of minorities and from the rural South. With this inmigration the demands for public expenditure by central city governments have risen. At the same time, population and economic activity have been decentralizing in urban areas, in part for reasons unrelated to central city fiscal problems (see Muth 1969, pp. 324–25). Though receiving large increases in grants from higher level governments, property and other tax rates in central cities have risen. It is widely believed that such tax increases have lead to increased urban decentralization.

In considering the fiscal implications of lower income migration into central cities, it is important to distinguish between the allocative and redistributive expenditures which central city governments make. Apart from external effects, which in my judgment are likely to be small for police and fire protection and for most other local allocative expenditure, one must reside in the

I am pleased to acknowledge the financial support of the Domestic Studies Program of the Hoover Institution during the preparation of this chapter.

taxing community to receive the benefits of this expenditure. Consequently, the effects of tax increases to support greater local allocative expenditure must be analyzed in conjunction with the benefits this increased expenditure provides in order for correct conclusions to be drawn.

Redistributive expenditure is a quite different matter, however, As pointed out by Olsen (1969) and by Hochman and Rodgers (1969), such expenditures benefit the taxpayers who finance it because of utility interdependence. If Mr. Brown's utility, his income or perhaps his consumption of housing or the quality of his childrens' education, is an argument of Mr. Green's utility function, then Green benefits indirectly from an increase in Brown's well-being. It is for this reason, presumably, that people contribute to private charities and vote to tax themselves for income redistributive expenditures. Unlike the benefits of allocative expenditure, though, the indirect benefits of income redistribution are not tied to location in the jurisdiction providing it. Indeed, while the effects of utility interdependence may be attenuated to some extent by distance, many in the United States contribute to victims of earthquakes in Central America or famine in Africa. For this reason, persons may enjoy the benefits of locally financial income redistribution toward lower income central city dwellers yet avoid its cost by locating in the suburban parts of an urban area. It is in this sense, rather than the fact that central city governments provide museums, parks, and zoos which suburbanites may use free of charge, that the suburban area may be said to "exploit" the central city in a quantitatively meaningful sense.[a]

It is quite difficult to draw a sharp line between those types of local public expenditure which are allocative and those which are redistributive. Net transfers toward the poor may result from local taxation and expenditure for police or for parks. The level of such services provided lower income families in central cities is probably greater than they would select for themselves, given their incomes and local tax shares. Such families may, however, be better off because of their smaller tax shares than they would be in a community composed wholly of taxpayers of similar income levels. Yet one suspects that the principal form of income redistribution is through programs such as public assistance, hospitals, housing programs, and, most important, public education. There are, of course, allocative arguments made in favor of the latter three kinds of expenditure. Clearly, though, support for better education of the children of lower income families stems principally from the belief that it will facilitate their escape from poverty.

It is important to realize, as well, that the primary shortcoming of the local property tax to finance public education is that it is a local tax rather than that it is a property tax. For, suppose a higher level of government were to levy a real

---

[a]It is naively said that suburbanites work and shop in the central city but pay no taxes there. But the buildings in which they work and shop are taxed by central cities through the real property tax, to say nothing of local sales and earnings taxes.

property tax at uniform rates throughout an urban area and return the funds to local school districts in fixed amounts per average daily attendence. In this situation, taxpayers could not escape their contribution to the education of lowerincome children by moving out of the central city. Alternatively, suppose that a local income tax were levied in lieu of a local property tax to finance central city schools. Higher income tax payers would have much the same incentive to relocate in the suburbs as under a property tax.

This chapter attempts to assess the degree of response of the distribution of real property as between central city and suburbs to central city taxation, the benefits of which are received irrespective of location. In Section II, a two-sector general equilibrium model similar to that made famous by Harberger (1962) is presented and solved. Section III develops plausible parameter estimates for the model, based primarily on housing, and calculates the effects of central city tax increases on before-tax returns to non-land capital and to land, the distribution of real property as between central city and suburbs, and the land area of suburban areas. The final section then considers non-allocative effects of differential central city taxation to finance income redistributive expenditure.

II

In the model presented here there are two sectors, central city designated by the subscript C and suburbs, S. A single output, real property, R, is produced using non-land capital, N, and land, L, under conditions of constant returns to scale in each sector. The rental value of real property per unit time is designated by p, while n and r are the gross-of-tax rental values of non-land capital and land, respectively. Throughout, the symbol $X^* = dX/X$.

Following Harberger (1962), the production equations in each of the two-sectors may be written

$$R^* = k_N N^* + k_L L^* \tag{22-1}$$

$$N^* - L^* = \sigma(r^* - n^*) \tag{22-2}$$

$$p^* = k_N n^* + k_L r^*. \tag{22-3}$$

Here, $k_N = R_N N/R$ is the share of real property rentals paid out to non-land capital under the assumption of competition in product and factor markets, k_L the share of land, and σ the elasticity of substitution of land for non-land capital in production. Attaching the subscript C or S to all quantities in (22-1) through (22-3) indicates which of the two sectors is being considered. Equation (22-1) is simply the production function, (22-2) the definition of the elasticity of substitution with the condition that the ratio of marginal products is equal to the factor price ratio. Equation (22-3) is essentially the condition that payment in accordance with marginal productivity exhausts revenues where production is carried on under conditions of constant returns to scale. The system (22-2)–(22-3) could be readily derived from the production function and the conditions that the value of marginal product equals factor price for each of the two factors.

The two sectors of the model are interrelated both in the product market and the market for non-land capital. Consider the latter first. I assume that a fixed stock of non-land capital is allocated between central cities and their suburbs, regardless of the earnings of non-land capital net of taxes.[b] Thus, $dN_C + dN_S = 0$ implies

$$N_C^* + \theta N_S^* = 0 \qquad (22\text{-}4)$$

where θ is the ratio of non-land capital in suburban areas to that in the central city. Further, the long-run equilibrium condition for distribution of the non-land capital stock is that earnings net of taxes be the same in central city and suburb. Thus, if an additional tax T is levied in the central city, $dn_C = dn_S + T$ or

$$n_C^* - \rho n_S^* = \tau \qquad (22\text{-}5)$$

where ρ is the initial ratio of gross non-land capital rental value in the suburbs to the central city and $\tau = T/n_c$.

Though non-land capital is assumed perfectly mobile as between central city and suburbs, land is, of course, highly specific as to location. Furthermore, for the past half-century or so there has been little tendency for annexation of surrounding populated areas as was the case in earlier years. It thus seems reasonable to suppose that the stock of central city land is fixed or

$$L_C^* = 0. \qquad (22\text{-}6)$$

The stock of suburban land is by no means fixed, however. As the rental values of suburban land rise, conversion of land from agriculture or other non-urban uses becomes profitable and the land area occupied by the suburbs increases.

---

[b]This assumption implies, in particular, that with a rise in central city tax rates, no non-land capital flows out of urban to rural areas. Though perhaps not wholly correct, adding a third sector would greatly complicate the model and its solution. In addition, I would have much less confidence to the numerical values I might attach to the parameters of the rural sector. Intuitively, it seems unlikely to me that the kinds of economic activity which characterize urban areas are likely to relocate outside them.

Therefore, let

$$L_S^* - \lambda r_S^* = 0 \tag{22-7}$$

where λ is the elasticity of land supply to the suburbs.

The formal model developed here largely neglects the spatial extension of the urban real property market for tractability. However, to form a judgment about the magnitude of the elasticity of land supply to suburban areas, it is useful to give explicit consideration to the variation of land rentals in urban areas. Suppose that the urban area is circular in shape with a radius of u_2 miles from the downtown area or central business district (CBD), and that the central city is circular with a radius of $u_1 < u_2$ miles. Land rentals decline at roughly a constant relative rate from the CBD (see Wieand and Muth 1972) or

$$r(u_2) = r(u_1) \, \epsilon^{-g(u_2 - u_1)}.$$

At the urban areas's edge, urban land rentals are equal to land rentals in non-urban uses, $\bar{r}$, assumed exogenously fixed. Therefore,

$$r_S = r(u_1) = \bar{r} \epsilon^{g(u_2 - u_1)},$$

since rentals for $u_1 \leqslant u \leqslant u_2$ vary proportionally with $r(u_1)$. Also,

$$L_S = \frac{\phi}{2}(u_2^2 - u_1^2),$$

where $0 < \phi \leqslant 2\pi$, ϕ reflecting the fraction of space surrounding the CBD which consists of urban land. Differentiating r_S and L_S with respect to u_2,

$$dr_S = gr_S du_2 \text{ and } dL_S = \phi u_2 du_2,$$

$$\lambda = \frac{dL_S/L_S}{dr_S/r_S} = \frac{2u_2}{g(u_2^2 - u_1^2)} = \frac{\phi u_2}{gL_S}. \tag{22-8}$$

The elasticity of suburban land supply then can be determined from a knowledge of central city and suburban land areas and the relative rate of decline of urban land rentals.

To complete the model it is necessary to specify the relation between the rental values of real property in the central city and suburbs. Most generally, the relative rental values of real property in the two locations are fixed by their differential advantages in production. In goods production, for example, differentials in transport costs on material inputs and final products and differentials in wage rates paid fix the relative amounts producers offer for real property. For housing, differential costs residents bear in transport, especially for CBD work trips, as well as other factors affecting the relative desirability of different locations, affect the level of housing prices. So long as taxation does not affect the relative desirability of different locations, real property rentals must bear the same ratio to each other as prior to the tax change.

Certain tax changes, such as income or sales tax increases do affect the relative desirability of different locations. The imposition of or an increase in a central city income tax, for example, will reduce the utility level obtainable by residents of the central city with the same before tax money incomes as their suburban counterparts at the previously existing level of housing prices. Consequently, housing prices in the central city must fall relative to those in the suburbs if members of a given income group are to continue to live in both locations. Specifically, let the utility functions common to residents of both locations be $U = U(x, q)$, where in equilibrium $Uq/p = Ux$. In the new equilibrium after the income tax change,

$$dU_S = dU_C = Ux(dx_C + p_C dq_C),$$

while from the budget constraint,

$$dx_C + p_C dq_C = dy_C - q_C dp_C.$$

Taking real asset rental values in the suburbs, p_S, as the numeraire, $dU_S = 0$, so

$$p_C^* = (pq/y)_C^{-1} y_C^* = -\alpha \tag{22-9}$$

where $\alpha > 0$ is the percentage change in disposable income of central city residents divided by the fraction of income spent on housing.

The development of the formal model is now complete. Equations (22-1)-(22-3) give production relations for both central city and suburbs, (22-4)-(22-7) the conditions of factor supply, and (22-9) defines real property rental values in the central city. The model determines three real quantities and three prices in each of two locations, all prices being expressed relative to property rental values in the suburbs.

The system is an especially easy one to solve. From (22-3) and (22-9),

$$r_C^* = -(k_{NC}/k_{LC})n_C^* - (\alpha/k_{LC}) \tag{22-10}$$

$$r_S^* = -(k_{NS}/k_{LS})n_S^*. \tag{22-11}$$

Equation (22-5) gives one equation in n_C^* and n_S^*, and a second is easily constructed in the following way. From (22-2) and (22-6),

$$N_C^* = \sigma(r_C^* - n_C^*),$$

(22-12)

while from (22-2) and (22-7)

$$N_S^* = (\sigma + \lambda)r_S^* - \sigma n_S^*.$$

(22-13)

Substituting (22-10) and (22-11) into (22-12) and (22-13) expresses N_C^* and N_S^* in terms of their rental values only, and (22-4) specifies the relationship between N_C^* and N_S^*. Carrying out these substitutions and solving.

$$n_S^* = -\frac{1}{\Delta}(\alpha + \tau),$$

(22-14)

where

$$\Delta = (k_{LC}\theta/k_{LS})(1 + k_{NS}\lambda/\sigma) + \rho > 0,$$

whence

$$n_C^* = -\frac{\rho}{\Delta}\alpha + \left(1 - \frac{\rho}{\Delta}\right)\tau$$

(22-15)

One interesting property of the solution is readily apparent from (22-14) and (22-15). Whether a real property tax or an income tax is levied in the central city, the effects on non-land capital rental values net of the tax are precisely the same. Thus, regardless of the form of the taxation,[c] raising taxes in the central city reduces the returns net of taxes to non-land capital in both central city (since $\rho > 0$) and suburbs. While it is unnecessary to solve for real quantities in order to calculate a solution, it is easily shown that their values too change in

---

[c]Except for a tax on labor incomes earned in the central city, which would have no direct effects upon relative disposable incomes of CBD workers residing inside and outside the central city, hence no direct effects on the prices they would offer for housing in the two locations. Such a tax, however, could induce producers to relocate from the central city to the suburbs. I do not consider the case of an earnings tax explicitly because relatively little is known about the locational determinants of goods producers within urban areas.

precisely the same way when an income tax is levied in lieu of a property by the central city. To exhibit only one, the most complicated,

$$R_S^* = k_{NS} \left[\frac{\sigma}{k_{LC}\theta} \left(1 - \frac{\rho}{\Delta} \right) + \frac{\lambda}{\Delta} \right] (\alpha + \tau).$$

The resource allocative effects of a local real property tax result not because it is a property tax but because it is a local tax, a tax levied differentially in relation to benefits received.

It is easy to see qualitatively what these allocative effects of central city taxation are. By (22–14) the rental value of non-land capital falls in the suburbs, so by (22–11) the rental value of suburban land rises. Hence, by (22–13) and (22–7) more of both non-land capital and land are used in the production of suburban real property. The latter's output must thus increase. From (22–10) and (22–15),

$$r_C^* - n_C^* = -(1/k_{LC}) \, (1 - \rho/\Delta) \, (\alpha + \tau)$$

so land rentals fall relative to those of non-land capital in the central city, in precisely the same way with either form of taxation. By (22–12), the stock of non-land capital in the central city falls as does its output of real property.

III

While the qualitative effects of central city taxation which provides benefits equally throughout the urban area are obvious enough, their empirical importance is less clear. In this section I was to assess the quantitative importance of these effects. I will base my assessment upon data for residential real estate only, principally because far more is known about it than non-residential real property. Though the largest single class of urban real property, the appropriate parameter values for other forms of urban real estate could, of course, differ considerably. The parameters whose numerical values must be determined are the shares of land in the production of central city and suburban real estate, the elasticity of substitution of land for non-land capital, the relative amounts of non-land capital invested in the central city and the suburbs, and the elasticity of supply of suburban land.

Probably the best source for estimating characteristics of residential real estate is data relating to new FHA-insured single-family housing. This source includes information not only on sales prices and amounts spent for land but also in the price paid per square foot of land. For the forty-seven U.S. cities I studied in an earlier paper (Muth 1971), the average site expenditure in 1966 was

$3,418, while the average price per square foot of lot size was $.448. The data on site expenditures, however, include expenditures for street improvements, utilities and landscaping which are more properly considered non-land capital. Schmid (1968, Ch. II) presents data which suggests such expenditures account for about half of developed land's value. It is thus appropriate to reduce site expenditure and cost per square foot by 50 percent and add half of site expenditure to construction expenditure per dwelling, which is the difference between sales price and site expenditure. Doing so yielded a per acre value for undeveloped land of $9,750, site expenditure of $1,709 and construction expenditure of $16,301, both per dwelling.

The figures just cited refer to newly-built dwellings, the majority of which one supposes were on the urban periphery. To calculate values in different locations, let the production function for residential real estate be

$$R = [a_N N^{-b} + a_L L^{-b}]^{-1/b} \qquad (22\text{-}16)$$

that is of the CES variety where $\sigma = 1/(1 + b)$. Equating the value of marginal products to factor prices and solving, one finds

$$(rL/nN) = (a_N/a_L)^{-\sigma}(r/n)^{1-\sigma}. \qquad (22\text{-}17)$$

With interest rates of 6 percent per year and property taxes of 2.5, $r = (.06 + .025)$ $9,750 \cong $829 per acre per year. Further, if a dollar's worth of structure has associated with it expenditures on depreciation maintenance and repair of 3.5 cents, $n = 0.12$ per dollar. Elsewhere (Muth [forthcoming]), after discussing available estimates, I argue that 0.75 is probably the best estimate of σ. Using the numbers cited above one readily calculates the ratio (a_N/a_L).

Wieand and Muth (1972) estimated that land values decline at a relative rate $g = 0.2$, using data for St. Louis in 1966. Furthermore, on the assumption that usable urban land surrounds the CBD in all directions (i.e., that $\phi = 2\pi$), census data shown in table 22-1 suggests that the radius of the typical urban area in 1970 was $u_2 = [(57.8 + 83.7)/\pi]^{1/2} = 6.7$ mi. Thus,

$$r(u) = 829 \, e^{.2(6.7-u)}.$$

Taking $u = u_1 = (57.8/\pi)^{1/2} = 4.3$ for the suburbs and $u = 0$ for the central city, substitution into (22-17) yields $k_{LC} = 0.13$ and $k_{LS} = 0.11$. Thus, despite great differences in land rentals per square foot as between central city and suburbs, land's share in the production of residential real property is not likely to vary appreciably as between the two sectors. Of course, land's share in the central city may be relatively higher than this because of the greater concentration of non-residential real estate there. I shall attempt to assess the possible consequences of this last consideration later on by taking $k_{LC} = 0.25$ as well.

Table 22-1

Population, Land Area, and Housing Output per Unit of Land, Typical[a] U.S. Central City and Its Suburbs, 1970

Item	Central City	Suburbs
Population (1,000's)	257.8	219.9
Land Area (sq. mi.)	57.76	83.70
Avg. Value per Dwelling ($'s)[b]	12,600	17,900
Value of Housing per Residential Area (1,000's of $'s)[c]	115	77.0

Notes:

[a]Means of totals for 248 metropolitan areas.

[b]Calculated from data on median value of owner occupied units and median monthly contract rent of rental units, assuming later is 0.01 times value.

[c]Assuming residential land is about 0.3 times total land area.

Source: Calculated from data in U.S. Bureau of the Census, *1970 Census of Population*, Vol. I, Pt. 1 (Washington: U.S. Government Printing Office, 1973), Table 20; and *1970 Census of Housing*, Vol. I, Pt. 1 (Washington: U.S. Government Printing Office, 1972), Table 2.

If residential real estate is produced according to the production function (22-16), it is easy to estimate the ratio of suburban to central city non-land capital from data in table 22-1. Rewriting (22-16),

$$a_N N^{-b} = R^{-b} - a_L L^{-b},$$

whence

$$\theta = \frac{N_S}{N_C} = \frac{L_S}{L_C} \left[\frac{(R_S/L_S)^{-b} - a_L}{(R_C/L_C)^{-b} - a_L} \right]^{-1/b} \tag{22-18}$$

The ratio (a_N/a_L) is given by (22-17) and data on factor shares and prices. This ratio together with (22-16) defines a_N and a_L separately as dependent upon the units selected for land, non-land capital and housing. Substituting the second and fourth lines of table 22-1 into (22-18) yields $\theta \cong 0.9$. This value, of course, refers only to residential real estate. To allow from the probable greater concentration of non-residential real property in the central city, I shall also calculate a solution for $\theta = 0.6$.

Finally, the value of λ, the elasticity of suburban land supply, is relatively easily calculated. As was noted earlier, the data on land areas imply a radius of 4.3 miles for the typical central city and 6.7 for the urban area as a whole. These together with $g = 0.2$ when substituted into (22-8) imply $\lambda = 2.5$. This figure, of course, refers to an urban area of about half a million people. For an area three times as large, (22-8) implies λ is $3^{-1/2}$ as large for the same average population

Table 22-2
Model Solutions for Central City Property Tax Increase of 0.01,
Alternative Parameter Values[a]

Variable	Parameter Values			
	Default[b]	$k_{LC} = 0.25$	$\theta = 0.6$	$\lambda = 1.4$
n_S^*	-.016	-.0091	-.022	-.022
n_C^*	.067	.074	.061	.062
r_S^*	.13	.074	.18	.18
r_C^*	-.45	-.22	-.41	-.41
N_C^*	-.39	-.22	-.35	-.36
N_S^*	.43	.25	.59	.39
L_S^*	.32	.18	.44	.25
R_C^*	-.34	-.17	-.31	-.31
R_S^*	.42	.24	.57	.38

Notes:

[a] Assuming $n_C = n_S = 0.12$ prior to the tax change. All parameters maintain their default values unless explicitly noted otherwise.

[b] $k_{LC} = 0.13$, $k_{LS} = 0.11$, $\theta = 0.9$, $\lambda = 2.5$, $\sigma = 0.75$.

density or approximately 1.4. The latter is probably more typical of the larger urban areas.

Table 22-2 shows solutions for alternative values of the parameters just discussed. Here it is supposed that the gross returns to non-land capital were initially 0.12 in central city and suburbs and that an additional property tax of 0.01 is levied in the central city. The first column presents the calculations for the base case, while the last three show the results obtained when various critical parameter values are varied one at a time. As a whole the calculations suggest that the precise outcome is rather sensitive to certain of the parameter values, so not much credence should be given to any particular number. One essential result stands out, though—the allocative effects of differential central city taxation relative to benefits received are likely to be large. Even small differences in taxes may bring about a substantial reallocation of resources as between central city and suburbs.

A few subsidiary conclusions that emerge are worth pointing out. Though partly reducing the before tax return to non-land capital in the suburbs, the principal effect of central city taxation is to increase the rental value of non-land capital to central city users. Secondly, differential central city taxation is likely to reduce the returns to central city land before tax rather drastically. This is the case because the reduction of non-land capital in the central city leads to a fall in the marginal product of central city land. Added to the fall in before tax rentals, of course, is the increase in taxes paid. Finally, central city taxation at differential rates is likely to lead to rather substantial coversions of agricultural and other non-urban land to urban land.

IV

To this point, this chapter has been concerned principally with the allocative effects of differential central city taxation relative to benefits received. The calculations presented in table 22-2 suggest these effects are likely to be large indeed. Differential central city taxation thus is likely to result in a substantial deadweight loss for the economy. In this section I wish to consider two other aspects of local taxation for purposes of redistributive expenditure, tax incidence and the effects of local financing and expenditure on the amount of income transfered.

The principal point in analyzing the incidence of central city taxation, whether through the property tax or an income tax, is that it reduces the returns to owners of non-land capital whether that capital is used in the central city or in the suburbs. In a sense, then, the incidence of the tax is on owners of non-land capital. Indeed, the owners of non-land capital are affected in essentially the same way as they would be if a real property tax were levied at uniform rates in the central city and in suburban areas. Of course, a central city tax also reduces the returns to owners of central city land, by relatively large amounts if the calculations in table 22-2 are anywhere near the mark. However, the returns to owners of suburban land rise with differential central city taxation. On balance though, tables 22-1 and 22-2 suggest that with central city taxation the incomes of land owners as a whole would fall, as they would, of course, with uniform property taxation throughout the area.

It is frequently said that, by raising rental values of real property in the central city, a central city property tax raises housing prices to poorer central city residents relative to prices paid by richer suburban ones. But surely this is mistaken. So long as the benefits of the expenditure undertaken by central city governments are received independently of location, the relative prices of housing in the two locations must, in the long run, remain unchanged. If housing prices were to rise relatively in the central city, persons moving would seek out suburban housing in greater numbers until the balance is restored. This is even the case for lower income families who are often said to be "trapped" in the central city. For, while living in the central city in greater relative numbers than in the suburbs, most suburban areas contain lower income families in significant numbers.

A condition for their intra-urban locational equilibrium, as for higher income families, is that utility level achieved be invariant with location. There is, therefore, no reason to believe that central city residents as consumers will be differentially affected by differentially high central city taxation. Consequently, it is only owners of land who are differentially affected by central city taxation.

Another consequence of central city taxation and redistributive expenditure is that income transfers to the central city poor are likely to be smaller than where taxation for redistributive purposes is levied throughout the urban area. To see this consider two income groups, higher and lower designated by the subscripts 1 and 2, respectively, and let $f < 1/2$ be the proportion of the lower-income group in the total population. Incomes before taxes and transfers are $\bar{y}_i$, and y_i after taxes and transfers. Following Hochman and Rogers (1969), let the utility function of the donor higher-income group be $U(y_1, y_2)$, with U_i standing for the marginal utility attached to income of group i. On the assumption that the recipients of transfers make up a minority of the electorate, majority rule implies the net transfers through the fiscal system are governed by the utility maximizing choice of the non-poor group. Neglecting deadweight losses, which may in fact be relatively large, the budget constraint facing members of the majority is

$$(1 - f)(y_1 - \bar{y}_1) + f(y_2 - \bar{y}_2) = 0.$$

Members of the majority, then, choose y_1 and y_2 so as to maximize

$$G = U(y_1, y_2) - \mu [(1 - f)(y_1 - \bar{y}_1) + f(y_2 - \bar{y}_2)].$$

The necessary conditions for a maximum are

$$\frac{\partial G}{\partial y_1} = U_1 - \mu(1 - f) = 0$$

$$\frac{\partial G}{\partial y_2} = U_2 - \mu f = 0$$

whose solution is

$$U_2/U_1 = f/(1 - f).$$

Thus, the larger the fraction of the poor population, in general, the smaller their after tax-transfer income. Indeed, let the utility function be Cobb-Douglas,

$$U = y_1^{(1 - \gamma)} y_2^{\gamma}$$

where γ may be thought of as a measure of tastes for redistribution on the part of the majority. Then

$$U_2/U_1 = [\gamma/(1 - \gamma)] \, (y_1/y_2)$$

so

$$(y_1/y_2) = [(1 - \gamma)/\gamma] \, [f/(1 - f)] \, .$$

Substituting into the budget constraint,

$$y_2 = \gamma \bar{y}/f,$$

where $\bar{y} = (1 - f)\bar{y}_1 + f\bar{y}_2$ is per capita income. After tax-transfer income of the poor thus varies inversely with their relative size, both because of the direct effect of a larger f in the last equation and because per capita income is smaller the larger is f for given before tax-transfer incomes of the two groups.

This last result is due to the fact that the tax price to members of the donor group of transferring a dollar of income to each poor family is higher the larger the fraction of the poor in the population. If in a population of 100 their are 10 poor, a dollar's aggregate income transferred increases the income of each of the poor by 10 cents and costs each of the 90 non-poor about 1.11 cents. The tax price per dollar transferred is thus 11.1 cents. With 20 poor each dollar transferred increases the income of each of the poor by only 5 cents and costs each of the 80 non-poor 1.25 cents. The tax price in the latter instance is 25 cents, or more than twice as much.

Local financing of income redistribution expenditure is thus likely to result in less redistribution where the poor are more numerous and in more where they are less numerous. One can thus readily account for the fact that payments under Aid to Families with Dependent Children are lower in Mississippi than in the Northeast. To the extent the poor are less than perfectly mobile as between Mississippi and the Northeast, local financing of income redistribution would result in unequal treatment of equals. Similarly, local redistribution of incomes would result in smaller transfers in central cities and larger transfers in suburban areas than if redistribution were nationwide. To the extent the poor are mobile as between central city and suburbs, however, the central city poor need not be worse off relative to those in the suburbs under local redistribution. Rather, locational equilibrium of the poor would result in the suburban poor paying higher unit prices for housing relative to their central city counterparts than they would under national financing. Regardless of this last finding, the preceding results suggest that local financing of income redistribution may result in a substantial deadweight loss to the economy as a whole.

References

Harberger, Arnold C., "The Incidence of the Corporation Income Tax," *Journal of Political Economy* 70 (June 1962): 215–40.

Hochman, Harold M. and James D. Rodgers, "Pareto Optimal Redistribution," *American Economic Review* 59 (Sept. 1969): 542–57.

Mieszkowski, Peter, "The Property Tax: An Excise Tax or a Profits Tax?," *Journal of Public Economics* 1 (1972): 73–96.

Muth, Richard F., *Cities and Housing* (Chicago: University of Chicago Press, 1969).

Muth, Richard F., "The Derived Demand for Urban Residential Land," *Urban Studies* 8 (Oct. 1971): 243–54.

Muth, Richard F., "Numerical Solution of Urban Residential Land-Use Models," *Journal of Urban Economics* (forthcoming).

Olsen, Edgar O., "A Normative Theory of Transfers," *Public Choice* 6 (Spring 1969): 39–58.

Schmid, A. Allan, *Converting Land from Rural to Urban Uses* (Washington: Resources for the Future, 1968).

Wieand, Kenneth, Jr., and Richard F. Muth, "A Note on the Variation of Land Values with Distance from the CBD in St. Louis," *Journal of Regional Science* 12 (Dec. 1972): 469–73.

23 "Inadvertent" Distributional Impacts in the Provision of Public Services to Individuals

Jerome Rothenberg

I. Introduction

This chapter is intended to supply a framework for examining the provision of public services to individuals, and to present informally a number of considerations that relate to crucial issues on that topic. It does not attempt to present a formal analysis of the area as a whole or, indeed, of individual pieces. Its aim and format are breadth and exploration rather than rigorous derivation.

In one sense all work on public sector economics refers to the provision of public services to individuals. I interpret the present topic as emphasizing the relation between the publicness of the services and the individuality of the recipients. Thus, usual assumptions about homogeneous citizenship are singularly inappropriate. The central focus of the present work will be on the heterogeneity of the public.

First we must dispel one literalism concerning individuality. Almost nothing in microanalytic theory refers literally to biological individuals; it is the household decision-making unit that we refer to as the individual. This usage will be continued here.

The emphasis on individuality is not at all new in economics proper. It is close to being the very raison d'être of microeconomics. But it is notably less comfortable in public sector economics—although it provides the distinctive substantive challenge for the modern renewal of interest in that field. The discomfiture stems from the fact that the concept of public goods emphasizes uniformity at least somewhere among production, distribution, and consumption: single, monopolistic production; distribution in which individual exclusion is infeasible or the calculation of individual benefit impossible; similarity, if not outright unanimity, of quantity and valuation in consumption. The upshot is a set of real world institutions, and at least a partial theoretical rationalization, of a distinctive, nonmarket relationship between individual and government. The decision-making of government, and the resulting interactions with individuals, are not based upon separate, voluntary, market-type transactions in which both parties enter into each only on the basis of mutually agreed-upon advantage.

Individual contacts with the public sector intrinsically involve nonvoluntaristic elements. Moreover, decision-making in the public sector to determine the nature of these contacts is accomplished not by unanimity but, generally, by some form of majority rule. As a consequence, in the presence of substantial individual differences, most public actions have nonneutral distributional effects of greater substance than "comparable" market actions. These distributional effects are typically "inadvertent" to the system in the sense that they stem from the interplay of attempts to obtain self-interested advantage by the different participants, not from the expression of some more or less consensual preferences about explicitly redistributional goals. They are not a deliberate social choice on welfare distribution. Hence they are likely to cut across genuine distributional goals in various ways. Their overall drift would be difficult to predict, either by observers or by the participants themselves, apart from the concrete constellation of political issues and participant preferences on those issues. Nonetheless, the welfare implications of these effects may be of real importance in evaluating both the particular public actions and the very structure of the public sector which generates them. In effect then, public sector activities are prone to generate political externalities, and these externalities, no less than market externalities, must be considered in evaluating the "efficiency" or overall desirability of public action.[1]

The purpose of this chapter is to describe the range of this sort of political externality, and the conditions that generate different types. Following that we shall examine two forms of solution that have been theoretically proposed (and which have real world counterparts) to lessen these externalities. They can be considered forms of a general "separate facilities" approach to the problem. We shall investigate some of their capabilities and limitations in this respect.

In the course of this investigation a number of ancillary issues will come in for emphasis: pure and impure public goods, the nature of Pareto optimality with regard to public sector activities, homogeneity and heterogeneity of public services, and operational differences between the public and private sectors.

Individual Differences and Political Externalities

There are six types of individual difference that we shall look at: (1) differences in tastes unrelated to tax base differences; (2) differences in tax base unrelated to taste differences; (3) differences in marginal valuations closely related to differences in tax base; (4) generic congestion (crowding-pollution) with unequal incidence; (5) differential access to use of public services; (6) unequal delivery of (eligibility for) public services. For each of these cases we shall indicate the socially efficient public action, the action actually likely to be forthcoming under majority rule decision-making, and the resulting political externality.

Political Choice Under Individual Uniformity

The point of departure for the analysis is the situation where individuals are alike with respect to both the valuation of public services and tax liability for financing them. For this situation the crucial assumptions are:

1. The public service(s) involved is (are) pure public goods in that their simple provision at all makes them equally available (accessible) to all individuals. The additional property—that neither service quality nor total resource costs vary when a given provision of such services is shared by fewer or more individuals—is not relevant at this point, since a fixed total population of constituents is assumed.

2. All individuals have the same tastes for the service(s). Their marginal valuations for different levels of general availability (quantity supplied) are equal.

Because of some of the complexities to be developed later, we shall introduce marginal valuation functions somewhat more roundaboutly. Let the utility function of the "individual" be given as:

$$U^i = U^i [Z_i, W_i] \qquad\qquad (23\text{-}1)$$

where Z is the vector of private goods consumed by individual i, and W_i is i's "consumption" of public services. Four issues must be raised at this point about this form of "consumption." First, the objects are termed "public services" rather than public goods, designating "commodities" produced by the public sector. All of these are assumed to have some degree of publicness, but they are not necessarily pure public goods, unless explicitly designated as such. Second, for simplicity they will be treated as a single homogeneous good; but this "good" is intended to be a composite of various separate types of good and service; and while some of these components are consumed as separately identifiable personal acts of consumption—as for example having firemen battle a blaze in i's house, or i visiting a public park or sending his children to a public school or using a road or drinking water pumped to his house—some are "impersonal"—for example, air quality over the rest of i's city or a welfare program that gives benefits to handicapped individuals but not to i. These components are assumed to be provided in fixed proportions. Occasions where this simplified, but more complex than usual,[a] treatment seems especially inappropriate will be noted below.

Third, the present work is making a distinction between what it is that the public sector supplies and what the individual consumes. The distinction applies primarily to the personal consumption components of the public service complex. Where such components have a high degree of publicness what the government is providing is often a *capacity*—or facility—to supply services, not the services themselves. Thus, the government provides roads, beaches, museums, a water system, hospitals, employment exchanges, etc. The individual is not a passive recipient of the services from these facilities but must opt to use them. The degree of use of these facilities depends on the individual's own choice. Thus, it is not the size or character of the government's provision of these capacities that

---

[a]Most theoretical treatments of the public sector deal with a single, homogeneous commodity.

properly enters into the individual's utility function, but the actual, personally discretionary use of these capacities, designated as W_i.

The two are connected in the following way. Let us consider W_i as a quasi-private good. It is linked to X, the public sector's provision of service capacity, in a final good-intermediate good relationship. In the general case the production of final good W_i requires an input of public capacity provision and some private operating resources used on i's behalf, N_i. Thus the production function for W_i is:

$$W_i = W(X, N_i). \qquad (23\text{-}2)$$

X is positively related to W for three reasons: (1) provision of higher levels of capacity can decrease the amount of private operating resources needed for each instance of consumption (e.g., the more parks provided the lower the expected cost of reaching a park from the individual's residence); (2) provision of higher levels of capacity can increase the quality level of the service in each instance of consumption because it affects the character of the service (e.g., "more" cultural services, or "more" education, may mean a wider variety of offerings—more paintings, more specialized services, a higher teacher-student ratio); (3) more capacity can increase the quality of each instance of consumption where crowding is relevant because it represents a more favorable balance of capacity to overall demand for simultaneous use.

It might be thought that W can simply be treated as a private good and that the present distinction is therefore not an apt one as a foundation for a theory of public sector decision-making. In fact, this is not so. It will be shown below how individual preferences concerning provision of public services X depend on the discretionary amount of consumption W. The demand for X is a derived demand and for some problems the explicit character of this derivative relationship is especially illuminating.

The fourth issue concerning W is that variations in W represent changes in the *level* of consumption during the relevant period. This level refers both to the quality of the service in each instance of its consumption and the number of consumption instances. In the present context we assume that quality is a function of the level of X only, and number of instances—*amount*—is a function only of the size of N.

Individual i faces a budget constraint as follows:

$$Y^i = P_Z Z_i + P_N N_i + T_i \qquad (23\text{-}3)$$

where Y^i is i's total income

P_Z is the price per unit of the composite private good

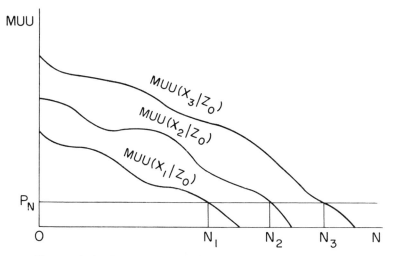

Figure 23-1. Determination of Optimal Use of Public Services

P_N is the price per unit of the operating resources

T_i is the total tax liability on i for provision of public service level X.

T_i is assumed to be determined by the political sector simultaneously with X and is exogenous to individual i's optimal budgetary allocation. He is assumed to allocate between Z_i and N_i to maximize utility, subject to (23-3), thereby determining—for given X—optimal W_i, $\hat{W}_i$, as well as $\hat{Z}_i$ and so $\hat{U}^i$.

To see the derivation of a marginal valuation function for X more intuitively we can look at individual optimization in partial equilibrium terms. Assume that P_N represents the operating cost per instance of consumption of W. So N_i can be interpreted as the number of instances—the amount—of consumption of W. Now, for initial Y^i, P_Z, P_N, and T_i, and an initial tentative choice of Z_i, Z_{i0} we calculate marginal utility for different amounts of consumption of W as a function of X, through equations (23-1) and (23-2). See figure 23-1 (for simplicity we omit i subscripts and superscripts). $MUU \equiv$ marginal utility of use (assumed a conventionally declining function of N).

For the given operating cost per unit, P_N, the chosen level of N is shown for provision of X_1, X_2, and X_3 as N_1, N_2, N_3 respectively. Let $P_N \hat{N}_i \equiv A_i$ (contingent access expenditure) and $A_i/X = z_i$ (marginal access cost).

Now allow Z_i to vary so as to maximize utility.[b] This gives optimal N, and thus also maximized utility, as a function of X. For the given T_i we can define

---

[b]Where the marginal rate of substitution between Z and W equals the price ratio P_Z/P_N.

individual i's marginal valuation function for X as the consumer surplus engendered by each additional unit of X provided—the maximum amount that i would be willing to give up in numeraire Z and be no worse off than at the lower level of X provided.[c] This T_i is of course arbitrary and a different total tax liability and access expenditure could in general have some influence on the shape and position of the marginal valuation function. We assume that

$$\frac{\partial MUU}{\partial X} > 0$$

and

$$\frac{\partial^2 MUU}{\partial X^2} < 0.$$

X_{i1}^*, X_{i2}^* are the most preferred levels of X by individual i when faced respectively with average tax liabilities of t_{i1} and t_{i2}.

In all the uses to be made of it, the marginal valuation function for public services refers both to a level of X and a level of individual use (N) optimally adjusted to that level of X. Moreover, the position and possibly even shape of the function depends somewhat on the individual's total tax liability (via an income effect), unlike the demand function for a private good, because, ceteris paribus, the individual's tax liability is independent of his level of consumption of $X(N)$: i.e., the tax liability is determined as soon as the level of X is and becomes part of the individual's budget constraint prior to his evaluating X.

The shape of the marginal valuation function is suggested by two things: (1) the conventional decrease of marginal utility of use at increasing rate with increasing use, (2) the fact that higher X means a higher marginal utility of use function and a larger optimal number of uses. Some rise is allowed at low X, since the second factor is likely to be strong and the first weak; but thereafter a falling segment is likely as the second factor begins to dominate.

With this analytical apparatus we can examine social decision-making in the uniformity case. By the assumption of individual sameness in marginal valuation functions, we have:

$$MV_i(X|Z_i) = MV_j(X|Z_j) \qquad \text{all } i,j \qquad\qquad (23\text{-}4)$$

where MV_i is individual i's marginal valuation (demand) function in money for the public service, Z_i is the amount of the composite private good consumed by i, and X is the capacity level of the public good made available by government.

---

[c]Thus in general, each X has a different optimal N associated with its marginal valuation.

The familiar condition for a Pareto optimal provision of public goods is:

$$\sum_{i \in J} MV_i(\hat{X}) = MC(\hat{X}) \qquad (23\text{-}5)$$

where $\hat{X}$ is the optimal level of X, MC is the marginal social cost of supplying X and J is the total jurisdiction population.

The individual citizen i is in equilibrium if:

$$MV_i(X) = t_i(X) \qquad (23\text{-}6)$$

where t_i is the marginal tax liability on i. This is not to be interpreted as the kind of active individual equilibrium assumed to occur in private markets, since the individual cannot himself vary the level of X, so neither $t_i(X_0)X$ nor $\int_0^X {}_0 t_i(X)dX$ is related to any activity involving X under i's control (but A_i is). It is, in fact, only an implicit "price" of X. Individual i's total tax liability is set as a function of his possession of tax base, not consumption of X. For each level of X to be provided, we assume that government is constrained to collect in aggregate taxes just enough to meet the total cost of providing it: i.e.,

$$T_i(X) = TC(X) \qquad (23\text{-}7)$$
$$i \in J$$

where TC is the total cost function.

t_i is obtained from T_i: it is simply the tax liability per unit of X provided: $t_i = T_i/X$.

Thus, individual equilibrium here is to be interpreted rather in the context of voting. Given the expectation that he will face a certain $T_i(X)$–via a social cost function for X and i's relative ownership of tax base–what level of X would i most prefer? Individual i's utility level would be maximized where (23-5) is fulfilled. So individual equilibrium is a predictor of a voter's preferred provision of X as expressible in voting. A simple three-person situation illustrates the case. Assume for simplicity constant costs in the provision of different quantities of X to the three-person community, as in figure 23-2. Benefits and costs (in \$) are measured on the vertical axis, capacity level of the public good (X) is measured on the horizontal axis. MC is the marginal social cost function, AC the average social cost function, for providing different levels of per capita availability of the public good. MV_i is individual i's marginal valuation function for each level of X.

In the unanimity case we assume that each individual pays the same tax per unit of availability (t_i), 1/3 of the marginal (and average) social cost. If each individual were to vote for his most preferred level of X, given the social cost and individual tax functions, all three would vote for $\hat{X}$, where $t_i(\hat{X}) = MV_i(\hat{X})$. It is

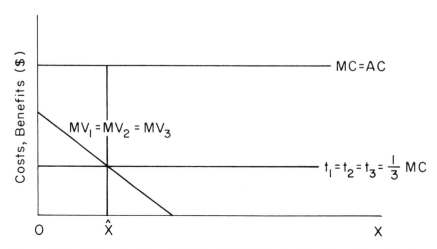

Figure 23-2. Determination of Optimal Public Service Provision: Equal Tastes, Equal Tax Liability Case

thus the unanimity equilibrium. Since (23-4) are also fulfilled here, and revenues are just met by total tax collections, it is also the social optimum—the Pareto optimum position.

In this situation, individual voting generates the social optimum resource allocation, one where there is no cleavage between majority and minority interests. All three individuals are better off for the production of the public service, and all are best off at $\hat{X}$. This is the situation to be compared with cases where distributional effects matter.

Differences in Tastes

Suppose now the three individuals have different tastes toward the public service:

$$MRS_{ZW}^{i}(Z_i, W_i) \neq MRS_{ZW}^{j}(Z_j, W_j) \neq MRS_{ZW}^{k}(Z_k, W_k) \qquad (23\text{-}8)$$

where MRS_{ZW} is the marginal rate of substitution between Z and W. From these we generate different marginal utility of use functions for the three, implying different optimal levels of expected use. Together with (23-7) these generate marginal valuation functions that differ. For simplicity, suppose these differences are of the form.

$$MV_2(X) = a_2 + MV_3(X) \qquad a_2 > 0$$

$$MV_1(X) = a_1 + MV_2(X) \qquad a_1 > 0 \qquad (23\text{-}9)$$

Differences in tastes can genuinely appear in the presence of the pure public goods we have posited because their purity is defined solely in terms of equal *availability of the facility* to the numbers of the population—not equal consumption of the services rendered by the facility and certainly not utility levels produced. It is important in this case that the differences among marginal valuations not be directly related to differences among the tax bases of the three individuals—assuming at this point that tax liabilities are nondiscriminatorily levied on a specific tax base. Figure 23–3 shows the situation.

In this case, if each voted for his most preferred level of X, individual 1 would choose X_1^*, 2 would choose X_2^*, 3 would choose X_3^*. Since there are differences in preferred candidates, we suppose that these three are placed in contention against one another in a sequence of paired comparisons to be decided by majority rule. The process envisaged here gives rise to transitive social choices (because of the monotonicity of the marginal valuation functions over X). By this voting process, X_2^* will be chosen: individual 2 always votes for it, and each of the two voters does also against the opposite extreme candidate.

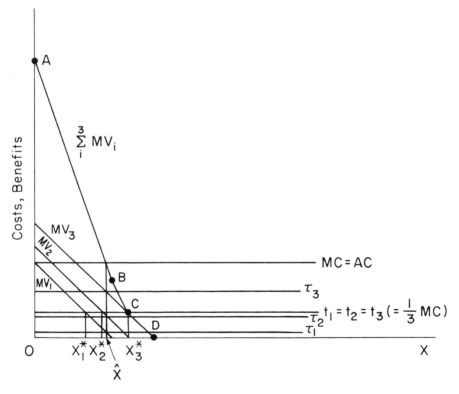

Figure 23–3. Determination of Optimal Public Service Provision by Voting and by Maximizing Aggregate Net Advantage: Unequal Tastes, Equal Tax Liability Case

In comparison with zero provision of the public service, provision of X_2^* represents a situation where individual 2 obtains the highest net gain possible to him with a tax liability of t_1 per unit of X provided; individual 3 gets the next highest percentage of what is possible for him at the same tax liability, and individual 1 gets the smallest. Notice that this is not a comparison of net gains for different individuals, but only a comparison across individuals of the discrepancy between potential and actual gain from public action for each. In direct comparative terms, individuals 1, 2, and 3 gain absolutely in that order. Both types of differences can be very dramatic. Suppose that MV_2 were much farther to the right, intersecting $t_1 = t_2 = t_3$ to the right of X_{3L}. Then that intersection would represent the majority choice, $X_2^{*\prime}$. At that level of X it would be individual 3 who was proportionately the least aided by public action—and he would in fact be worse off than if no public service at all had been provided! So majority rule can lead to changes in real income distribution among voters—redistributions not only in terms of different divisions of the gains from government action, but also in terms of positive vs. negative net impacts from such action.

The size of such potential redistributions can be suggested by considering the much broader range of government actions available in practice. The above example speaks of "public services," implying a single composite "public good." Individual appreciations are unlikely to vary greatly for such a composite. But in the real world of many different kinds of public services, including not only tangible goods and services but also various forms of regulation and control, and policies affecting welfare distribution via resource transfer programs, preferences for any one or subset of such "public services" can vary extremely. Besides these differences, there will be differences in the evaluation of different combinations of services—i.e., preference tradeoffs will be likely to vary substantially. Thus, majority choice can lead to substantial income redistribution, depending on the pattern of taste clusters. In general in the M-person case, the greater the deviation of those respective clusters, the greater will be the real costs imposed by the majority on the minority.

These potentially wide discrepancies in net benefits (value of services consumed less taxes)—with even the possibility of negative net benefits—stem from the ability of the majority to impose a public service level-tax liability combination on the minority against the latter's will. If unanimity were required, of course, the situation would be quite different. Unanimity can be implemented by institutionally requiring that *all* participants prefer the socially chosen level to all others. In the present example, individual 3 has to be induced to prefer a level greater than X_3^*. This has come about by compensation being paid to him from 1 and/or 2 for his decreased net gains in moving above X_3^*. Instead of by side payment we may suppose that the compensation is integrated with the tax payment to form adjusted tax liabilities.

A behavioral and a normative theory of compensation are not equivalent, since relative bargaining power helps determine participants' final positions. But if relative bargaining powers consist only in the locations of the individual marginal valuation functions, then the final level agreed on will be $\hat{X}$, and the adjusted tax levels T_1, T_2, and T_3. Since both X_3^* and X_2^* are to the left of $\hat{X}$, individual 1 is forced to compensate both individual 3 $(t_3 - T_3)$ and individual 2 $(t_2 - T_2)$. $\hat{X}$ balances the amount that individual 1 can afford to pay to move the level closer to X_1^* and the amount that he is required to pay to the others to gain their agreement.

$\hat{X}$ is the expected level arrived at by this compensation process because it is the level at which:

$$\sum_{i=1}^{3} MV_i(\hat{X}) = MC(\hat{X}) = AC(\hat{X}) \tag{23-10}$$

as shown in figure 23–4 as the intersection between the sum of marginal valuations function (ΣMV_i) and the marginal social cost function (MC). It represents the Pareto optimal level of X. Figure 23–3 also shows that $\hat{X}$ is the level at which the aggregate net benefits of the three individuals are maximized:

$$\hat{X} = \left\{ X | \max \int_0^X \left(\sum_{i=1}^{3} MV_i - \sum_{i=1}^{} t_i \right) dX \right\}. \tag{23-11}$$

Since the overall potential surplus in monetary terms is greatest here, it means that in principle a set of compensatory transfers from potential gainers to potential losers can be arranged to make this level preferred by all three individuals to any other level. It is the social optimum in this sense (and in the example given is unique). Thus, any movement toward unanimous agreement from the majority choice X_2^* could reach levels unanimously preferred to X_2^* in the direction of $\hat{X}$; but each of these would in turn be subject to further unanimous preference by other alternatives until $\hat{X}$ was reached; and $\hat{X}$ itself could not be so superseded by any.

As is well known, this optimal level can be converted to a decentralized Lindahl equilibrium by the government directly charging discriminating taxes equal to individual marginal valuations at that X for which the sum of these valuations equals the marginal social cost of public service availability. In that circumstance each individual selects the X which equates his marginal valuation with his marginal tax liability, and all select the same X—i.e., $\hat{X}$. This is shown in figure 23–3 by Lindahl tax functions τ_1, τ_2 and τ_3.

Comparison of the majority choice with the social optimum is illuminated by referring to the Lindahl equilibrium. Net benefits for each individual under both choices are shown by:

$$B_i^* = \int_0^{X_2^*}(MV_i(X) - t_i(X))dX \qquad\qquad (23\text{-}12\text{a})$$

$$\hat{B}_i = \int_0^{\hat{X}} (MV_i(X) - \tau_i(X))dX. \qquad\qquad (23\text{-}12\text{b})$$

All three individuals are guaranteed $B_i > 0$, while under majority choice, $B_i^* \lesseqgtr 0$. In comparison with X_2^*, the provision of X is closer to what individual 1 would like, farther from what individuals 2 and 3 would like; but the latter two are better off than under majority choice because of the lower taxes they are required to pay—individual 2 slightly better off and individual 3 much better off. Despite a level of X more favorable to individual 1, however, he is actually worse off than at X_2^* because his total tax liability is much higher than previously. Achievement of the social optimum $\hat{X}$ considerably bunches the distribution of the gains from public action relatively to uniform tax majority choice.

The net loss by individual 3 relative to X_2^* suggests that the Lindahl equilibrium is not the same thing as establishing uniform taxes and requiring unanimous agreement via compensation. This is ratified by noting that the latter situation is not represented by tax liability functions τ_1, τ_2, and τ_3. Up to level X_2^* all three individuals face $t_1 = t_2 = t_3$. It is only for levels above X_2^* that they face net liabilities other than these; and at $\hat{X}$, τ_1, τ_2, and τ_3 are only *marginal* liabilities; the respective average liabilities—unlike in the original situation—are different from these (less for individual 1, greater for individuals 2 and 3). Thus, individual 1 is better off, individuals 2 and 3 worse off, at $\hat{X}$ when that level is achieved through uniform taxation and compensation rather than by Lindahl taxation.

Indeed, with monotonic individual marginal valuation functions the income distribution consequence of determining public resource use through Lindahl taxation is unique. Contrariwise, the distributional consequence of uniform taxation with separate voluntary compensation to establish the same expected level of public provision is dependent on what the majority choice level would be and its relation to the social optimal level. Of course, given a particular set of marginal valuation functions and the marginal social cost of providing public services, the majority choice is determined as well as the identity of the social optimal level—so the expected welfare impact of the compensation-induced unanimity is also established in principle.

By the way, it is not the possibility of compensatory side payments but the requirement for unanimity, that mitigates the substantial distributional inequality, relative to both zero services and the social optimal level, that arises from unadorned majority choice. Thus, with only majority choice required, a minority extremist group could pay a centrist group to establish a majority position closer to its extreme and thus farther pass that of a sizable minority at an opposite extreme—thereby *increasing* the negative political externality of majority rule.

This requirement for unanimity raises two deep issues about the very concept of social (Pareto) optimality. Suppose social choice is defined solely by majority rule, and no side payment compensations are permitted, let alone required. Then, since Pareto optimality is defined solely with respect to the set of feasible alternatives, it has sometimes been argued that *every* alternative for which at least one voter will vote as most preferred outcome (like X_1^*, X_2^* and X_3^*) is a Pareto optimal level of X—since there is no other feasible alternative which will make someone better off in comparison with it without making someone worse off.

This is not strictly true, since a voter may vote for alternatives other than—and sometimes even against!—his most preferred alternative for strategic reasons. In general, all alternatives must be considered feasible. In the exclusively majority rule process many such alternatives will be Pareto optimal, depending on the number of voters and the pattern of their preferences. Yet almost all of these will fail to fulfill the condition of optimal resource use, (23-4). It is only when unanimity is required for legitimate social choice, and voluntary compensatory side payments are permitted to facilitate this by balancing different preference intensities, that one alternative (where (23-4) is fulfilled uniquely) can in principle reveal itself to be Pareto superior to all others.

Unanimity of this sort can in fact be wrought only out of a multi-person bargaining process. Even with three voters this is not easy. With a realistically much larger number of voters the attempt to achieve an n-person agreement may well be extremely costly in time and effort, given the variety of strategic interplay possible, and often may fail. There is reason to believe, moreover, that the cost of achieving agreement is a positive (even nonlinear) function of the number of individuals required to agree. These agreement costs are not different in kind from any other form of resource cost. They subtract, therefore, from the resources available for producing other public and private commodities and must therefore be considered in evaluating the overall desirability of any alternative.

Assume that we begin with an equal assignment of tax liabilities, as $t_1 = t_2 = t_3$, and a first stage majority choice of X_2^*, the requirement for unanimity may well result in no alternative dominating X_2^*, or at least in a choice favoring an alternative other than $\hat{X}$, because it is too expensive actually to achieve the agreement *at* $\hat{X}$—i.e., when agreement costs are considered, the sum of compensatory payments possible is too small for everyone to prefer $\hat{X}$ to every other alternative, even perhaps to X_2^*.

It might be objected that $\hat{X}$ can be brought about by resort to Lindahl taxing. But this requires prior knowledge of the individual MV functions, and the usual difficulties lie in the way of obtaining truthful revelation of these preferences.[5] Techniques can be established to approximate these underlying preferences, but they too are costly, and their costliness is probably a rising function of the closeness of the approximation. Thus, when this variable schedule of costs is integrated within the overall choosing situation, a choice other than $\hat{X}$ may result.

What this means is that the usual definition of the social optimum as that for which (5) holds strictly follows only if there exists a costless regimen for achieving unanimous bargaining agreement, or correct Lindahl taxation. Failing that, the social optimum will be that which fulfills a condition analogous to (5), but where actual agreement or preference revelation costs are included. This is much more difficult to specify than the conventional condition. Moreover, if the voting rules of the system being examined do not call for unanimity, then even this *modified* condition (23-4) becomes irrelevant to social optimality, since alternatives comparable to $\hat{X}$ may simply not be attainable under the existing voting rules.

In what follows we shall assume that the conventional specification *is* applicable, not so much for its normative force, as to have a point of reference for characterizing the dispersion of distributional consequences resulting from nonunanimous forms of decision-making. The normative thrust of the analysis must not, therefore, be misunderstood. Resolution of the problem of these political externalities does *not* reside simply in asserting that majority rule must be replaced by unanimity. Indeed, the latter section of the chapter delves into the question of how a nonparalyzing form of near-unanimous consensus can be practically achieved. Its conclusions give no cause to celebrate the practicality of effective unanimity.

To summarize this section, then, majority rule leads to negative political externalities on some minorities. These can involve substantial real income effects. The possibility of side-payments in any form changes the pattern of, but does not necessarily decrease, these nontrivial redistributional impacts.

Tax Base Differences

In the last section we treated differences in preferences toward public services as the cause of distributional externalities. In fact, since what is really involved is differences in valuation of public services received less the tax liability incurred per household—i.e., in household net benefits—these may come about as a result of differences on the tax liability side. Arbitrarily discriminatory taxation is one such case. All of the patterns of the last section can be reproduced via discriminatory taxation that has the same effect.

We have so far implicitly proceeded on the simplifying assumption that tax liabilities are based on ownership of tax base property, and that tax rates are uniform on such property, regardless of their ownership. This assumption should be made explicit now. It is not a trivial assumption. It excludes taxation based precisely on benefit. The consequences are important. Lindahl taxes are, in effect, an extremely efficient form of such benefit taxation, setting marginal (and average) liabilities for each individual equal to his marginal valuation of public service. But in the real world taxes formally imposed on nonexplicitly benefit tax bases are often related implicitly to benefit. Insofar as income levels, or real property owned, or retail purchases are positively contributed to by provision of public services, most real world taxes will bear implicit shadows of benefit taxation. But these taxes are not very closely related to benefit. Some forms of public charge do closely approximate benefit—museum charges, park admissions, etc.—but this is where the services are most nearly private goods. Where significant degrees of publicness inhere in the services, taxes to finance them cannot closely link with relative benefits, even where such a link is desired. In fact, because of the explicit welfare redistributional goals of government, a tight link of this sort is not even desired. So we assume an absence of perfect benefit taxation in the model. Tax bases chosen may reflect benefit, but only distantly, if at all.

What else is excluded is outright tax discrimination: different rates on the same tax base are permitted (taxes may have uniform, progressive or regressive rates), but arbitrary selection of different tax bases for different individuals are not. In the real world political power is sometimes used to select tax bases that will differentially favor those wielding the power relative to others. Indeed, that is akin to those in power adopting spending programs that will differentially benefit them. Admission of this phenomenon does no violence to our thesis, indeed amplifies it. We omit it from the present discussion simply for convenience.

In the present section, therefore, we assume that tax liabilities derive from a uniform tax rate on a single, universal tax base. Our case here deals with differences in tax liabilities stemming only from differences among our individuals in ownership of this tax base.

In this category belong individual differences in ownership of tax base. Symmetric with the last category, these latter differences are assumed not to be closely related to differences in marginal valuation. As indicated above, this is not a trivial requirement, since where the major tax is on household income, marginal valuations for superior goods *are* tied to the overall level of the tax base via monotonic falling marginal utility of money income. It is less closely related to relevant tax bases for state and local taxation: real property and retail purchases. By assumption, the situation is as follows for the three-person community:

$$MV_1(X) = MV_2(X) = MV_3(X) \tag{23-13a}$$

$$t_2 = c_2 + t_3 \qquad c_2 > 0$$

$$t_1 = c_1 + t_2 \qquad c_1 > 0 \tag{23-13b}$$

and in figure 23-4. Here X_1^*, X_2^*, and X_3^* are the individual preferred X levels, and X_2^* is the majority rule choice. Again there are differences in the discrepancy between actual and most preferred choice among the three. And again there is a discrepancy between actual and group optimal choice, the latter being at $\hat{X}$

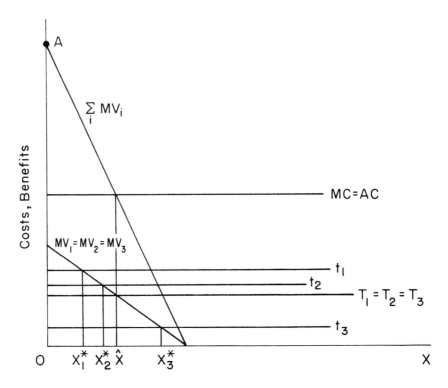

Figure 23-4. Determination of Optimal Public Service Provision by Voting and by Maximizing Aggregate Net Advantage: Equal Tastes, Unequal Tax Liability Case

(where the sum of individual marginal valuations equals the marginal social cost) because the common valuation function requires an equal marginal tax liability for all if $MV_i(X)$ = marginal tax$_i(X)$ is to be fulfilled. $\hat{X}$ will become a unanimously chosen alternative only if virtual compensations make the effective marginal tax rates equal to $MV_i(\hat{X})$ for all—i.e., $\tau_1 = \tau_2 = \tau_3$. This comes about by individual 3 in effect subsidizing the tax liability of both 2 and 1, mostly 1. The possibility of side payments without unanimity does not dependably decrease the redistributions, since without it each of 1 and 3 alone can compete for 2's support on a shift favorable to each but unfavorable to the excluded one. Thus, this case gives rise to the same kinds of political externality, and with magnitudes probably not unlike those of case 1.

Related Taste and Tax Base Differences

Here is the category where taste and tax base differences are directly related to one another, perhaps through the agency of a marginal utility of expenditure that falls with income and a tax base positively related to income. Individuals with lower marginal valuations have a smaller tax base, individuals with higher marginal valuations have a larger tax base. Clearly the two sets of differences tend to cancel one another out in the vote analysis. Differences in net benefit-tax incidence may still exist, but they will be smaller—probably much smaller—than differences generated by either taste or tax liability differences. They may even disappear entirely. This is the sort of situation where political externalities may be moderated. The reason is that because of the fortuitously offsetting directions, public sector taxation becomes a benefit tax analogous to private sector discriminatory pricing. The complete offset case is shown in figure 23-5.

Generic Congestion with Unequal Incidence

With this category we enter the realm of the nonpure public good. In the previous, pure public good cases, equations (23-1) and (23-2) established U^i

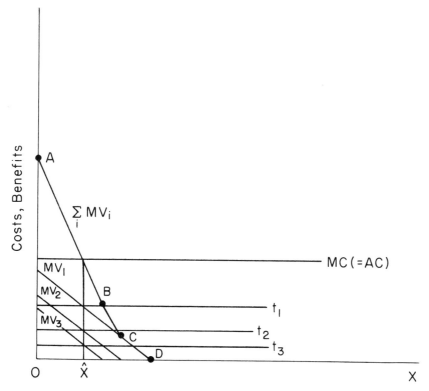

Figure 23-5. Determination of Optimal Public Service Provision by Voting and by Maximizing Aggregate Net Advantage: Exactly Offsetting Taste and Tax Liability Differences Case

as a function of Z_i, X, and N_i alone; which means that for a given amount of X provided, individual i's utility depended only on the amount of *his own use* of the facility supplied, and regardless of how much use others made of it. There was no crowding or pollution due to many-person use of the public facilities made available. In fact, most public services do experience genuine congestion in the sense that as a given sized facility for providing public services is beset by a larger and larger number of clients, the quality of the service declines at least to some—and a growing—proportion of the clients. In a different place I have presented an integrated analytic framework for such phenomena, referring to them as instances of "generic congestion."[3] This interference or crowding phenomenon can have important distributional effects if its incidence is uneven among the population. Thus, instead of equation (23-2), we have:

$$^c W_i = {}^c W(X, N_i, M) \qquad\qquad\qquad (23\text{-}14)$$

where

$^c W$ is the size of commodity W under conditions of congestion,

M is the number of users of the facility.[d]

For any given X_0 and N_i, an M larger than the threshold level M_{X_0} will cause congestion (pollution) and hence decrease W_i. Thus, the whole marginal utility of use schedule will fall and, for given P_N, so too will the optimal number of uses. As a result both of the decreasing utility per use and the decreasing use, the marginal valuation of the last unit of X (at X_0) will decline.

The threshold value of M at which congestion sets in, and the schedule of congestion effects of different M values thereafter, are not independent of X. The smaller the X, the smaller need be M to produce a given degree of congestion; the larger the X, the larger the required M. Thus, a reasonable form for $^c W$ is:

$$^c W_i = {}^c W\left(\frac{X}{M}, N_i\right). \qquad\qquad\qquad (23\text{-}15)$$

Unequal incidence is the typical situation where crowding of public services occurs. Because their frequency and character of use differ, art lovers and nonart lovers experience different degrees of museum crowding, fishermen and pulp processors experience different degrees of damage from water pollution, rush hour and nonrush hour traffic experiences different degrees of highway conges-

---

[d]If use varies by time, $^c W$ should separately list the number of users in each instance. If use is effectively constant over time, and number of users is a dependable function of the size of the relevant community, then M can refer to community size.

tion. Thus the marginal valuation functions for an unlike pair of individuals are as follows in the presence of any number M of inhabitants larger than the threshold size M_X at which generic congestion sets in:

$$MV_i(X,M) \neq MV_j(X,M) \tag{23-16}$$

for some i,j pairs ϵJ when $M > M_X$.

This case formally resembles that of differences in tastes. The consequences are similar; what differs are the kinds of policies appropriate to rectify the situation, since under the latter a promising approach is to price differentially in terms of differential marginal valuation while under this case the more promising approach is to price differentially in terms of differential contribution to creating the generic congestion. The two can diverge markedly.

This category also suggests another deficiency in the treatment of earlier categories. Crowdedness, and differential incidence of crowdedness, are quite unlikely to be characterizable for "the" public good. In the real world they are likely to exist, but to exist in different configurations for different types of public service. Multiplicity of public services is crucial to reflect the real significance of many of the differences in this category. Indeed, it is important to reflect adequately the differences in marginal valuation (taste) case as well. Tastes for a somehow-aggregated complex of public services are likely to differ far less among individuals than for individual types of services. Insofar as provision for different types of services is decided separately, very substantial political externalities can be created.

This argues for a model that explicitly treats more than one type of public service. Most models contain a single homogeneous public good and are used as if this treatment were adequate to express most theoretical issues in public sector analysis. In fact, the homogeneity treatment misrepresents important issues on both the demand and supply sides: taste and congestion considerations, as well as the topic of the next section, "accessibility," for the former; scale, administration, and mix considerations, for the latter. In addition, the whole question of the decision process where side-payments via logrolling are included, really requires a multiple public service treatment. Where direct money payments are illegal, and where institutional (say constitutional) constraints make discriminating tax treatment illegal as well, side payments will not take place unless there exists another form of tender in which the transfers can be made. The most important one in the real world is vote-trading—with respect to different kinds of public service. Participant 1 sells his vote (or representation) to 2 on the provision of service A, in exchange for 2's sale of a vote (or representation) on service B. This is a barter transaction. Like a barter system the ability of the market to approach Pareto optimality in vote trades depends on the degree to which traders can make use of a *generalized* purchasing power—"money"—so as to avoid the narrow coincidences of bilateral or even small multilateral trade pat-

terns. This is approximated the greater is the number of public services on which
to trade votes. Thus, insofar as solutions to minority exploitation depend on fa-
cilitating side payments (compensation), the potential for such payments cannot
be adequately rendered by one-commodity public service models.

Differential Access to Use of Public Service

This category also refers to public services which are not pure public goods:
here because, while their sheer provision makes them available to all, they are
not available to all on equal terms. Unlike the category to follow, where there is
inherent discrimination in how the government allows the services to be distributed among individuals, here the inequality rests on the fact that in order to consume the public service, each individual must use supplementary private resources,
and this private auxiliary cost differs from person to person. The most obvious
example is where the provision of the public service has a specific location and
persons must either travel to this site or have the service shipped to them. Travel
or transport costs will differ in terms of the individuals' different origins. Thus,
in our terminology of equation (23-3), individuals face different prices in terms
of operating resources in order to use the public facility provided:

$$P_{N_i} \neq P_{N_j} \tag{23-17}$$

for some i, j pairs in the community.

Besides travel costs there are, in addition, more subtle forms of "differential
access." An important component of what are treated as taste differences is really differences in experience or skill. One may invest resources to develop both
experience and skills. In effect, such investment is like the auxiliary travel cost
needed to enjoy some fixed site commodity. So art exhibitions, musical presen-
tations, sports facilities, all require private auxiliary expenditures in order to be
appreciated, and at any time different individuals will be required to make different *new* amounts to attain any given level of satisfaction from the public service, depending on their past investments and amounts of experience with the
public service.

It should be clear that with this category, as with the last, we are speaking
of a world of many public services. Characterization of the phenomenon in
terms of a single composite public service very inadequately, if at all, captures
the spirit of the central issue. Within the basket of public services there will be
some that appeal differently to different persons because of their past training
and experiences. Similarly, not all types of public service are significantly localized. Different types of service will, because of technology and mode of consumption, have quite differing degrees of localization and hence involve quite
different patterns of required private auxiliary payment. Figure 23-6 shows a

simple version of the situation for a particular public service with significant localization. In this illustration we assume that differential access can be interpreted as differences in the cost of consuming the public service at a "normal
quality" typical of the level of X supplied. Thus, in figure 23-7, each $MUU(X)$
curve is equal for all individuals (assumed to have the same utility function and
same income), and their differential access is shown by having each face a different operating cost per unit, $P_{N1} < P_{N2} < P_{N3}$. This simplifies the situation in
two ways. First, larger levels of X may well involve greater decentralization in
the provision of the public service and so both lower the P_N curve for all and
probably decrease the spread between them. Second, differential access interpreted in the broader sense of differential experience or training as a determinant of current "tastes" may involve the MUU function as well. We simplify by
assuming that all those influences can be summarized in the P_N function. For
present, purely illustrative purposes this seems adequate.

Each $MUU(X)$ function shows the marginal utility use schedule for a given
level of X provided. Higher levels of X correspond to higher MUU curves. P_{N1},
P_{N2}, and P_{N3} are the per unit operating costs facing individuals 1, 2, and 3 respectively. For provision of X_3, individual 1 chooses N_{13} instances of consumption, individual 2 N_{23} and individual 3 N_{33}—a declining order. Thus, with the
same utility function, their total utilities differ in the same order, as does their
marginal valuation of X at that level. In the same way, at X_2, individual 3, facing
the highest accessibility cost, chooses zero consumption of the public service,

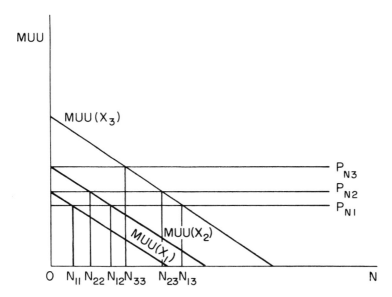

Figure 23-6. Determination of Optimal Use of Public Services with Unequal
Accessibility Cost

despite the fact that it is offered "free" as a public good: (and he thus has a zero marginal valuation of X at that level)! The same is true for individual 2—and even more so for individual 1—at X_1. So from level X_1 only individual 1 will avail himself of the public good (and thus have a positive marginal valuation of X).

From these considerations we can show the individual and aggregate marginal valuation functions of X and the resulting individual votes for X (see figure 23-7). Individual 3's $MV = 0$ from $X = 0$ to $X = X_2$, individual 2's $MV = 0$ from $X = 0$ to $X = X_1$. All three MV functions begin with a rising segment (which is not essential to the exposition: the preferred level of X for each is always on the declining segment) because at these points where $MV = 0$, $N = 0$; as X rises the optimal number of uses of the public service rises, and this acts to offset the marginal utility of use in influencing total utility. Thus, with tax liabilities equal at $t_1 = t_2 = t_3$, individual 1 votes for X_3^*, individual 2 for X_2^* and individual 3 for 0 (despite the local maximum for him at the downward intersection with t_3, the total tax liability exceeds total benefits there, so he votes for zero provision of X); X_2^* is the majority choice. At this level only individuals 1 and 2 use the public service, quite unequally, but individual 3 does not use it at all. Since ΣMV_i = discontinuous curve ABCDEFGHIJ, $\hat{X}$ is the social optimum. At this level, all three individuals consume the public service.

The particular distribution of users and nonusers in this illustration depends on the specifics of the case. More generally, out of any population greater than 2, a subset may consume none of the public service at the majority choice and a different subset consume none under the social optimum—and either subset may

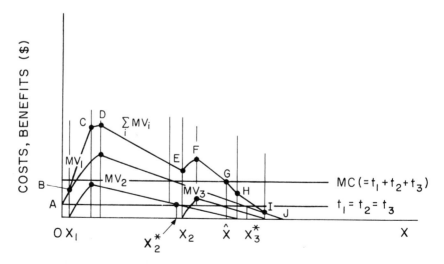

Figure 23-7. Determination of Optimal Public Service Provision by Voting and by Maximizing Aggregate Net Advantage: Unequal Accessibility Cost Case

be larger than the other, depending on specifics. But the two distributions will generally differ.

These zero consumption instances represent even more substantial real redistribution impacts than under the previous categories. But since differential private resource costs are involved here as well, the social optimum may require quite considerable inequality of impact as well as majority choice. An intuitive rationale for this is that the height of private access costs in effect represents the efficiency with which different individuals can take advantage of the public service. If, even given the provision of the public capacity X (a sort of fixed cost), the required expenditure of variable costs would gain less benefits than these variable—and optional—costs, the costs should not be incurred: the individual should consume nothing.

This last consideration raises the question as to whether the present category should not simply be decomposed into separate cases of a public good (X) and a private good (N) market. To do so would be misleading. The two are genuinely and tightly linked together. The individual's interests in the provision of X depend on his expected use of it. Thus, he must calculate how much use he is likely to make of each level of X before he knows what that level is worth to him. Similarly, he generally needs to know how much of X is to be provided before he can decide how much use of it to make. It is only by dealing with the two as part of a single market that these linkages become central.

A final point should be made about this analytically somewhat strange but not at all unnatural, category. Figure 23-7 suggests that the situation is similar to that of the unequal tastes case, and therefore that imposition of Lindahl prices would be a technique for eliciting the social optimum $\hat{X}$ by unanimous choice. In fact, this is not generally so. In that earlier case we could neglect the zero and rising portions of the individual marginal valuation curves (where typically marginal value exceeded marginal tax liability for much of the interval) because we could reasonably assume that everyone would use the public service if at all provided, and thus that the MV curves would be positive at X levels near zero, and the declining segments would begin at reasonably low levels of X. In such a situation fulfillment of the first order conditions for utility maximization would warrant the expectation that the total conditions would be fulfilled also— i.e., that some X was better than none. The key assumption in this chain is that access costs were negligible. But in the present category we are dealing with access costs that may be very large for some individuals (the interesting cases—indeed, where differential access costs are worth paying attention to, probably the typical cases). For these individuals only substantial levels of X can elicit positive use. But such high levels of X are expensive to provide, so per capita tax liabilities are high. Therefore an overall tax whose marginal rate(i.e., per unit of X) equals marginal benefit at some level of X for an individual with high access cost may elicit a vote for zero level of X, because at the former level the individual would be paying a total tax that exceeded the total benefit desirable from X. This is seen in figure 23-7 for individual 3.

The upshot of this is that a set of Lindahl prices may fulfill first order conditions for all individuals to vote for the same level of X, yet fail to meet the total conditions for some and therefore fail to obtain a unanimous choice. Under extreme conditions it might even fail to elicit a nonzero majority choice (the majority preferring zero X). So the special features of this mixed public-private category deserve further study. It certainly does not deserve neglect on grounds of improbability in the real world. Indeed, its characteristics may be discerned in many types of public services for which such considerations have simply been overlooked as unimportant. Where it does occur, however, it can be responsible for some of the most important of the sources of political externalities.

Unequal Eligibility and/or Delivery of Service

This category is in a sense a generalization of differential access; but the source of the difference is a deliberate, policy-intended inequality in the distribution of the public services. Here there are eligibility criteria for receipt of the services which designedly include a special group and exclude all others. One form is extreme localization, where a person is eligible only if he resides in the particular political jurisdiction which furnishes the service. This presupposes that the public sector in the system as a whole provides at least some of its services on a decentralized basis by partitioning its overall jurisdiction into local authorities, with residence location the desideratum for membership eligibility.

Another form is occupation—as for example, benefit programs for farmers— or economic activity, as in government insurance of savings deposits. Another is economic status, as in the whole panoply of welfare services for the poor and otherwise economically disadvantaged.

In some respects this case operates like an extreme version of taste differences: for any given x level of provision of the good, those who will receive it have a nontrivial marginal valuation while those who are excluded are legally defined as having a radically lower—often zero—marginal valuation. There are two main differences. First, some of the goods involved are meant to ameliorate the woeful condition of unfortunates. Many of the more fortunate citizens *want* to help these people through public sector programs, and at their expense. They value the selective provision of these goods to others as something considerably greater than zero—perhaps even approaching the valuation of the selective recipients themselves. Such redistribution is *intended*—nearly unanimously so—and so falls outside our present forms of unwanted or controversial redistribution. Second, where extreme localization is involved, excluded persons do not even vote on what level of public services to provide, nor do they share in the cost of providing them. Here again, therefore, no unwanted redistribution occurs. Thus, the part of the category that concerns us in where selective eligibility is controversial and the burden of supplying the goods is borne by all. Many situations meet these conditions. As noted above, the process operates like that of taste differences, except that often the nature of the majority that succeeds in imposing such programs is not the same.

The majority envisaged in the earlier category related to a single, composite public good. The same is scarcely credible where total exclusion is exercised. The present case, like a number of the others, must refer to provision of a variety of different public goods, and on different terms. Special benefits to walnut growers can scarcely come about because these are in the majority. Rather, they arise typically from logrolling procedures, whereby walnut growers join with other special minority groups to vote majority special benefits to each of the others in return for *their* help in voting majority benefits for the walnut growers. It is *conceivable* that the circle of minorities so benefited is so broad as to comprise most of the population. Logrolling in such a case then generates not controversial redistribution but a relatively equal flow of benefits throughout the population. On the other hand, it is at least as conceivable—and probably much more prevalent existentially—that the circle of mutually enhancing beneficiaries will exclude substantial minorities who thereby bear the chief net burden of these benefits. Thus, negative political externalities are created.

III. Types of Solutions

Are negative political externalities intrinsic to the public sector, or can something be done to ameliorate them? It is beyond the scope of the present chapter to delve deeply into this question, but a number of approaches can be briefly considered.

Unanimity

The first approach is to drop majority rule and require unanimity for public decisions. Where institutionally no side-payment compensation transactions are permitted, this would result in virtual paralysis of the public sector, since few programs could gain unanimous consent. It would especially halt public action if only one fixed composite public good were involved, since even legal legislative compromise would be largely powerless for lack of anything approaching a legal tender in which to pay legislative compensation.

Multiplicity of public services augments the possibility of achieving multilateral legislative trades. The possibility of side payments—outside of legislation— amplifies this further. But the requirement for complete compensation even under the most favorable conditions leaves the system open to the enormous costs of multiparticipant strategic bargaining. The real resource costs in delay and manhours used up must be extremely great. Numerous opportunities will exist for small minorities to exert effective veto power over near-unanimous majorities. Public sector paralysis even here is a real possibility.

It must be pointed out that formally to require unanimity, and to permit—even foster—vote trading to facilitate it, again raises the question of the identity of the social optimum choice. As we argued early in this chapter, the hypothetical unanimity allocation reached by a costless compensation process of specified character (i.e., with relative bargaining power represented solely by linear differences in first choice levels of X) is not likely closely to resemble a real world general agreement hammered out through complex bargaining strategies in the context of significant agreement costs. Our designated $\hat{X}$ levels in the cases shown will not generally be feasible unanimous agreement points—i.e., some of the potential gains from arriving there will be inherently lost through the agreement process. Within the real agreement process other levels of X may dominate these hypothetical $\hat{X}$ levels. Automatically to define these real agreement points as the social optima, however, may be inappropriate. The resources used up in seeking agreement, and the resulting distribution of welfare, imply tradeoffs with non-public goods. It is conceivable that a less demanding criterion for legitimate political choice can induce more preferred overall allocations of resources between private and public sectors and within the public sector. Buchanan and Tullock, in *The Calculus of Consent*, attempt to formulate such a compromise criterion, and while their particular formulation has serious shortcomings, it is supportive of the central double thesis of the present chapter: that the problem of political externalities must be taken seriously, and that it is not an easy one to resolve.

Effective Logrolling and
Legalized Side Payments

We have already discussed these in the context of a requirement for unanimous choice. Can they help where majority rule is kept? The basic argument is that, while they do not at all promise to do away with unsatisfied minorities at the exploitative hands of the majority, they can change both the identity of the majority and the decisions made by whatever majority emerges—and that both will tend to obtain a better balance between the size of gains and losses. For example, a given majority group C may be able to exploit either minority group A *or* B, but not both. It selects its action on the basis of gains to itself. Where logrolling is absent or highly rudimentary, the gains to C may bear little relation to the losses to A or B, and thus it may choose an action which carries a slight advantage to itself but an enormously greater minority loss than if it had chosen differently. In other words (assuming as throughout, aggregative comparability among gains and losses to different individuals), if A would suffer far more than

B, but C chooses to exploit A because of a slight advantage to itself, aggregate net advantage will be lower than if B had been exploited.

With effective logrolling or side-payments, A and B both have the opportunity to bid effectively for C's indulgence by offering compensation in one form or another that accurately mirrors their respective potential losses. A would generally be able to outbid B, and thus C's choice *cum* transaction would result in a larger aggregate net advantage. Very large minority losses would tend to be mitigated, but minority losses would still exist, and the number of losers might be affected either way.

As indicated above, effective logrolling, and even side-payments which are not in the form of general purchasing power, require the existence of a multiplicity of public goods which are obtainable and dispensable on different terms. The fewer the kinds of public goods, the more each transaction resembles bilateral barter in which a double coincidence of wants must be present to permit the transaction. The larger the number, the more transactions resemble multilateral trade in which triangulation occurs—no bilateral balancing is necessary, either for type of good or size of "package." As the number gets very large, the system of bargaining can proceed as though a form of general purchasing power existed, and thus trade can be carried out to its fullest. Because extensive and complex bargaining and transactions are involved, much more overt information is required to lubricate the process. For this to occur the process must be made legal and respectable.

Two problems must be faced, however. As under unanimity, very large, but somewhat smaller, bargaining costs are involved. Paralysis is much less likely, though, since no one potential loser has a veto power. The second problem may be even more serious. Effective transacting proceeds out of, and helps in turn to generate, a general purchasing power for political influence, a form of property right value to political power. This increases the leverage—and so the expected gains out of—political influence. Insofar as a group must pay its way to gain political influence, its use of it is determined and constrained in that network of payments. But there are groups that achieve majority status in more unencumbered fashion. In such a system of effective trading they now have an incentive to create the threat or actuality of obtrusive acts which it was never before in their interest to do, since they could not previously turn it to their own advantage. Under the more articulated—but not necessarily under the more rudimentary market—more trouble to others represents larger payoffs to themselves. The political process could well take on the character of a struggle for control of a lucrative protective racket. Total obtrusiveness stemming from the public sector could well increase, instead of decrease!

Because this is a distinct possibility, the aura of supposed social responsibility for actions within the public sector would be dissipated. The moral impugning—as well as illegality—of political bribery is not lightly to be cast aside.

Separate Facilities

This approach attempts to mitigate redistributional impact by furnishing a variety of specialized services to meet the differing tastes among the population, and/or by physically separating different taste-tax base combinations in different jurisdictions.

Intra-Jurisdictional Variety. The first is feasible where there is a rather even distribution of different taste and access characteristics among the population, so that each realizes the general mutuality of dependence in obtaining satisfaction of everyone's specialized—or localized—tastes. In this case political power will be scattered, and rings of logrolling exchanges will be elicited for political action, promoting reasonable overall representation and no heavy controversial redistribution. In order that this come about, however, the distribution of tax base must not be unevenly clustered among certain taste-access groups, since there will then tend to come about exploiting majorities and exploited minorities.

Thus, logrolling can be an instrumentality for a type of intrajurisdictional separate facilities solution. It must be emphasized that it is not logrolling per se, but logrolling in the presence of certain political representational configurations that makes this possible. In other circumstances, as for example, with an entrenched majority, logrolling may increase the degree of controversial redistribution, as we argued in the previous section. Indeed, where the pattern of representation permits real exploitation of minorities (either minorities of taste or minorities of high tax-base), the latter will "vote with their feet" and seek jurisdictions more politically congenial to their adequate representation. Where such jurisdictional mobility is legally possible and economically inexpensive, we enter the second form of the separate facilities approach—the system of spatial jurisdictions, each specializing in a relatively homogeneous population and, as a result, in a specialized, distinctive public sector posture including level and mix of public services and distribution of tax liabilities.

Jurisdictional Separations and Specialization: The Tiebout Case. As the uniform taste, uniform tax base example at the beginning indicated, majority rule does not inherently give rise to unwanted redistribution. Highly homogeneous populations generate minimal unwanted redistributions. It is heterogeneity in combination with majority rule that results in significant redistributions.

The present approach emphasizes the desirability of establishing or permitting to be established a large set of jurisdictions, in each of which would reside a highly homogeneous population with respect to tastes for, and ability to finance, public services. The well-known Tiebout model is of this sort. It assumes that a number of political jurisdictions exist, each one offering to residents who wish to reside there a particular public output-tax configuration. The argument is that the assortment is like a private market place, where a large variety of commodities are offered to voluntary transaction. The population is assumed to be free to choose to "enter" any jurisdiction—and free to leave—so their several choices resemble those of a competitive market. So long as the variety of available output-tax configurations is as great as taste-tax base configurations in the population, the resulting self-selection of jurisdictional residences is alleged to have the same equilibrium-optimum properties as that of the private competitive market. Negative political externalities will have been entirely dispensed with, because each individual will have attached himself to that jurisdiction which offers just the output-tax combination which his own taste-budget situation would have induced him to buy if these goods had been offered on the private market.

This is a most attractive prospect. In fact, there are many very serious difficulties with it when important features of the real world are allowed to enter. There is space for only a brief statement of each.[5]

Public Good vs. Private Good.   At the outset we remarked that the adequate treatment of individual differences is hampered in the presence of public goods. This is because: (1) public goods, unlike private goods generally, involve extreme economies of scale in planning, production, or consumption over at least some nontrivial range of population size; or (2) benefits from the sheer provision of many public goods cannot be feasibly excluded from flowing to many members of the affected population; or (3) even where benefits might be selectively shut off, there is often no ability to gauge the amount flowing to any individual.

As a result of these: first, it is inappropriate to treat public service production as essentially a constant cost phenomenon with respect to jurisdictional size. Jurisdictions smaller than nontrivial minima may experience significant cost disadvantages and so bias individual choices of residence toward larger, more heterogeneous jurisdictions. Second, taxation in any jurisdiction cannot be closely metered to individuals on the basis of actual benefit flows to them (unlike what is approximated in private markets). If the jurisdiction is homogeneous this is not a problem. But if someone different wishes to enter, his flow of benefits and tax liability cannot generally be controlled so as to leave everyone else in the jurisdiction as well off as before.

This consideration represents a real political externality, not simply a pecuniary one: what is at issue is not simply a gradation in the quantity of some commodity consumed as its unit price changes, but an all-or-nothing choice of one or another jurisdiction in which to reside. These entry and exit impacts affect the quality of each such lumpy commodity to those who do or might consume it.

Depending on circumstances a new, different entrant will almost invariably leave the earlier residents better or worse off, but not unchanged. In a jurisdiction that is too small for efficiency the entry will often improve their condition. Where the entrant has a considerably smaller tax base than the present average, and no further population scale economies exist, the entrant will typically incur greater social cost for public services than he is required to finance, so the entry worsens conditions for the earlier residents.

Why would anyone wish to enter a jurisdiction in which he differs from the prevailing population? It is just this possibility of taking advantage of an average fiscal base greater than one's own. While the output mix and level might not be what he would most have preferred—especially if he had had to pay a proportionate share—his ability to pay a smaller than proportionate share may well give gains higher than the costs of the somewhat inappropriate output. With this possibility it is no longer clear that self-selection *will* lead to highly homogeneous jurisdictions. Poorer individuals, for example, will often try to reside in wealthy communities. If they succeed,[e] then this may seriously lessen the advantages of the wealthy in locating where they did. Either a repetition of flight for the rich to a new jurisdiction with pursuit by the poor, or some form of entry control before the poor move in, may well be resorted to.

These phenomena are important, because they significantly differentiate the market for local jurisdictions from private competitive markets. The latter are a model for efficient performance only where they do not possess significant externalities. But, since each individual decision about entry and exit will typically impact the welfare of many others, the former market is inherently rife with externalities. A decentralized decision process of this sort will surely not unerringly achieve Pareto optimality if left to its own devices.

Indeed, this is recognized in the real world. Since the fact and character of entry into a jurisdiction is not a matter of indifference to its inhabitants, they have often employed both implicit and explicit techniques to control such entry. Various forms of exclusion are practiced: through zoning, code enforcement, or public preclusion by purchase of development sites which were intended to attract a kind of migration deemed undesirable by the present population. While the uncontrolled jurisdiction market does not conform to the criteria for competitive market optimality, neither does it when supplemented by these barriers to entry erected on grounds of narrow sub-group advantage.

Degree of Public Product Differentiation. Close approximation to the ideal of a variety of jurisdictional alternatives sufficient for the possibility of highly homogeneous jurisdictions would require an extraordinarily large number of jurisdictions, far more than other considerations appear to warrant. Even if tastes referred to marginal valuations of a single composite public service, the variety would be great and the number of taste-fiscal base combinations formidable. But we have remarked at several places that a relevant formulation of the present problem should recognize the multiplicity of public services. If this is done, the variety of tastes with respect to all the public services would be enormous for a

---

[e]A variety of considerations restraining this will be presented below.

population the size of a large metropolitan area. The number of required jurisdictions would be unfeasibly large and their size inefficiently small.

The inefficiency of so large a number of jurisdictions stems partly from the high cost of providing public services in very small jurisdictions, which derives from the existence of some marked economies of scale for nontrivial ranges; but also from another real-world feature that should now be recognized: the organization cost of the public sector. Government represents a special organization of decision-making and administering resources. There are basic costs of setting up and operating the infrastructure of government. In this, scale economies are important. To set up a full complement of legislative, administrative and judicial authorities for a small community is very little cheaper than setting it up for a population twice as large, so long as the same governmental functions must be performed. This enormous proliferation of the sheer *number* of jurisdictions, with their required governmental infrastructure, entails very heavy resource costs, enough to discourage many individuals from seeking the most finicky accommodation of their taste-fiscal base configurations by complete jurisdictional stratification. Thus, practically speaking, public sector cost considerations alone are likely to determine a set of jurisdictions far smaller in number than would be needed for near-perfect homogenization of jurisdictions. Add to this the earlier factor of deliberate unhomogeneous choices to take advantage of political externalities (where not prevented by exclusionary controls) and a good deal of self-selected nonhomogeneity is likely to come about.

Spatial Differentiation of Non-Public Economic Opportunities. Basic to the Tiebout formulation—and to many succeeding treatments in the same spirit—is that space does not matter. Economic opportunities are equally available over space, so jurisdictional choice can be rationally based on public sector attributes alone. This is significantly false. For a number of locational reasons that cannot be examined at this time (production and localization and agglomerative economies, transportation factors, resource availability clustering, etc.), economic activities are distributed notably unequally over space. Degree of accessibility to the sites of these activities influences productivity and welfare. Within a metropolitan area, for example, accessibility to desired destinations will be distributed significantly unequally over space. More accessible sites will be more attractive and hence valuable then less accessible sites. Moreover, because of the important nonconvexities that locational factors determine, social and physical environmental features, all welfare-relevant, will differ markedly over space. Thus, space and location will possess differential welfare significance from these nonpublic sector attributes at least as important as from public sector attributes.

Locational-jurisdictional choices will rationally have to consider the whole private sector-environment-public sector *mix* of attributes.

A number of consequences follow from this. First, there will be an inherent scarcity of locational alternatives: it will simply not be possible to offer the population a jurisdiction with every possible public output-tax mix that possesses the same accessibility-environmental attributes, and vice versa. As a result, individuals will have to compromise among the several public sector-private sector-environmental components in choosing locations. Jurisdictional homogeneity will recede even further than the preceding sections suggested.

Next, given the character of the specific overall population and the economic activities in the area, some of these intrinsically scarce attribute mixes will come to be differentially attractive relative to others. Therefore, the market for land sites will capitalize these relative desirabilities into land prices and rentals. Individuals will have to choose locations on the basis of whether their personal valuations exceed or fall short of the preponderant differential market valuations. It is clear that relative land prices will capitalize not only public sector attributes but also private good and environmental components.

Capitalization will perform a rationing function. Where there are highly prized fiscal base shelters, for example, poorer people who might otherwise wish to locate there to take advantage of the community's fiscal base will be discouraged away by the high land prices which reflect the market's valuation of those advantages. This to some extent mitigates the earlier cited need for explicit exclusionary actions by the community.

The upshot of this section, in conjunction with the preceding, is to indicate that jurisdictional choice is likely to fall well short of public sector purity. Many attendant considerations will mongrelize political representation in each community, and will establish far fewer jurisdictions than the avoidance of political externalities alone would warrant.

Inter-Jurisdictional Externalities.   The nonneutrality of space for economic welfare has further significance. Members of one jurisdiction are likely to be economically interdependent with members of and activities in, others. These patterns of interdependence mean that the welfare impact of public sector variables in one jurisdiction depends partly on what activities are being carried out in that jurisdiction by members of other jurisdictions, and vice-versa. Road expenses, police and fire protection, water supplies and other services may depend heavily on such factors.[6]

The implication of heavy inter-jurisdictional externalities of these sorts is that the purely decentralized determination of the number, location, size, and character of the set of jurisdictions must diverge from an optimal set so long as the aggregate, nonwelfare neutral, coordinational considerations are not heeded. Some centralization is required to create an optimal public sector structure, whether directly or by imposing modified incentives for decentralized decision makers.

Endogeneity of Public Sector Decisions. Much of the foregoing argument about discrepancies from perfect homogeneity calls for recognition of another important feature of real world public sector processes. It is to repudiate the emphasis in Tiebout-type models that the public sector can be viewed as some fixed display which individuals are free either to accept or reject. Rather, the distinctive posture of any jurisdiction is determined *by* those individuals who have chosen to reside there—and determined by them *for* their interests. Public sector decisions are endogenous with respect to the wants of their populations. When either the wants or the populations change, the posture of the public sector responds accordingly. Thus, the self-selection migration process and the nature of the array of public sector opportunities change hand in hand. The optimality of such a process is by no means firmly established, since public objective functions are not fixed, but are a function of the induced relocation choices that arise out of their own decisions. Each set of public choices by a jurisdiction induces changes in its—and others'—population, and these define new welfare criteria for it to satisfy.[7]

Imperfect Mobility. Tiebout-type models assume very high degrees of interjurisdictional mobility on the part of individuals. Individuals are assumed ready to move to adjust to any changes in public sector opportunities. In fact, mobility is considerably limited by two factors: high information costs and high moving costs. If what really has to be perceived is the public good-private good-environment mix, and if this must be done for a very large number of jurisdictions—or even for the much smaller but still respectable number we argued was more likely—the cost of adequate information will be high. Moreover, even if advantage over a present location should be discovered, the cost of shifting is very high. There are substantial costs of moving one's belongings; and there are the large psychological costs of changing the whole socioeconomic-environmental milieu represented by a residence. Together they add up to an important friction, a strong inertial force tending to slow down, postpone, and even reject adjustments to small or moderate and especially to temporary, perceived improvements. A process replete with significant frictions of this sort is not likely to display the vigorous oscillations of highly competitive markets.

Conclusion. This has been a long discussion of the separate facilities approach. It seems warranted because the approach has been rather popular. What has been argued here is that the analogy with a highly competitive private market is faulty, both in predictive power and normative thrust. Many elements must be added to the model before a less misleading view of the prospects for mitigating distributional externalities through jurisdictional proliferation can be discerned.

Adding this agnostic emphasis to the rest of the chapter suggests that the distributional impacts in furnishing public services to individuals are worthy of concern; and that our concern up to now has not clearly indicated how sometimes serious problems arising from this can be satisfactorily resolved.

Notes

1. Cf. Buchanan, James, and Tulloch, Gordon, *The Calculus of Consent.*
2. Individuals have a strategic incentive to misrepresent their preferences where public goods are involved. See, T. Nicolaus Tideman, "The Capabilities of Voting Rules in the Absence of Coalitions", *Public Choice*, forthcoming.
3. Jerome Rothenberg, "The Economics of Congestion and Pollution: An Integrated Analysis," *American Economic Review,* May 1970.
4. See my review in *Econometrica* 32, 3 (July 1964).
5. Compare this with the criticism of the model in J.M. Buchanan and C.J. Goetz, "Efficiency Limits of Fiscal Mobility: An Assessment of the Tiebout Model," *Journal of Public Economics*, 1, 1 (April 1972).
6. See my "Local Decentralization and the Theory of Optimal Government," in Julius Margolis (ed.), *Economics of Public Output* (Universities-National Bureau of Economic Research, New York: Columbia University Press, 1971).
7. Compare this with the welfare analysis of such alternative population assignments in Bryan Ellickson, "A Generalization of the Pure Theory of Public Goods," Discussion Paper 14, UCLA, October 1971, and "The Politics and Economics of Decentralization," Discussion Paper 31, UCLA, December 1972.

24

Congestion, Road Capacity and City Size

G.S. Tolley
Peter Zadrozny

Introduction

Traffic congestion is one of many types of external costs associated with the growth of large cities. The externality arises from the fact that an individual driver does not take account of the costs he imposes by slowing other drivers down. The externality could be internalized by a toll: a tax on trips raising marginal private cost of a trip by the extra costs the driver imposes on others. Vickrey[1] has been a leading analyst of the effects of congestion on speed and the possibility of eliminating external costs through congestion tolls.

The analysis of congestion needs to be extended to consider more explicitly the responsiveness of commuting decisions to costs of driving at peak times. When costs of driving rise due to congestion, commuters have incentives to switch from automobiles to mass transit. Many commuters can arrange to travel at off-peak times. There is an elasticity of demand to commute by auto at peak periods.

Another need is to allow for road building responses. Because amount of peak travel affects the marginal productivity of road expenditures, road builders can be expected to vary the characteristics of the road network in response to changes in peak demand. Capacity is likely to be expanded to accommodate increased traffic.

These extensions are of particular importance when congestion is considered as one of the environmental costs of growth of large cities. An earlier paper by Tolley[2] considered qualitatively the effects on city size of the externalities from failure to impose congestion tolls. A person migrating to a city does not take account of the slowing down he imposes on others already in the city. The distortion in migration incentives depends on differences in externalities. If congestion is greater in large cities than in the rest of the economy, a person migrating to a large city raises external costs by more in the large city than he reduces them in leaving the rest of the economy. Because of the difference in externalities, a tendency is imparted for large cities to be too large; though, large cities may be too small relative to their optimal size in the presence of congestion tolls.

Using this framework, another paper[3] quantified the divergence between private and social gains from migrating to a large city under the assumptions that (1) per person travel in the city is unaffected and (2) the road network of the city does not expand in response to the migration.

405

The present chapter relaxes these two restrictive assumptions. First, a model is developed of equilibrium traffic speed and traffic volume for given road building expenditures and city population. The model contains a demand schedule for auto trips and a relation which indicates how traffic speed is affected by traffic volume.

Second, road expenditures are allowed to vary in response to city size. This is done by adding a road building decision to the model. When a city grows, additional inhabitants cause an increase in the demand to use the local road network. The road building decision indicates how the increased demand is met through some combination of allowing congestion to increase and building new road capacity. The expanded model is used to make illustrative numerical estimates of changes in congestion due to an increase in population.

Third, the expanded model is used to consider the question: to what extent do immigrants coming into a city bear the additional transportation costs which they impose? A condition for optimal migration incentives is derived. The condition has two parts, taking account of effects of immigrants both on congestion and road expenditures, and generalizes earlier analyses.

An expression is developed for the external costs imposed by non-optimal migration incentives. This is used to calculate numerical examples suggestive of the magnitude of external commuting costs being imposed by the growth of large cities in the U.S. economy.

Commuter Response with Fixed Capacity

Following a standard approach[4] an illustration was given in a previous paper[5] of a congestion cost of $0.10 per mile driven in a large city, amounting to $0.50 per day per worker.

To extend that analysis, note that for the person deciding to make the trip, the cost of an auto trip of length D is the car operating cost plus the time cost of the trip or

$$p = D(c + w/s) \tag{24-1}$$

where p is the cost per trip, c is the car operating cost per mile, w is the wage or other amount at which the time cost per hour of travel is valued, and s is speed of travel.

The number of auto trips made at times of day when there is traffic congestion depends on the cost of making the trips. At higher costs per trip, people will be increasingly willing to bear the costs encountered in reducing auto trips at congested times. The demand schedule for auto trips at congested times can be expressed as

$$p = p(x), \tag{24-2}$$

showing cost per trip corresponding to a given x, where x is the number of trips per person.

The number of trips taken per person is the number of trips on the demand schedule indicated by the cost for a person deciding to make trips or

$$D(c + w/s) + t = p(x) \tag{24-3}$$

where t is the congestion toll per trips. Since the normal situation is to collect no congestion toll, t will be assumed to be zero.

The speed of travel s depends on the total number of trips taken by all persons. Speed also depends on characteristics of the road network such as the number of roads, their width and arrangements provided for avoiding delays due to intersecting traffic. The relation determining speed can be written

$$s = s(v, k) \tag{24-4}$$

where the total amount of resources devoted to providing the road network is denoted as k, and

$$v = nx. \tag{24-5}$$

The symbol n refers to the total number of persons in the city, so that v is total number of trips taken in the city under the above conditions. Conditions (24-3), (24-4) and (24-5) jointly determine x (number of trips taken per person), s (speed of travel) and v (total number of trips), given population of the city n, the road network characteristics as determined by k and the cost parameters D and W.

Knowledge of the relation determining speed enables estimating the cost imposed by taking a trip which a person deciding to take the trip does not pay for. To find the cost not paid for, due to the slowing down of other cars, note that the total cost of travel is traffic volume times cost per trip of $vD(c + w/s)$. The cost of an extra trip is the derivative of total cost with respect to traffic volume $d[vD(c + w/s)]/dv$ or $D(c + w/s) - (vDw/s^2)(\partial s/\partial v)$. The second part of this expression is the cost not paid for. It depends on the partial derivative $\partial s/\partial v$, which is the effect of a unit increase in traffic volume on speed. Letting e_v equal the absolute value of the elasticity of speed with respect to volume, or $-(\partial s/\partial v)$

(v/s), and expressing cost on a per mile basis by dividing by length of trip D, the cost not paid for is $(w/s)e_v$ per mile of travel or the time cost of traveling a mile multiplied by the volume elasticity.

In the earlier paper, taking k as given, the speed relationship (24-4) was approximated linearly by passing a line through an estimated noncongested speed at zero volume and the observed speed at the observed volume. Specifically if the noncongested speed is 35 miles per hour and the observed speed is 20 miles per hour, $\partial s/\partial v$ is $(20-35)/v$ giving $e_v = [(35-20/v] \, (v/20)$ or 0.75. With a value of travel time per car of $3.00 per hour, the earlier estimate of the cost not paid for is $0.10 per mile.

Another approximation may be obtained by considering the excess of traffic volume over that at which congestion begins. Suppose the estimate is that the maximum noncongested traffic volume is one-half the observed volume. The estimate of e_v becomes $[(35-20)/(v - 0.5v)] \, (v/20)$ or 1.5, giving cost not paid for of about $0.20 per mile. To obtain yet another estimate, suppose uncongested speed is 50 miles per hour. The estimate of e_v is then $[(50 - 20)/(v - 0.5v)] \, (v/20)$ or 3 giving cost not paid for of $0.45 per mile.

The results may be used to estimate external costs of growth of a city. For purposes of illustration, consider the effects of a 10 percent increase in the population of a city of six million. Assume that the congestion cost is the average of the three estimates, or $0.25 per mile. If there is an average per worker of five miles each work day of driving under congested conditions and if there are 250 work days a year, a worker imposes extra travel cost on others each year of $312.50. If one quarter of the 600,000 residents added to the city by 10 percent growth are workers, the total cost is $312.50 times 150,000 or about $47 million per year.

This is the estimate obtained if commuter response is ignored. One of the uses of the model of the present chapter is to take account of the response of automobile commuters to cost per trip. From the end of the next section, the elasticity of speed with respect to population is -0.86, when road capacity is fixed and when the elasticity β of travel with respect to cost per trip is -1. A 10 percent growth of city population reduces speed only 8.6 percent instead of the 15 percent just estimated for zero response (where β was assumed to be 0 instead of -1).

The difference in speed effects reduces the estimate of the cost of the existing number of trips per person in the ratio of speed reductions or 8.6/15, reducing the increase in cost of the existing number of trips to $27 million. In addition, there is a triangle effect associated with the change in number of trips per person. The reduction in travel leads to a saving in consumer outlays as compared to the existing number of trips which is, however, partially offset by the reduced benefit of travel. The change in net benefits per trip is the average of the change for the first and last trips cut or $\Delta P/2$, which is multiplied by the change in amount of travel ΔQ to obtain the triangle effect. The triangle effect is $0.6 million.

Subtracting the triangle effect from the increased cost of existing trips gives an external cost due to 10 percent city growth of $26.4 million when the elasticity of demand for auto commuter trips is -1.

The Road Capacity Decision

The estimates so far have assumed no change in road building expenditures. Ordinarily as a city grows more road building will be undertaken. The extent of this road building will determine how speed of traffic is affected by city growth. A more general framework will now be developed allowing for changes in road building expenditures.

It is reasonable to suppose that road expenditures are influenced by the marginal benefits from them, without assuming an exact optimization is achieved. As indicated in (24-22) below, the total benefit from a road is the number of persons in the city times the travel benefit per person, minus the number of persons times the travel cost per person, minus road cost. Differentiating (24-22) with respect to k and using (24-3) through (24-5) to determine the equilibrium responses of x and s with respect to k, gives the following as the net marginal benefit of road expenditures: benefits of extra trips, $nt\ dx/dk$, plus travel cost savings due to higher average speed, $nxDw/s^2\ ds/dk$ minus the dollar of expenditure, 1. The change in traffic volume (dx/dk) is governed by (24-3) through (24-5) determining traffic flows. A road planner contemplating extra road capacity can be visualized to differentiate (24-3) through (24-5) with respect to k obtaining three equations in the derivatives dx/dk, dv/dk, and ds/dk. The solution of the three equations for dx/dk is $-(x/k)\ [e_k/(-e_v + 1/\rho\beta)]$ where e_k and e_v are the absolute values of the elasticities of speed with respect to road expenditures and traffic volume, ρ is $D(w/s)/[D(c + w/s) + t]$ or time cost as a fraction of total travel cost and β is the elasticity of demand for trips.

With perfect optimization, the road planner would choose capacity making net marginal benefit equal to zero. However, road expenditures are decided by a public process, and the benefits are difficult to evaluate precisely. Tax and borrowing decisions at the local and state levels may impart a tendency for rich communities to overbuild and for poor communities to underbuild. Growth-minded communities may tend to build beyond the point suggested by the criterion, while communities not desiring growth may deliberately underbuild. Subsidies for expressways can give incentives to build beyond the point suggested by the criterion.

Let m be the difference between the marginal benefits and marginal cost of extra road building expenditures. Then substituting the solution for dx/dk into the expression for net marginal benefit, the relation being sought specifying road building expenditures k is

$$m = \left(\frac{nx}{k}\right) [t - p(x)/\beta] \ [-e_k/(-e_v + 1/\rho\beta)] - 1. \qquad (24\text{-}6)$$

Conditions (24-3) through (24-6) determine trips per person, total number of trips, speed, and road building expenditures for a city of given population. We are now in a position to consider how these magnitudes are affected by a change in population. Taking the differentials of the four conditions, dividing through by absolute values and making divisions and multiplications as necessary to obtain elasticity expressions gives

$$\dot{x}/\beta = -\rho\dot{s} \qquad (24\text{-}3')$$

where β is price elasticity of demand for trips $p/xp'(x)$ and ρ is time cost of a trip as a percentage of total cost of a trip or $(Dw/s)/[D(c + w/s) + t]$;

$$\dot{s} = -e_v\dot{v} + e_k\dot{k} \qquad (24\text{-}4')$$

where e_v and e_k are the absolute values of the elasticities of speed with respect to volume and road expenditures.

$$\dot{v} = \dot{n} + \dot{x} \qquad (24\text{-}5')$$

and

$$(1 + e_{kv} + \epsilon e_{vv})\dot{v} + (e_{kk} + \epsilon e_{vk} - 1)\dot{k} + \dot{x}/\beta = 0 \qquad (24\text{-}6')$$

where e_{kv} and e_{kk} are the elasticities of e_k with respect to traffic volume and road expenditures or $e_{kv} = (v/e_k)\partial e_k/\partial v$ and $e_{kk} = (k/e_k)\partial e_k/\partial k$; similarly e_{vv} and e_{vk} are the elasticities of e_v with respect to traffic volume and road expenditures or $e_{vv} = (v/e_v)\partial e_v/\partial v$ and $e_{vk} = (k/e_v)\partial e_v/\partial k$; and ϵ is a negative number whose absolute value is less than one and specifically is $\epsilon = \rho\beta e_v/(1 - \rho\beta e_v)$.

In taking these differentials it has been assumed that t is zero which is realistic inasmuch as congestion tolls are essentially nonexistent. It has also been assumed that $\dot{m}$ is zero. This assumption will definitely be fulfilled if road expenditures are optimal ($m = 0$). Equation (24-4') is also consistent with departures from optimality. The assumption that $\dot{m}$ is zero implies there is no systematic change one way or the other in the difference between marginal gain and marginal cost of road expenditure as city size increases. Economies or diseconomies of scale, in connection with average cost financing, might lead to $\dot{m}$ not being zero. Economies and diseconomies will be considered later in this paper.

Equations (24-3') through (24-6') determine the percentage changes in trips per person, speed, traffic volume and road expenditures ($\dot{x}$, $\dot{s}$, $\dot{v}$, and $\dot{k}$) given the percentage change in population $\dot{n}$. Equations (24-3') through (24-6') can be solved by any method applicable to linear equations. The solution for the percentage change in speed is

$$\dot{s} = -\dot{n} \; [(1 + e_{kv} + \epsilon e_{vv})e_k + (e_{kk} + \epsilon e_{vk} - 1)e_v] \, /$$

$$[(1 + e_{kv} + \epsilon e_{vv})(-\rho\beta e_k) + (e_{kk} + \epsilon e_{vk} - 1)(1 - \rho\beta e_v) - \rho e_k] \, . \; (24\text{-}7)$$

The special case of no change in trips per person is obtained if the elasticity of demand for trips β is zero, in which case ϵ is also zero. Inserting these conditions into (24-7), the percentage change in speed becomes

$$\dot{s} = \dot{n} \; [(1 + e_{kv})e_k + (e_{kk} - 1)e_v] / (1 + \rho e_k - e_{kk}), \text{ if } \beta = 0. \qquad (24\text{-}8)$$

Another special case occurs if no changes in road building expenditures are allowed as city size changes. Then $\dot{k}$ is zero, and equation (24-6') is dropped. The solution for the percentage change in speed is

$$\dot{s} = \dot{n} \; [-e_v / (1 - \rho\beta e_v)] \, , \text{ if } \dot{k} = 0. \qquad (24\text{-}9)$$

A final special case occurs when there is no change in trips per person and road capacity does not change. Letting $\beta = 0$ in the foregoing equation gives percentage change in speed

$$\dot{s} = -\dot{n}e_v, \text{ if } \beta = 0 \text{ and } \dot{k} = 0. \qquad (24\text{-}10)$$

To further examine changes in speed, the following form for the speed relation may be considered:

$$(s/\bar{s}) = 1 - a \, [v/\bar{v}) - 1] \qquad (24\text{-}11)$$

where $\bar{s}$ is maximum uncongested speed attained, when traffic is light enough so that cars do not slow each other down, and $\bar{v}$ is the maximum uncongested traffic volume, above which the cars slow each other down. Both $\bar{s}$ and $\bar{v}$ may be increased by road building expenditures, i.e.,

$$\bar{s} = \bar{s}(k) \qquad (24\text{-}12)$$

and

$$\bar{v} = \bar{v}(k) \qquad (24\text{-}13)$$

where $\bar{s}'(k)$ and $\bar{v}'(k)$ are positive.

Taking the partial of (24-11) with respect to v and using the substitution from (24-11) that $-a\,[(v/\bar{v}) - 1] = (s/\bar{s}) - 1$ gives $\partial s/\partial v = (s - \bar{s})/(v - \bar{v})$. Using this result in the definition of e_v gives

$$e_v = [(\bar{s}/s) - 1]/[1 - (\bar{v}/v)]. \qquad (24\text{-}14)$$

Substituting (24-12) and (24-13) into (24-11), differentiating with respect to k, and substituting in the expressions for $(s/\bar{s})$ and $(s/\bar{s}) - 1$ obtained from (24-11) gives $\partial s/\partial k = (s\bar{s}'/\bar{s}) + (v\bar{v}'/\bar{v})(\bar{s} - s)/(v - \bar{v})$. Using this result in the definition of e_k gives

$$e_k = \eta + \pi\,[(\bar{s}/s) - 1]/[(1 - (\bar{v}/v)] \qquad (24\text{-}15)$$

where $\eta = k\bar{s}'/\bar{s}$ is the elasticity of uncongested speed with respect to road expenditures and $\pi = k\bar{v}'/\bar{v}$ is the elasticity of maximum uncongested traffic volume with respect to road expenditures. The values of η and π are determined by (24-12) and (24-13), as $\bar{s}'$ is the first derivative of (24-12) and $\bar{v}'$ is the first derivative of (24-13).

Using (24-11) we can evaluate e_{vv}, e_{vk}, e_{kk}, and e_{kv} in terms of e_k, e_v, η, and π. The following two relations help simplify these derivations: (a) $e_k = \eta + \pi e_v$ which follows from substituting (24-14) into (24-15), and (b) $e_v = a(v/s)(\bar{s}/\bar{v})$ which follows from (24-11) and (24-14) along with some algebraic manipulation. This form of e_v simplifies the task of taking logarithmic differentials. Recalling that a is a constant, s is a function of v and k, and that $\bar{s}$ and $\bar{v}$ are functions of k only, we can readily calculate e_{vv} after taking logarithms of $e_v = a(v/s)(\bar{s}/\bar{v})$. This yields

$$e_{vv} = 1 - e_v. \qquad (24\text{-}16)$$

Similarly $e_{vk} = -e_k + \eta - \pi$ and using $e_k = \eta + \pi e_v$. This implies

$$e_{vk} = -\pi(1 + e_v). \qquad (24\text{-}17)$$

In order to calculate e_{kv} and e_{kk} use $e_k = \eta + \pi e_v$. It will be assumed that (24-12) and (24-13) are constant elasticity functions. This has the advantage of allowing for diminishing returns to road building expenditures and it implies that η and π are constants. Differentiating logarithmically gives $e_{kv} = \pi(e_v/e_k)e_{vv}$ which together with (24-16) implies

$$e_{kv} = \pi(e_v/e_k)(1 - e_v). \qquad (24\text{-}18)$$

Similarly we can derive $e_{kk} = \pi(e_v/e_k)e_{vk}$ which together with (24-17) implies

$$e_{kk} = -\pi^2(e_v/e_k)(1 + e_v). \qquad (24\text{-}19)$$

The conditions for observed traffic $\bar{s}/s = 35/20$ and $\bar{v}/v = 0.5$ inserted into (24-14) give $e_v = 1.50$. Consider the increase in road expenditures that would be necessary to maintain the same speed if traffic volume were increased. The assumption that a 10 percent increase in volume would require a 10 percent increase in road expenditures to maintain the same speed implies that e_k equals e_v. Since $e_k = \eta + \pi e_v$, with $e_k = e_v = 1.50$, the assumed values of η and π must then be consistent with $1.50 = \eta + 1.50\pi$. As road expenditures are increased, there is some optimum division of expenditures as between increasing uncongested speed and traffic volume possible before congestion is encountered. This division determines the relative values of η and π. Intuitively, it seems likely that most effort would be devoted to increasing the capacity to handle traffic at existing speeds, rather than attempting to increase maximum speed as city size increases. In obtaining a numerical result here, it will be assumed that all additional road expenditures are devoted to increasing traffic volume with no increase in maximum speed, i.e., $\eta = 0$, $\pi = 1$. Using (24-16) through (24-19), the following values are then obtained: $e_{vv} = -0.50$, $e_{vk} = -2.50$, $e_{kv} = -0.50$, and $e_{kk} = -2.50$.

The values in the preceding paragraph can be used to estimate how speed will change as city population increases. From (24-10), if the elasticity of demand β is 0 and if road expenditures are not allowed to change, the percentage change in speed resulting from a one percent increase in population $\dot{s}/\dot{u}$ is -1.50. From (24-9) if β is -1 and the ratio ρ of time cost to travel cost is 0.5, still retaining the assumption that road expenditures do not change, $\dot{s}/\dot{n}$ is -0.86. From (24-8) if β is zero but road expenditures are allowed to change, $\dot{s}/\dot{n}$ is -1.06. From (24-7) if β is -1 and road expenditures are allowed to change, $\dot{s}/\dot{n}$ is -0.66.

Road Taxes for Optimal Migration Incentives

To use these results to examine the effects of population redistribution on national income, let y refer to all income earned by a person in the city in question other than the net benefits b of using the city's congested roads, so that $y + b$ is all income earned in the city including net benefits of using its roads. Let y' refer to the income the person would earn if he were outside the city in question, where y' is all income from being elsewhere including benefits from using any roads in other cities. Labor will have incentives to migrate until the benefits from an extra person moving to the city in question are zero, implying $b + y - y' = 0$, or $b = y' - y$. The effect on national income is the change in benefits from road use dB/dn plus other income earned in the city minus total income the person could earn elsewhere, or $dB/dn + y - y'$. Substituting b for the difference between y and y' as expected in view of migration incentives gives the effect on national income when a person moves to the city:

$$dB/dn - b, \qquad (24\text{-}20)$$

that is, the difference between the marginal effect of a person on road benefits and the benefit b a person receives from the road when he moves to the city.

Confining attention to that part of the road system which is congested, the benefit to a person from using the roads when he moves to a city is

$$b = {}_0\int^x p(X)dX - xD(c + w/s) - k_n. \qquad (24\text{-}21)$$

The first term on the right hand side is the area under the demand curve of a person to travel on the roads from zero trips up to the actual number of trips taken. It is the sum of the amounts that he would be willing to pay to use the road system and is greater than his travel expenditures due to willingness to pay higher prices per trip at smaller numbers of trips. The second term on the right hand side is the travel cost borne by a person using the roads. It is the cost per trip $D(c + w/s)$ times x, the number of trips per person. The third term k_n is the person's contribution to road expenditures. It is the amount his taxes are higher because of provision of the roads.

The total benefits from using the roads are

$$B = n \, {}_0\int^x p(X)dX - nxD(c + w/s) - k. \qquad (24\text{-}22)$$

The first two terms on the right side of (24-22) are equal to the population n multiplied by the first two terms of (24-21) which are travel benefits and travel costs in the expression for individual benefits, and the third term k is the total cost of providing the roads. To find the effect on the road benefits of an extra person entering the city, differentiate (24-22) with respect to n:

$$dB/dn = {}_0\int^x p(X)dX - xD(c + w/s) - dk/dn$$

$$+ n\,[p(x) - D(c + w/s)]\,(dx/dn)$$

$$+ (nxDw/s^2)(ds/dn). \qquad (24\text{-}23)$$

When road capacity expands optimally due to an increase in city population, we can relate the changes in trips per person dx, average speed ds, and total road expenditures dk to the changing city population dn using equations (24-3′), through (24-6′). Hence for given road contributions per person k_n we can view road benefits per person b and the change in total benefits due to an extra person entering the city dB/dn to be determined by the city population n. In other words—mathematically speaking—$db/dn - b$ is a function of the city's population n for given k_n, and it correctly measures the addition to national income of a person entering the city only when it is evaluated at the level of population consistent with the zero net migration condition $b = y' - y$. Subtracting (24-21) from (24-23) allows us to write (24-20) explicitly as

$$dB/dn - b = (xDw/s)\dot{s}/\dot{n} + (k_n - dk/dn) \tag{24-24}$$

where percentage change notations $\dot{s}$ and $\dot{n}$ have been substituted for ds/s and dn/n. Suppose that k_n is a neutral tax except to the extent that it affects city population. This means that the level and method of collection of road contributions per person does not influence allocative decisions with respect to trips taken within the city. Therefore for a given city population n, the level of k_n does not affect average speed or the external cost due to the slowing down of traffic (this assumption is implicit in the fact that k_n does not appear in equations (24-3') through (24-6')). Of course, k_n affects the external cost indirectly because it is a factor determining migration into the city. Lowering k_n will stimulate migration into the city by increasing b, the benefit to a person from using the city roads. Consequently, in the absence of an optimal toll, national income will be maximized when personal contributions to road expenditures k_n determine a city population such that $dB/dn - b = 0$.

Setting the left side of (24-24) equal to zero and solving, indicates the condition to maximize national income is:

$$k_n = dk/dn - (xDw/s)\dot{s}/\dot{n}. \tag{24-25}$$

People should be charged for *the extra cost of road capacity*, dk/dn, *plus the extra travel costs imposed on other drivers due to the reduction they cause in average traffic speed*, $- (xDw/s)\dot{s}/\dot{n}$.

To derive numerical estimates assume $dk/dn = k_n$, i.e., that the city tax levied per person to finance roads equals the cost of adding to road capacity to accommodate an additional person. Then $dB/dn - b = (xDw/s)\dot{s}/\dot{n}$, indicating that to find external costs of city growth the results for $\dot{s}/\dot{n}$ obtained above should be multiplied by xDw/s. Following the earlier example, assuming that yearly congested driving per worker is 1,250 miles or per person xD is 312.5 miles and that w/s is $3 per hour divided by 20 miles per hour or $0.15 per mile, then xDw/s, which is the yearly time cost of congested driving per person in the city, is $46,875. Multiplying xDw/s by $\dot{s}/\dot{n}$, as obtained for alternative response assumptions in (24-7) to (24-10), gives the effect of growth of the city by one person. Further multiplication by 600,000 gives the effect of growth of a city of six million persons by 10 percent.

The estimated effect is $42 million if $\beta = 0$ and $\dot{k} = 0$, which is close to the $47 million estimate given initially. Applying other assumptions, the effect is $24 million if $\beta = -1$ and $\dot{k} = 0$, $30 million if $\beta = 0$ and road expenditures are allowed to change, and $17 million if $\beta = -1$ and road expenditures are allowed to change.

In practice k_n may not equal dk/dn as assumed in these estimates. In the absence of transfers between cities such as due to federal subsidies to urban expressways, road expenditures will be self financing within the city, and k_n may tend to equal average road expenditures per person. Real methods of financing probably come closer to charging an average than a marginal cost. If there are road diseconomies of scale with respect to city population, i.e., dk/dn rises with n, with average cost pricing migrants to the city are being charged for roads less than the marginal road building costs they impose. This means $(k_n - dk/dn)$ is negative. Using equation (24-24) there is an additional external loss by the amount $(k_n - dk/dn)$ as compared with the case where people are charged the marginal cost of road expenditures. The external costs would be higher than in the estimates just given.

Conclusion

To illustrate the external congestion costs associated with growth of large cities, the growth of a city of six million persons by 10 percent (roughly a dec-ade of growth of the Chicago SMSA) leads to external costs on the order of $42 million per year if the customary type of speed volume relationship is assumed, where there is neither change in road capacity nor any response of auto commu-ters to higher travel costs. Using the model developed in this chapter, if the elas-ticity of auto commuting with respect to the cost per trip is –1 (still assuming no change in road capacity), the external costs of the 10 percent growth are brought down to $26 million.

The congestion resulting from growth of a city will increase the marginal benefits from adding to road capacity, leading road decisionmakers to expand the carrying capacity of the existing road network as the city grows. The margin-al benefits are determined by a road production function showing (a) how in-creases in traffic volume reduce speed below free-flow speed and (b) how road building expenditures can be used to increase the free-flow speed. Road building expenditures reduce the congestion resulting from growth of cities. In the simple case of no response of amount of auto commuting to costs, the elasticity of speed with respect to population is reduced from –1.5 with no change in road expenditures to –1.06 if the change in road expenditures is allowed for. In the more general case of a response of auto commuting to costs, if the commuting response elasticity is unitary, the elasticity of speed with respect to population is reduced from –0.86 to –0.66.

For optimum migration incentives, people should be charged for the exter-nal congestion costs they impose plus the costs of extra road capacity built if they come to a city. The major estimate of this study is that the external conges-tion coats from 10 percent growth of a city of six million population are $19 to $30 million dollars per year if changes in road capacity are allowed for. It is like-ly that migrants do not bear the full costs of extra road capacity, and so the ex-ternal costs of city growth due to increased traffic are probably higher than indicated by this estimate.

Beyond these specific results, a contribution of this study is to explain urban congestion as an equilibrium phenomenon determined by commuter response to travel cost, the physical relations governing speed, and road builder behavior.

Another contribution is to add to ability to evaluate urban policies in a number of areas including congestion tolls, road finance, and city size. Most discussions of such policies have been at best qualitative. The present study has developed means for considering the benefits in quantitative terms.

Notes

1. W.S. Vickrey, "Pricing in Urban and Suburban Transport," *American Economic Review* 53 (May 1963): 452–465; W. S. Vickrey, "Congestion Theory and Transport Investment," *American Economic Review* (May 1969): 251–260.
2. G.S. Tolley, "Welfare Economics of City Bigness," *Journal of Urban Economics* 1, 3 (July 1974): 324–345.
3. G.S. Tolley, "Population Distribution Policy," *Increasing Understanding of Public Problems and Policies* (Chicago: Farm Foundation, 1971), pp. 52–59.
4. See for instance, A.A. Walters, "The Theory and Measurement of Private and Source Costs of Highway Congestion," *Econometrica*, 29 (October 1961): 676–699.
5. G.S. Tolley, "Population Distribution Policy."

List of Contributors

Kenneth J. **Arrow**, Professor of Economics, Harvard University
A.B. **Atkinson**, Professor of Economics, University of Essex
Martin J. **Bailey**, Professor of Economics, University of Maryland
William J. **Baumol**, Professor of Economics, Princeton University and New York
    University
Jeffrey I. **Chapman**, Professor of Economics, University of California, Los
    Angeles
Jacques H. **Dreze**, Professor of Economics, C.O.R.E. Louvain
Martin **Feldstein**, Professor of Economics, Harvard University
Ronald E. **Grieson**, Associate Professor of Economics, Columbia University
C. Lowell **Harriss**, Professor of Economics, Columbia University
Werner **Hirsch**, Professor of Economics, University of California, Los Angeles
John F. **Kain**, Professor of Economics, Harvard University
Kelvin **Lancaster**, Professor of Economics, Columbia University
John **Ledyard**, Professor of Economics, Northwestern University
Maurice **Marchand**, Professor of Economics, C.O.R.E. Louvain
Peter **Mieszkowski**, Professor of Economics, University of Houston
Edwin S. **Mills**, Professor of Economics, Princeton University
Ezra J. **Mishan**, Professor of Economics, London School of Economics
Herbert **Mohring**, Professor of Economics, University of Minnesota
Leon N. **Moses**, Professor of Economics, Northwestern University
Richard F. **Muth**, Professor of Economics, Stanford University
Edmund S. **Phelps**, Professor of Economics, Columbia University
Jerome **Rothenberg**, Professor of Economics, Massachusetts Institute of Tech-
    nology
Paul A. **Samuelson**, Institute Professor, Economics, Massachusetts Institute of
    Technology
Carl S. **Shoup**, McVickar Professor of Political Economy, Emeritus, Columbia
    University
Robert M. **Solow**, Institute Professor, Economics, Massachusetts Institute of
    Technology
Sidney **Sonenblum**, Professor of Economics, University of California, Los Angeles
Joseph E. **Stiglitz**, Professor of Economics, Stanford University
G.S. **Tolley**, Professor of Economics, University of Chicago
Peter **Zadrozny**, Professor of Economics, University of Chicago

About the Editor

Ronald E. Grieson, associate professor of economics at Columbia University, received the Ph.D. at the University of Rochester. He was assistant professor of economics at Massachusetts Institute of Technology and associate professor of economics at Queens College and the Graduate Center, C.U.N.Y. He has published in the *American Economic Review, National Tax Journal, Journal of Urban Economics, Journal of Public Economics* and various other journals and collections of essays. He is also the editor of *Urban Economics: Readings and Analysis.*

Biography of William S. Vickrey

William S. Vickrey (born June 21, 1914, Victoria, B.C.) received the B.A. from Yale University and the M.A. and Ph.D. from Columbia University and is McVickar Professor of Political Economy at Columbia University. His honors and awards include a Guggenheim Faculty Fellowship, a Ford Research Professorship, and fellowships in the Econometric Society and the American Academy of Arts and Sciences. He is currently on the editorial boards of the *Journal of Economic Literature* and *Public Finance Quarterly* and is on the board of directors of the National Bureau of Economic Research. His publications in public finance and urban economics are far too numerous to mention and include every leading journal in economics, law and taxation, including the *American Economic Review, Econometrica, The Journal of Political Economy, Yale Law Review, Columbia Law Review, Review of Economics and Statistics,* and *Encyclopedia of the Social Sciences.* His *Microstatics* and *Metastatics and Macroeconomics* are widely used texts. He has done much of the seminal and inspirational work in public and urban economics and the profession and public often discover his oldest work to be the newest.